Honduras in Dangerous Times

Honduras in Dangerous Times

Resistance and Resilience

James J. Phillips

LEXINGTON BOOKS
Lanham • Boulder • New York • London

Published by Lexington Books
An imprint of The Rowman & Littlefield Publishing Group, Inc.
4501 Forbes Boulevard, Suite 200, Lanham, Maryland 20706
www.rowman.com

Unit A, Whitacre Mews, 26-34 Stannary Street, London SE11 4AB

Copyright © 2015 by Lexington Books

All rights reserved. No part of this book may be reproduced in any form or by any electronic or mechanical means, including information storage and retrieval systems, without written permission from the publisher, except by a reviewer who may quote passages in a review.

British Library Cataloguing in Publication Information Available

Library of Congress Cataloging-in-Publication Data

Phillips, James J., 1945- author.
 Honduras in dangerous times : resistance and resilience / James J. Phillips.
  pages cm
 Includes bibliographical references and index.
 ISBN 978-0-7391-8355-7 (cloth : alk. paper) — ISBN 978-0-7391-8356-4 (ebook) 1. Honduras—Social conditions—21st century. 2. Social movements—Honduras. 3. Protest movements—Honduras. 4. Government, Resistance to—Honduras. I. Title.
 HN153.5.P55 2015
 306.097283—dc23
 2015030260

∞™ The paper used in this publication meets the minimum requirements of American National Standard for Information Sciences Permanence of Paper for Printed Library Materials, ANSI/NISO Z39.48-1992.

Printed in the United States of America

Contents

Acknowledgments	vii
Acronyms and Organizations	xi
1 Encounters with Honduras: Resistance and Resilience	1
2 A Culture of Domination	17
3 Rituals of Control	39
4 Evolution of a Culture of Resistance	65
5 Patterns of Indigenous Resistance	91
6 Nourishing Resilience: Food, Environment, Community	126
7 The Legal Order: Challenging Judicial and Political Systems	148
8 Ancient Weapon of the People: Popular Culture	170
9 A Spiritual Struggle	192
10 The United States in Honduras: Intervention, Solidarity, and Resistance	220
11 Conclusion: Honduran Resistance in a Global Context	236
Bibliography	246
Index	254
About the Author	268

Acknowledgments

This book is a product of almost forty years of interest in Honduras and various visits, usually for short periods ranging from a few weeks to a few months. This means that I have incurred four decades of debt to many people, and it will be impossible to name them all here. I have had the privilege of meeting, interviewing, and accompanying many Hondurans and some internationals in Honduras who have provided me with much information, opinion, and analysis of many aspects of life in their country. In my first visit to Honduras, one that inspired my further interest, I was a guest of the Jesuit community at La Fragua in El Progreso, and their then-superior, Patrick Wade, SJ. Phil McManus and the team of Witness for Peace based in Nicaragua facilitated my next encounter with Honduras in 1984 as part of an observer delegation. During two years based in Nicaragua (1985–1987) Witness for Peace also provided organizational support that allowed me to make several visits across the Nicaraguan border to Honduras, especially to refugee camps in the south of the country and later to interview Honduran human rights activists in many areas. That research was also supported generously by many kind friends and members of solidarity groups and churches in different areas of the United States, especially folks in southern Michigan and the Institute for Global Education in Grand Rapids, Michigan, and solidarity groups in the San Francisco Bay area and Santa Barbara, California. In addition to financial support, many of these individuals and groups provided opportunities for me to make public presentations and radio interviews about what was happening in Central America during those turbulent war years.

During that period in Honduras, many people graciously gave me time for interviews, including Dr. Ramón Custodio, then-director of CODEH; Victor Meza, director of CEDOH; Berta Oliva, director of COFADEH; Honduran staff members of both Caritas and the Christian Development Commission in the south of the country; faculty and members of student groups at the National University; Efrain Diaz, then Christian Democratic member of the Honduran Congress; a young family in the Department of El Paraiso who remain to this day dear friends; and several Jesuits, including especially Joseph V. Owens, SJ, who introduced me to the beautiful and much-conflicted Aguán Valley, and who served at different times as the Catholic pastor in several communities there and as director of Radio Progreso in El Progreso, Yoro. These are only a few of the many to whom I am indebted for assistance during that period and since.

In more recent visits to post-coup Honduras, the director of ERIC and Radio Progreso, Ismael Moreno Coto, SJ, and the staff at ERIC and Radio Progreso provided me with office space and very patiently and cheerfully allowed me to accompany them to various meetings of popular organizations, coverage of news events related to resistance organizations and actions, and rural communities engaged in forms of community development, and allowed me to participate in ERIC's own analysis and reflection sessions on the "national reality" (*la realidad nacional*). Their energy, humor, and dedication to improving their country and serving its people gave me much inspiration on long, hot, and sometimes uncomfortable journeys. They also agreed to my requests for interviews and spent time answering my questions and providing their own analysis and insights. I am especially grateful for the way in which they were available and helpful while allowing me the physical and mental space to arrive at my own analyses and conclusions.

Members of the ERIC staff introduced me to the work of historian Marvin Barahona, whose writing I found useful and inspiring. I also benefited greatly from the willingness of many other Hondurans to share their experiences and insights, including leaders and members of indigenous, human rights, and other organizations, and several pastors and religious leaders, all who must remain anonymous here. Their courage and resilience is what has most inspired and motivated me to write this book.

Some of the material is drawn from some of my earlier articles and book chapters. In particular, I acknowledge the patient encouragement I received from Barbara Rose Johnston, editor of several books to which I contributed chapters about resistance, environment, and human rights in Honduras. I am also grateful to colleagues in the small network of Honduran scholars in the United States whose conversation and published scholarship have helped to introduce me to aspects of Honduras with which I was less familiar. These colleagues include in particular Mark Anderson, Jeff Boyer, Jon Carter, Darío Euraque, Dana Frank, Jordan Levy, Adrienne Pine, and Jon Wolseth, among others.

Brigitte Gynther kindly and efficiently provided an initial edit of the manuscript, using her broad and detailed knowledge of contemporary events in Honduras to check the accuracy of many of my details about recent events.

My editor at Lexington Books, Amy King, and her associates were most patient with my extended deadlines and my various editorial questions and anxieties.

To Dwight Heath, my doctoral adviser at Brown University in the 1970s, I owe a large lifetime debt for introducing me to the enormously rich and vibrant study of the anthropology of Latin America that has provided me with endless sources of wonder and much adventure over many years, and for giving me some solid scholarly resources to explore the wonder and interpret the adventure. Robert Jay at Brown University also encouraged my study of post-colonialism and social change and became an important part of the network that supported me in my fieldwork in Honduras and Nicaragua during the 1980s.

My wife, Lucy Edwards, has been my constant companion and strongest support in many trips to and adventures in Honduras and Nicaragua since we first met in Tegucigalpa in 1984. In conversations with her I have gotten many insights and "ah-ha!" moments.

Acronyms and Organizations

ADCP	*Asociación de Desarrollo Campesino de El Progreso*
ADJ	*Asociación de Jueces por la Democrácia*
AID	Agency for International Development (United States)
AIFLD	American Institute of Free Labor Development
ALBA	*Alianza Bolivariana*
ANACH	*Asociación Nacional de Campesinos de Honduras*
ANDROH	*Asociación para el Desarrollo de Honduras*
APROH	*Asociación para el Progreso de Honduras*
ASONOG	*Asociación de Organizaciones No-Gubernamentales*
CAFTA	Central American Free Trade Agreement
CARSI	Central American Regional Security Initiative
CCD	*Comisión Cristiana de Desarrollo*

CCUC	*Comité Central de Unidad Campesina*
CDV	*Comisión de Verdad*, independent international truth commission
CEB	*Comunidad eclesial de base*
CEDOH	*Centro de Documentación de Honduras*
CEH	*Confraternidad Evangelica de Honduras*
CIA	Central Intelligence Agency (United States)
CNTC	*Comité Nacional de Trabajadores del Campo*
CODEH	*Comité para la Defensa de Derechos Humanos en Honduras*
COFADEH	*Comité de las Familias de los Detenidos/Desaparecidos en Honduras*
Comité de Mujeres	*Comité Hondureño de Mujeres por la Paz Visitación Padilla*
CONADEH	*Comisión Nacional de Derechos Humanos de Honduras*
CONATRIN	*Concilio Nacional de Tribus Indígenas*
COPIN	*Comité de Organizaciones Populares e Indígenas de Intibuca*
COPINH	*Consejo Cívico de Organizaciones Populares e Indígenas de Honduras*
CVR	*Comisión de la Verdad y Reconciliación* (Honduran Government)
DEA	Drug Enforcement Agency (United States)
ERIC-SJ	*Equipo de Reflexión, Investigación, y Comunicación (de la Compaña de Jesús)*

FECORAH	*Federación de Cooperativas Agropecuarias y Empresas de la Reforma Agraria de Honduras*
FENACH	*Federación Nacional de Campesinos de Honduras*
FENATRINILH	*Federación Nacional de Tribus para la Liberación del Indio Hondureño*
FETRIXY	*Federación de Tribus Xicacques de Yoro (Tolupan)*
FMLN	*Frente Farabundo Marti para la Liberación Nacional* (El Salvador)
FNRP	*Frente Nacional de Resistencia Popular* (Honduras)
FSLN	*Frente Sandinista de Liberación Nacional* (Nicaragua)
FUNACAMH	*Frente Nacional Unitario de Campesinos de Honduras*
FUSEP	*Fuerza de Seguridad Pública*
ILO	International Labor Organization
INA	*Instituto Nacional Agrario*
LIBRE	*Partido de Liberación y Refundación*
MADJ	*Movimiento Amplio por la Democracia y Justicia*
MARCA	*Movimiento Auténtico Reivindicador Campesino del Aguán*
MASTA	*Moskitia Asia Takanka* (Miskito)
MCA	*Movimiento Guadalupe Carney*
NAFTA	North American Free Trade Agreement
ODECO	*Organización para el Desarrollo Étnico Comunitario* (Garifuna)
OFRANEH	*Organización Fraternal Negra de Honduras* (Garifuna)
ONILH	*Organización Nacional Indígena Lenca de Honduras*

PATH	*Proyecto de Administración de Tierras de Honduras* (government plan)
RED	*Regiones Especiales de Desarrollo*
SOA	School of the Americas
SOAW	School of the Americas Watch
Sociedad Cultural	*Sociedad Cultural Abraham Lincoln* (Garifuna)
UFCo	United Fruit Company
UNC	*Unión Nacional de Campesinos*
ZEDES	*Zonas de Empleo y Desarrollo Económico y Social*

Chapter One

Encounters with Honduras

Resistance and Resilience

One night in May 2012, fifteen-year-old Ebed Yanes waited until his parents had gone to bed. Then, on his father's motorcycle, he drove through the darkened streets of Tegucigalpa, the Honduran capital, to see a girl he had met on Facebook. He knew it was dangerous to be out in the city at night, but romance got the better of prudence. As he turned into a street, Ebed ran headlong into a military checkpoint, and drove through without stopping. Soldiers pursued him in their vehicle and shot him. He was unarmed. A young soldier in the patrol who had witnessed the killing was troubled by it and went to the public prosecutor's office (*Ministerio Público*). A neighbor who saw the shooting told Ebed's father. The father began his own investigation while military officers attempted a cover-up. One year later this led to a very rare event—charges filed against several military officers—but not until the young soldier had struggled with his conscience, and Ebed's father and some very brave lawyers had struggled through the Honduran judicial system to obtain a measure of justice.

This book is about Honduras and its people. It is a book about human resilience because this is at the core of much of Honduran history and society. The dominant narrative about Honduras—a tale of violence, fear, and oppression—does indeed express the context and circumstances in which Hondurans too often live, but alone it becomes disempowering and often obscures the ways in which the Honduran people survive, resist, and transform the conditions that would destroy them. My intent in this book is to contribute to an appreciation and understanding of how Hondurans have fashioned and carried forward a way of life and a particular culture of resistance that at times embodies and sustains this resilience. In this way, this study can also contribute to the developing analysis and understanding of social transformation, popular resistance, and the so-called weapons of the weak.[1]

Resistance to violent and oppressive conditions is often understood in terms of small acts of subversion, public acts of denunciation, or armed struggle. In Honduras, one also encounters another form of resistance, a more positive response. People are busy building patiently and piece by piece a new model of a better society, practicing daily in a thousand ways their vision of the future they want, as if in defiance of the reality that is around them. This can be an enormously dangerous enterprise, but Hondurans often say that not to engage it would be even more costly.

ENCOUNTERING HONDURAS: STRUGGLE AND RESILIENCE

I first encountered Honduras in 1974. As a graduate student in anthropology at a university in the United States, I had been doing fieldwork in Jamaica for my dissertation on land tenure and social change when I heard stories from Honduras that the government under General Lopez Arrellano had, quite uncharacteristically, passed an agrarian reform law that seemed to hold the possibility of land for hundreds of thousands of poor and landless peasant farmers. Since I was at that time a Jesuit, I arranged a visit to the Jesuit community in El Progreso, a city in northern Honduras near the heart of what had been the huge banana plantations owned by United Fruit and other United States companies. The afternoon of my arrival, one of my hosts took me for a short ride to what he said was an important thing to see. We stopped near a unit of soldiers standing idly in the road as a group of peasant farmers in a nearby field were busy preparing part of the field for planting. My host explained that we were witnessing a *toma de tierra* (land taking). The land was an unused portion of a large cattle ranch owned, I was told, by the McDonald's hamburger and fast food corporation. These landless peasant farmers were occupying this piece of company land, without permission, to grow food. At another moment in Honduran history, the military would have evicted and possibly arrested the peasants, or the landowner's private security guards would have shot a few peasants and run the rest off the land. Land takeovers by peasant farmers were characterized as terrorism, while the harsh and sometimes deadly response of landowners and authorities was not considered terrorism. But on that particular day in 1974, in the middle of an all-too-short period of reform, the government seemed to ignore the company's complaints, and the soldiers simply observed—and probably prevented the company's own guards from interfering as well. This was my first encounter with the resilience of Honduran peasants and small farmers, the precarious world in which they live, and some of the forces seemingly arrayed against them.

When next I saw Honduras in 1984, the country was experiencing the effects of one of the more repressive episodes in its history, in part a reaction to events in neighboring El Salvador and Nicaragua. In El Salvador the Farabundo Marti Front for National Liberation (FMLN) had been waging a guerrilla-style war against the government and trying to advance a program of major change to improve the lives of the poor and reduce the dominance of a small group of wealthy families. In Nicaragua, in July 1979, the Sandinista Front for National Liberation (FSLN) overthrew the brutal dictatorship of the Somoza family that had ruled Nicaragua for forty-five years. The FSLN declared a revolutionary government and a program of major economic and social change focused on improving the lives of the rural population and gaining national sovereignty over the country's economic assets.

These events raised major concerns among the economic and military elite that controlled the Honduran government, and for the Reagan Administration that took office in Washington in 1981. The reaction was swift. Honduran military chief Gustavo Alvarez adopted in full measure the doctrine of national security, claiming that the Sandinista government in Nicaragua was planning an invasion of Honduras to establish communism there, and that drastic measures were called for to defend the country—an assertion that the Reagan Administration also used to develop a massive U.S. military presence in Honduras.[2] The country became thoroughly militarized. In Tegucigalpa, the capital, Honduran military units routinely rounded up young men from the streets, pressed some into the army, and jailed or disappeared others deemed potentially subversive. In the countryside, military roadblocks stopped busses to search male passengers. In an interview, an opposition member of the Honduran Congress said, "This is an occupied country with four armies, and it is run out of the United States Embassy." He listed the armies: Honduran, United States, Salvadoran military receiving training from U.S. advisers, and the anti-Sandinista Contras who had camps along the Nicaraguan border. The Honduran military developed Battalion 316, characterized by many Hondurans as a death squad that targeted opponents of the government and "subversives." The latter category included peasant and labor union activists, university students and professors, priests, and many others.[3]

In response to this repressive context, new organizations were born, such as the Honduran Committee for the Defense of Human Rights (CODEH), the Committee of the Families of the Disappeared/Detained in Honduras (COFADEH), the Honduran Documentation Center (CEDOH), the Reflection, Investigation, and Communication Team in Progreso (ERIC), religiously based human rights groups, student and environmental organizations, and others. In several visits to Honduras in the 1980s, my wife and I met some courageous and mostly middle-class leaders of these organizations. Many of them lived with daily threats against their lives. The CODEH office in Tegucigalpa was bombed and its outside wall was painted with graffiti linking its director to the Nicaraguan Sandinistas ("*Doctorcito Sandinista*"). But the organizations continued (most of them are still active today). This was my second encounter with the resilience of many Hondurans.

During the 1980s, Honduras received thousands of refugees from Guatemala and especially from El Salvador and Nicaragua. By the latter part of the decade, almost ten thousand Salvadorans were gathered in two large refugee camps in southwestern Honduras. Some of them were survivors of the so-called Rio Sumpul massacre of May 14, 1980, in which Salvadoran and Honduran military units killed many refugees who were trying to cross the river that separates the two countries.[4] Salvadoran military units were said to pursue fleeing refugees into Honduras without much interference from the Honduran military. As a staff member in the Boston headquarters of Oxfam America in the early 1980s, I heard stories from our field representative in Honduras about this refugee exodus. A typical example involved a group of about twenty weary, frightened, and hungry Salvadorans who reached the house of a peasant family on the Honduran side of the border. The elderly grandfather and his extended family welcomed them, fed them, and allowed them to stay and rest. Before long a unit of Salvadoran soldiers arrived at the house. The grandfather came out to meet them. The lieutenant said he was there to take custody of the refugees. The grandfather replied, "This is Honduras and this is my house. I own this house, and you get lost!" The Salvadoran soldiers left without the refugees.

Such accounts of the hospitality that ordinary Hondurans offered Salvadoran refugees in those difficult days were impressive and raised questions about why and how Hondurans acted thus. A few years later with my wife I was able to make several visits to the major camps of Salvadoran refugees at Colomoncagua and Mesa Grande in southwestern Honduras. We also visited the large camp of Nicaraguan refugees near Jacaleapa in southeastern Honduras along the Nicaraguan border. The area was not far from the training camps of the anti-Sandinista Contras. Local staff of the Catholic organization Caritas told us that as many as ten thousand Hondurans in this rural area had been displaced from their land or had seen their lives disrupted by the Contra presence and the refugee influx.

The 1990s brought some changes in Central America, including a more conservative, non-revolutionary government in Nicaragua, and a relative softening of the most oppressive aspects of the national security doctrine in Honduras, although the old and deeply entrenched attitudes and practices continued. A small elite continued to regard the majority of the population as resources to further the development plans of the elite or as hindrances that had to be moved aside. The number of landless peasants grew, and their efforts to obtain land to feed their families continued to follow familiar patterns such as widespread incidents of organized *tomas de tierra* especially at the start of planting season each May and June. Land conflicts and incidents of violence related to land went on unabated, and even increased.[5] Central American countries encountered a globalized world economy where neoliberal policies of privatization, lack of government economic intervention, reduction of social services and social safety nets for the poor, increasing concentration of wealth among fewer families, and an expansion of extractive industries—mining, logging—as well as a rapidly expanding narcotics trade were the order of the day.

In this context a remarkable convergence of sorts seemed to be evolving. The older popular organizations, especially the labor and peasant unions and indigenous organizations that had emerged as political forces to be dealt with in the 1950s, 1960s, and 1970s, and newer organizations that had emerged especially in the early 1980s to promote human rights, indigenous rights, and environmental protection often found themselves working toward similar goals using, at times, similar means. One example was the popular protest that formed to challenge the 1991 agreement between the Honduran government and Stone Container Corporation, a major foreign cardboard manufacturer. When it was known that the agreement gave the corporation rights to extract timber from thousands of acres of eastern Honduras (Olancho), peasants, indigenous communities, students, environmentalists, and many others joined the protests. While not entirely new in Honduras, this convergence of interests seemed to be increasing during the last decade of the twentieth century. Human rights groups saw peasant, indigenous, and environmental activism as human rights concerns, especially when activists were threatened and killed. In 1997, I wrote about a gradually evolving culture of protest that seemed somehow and tenuously to unite social classes and local and particular concerns.[6]

Early in the morning of June 28, 2009, a unit of the Honduran military acting on orders from the Congress and the Supreme Court entered the home of President Manuel Zelaya, took him—still in his pajamas—to the airport, and sent him into exile in Costa Rica. The president of Congress assumed an interim presidency until elections were held in November in a context of widespread popular protest against the "coup" (*golpe de estado*) and widespread military and police repression of the massive popular protests that arose in reaction to the coup. This was the first coup against a duly elected civilian president in the Western Hemisphere in the new millennium. People had imagined that such things belonged to the region's past. The coup gained attention in world media, but the mounting popular protests and the repression that followed gained the attention of many outside Honduras who cared about or had a connection to the country and its people. Some Hondurans said the repression was as bad as or worse than that of the national security state of the early 1980s.

The protests and the repression that grew after the coup had roots in long-standing social and economic inequities going back decades, perhaps centuries. By the mid-1990s, this long-standing situation had become increasingly complicated by narcotics trafficking (Mexican and Colombian drug cartels had moved into Central America), expanding official corruption, a lucrative enterprise in arms sales seemingly controlled by senior and retired members of the Honduran security forces, and a crisis of identity, opportunity, and security among the country's disillusioned youth. Added to older conflicts over land and resources, these were ingredients for a perfect storm of violence and repression. Yet within this context, Hondurans often used the Spanish term *resistencia* to connote both resistance and resilience, the active construction of a better life in the midst of the present reality.

SOCIAL CHANGE AND THE BETTER LIFE

I have had a lifetime interest in the question of how people envision a better life and engage in changing their society toward that vision. This interest is personal. I was a child in an immigrant, working-class community, son of a family of labor union activists, and had a religious upbringing that emphasized social justice and the dignity of the "ordinary" person. It is personal not only because of my own early experiences but also because fieldwork and research among a people so often leads to friendships and involvements in the lives of those among whom one attempts such enterprises. Caring deeply about those you "study" is a major occupational hazard among anthropologists. In my visits to Honduras over several decades I have made friends with people whom I have come to regard as generous, courageous, committed to bettering the lives of others, and often deeply reflective and spiritual humans. That they live in and confront violence and oppression concerns me. This is all the more personal inasmuch as I live in a society that has had a long and intimate, albeit problematic, relationship with the people of Honduras. One need only study the history of United States involvement to see how deeply that involvement has affected the lives of Hondurans.

My interest in social change is also the focus of my professional training. This book is the product, in part, of an anthropological, social scientific perspective. The example of colleagues in Latin America and the Caribbean has taught me that the social sciences are almost always a matter of urgency. In Central America, the social sciences are critical in at least two ways. They deal with critical issues that deeply affect the lives of people and nations, and they constitute a critical interrogation of what is or seems to be. A sense of both the urgency of daily lives and the analytical interrogation of context are required and mutually complementary in the "dangerous anthropology" of situations in which human lives may be lost or saved daily.

NOTHING IS SIMPLE

With each bit of research and each engagement with situations, my understanding of social change has become increasingly complex. It is necessary to disabuse oneself of the idea that people guide their daily actions toward the actualization of fully developed ideals of societal change. How people envision change and work for it seems so often to be a gradual and almost imperceptible process. Daily life is pragmatic. How does one survive and make this here-and-now a bit easier or more secure? How to exercise some measure of control over the essentially uncontrollable? Yet in some fashion people do construct and are guided by larger dreams and visions of what is right and good and how their society should function. The relationship between daily action and larger visions is an enduring concern of human inquiry.

A related complexity arises with the observation that the question of acting to make a better life seems to be most urgent when the current life is experienced as particularly oppressive, unstable, or even unbearable. One is led to ask whether there is a continuum between everyday acts of resistance and empowerment in what people experience as "ordinary" oppressive conditions and those experiences that seem especially oppressive. When does the agenda move from daily survival to societal change? Put differently, when, if ever, do daily survival and societal change become one and the same in a community's thoughts and actions? Is it as Eric Wolf described? "[By the time] the peasant protagonist lights the torch of rebellion, the edifice of society is already smoldering and ready to take fire."[7] Do Hondurans live in a context where this question is always near at hand?

The terms we use to identify or describe people often hide complex realities. We shall be forced constantly to remember that the Honduran "elite" is really a diverse set of individuals who, although they share certain commonalities and interests, are yet quite different in other ways. Differences and even conflicts among the economically and politically powerful in Honduras have appeared throughout the country's history, sometimes in ways that affect the prospects for popular resistance and change. In 2013, for example, when the Honduran Congress passed a statute to create *Regiones Especiales de Desarrollo* (Special Development Regions, RED) four judges in the Honduran Supreme Court declared the statute unconstitutional, but the Congress simply (and outside of due process) dismissed the four judges and replaced them with others who approved the law. Economic interests in the Congress that had proposed the statute clashed with judges who saw the law as a threat to national sovereignty. Similarly, groups sometimes referred to as the popular resistance, the popular organizations, or other such terms are also a diverse population with similarities and important differences. Moreover, there are situations in which individuals among the powerful and the popular see some common interest. These instances are many and the results can range from opportunities for positive improvement in people's lives to situations of cooptation, division, and even a sense of "betrayal" within popular organizations.

In Honduras no story is simple, and things are too often not quite what they seem. But then, discerning the complexity is what anthropologists are paid the "big bucks" to do. For Hondurans, discerning the complexity is quite often a question of survival, of life or death.

CULTURE AS CHANGE

Culture has been defined and understood in many different ways.[8] The term arose in part out of the nation-building and empire-building epoch of Europe in the nineteenth century. Culture referred to those material and ideological traits that characterized a group of people and their daily way of life. Culture implied a discrete and bounded set of characteristics, a "complex whole" that defined a particular human group and distinguished the members of that group from others who did not seem to share the same culture. This was sometimes labeled an "essentialist" understanding of culture because it implied that a particular set of characteristics defined the essence of a group of people.

There were potential problems with this essentialist understanding of culture. It tended to exclude or subordinate human diversity and to ignore the presence of social and cultural conflict. It had little to say about the relationship of the individual to society and the question of human particularity, and it seemed to imply that everyone acted in concert. The essentialist idea of culture implied that "culture" was static rather than dynamic when, in fact, human groups are constantly adopting ideas, traits, language, and much more from each other, and conflict among people and groups is normal. Few, if any, human groups continue to live the same way they lived a century ago. This static idea of culture also implied that the world was a set of discrete, bounded, and essentially disconnected entities within which harmony was always maintained. At least since the advent of modern colonialism, the lives of people in even the most isolated human groups have been continually altered and shaped by external forces that may be close at hand or far away. In short, the essentialist idea of culture seemed inadequate to describe and understand a changing, interrelated, dynamic world.

Since at least the 1960s, the processes by which human groups function has been a focus of inquiry and theory, and a more processual and dynamic idea of culture has emerged in which individuals and groups negotiate such basics as identity, meaning, and adaptation to changing environments, and are part of larger, global economic, political, and social systems. By the 1970s, theorists such as the Brazilian educator Paulo Freire emphasized that human adaptation could be understood not merely as acquiescence to necessity or limitation, but as a form of active empowerment and a vehicle for change. Freire called this *integration* with one's environment as opposed to "mere adaptation."[9] For Freire, the symbols and language that people use to express their reality provide powerful "cultural" resources in giving voice to the voiceless and in forming a community for change out of a collection of isolated individuals. In Freire's terms, people *become* subjects that act upon their environment. In this sense, people begin to claim identity—an expression of the self in relation to others—and subjectivity, "insight into a person's embodied experience of who he or she is within a hierarchy of power."[10]

One great advantage of seeing culture as constructive and conflictive processes in which humans engage is that it understands humans as active agents in shaping their lives. In Honduras there are people who go beyond simply adapting passively to a changing environment. They mount collective resistance to mining, agribusiness, logging, and other corporate and government enterprises that would radically alter the natural environments that sustain people and communities. They contest the identification of peasant and labor leaders as terrorists or common criminals; instead they identify as martyrs those who are killed defending the interests of the people. What officialdom means by justice, the popular resistance understands to mean official impunity. What elites call economic development is understood to mean perpetual inequity and poverty for the majority and the violation of national sovereignty. People do all of this by constructing images and expressions of the reality they see and the one they want, and they do so using cultural resources in a creative process.

CULTURE AND RESISTANCE

The term "culture of resistance," or its associate term, "cultural resistance," has come into common usage in scholarly and activist networks in recent years, although the concept is sometimes said to be almost as old as human civilization.[11] There is something slightly disconcerting about the juxtaposition of the idea of culture tied to the image of resistance. Culture often conjures pictures of creative yet orderly daily life, a sense of normalcy and tradition. Culture is often linked to ideas of "civilized" life as opposed to the wildness of nature or to barbarism and chaos. Resistance, however, evokes something not quite normal, a disruption of ordinary life, a situation in which the outcome is uncertain, not like the security that the idea of culture seems to provide. Resistance seems inherently negative and insecure, as if it were somehow a living critique of what passes for ordinary daily life. Those charged with maintaining and perpetuating what passes for culture, the orderly daily life, often characterize forms of resistance as threats to security and tradition.

The idea of a culture of resistance raises the question of the relationship between two fundamental experiences of human life—culture and power. Human life is shaped not only by tradition, custom, and whatever else one thinks of as culture, but also by the exercise of power in its economic, social, political, and physical forms. How is power used to shape or reshape culture? How does culture structure the forms of power and the manner in which it is used?[12]

The term culture of resistance implies the question, how do humans use cultural resources to obtain and exercise power over daily life? Traditionally there have been at least two answers to this question, two ways to use culture in the pursuit of power—hegemony (the appropriation of cultural symbols, values, ideologies to impose control over others) and resistance (the use of cultural resources to critique, challenge, or weaken hegemonic power or to provide an alternative empowerment). Typically hegemony has been ascribed to the machinations of elites, while resistance is identified as the work of subordinated groups. In chapter 2, we shall explore more thoroughly how an ideology of dominance is constructed and employed by the powerful who control Honduran society. In later chapters, we examine the ways in which Hondurans critique and challenge the images of reality presented in this ideology, and how they use cultural resources to construct a different image of reality—not just a desired future but one constructed, haltingly and at great cost, in present everyday life. The very act of constructing the better society in everyday and often apparently mundane ways, may be interpreted as a work of resilience and a critique of the current situation and of those who seem to control it. This book suggests that this construction of a better society is at the core of resistance and resilience in Honduras.

CULTURAL RESOURCES AS INSTRUMENTS OF POWER

Cultural values, beliefs, terms, rituals, and symbols are resources used by both politically and economically dominant and subordinated people in their everyday struggles over power and empowerment. Framed into ideologies—systems of values, symbols, beliefs, and expectations—they codify, instruct, motivate, and justify actions, either as statements of how things are or of how they should be but are not. Ideologies are not synonymous or co-extensive with the entirety of "culture," but are rather selective in the cultural resources that are referenced in constructing the ideology at hand.[13] Ideologies can move people to engage the current political, economic, and social reality in ways that are meant either to reinforce or to alter that reality. This engagement, this mobilization is a question of power. Cultural resources of the current reality may be used and fashioned to enliven and mobilize the social, economic, and political power to fashion a new reality. In this sense, people make and remake cultures—ways of living—as they "engage each other in diverse social, economic, and political arenas," and culture is constructed, reconstructed, and altered through the exercise of power.[14] In this way, any essentialist view of culture becomes misleading or useless. Instead, cultural elements may be assembled and reassembled in a particular place and time out of a global pool of cultural resources through the exercise of various kinds of power.[15] This power may take the form of constructing systems of economic dependency or developing means of breaking that dependency; isolating individuals and dividing communities or mobilizing massive social or political resistance. Ideologies are not the source of power, but are often the means of tapping, mobilizing, and channeling economic, social, and political power in a society, either to maintain or to change the current situation.

Hondurans use many different cultural resources to construct critiques of what is wrong and models of a new or different reality. These resources include such things as indigenous traditions and patterns of survival and resistance; religious and spiritual beliefs, values, and symbols; laws and statements of justice and rights, both national and international; farming technologies that lessen reliance on foreign or expensive chemical inputs; food, diet, and cuisine as expressions of empowerment; traditional forms of organization that emphasize democratic participation and sharing across social class; popular and public art, music, theater, and poetry; preservation of history and collective memory; reclamation of public spaces for everyday social activities; and more. It is important to realize that these ways of constructing a new reality involve not just thought or occasional protests but also actually beginning to live the desired change. It is Gandhi's famous quote about being the change you want, but in a context where living the change can be dangerous, as Hondurans know well. There are boundaries and constraints on the deployment and efficacy of cultural resources that should become evident in later chapters.

ABOUT THE BOOK

I see the writing of this book as one small piece in the "urgent social science" mentioned above. It will quickly become apparent that I have an interest in seeing Hondurans succeed in overcoming or transforming the oppression and violence that troubles their lives, although there are various images of what that success might look like. The subject of this book makes apparent my concern for the question of how people survive, resist, and transform an oppressive reality. To explore this question is difficult without some understanding of what people are resisting, what policies, conditions, or situations drive people to resist. Describing these conditions, in turn, is difficult without describing a society seemingly divided between those who dominate and those who are oppressed. But the intent of this book is not so much to portray these as distinct groups, and not to vilify one group and champion the other. Honduran society is evolving, moving toward some future as yet unknown, but it cannot do so without the evolution of all sectors of society. While this book focuses on those who "resist," it should be clear that their resistance is one important force and influence in a complex social system in which everyone is influenced and shaped by various social and cultural forces.

I try to understand something about the popular resistance of Hondurans through a combination of external observation and interpretation combined with glimpses, when possible, into the ways in which some Hondurans, at least, understand their resistance. Students of anthropology will recognize this as the etic (outside) and emic (inside) perspectives. This book does not pretend to portray fully and accurately a "Honduran perspective" on resistance. I cannot do so both because of the limitations of my own experience and methods, and because there is no one "Honduran perspective" on anything. The many perspectives that exist are always changing. At best, this book tries to offer a few glimpses of how some Hondurans see things, as it also provides a structured interpretation of recorded and recordable events. The perspective is often historical or, rather, evolutionary—not a history but an attempt to see some patterns in historical developments that conduct Honduran society to the present and may perhaps suggest something about a possible future.

This book combines certain features of ethnography and history, but it does not pretend to be an ethnography or a history. It is an attempt to discover patterns, trends, and characteristics that can promote a deeper understanding of how Hondurans manage to survive, engage, and transform the difficult conditions of their society and their country. I combine information and insights gained from my visits and short periods of fieldwork in Honduras stretching over forty years, materials from some of my own previous articles and writings, scholarly studies by other anthropologists and writers, and a variety of news items and analytical and interpretive articles in both Honduran and international news media and journals and in publications of Honduran organizations in the period between 1980 and 2014. I also incorporate ideas and perspectives from long discussions and shorter interviews with activists and scholars in Honduras and in the United States.

Writing this book presented several challenges. During the most recent period, and especially at the time of writing, events and conditions in Honduras seemed to be changing daily. Every morning my wife or I found fresh news items online that could range from new laws passed or policies outlined by the Honduran government, to the latest political or drug-related assassinations, or the most recent letter about Honduras from members of the U.S. Congress to the secretary of state. The "crisis" of thousands of Honduran young people seeking asylum at the southern U.S. border exploded onto national media and consciousness while I was writing. I once remarked to a fellow student of Honduras that trying to understand—much less write about—Honduras during this time was like shooting at a fast-moving target. The phrase expressed the feeling, but was perhaps morosely appropriate, given the prevalence of gun violence in Honduras at the time. I kept reminding myself that the purpose of this study was not to describe the mountain of details but rather something of the geology of the mountain. A more important challenge was the sensitive nature of trying to explore popular resistance in a country where political and other retribution and violence are widespread. Discretion is a standard feature of any ethnographic study, especially in potentially conflictive situations such as described in this book. I have employed a fairly standard anthropological practice of using pseudonyms or general anonymous descriptions when referring to people who are not already widely known or "high profile" in Honduras, or whose actual identity is incidental to the meaning. Individuals and organizations already publicly prominent are usually identified.

This study mentions many Honduran and some U.S. and international organizations, each with its acronym and a Spanish or English name. A list of these is provided early in the book. Translations from Spanish to English of both organizational titles and texts quoted from Spanish originals are my own unless otherwise noted. Occasionally, I retained the original Spanish word or phrase in parentheses in the English translation if the word's meaning is complex or especially nuanced.

The next two chapters examine the ideology and practices of domination deployed by members of the Honduran economic and political "elite." This provides an idea of what the popular resistance is actually trying to resist. Chapter 4 traces aspects of the evolution of a broad culture of resistance in Honduras. Chapters 5 through 9 explore different manifestations of the culture of resistance in different aspects of daily life and national institutions. Chapter 10 deals with U.S. involvement with Honduras because of its importance to Honduras and to Honduran popular resistance.

NOTES

1. James C. Scott, *Weapons of the Weak: Everyday Forms of Peasant Resistance* (New Haven, CT: Yale University Press, 1985).
2. Maria Oseguera de Ochoa. *Honduras hoy: Sociedad y crisis política* (Tegucigalpa: Centro de Documentación de Honduras, 1987), 64–67.
3. Alison Acker, *Honduras: The Making of a Banana Republic* (Boston: South End Press, 1988), 64–67. For a discussion of the national security doctrine and its application in Honduras, see Leticia Salomón, "La doctrina de la seguridad nacional en Honduras," *Honduras Boletín Informativo* (Tegucigalpa: Centro de Documentación de Honduras, May, 1984).
4. Yvonne Dilling, *In Search of Refuge* (Scottsdale, PA: Herald Press, 1984), details this incident and the events surrounding it. Dilling was an eyewitness and participated in trying to rescue people from the Sumpul River during the incident.
5. Tanya Kerssen, *Grabbing Land: The New Struggles for Land, Power, and Democracy in Northern Honduras* (Oakland, CA: Food First, Institute for Food and Development Policy, 2013) provides an extended discussion of such land conflicts as they continued and developed.
6. Greg Grigg, "Honduran People Say No to Stone" (*Focus on Honduras*, Summer, 1992), 1–3. James Phillips, "Resource Access, Environmental Struggles, and Human Rights in Honduras," *Life and Death Matters: Human Rights and the Environment at the End of the Millennium*, ed. Barbara Rose Johnston (Walnut Creek, CA: AltaMira Press, 1997), 173–84.
7. Eric R. Wolf, *Peasant Wars of the Twentieth Century* (New York: Harper and Row, 1969), 284.
8. A. L. Kroeber, Clyde Kluckhohn, and Wayne Untereiner, *Culture; A Critical Review of Concepts and Definitions* (New York: Vintage Press, 1952). See also Robert Winthrop, *Dictionary of Concepts in Cultural Anthropology* (New York: Greenwood Press, 1991).
9. Paulo Freire, *Pedagogy of the Oppressed* (New York: Herder and Herder, 1970). Paulo Freire, *Education for Critical Consciousness* (New York: Seabury, 1973). See also, Paulo Freire, Ana Maria Araújo Freire, Walter de Oliveira, and Donald Machedo, *Pedagogy of Solidarity: Qualitative Inquiry and Social Justice* (Walnut Creek, CA: Left Coast Press, 2014).
10. Adrienne Pine, *Working Hard, Drinking Hard: On Violence and Survival in Honduras* (Berkeley: University of California Press, 2008), 12.
11. Stephen Duncombe, "Cultural Resistance," *Blackwell Encyclopedia of Sociology*, ed. George Ritzer (London: Blackwell, 2007) argues that while the general idea of using culture to resist oppressive power is ancient, the modern idea was born with Matthew Arnold's essay, "Culture and Anarchy" (1869), in which Arnold held out his idea of culture as "the best which has been thought and said" in opposition to what he saw as the anarchy of industrialized nineteenth-century England. Dunmore argues that Arnold thought of culture as representing a principle of authority to challenge anarchy. Arnold's idea seems quite different from the more recent use of the term in such examples as Eben Bernard's review essay, "Cultural Resistance: Can Such Practices Ever Have a Meaningful Impact?" (*Critical Social Thinking: Policy and Practice*, vol. 3, No. 2, 2011. This is also explored in the feature-length film by filmmaker Iara Lee, entitled *Cultures of Resistance*, (released 2010) that has received various film awards; and a website, http://www.culturesofresistance.org, maintained by the Cultures of Resistance Network.
12. For a discussion of this idea, see Skidmore and Smith, *Modern Latin America*, fifth edition (New York: Oxford University Press, 2001), esp. prologue and epilogue. The idea that culture and power are dynamically related underlies much of modern anthropology. The idea that power is used to reshape or transform "culture" underlies much of the critique of colonialism and Marxist-inspired analysis. Much of the work of Eric Wolf and Sidney Mintz, for example, explores aspects of this relationship, for example, Wolf's *Europe and the People Without History* (Berkeley: University of California Press, 1983); and Mintz's *Sweetness and Power: The Place of Sugar in Modern History* (New York: Viking, 1985).
13. Jean Comaroff and John Comaroff, *Of Revelation and Revolution* (Chicago: University of Chicago Press, 1991), 20.

14. Eric R. Wolf, *Envisioning Power: Ideologies of Dominance and Crisis* (Berkeley: University of California Press, 1999), 274–75. E. Paul Durrenberger, "Anthropology and Globalization," *American Anthropologist* 103:2 (June 2001): 531–35.

15. Arjun Appadurai, "Disjuncture and Difference in the Global Cultural Economy, *Theory, Culture, and Society* 7 (1990): 295–310.

Chapter Two

A Culture of Domination

To understand the nature of popular resistance in Honduras it is important to understand what occasions such resistance. What provokes popular resistance is a system of social, economic, and political domination exercised by the few over the lives and resources of the many manifest in hundreds of large and small ways every day. Fundamentally, this domination works by redefining reality in ways that debilitate and delimit the human possibilities and potential of whole groups, as James Scott points out. "The function of a system of domination is to accomplish precisely this: to define what is realistic and what is not realistic and to drive certain goals and aspirations into the realm of the impossible . . . the realm of idle dreams and wishful thinking."[1] In this chapter, we explore the ideological bases of this construction of reality. In the next chapter, we examine some of the everyday ways in which domination is enforced.

THE MASSACRE AT EL ASTILLERO

On May 5, 1991, five peasants were shot and killed as they slept on a piece of land they had peacefully occupied in northern Honduras. The peasants were part of a group to whom the government had awarded title to the land fifteen years earlier, but several large landowners including an army colonel had continued to claim it. The colonel was accused of sending his security guards or hired hands to attack the peasants and drive them off the land. According to survivors, the attackers sprayed the area with machine gun fire. Known throughout Honduras as the El Astillero massacre, this incident and others like it gave rise to popular songs in peasant communities, including one with these words: "The land is for sustaining life, not just for the powerful. The life of a peasant is worth the same as a rich man's."[2] In May 1995, an immigration judge in the United States granted political asylum to two survivors of the El Astillero massacre.

This incident and so many more form part of an historic pattern that illustrates a set of power relationships shaped by attitudes and supported by an ideology of dominance and subordination that seemingly justifies the actions of the powerful over the land, resources, and people of Honduras. This chapter begins with a more extended, complex, and layered example of this pattern of power relations from the Department of Yoro, then discusses the evolution of societal roles of class dominance and subordination in Honduras, and ends with an exposition of the ideology that supports and tries to justify the control of the few over the many that was played out at El Astillero and elsewhere.

PATTERNS OF DOMINATION IN YORO

The Department of Yoro occupies a central portion of Honduras. Between the city of El Progreso and the sugar plantations of the Ulua Valley in the west and the old colonial city of Yoro in the east, much of the Department is a series of rugged mountains where Tolupán communities (*tribus*) have lived for centuries as small farmers. The Tolupán (also know as Hicaque or Xicaque) claim to their land rests on traditional legal treaty rights that go back at least to the mid-nineteenth century, and perhaps to Spanish colonial times, as J. M. Tojeira discusses at length.[3] Beginning in colonial times and continuing to the present, a small group of mostly non-Tolupán families began to amass landholdings in parts of Yoro. Today, some members of this local landed class feud among themselves over land, political office, and who will control and benefit from drug trafficking in the region.

In recent decades, the older bases of dominance that centered on control of land, patronage, and natural resources have expanded to include the wealth and power of the international narcotics trade. Local people say that certain politicians and prominent landowners are involved in narcotics trafficking. How heavily fortified one's house is—with guards, fences, weapons—is seen as a sign of who might be important in the drug trade. According to local accounts, around 2010 the mayor of the city of Yoro was killed in what seems to have been a feud between large landowning families. The man who was finally charged—there is a common belief that he was probably not guilty of the murder—was said to be involved in drug traffic in collaboration with large landowners. This incident perpetuated a feud between prominent families over land, resources, power, and the narcotics trade.

Evictions of peasants and peasant communities are an important part of the patterns of dominance in the area. Expulsions of entire communities occur with some frequency in this region. The following are cases of evictions reported by members of the local community in Yoro city. In October and November of 2012, gunmen came to Loma Alta (pseudonym), a community of nine peasant families, and told the community to abandon the land soon or they would be killed. Gunmen returned during the week before Christmas, ordered the community off the land at gunpoint, and told them not to return or they would be killed. Not trusting the local authorities in this matter, the Catholic parish and others sent a *carta de denuncia* to national authorities in Tegucigalpa detailing and denouncing this incident. Although the denunciations received no formal response, women of the community soon began to move back to their homes. Some people took this as a sign that national authorities had quietly exerted "pressure" on the local perpetrators. Most of the men of the community stayed away.

Quebrada Alta (pseudonym) is a community of 112 people, nineteen houses or compounds, and an extensive area of land. On August 19, 2013, about twenty-five heavily armed men arrived during the night and ordered the entire community to leave immediately and not to return or they would be killed. The entire community fled, and some found temporary refuge in the city of Yoro. At the time of this eviction, the community was said to be preparing to harvest the coffee crop and had also been trying to protect extensive stands of mahogany higher up the mountain. Quebrada Alta was located on land of a local Tolupán tribe. A large landowner claimed that the tribe had sold the land to him, but community members claimed the tribe had given or leased the land to the community. No papers were produced to support either claim. Small amounts of antimony had been mined by hand in the area for some years, but in 2012, a company began mining with machines, raising concern among local communities that the land and water in the area might become contaminated.

In Honduras, individual large landowners stage takeovers of the land in different parts of Honduras for several reasons. Some want to expand their production of lucrative export commodities, such as palm oil on plantations of African palm in the north of the country. In regions such as central and eastern Yoro, takeovers are sometimes a form of revenge against other landowners who may have relatives, connections, or economic interest in a particular community, or they are preemptive actions to take control of more land before other prominent families do. Evictions are direct means of acquiring control of more land and especially resources, in particular coffee harvests and higher altitude forest stands of precious mahogany (*caoba*) that may be claimed by local Toulpan and other peasant communities. If challenged, large landowners who displace Tolupán communities from land usually supply some form of legal argument to contest a community's land rights. But legal processes are often a formality, since threat and force are usually all that is needed. According to local people, there are many poorer, unemployed men willing to make money as hired guns, and large landowners hire them to stage expulsions and assassinations against local communities.

On August 21, 2013, the first report I heard of Quebrada Alta's eviction included speculation that local landowners involved in narcotics trafficking might have wanted the community's land to facilitate drug transshipment. The actual story shows a more complex picture of old family feuds and old land conflicts in an evolving new context of narcotics trafficking and political corruption. A Catholic priest who had some familiarity with the community at Quebrada Alta and others like it said that the violence of this eviction was particularly heinous inasmuch as the people of these communities were "*muy humilde*" (very humble). He did not mean that they had simply accepted the identity that the powerful had imposed upon them for so long, but rather something deeper, older, and more complex. The traditional cultural resources of the people seemed to combine indigenous and Christian values emphasizing community, restraint, and the example of Jesus. They had also learned from perhaps centuries of experience the cost of resistance, and how to survive in a world dominated by others deploying power and force. These cultural and historical experiences became resources of survival even though in the short run they seemed to guarantee neither individual nor community survival nor the protection of community resources.

These incidents are a few of the many evictions of peasant communities that occur in Yoro and elsewhere in Honduras. They illustrate how many of the major forces and sources of dominance and violence come together—land and resource conflicts, elite infighting, drug traffic, political corruption and impunity, the extent of desperation from unemployment and poverty, and the wide availability of arms. They also reflect a sense of entitlement, and a set of beliefs, values, and assumptions—elements of an ideology of dominance—that can inform the actions of powerful members of Honduran society.

EVOLUTION OF AN "ELITE" CLASS

Some patterns of economic, political, and social dominance and power in Honduras today are rooted in mechanisms of control that were established in colonial times throughout many areas of Latin America. Under systems such as the *encomienda*, Spanish explorers and colonizers and their descendants received from the Spanish Crown, or they managed to acquire, the right to large tracts of land and the labor of the mostly indigenous peoples living on or near these tracts. A later version of this land and labor control system, the *hacienda*, continued in many areas of Latin America well into the middle of the twentieth century.[4] These systems were justified by racial ideas about the "inferiority" of indigenous people and the need for a prominent class to control the land and labor if civilization were to thrive in the region. These regimes of control reinforced the idea that a small group of prominent individuals had a natural right to use the land and its people for their own advancement and the development of civilized society.

Honduras today is a society dominated economically and politically by a small group of families totaling less that three hundred individuals. Members of these families control much of the country's land, large-scale agriculture, mining operations, and major industries from banks to breweries.[5] What they do not own is controlled largely by foreign transnational companies. In the past fifty years, the land base controlled by peasant and small farm communities has been under increasing pressure from several sources.[6] Urban expansion, environmental degradation, and population increase have taken a toll. But much of the land of peasant communities has been claimed by economically and politically powerful individuals or families or by government sponsored or supported projects—including foreign extractive enterprises—that displace peasants and rural communities. Since the government is regularly in the hands of two major political parties whose leaders are themselves usually members of the economic elite, these projects amount to another form of control over the development of the country by a small group, often resulting in the dispossession of peasants and rural communities.

The Honduran economic and political ruling class of today is the result of a turbulent history in which contending forces vied for control over major aspects of the country's development. Families descendant from the educated and socially dominant Criollos during and after the colonial period, and those who controlled the early development of mining in the south of the country in the nineteenth century formed an economic and political class based in and around Tegucigalpa in the last decades of that century. By the early 1900s, the Honduran north (Caribbean) coastal region and the Aguán Valley saw the expansion of foreign fruit companies and their plantations that displaced thousands of peasants and small farmers, many of whom were turned into plantation workers. The region also saw an influx of immigrants from the Middle East and elsewhere who became the core of a business community that thrived by serving the needs of the foreign companies and their workers in the expanding urban areas, especially San Pedro Sula. This commercial class provided capital for new industrial and agricultural ventures.[7] Although the interests of the southern mining barons sometimes conflicted with those of the northern commercial capitalists (who tended to be more aware of the concerns of the local working class populations and foreign investors such as the fruit companies) both groups had a common interest in directing and managing the country and its economic and political development.

Honduras also developed a small middle-class of educated clergy, physicians, government clerks, teachers, artisans, journalists, writers, and mid-level military officers. While much of the work of this middle-class was to serve the dominant institutions of society, individuals among them developed an ongoing level of criticism of those institutions and of the ruling class. During the late nineteenth and early twentieth centuries, newspapers, literary journals, and semi-fictional writing were important but limited outlets for these middle-class critiques of Honduran society.[8]

EVOLUTION AND CRISIS OF A "COMPLIANT" SOCIETY

Historical conditions that reinforced a behavior of acceptance and compliance among the poor in rural communities during the nineteenth century have in more recent years begun to change in ways that undermine compliance and the apparent passivity of these communities. Until the early decades of the twentieth century, in areas where the hacienda pattern or its remnants remained, large landowner, small farmer, landless peasant interacted in a narrow system of local relationships that was often maintained for generations. The closeness and interdependency of groups in this context promoted a sense among the powerful that harsh measures of control and dominance should be tempered prudently with practical measures that to some extent could mask or blunt the harsher edges of the system. In this kind of rural society, especially where the local economy was not well connected to a larger national or international economy, landlords could allow landless or land-poor peasants to sharecrop or rent unused portions of land, and they could adopt a sense of patronage over local rural communities—both lord and protector of these communities.[9] There was certainly resistance to this system among peasants and rural communities, but much of it was covert and tended to small acts of subversion done primarily to ease the burdens of daily life rather than to overthrow the system.

The relative isolation of many rural communities, especially in the nineteenth and the early twentieth century, meant that a sense of hierarchy, authority, and submission could be reinforced through the local power brokers such as the large landowners themselves or the priest, the schoolteacher, the local government official who mediated whatever relationship the local community and the peasants had with the larger world. The major institutional functions were church, administration of justice and collection of taxes, and perhaps maintenance of the few local roads. Local people had relationships to the large landowners who were also the holders of offices of justice and administration for the area, and more limited relations with the priest when he was able to come, and possibly a teacher who might also be a local person. There were few other relationships to larger institutions, and the institutions of national government were, in any case, relatively weak and limited in reach. This relative isolation made local communities more dependent on the few figures that represented larger institutions, and these were persons who could carefully filter information and influences coming from beyond the area. Isolation also meant that knowledge of alternatives or even basic education was often minimal among rural populations.

In Honduras since Spanish colonial times, and throughout much of the early history of independence, the rulers often implemented a system of political authority in indigenous communities that selected and placed certain local indigenous leaders or prominent people in positions of local political authority (*caciques* was the most common term) over indigenous communities. Caciques occupied a place as power brokers who carried out the mandates of the powerful who ruled the society, but were also culturally and socially connected to the local indigenous community. This "indirect rule" introduced a layer of authority and rule between the rulers and the local indigenous community that could complicate and blunt the question of who was responsible for oppressive measures.[10]

Changes in Honduran life that have accelerated since the 1950s have undermined some aspects of this older system of control and compliance, and introduced conditions and opportunities for the rise of more open resistance by local populations. The expansion of the banana companies in northern Honduras in the first half of the twentieth century often involved the forceful displacement of local communities, peasants, and small farmers. Some of these displaced people were already part-time workers on the banana plantations. This uprooting is often seen as a major contributor to the banana workers' strike of 1954 and the rise of labor and peasant unions and militancy. By the 1980s, the expansion of corporate sugar production by both Honduran and foreign interests and of African palm plantations geared to palm oil export involved sometimes violent displacement of rural communities and small farmers. The model of national development promoted new mining enterprises and hydroelectric dam construction in rural areas, further disrupting the older patterns of society. Many of the large landowners were foreign corporations with little or no network of personal relationships to the local communities. These communities experienced displacement by force and threat or by increasing environmental degradation that made small farming life untenable. Road construction into previously isolated areas brought extractive industries to rural areas, but also increased opportunities for local populations, peasants and others, to encounter the larger society, absorb new ideas, and make contact with other communities.

All of these changes combined to undermine the older system of interdependent dominant-subordinate relationships, and to rip away some of what masked the oppressive nature of these relationships, making the oppression more apparent or more directly felt. This was a Honduran variant of a process that has been occurring worldwide in many peasant and small farming communities since at least the 1960s.[11] In Honduras, it contributed to increased public forms of resistance and militancy such as the rise of peasant and rural workers' movements and agrarian conflict in the Aguán Valley and elsewhere. This revealed the dilemma of those who controlled the old order and had now abandoned or transgressed it for the new neoliberal global economy.

> The rich, the precondition of their new wealth has been the systematic dismantling of the practices that previously rationalized their wealth, status, and leadership. Their economic domination has come at the cost of their having broken their own hegemony.[12]

Consequently, by at least the 1980s, it was necessary for new ideologies and practices of dominance to replace the older order. The replacement was far from complete. It would be more accurate to say that the new ideologies and practices of control were in part a continuation of the old and built upon the old with changing emphases as needed to meet the contradictions of a rising popular resistance. This brings us to examine the major characteristics of the system of dominance and control that emerged in Honduras since the 1950s—in this chapter, the ideology that guides and tries to justify it; in chapter 3, the mechanisms through which control is maintained. An important part of the ideology of control is the writing and interpretation of the nation's history.

THE OFFICIAL HISTORY

In the nineteenth century, Honduras seemed to be little more than a collection of local and regional interests often at odds with each other. In addition, "economic relations connecting Honduras and world markets from the 1830s to the 1870s did not sustain a state capable of producing the 'nation' imagined by elite Hondurans."[13] By the 1870s, as the region's economy became more integrated into international economies, the country's ruling elite undertook the task of nation building during a period of liberal reform beginning in the last quarter of the nineteenth century, aided by a small group of intellectuals who generally saw themselves as part of the nation-building enterprise. They constructed a sense of nation in part through the elaboration of a history that they promulgated through the education system and the national imaginary as the exclusive memory of the nation. This official history magnified the deeds of the ruling elites and their educated social class members—for example the nineteenth century independence leaders Morazan, Valle, others—while ignoring or minimizing the role of peasant farmers and workers and of indigenous and Afrocaribbean peoples who were regarded as primitive or regressive. This historical narrative and imaginary obscured, subsumed, or ignored indigenous peoples and the uniqueness of ethnic minority identities within a national history that characterized Honduras as a *mestizo* nation.[14] Almost the sole exception to this was the figure of

Lempira, the indigenous leader of resistance to Spanish colonial rule. But the national historical narrative and especially the folk imaginary that accompanied the construction of the national heroes carefully stripped this indigenous figure of his historical reality and made him a sort of parallel elite figure, another "great man" or hero separate from the power of the indigenous masses whom he led. The ultimate ironic symbol of this co-optation was the image of Lempira on one of the lowest denominations of the national currency (also called *lempiras*). The nation-building elite assigned the great indigenous leader to a token of the economic power of the "liberal oligarchic state." Today a few Afrocaribbean and indigenous Hondurans occupy positions of some responsibility in the Honduran government and bureaucracy. Their situation does not substantially change the marginalized position of these sectors of the population.

The national ideology expressed through the official history insisted on concepts of progress and equality, the former personified in the accomplishments of the governing classes, the latter expressed in the idea and the legal fiction of common citizenship but not in any attempt to ensure more equitable access to or distribution of economic or other resources.[15] Concepts of progress and citizenship acted as implicit critiques of the backwardness of indigenous and peasant communities, and minimized the importance of unique ethnic identities under the guise that all Hondurans were citizens of a mestizo nation. In Honduras, this had important implications for the political life of indigenous and Afrocaribbean communities such as the Garifuna.[16] Beginning in the late 1800s, Honduran intellectuals and politicians were already formulating an aspect of the national mestizo identity that acknowledged the country's indigenous roots, but chose the archaeological ruins of Copan and their reputed Mayan origins as the representation of the indigenous strands of the national mestizo identity. The actual influence and presence of Mayan cultural groups in Honduras is still debated and contested among scholars but, as historian Darío Euraque argued, this debate is irrelevant to the proponents of a policy of "mayanization" that ignores the presence and influence of the many other indigenous groups in Honduras. In recent decades, this has served as a policy geared to packaging and selling folk culture to tourists, suppressing the voices of indigenous movements, and erasing the history of indigenous resistance to colonial and national dominance.[17] This national cultural policy serves to disarm indigenous and autochthonous groups as political bases of power by redefining them as aspects of the colorful folklore of the Honduran nation rather than as living communities.

Chapter 2
IDEOLOGY AND DISCONTENT

Ideology is a field on which struggles of dominance and resistance are engaged. Ideologies are socially and culturally constructed systems of symbols, ideas, beliefs, stereotypes, and values that present a particular version of reality in order to justify or legitimize certain policies and practices. But as James Scott has written, "Properly understood, any hegemonic ideology provides, within itself, the raw material for contradiction and conflict."[18] As we shall see in Honduras, the practical implications and consequences of an ideology may not be fully accepted or wanted by all members of a group.[19]

Hegemonic or controlling ideologies work their magic in several ways. Those over whom control is to be exercised accept images, "truths," and the interpretations of reality that the powerful present as the only reality, and they internalize them as their own. Adrienne Pine argued that the dominant ideology in Honduran society promoted in various ways the image of Hondurans as a "violent" people, that violence was part of Honduran identity and life, especially for certain lower-middle and working classes of Honduran society. The mainstream Honduran media, the statements of some political, religious, and other prominent persons reinforced this image of a violent society with reports that highlighted criminal violence as well as by calling attention to popular images of heavy drinking, reformist movements for temperance, and religious admonitions. Writing in the years before the 2009 coup d'etat, Pine noted the degree to which many Hondurans seemed to accept and internalize this image of an inherently violent people. This served the purposes of an elite class that could thereby absolve the state of its violence by laying the blame squarely in the inherent character of the people.[20]

Most often, however, this internalization is partial, incomplete, and contested. Under certain conditions, resistance may take the form of using the ideologies presented by the powerful as standards against which to measure and critique the gap between the reality presented and the reality that people live every day. Put another way, "the ideology formulated by the ruling class to justify its own rule [provides] much of the symbolic raw material from which the most damning critique could be derived and sustained."[21] This may occur when people are acutely aware of the contradictions between the reality portrayed by those in control and the daily reality of people's lives. In May 2011, the Honduran government began trying to lure foreign investment back to Honduras following the 2009 coup d'etat, by sponsoring a large economic forum in San Pedro Sula, with the title, "Honduras is Open for Business," even as government security forces were repressing massive anti-coup demonstrations. At the same time, the Honduran Congress moved toward passage of a law for the promotion and protection of investment.[22] The contradiction between the official image of a stable, orderly situation and the very unstable daily reality was not lost on many Hondurans. In such situations, people may seem to take the values symbolized or promised in the dominant ideology more seriously than do the elites themselves. As such contradictions have become more apparent and widespread in Honduran society, they have fuelled popular resistance and discontent. "Hegemony is, after all, fundamentally about the misrepresentation of 'objective' interests."[23] When a dominant controlling ideology loses legitimacy and is increasingly questioned, it can sometimes be reworked to try to ensure the acquiescence of people.

IDEOLOGIES OF DOMINANCE AND SUBORDINATION

Reflected in the daily events of Honduran life are differing images of reality, of the way things are and should be. Two images of reality complement each other in justifying or rationalizing the way things are in the culture of domination. One image of reality portrays the prominent and powerful and the rightness of their role in controlling Honduran society. I call this an ideology of dominance. The other constructs an image or identity of subordination for most of the rest of Honduran society. This ideological construction achieves its greatest success when the subordinated population accepts and even internalizes both portrayals—how the powerful describe themselves and their role in society, and how they describe or characterize the rest of Honduran society. As we shall see, Honduran society presents too many differences, challenges, practical dilemmas, and forms of resistance for such a process of internalization to be completely successful. In fact, it may have a very different outcome, as Scott suggests. "The most common form of class struggle arises from the failure of a dominant ideology to live up to the implicit promises it necessarily makes."[24]

An Ideology of Dominance

The stories of community displacements (*desalojas*) at El Astillero and in Yoro—and hundreds of other examples—reflect elements of a belief and value system, an ideology. Marvin Barahona describes the basic elements of a dominant ideology in what he characterizes as "the liberal oligarchic state" of Honduras.[25] From the beginnings that Barahona described for the late 1800s, this ideology of dominance assumed the natural and cultural superiority of some and their right to govern others. The land, the natural resources, and most of the population, especially the large population of rural poor, were resources at the disposal of those who have a right to control the nation and to direct and use its resources. The political and economic leaders seemed to believe that economic and social inequity were necessary for national development. They tended to see themselves as partners of international economic elites, and they generally invited foreign involvement in the economic development of the country. But this posed a practical problem inasmuch as international involvement by foreign companies and investors could be seen to threaten the control of the local elites themselves.

These basic aspects of an ideology of dominance—how the "elite" saw and portrayed themselves—began to accumulate added dimensions in response to both the rising voice of labor and peasant groups after the 1950s and the extension of neoliberal globalization as a model for Honduran development after the 1980s. One added dimension was the tendency to raise the personal accumulation of great wealth to the level of a patriotic act or duty. Personal accumulation of wealth was both a sign and a guarantee that the country was developing and wealth was being created. Personal wealth creation was essential to national wealth creation, and national development could be understood in terms of wealth creation by and for a relatively small class. In an odd, seemingly perverse way even the introduction of drug trafficking and the arms trade could be further opportunities for wealth creation. From one perspective, drugs and arms became simply more ways to use the country's resources—the land for production and transshipment areas and the people as labor or as consumers. But here again, the growth of narcotics trafficking in Honduras gave others in the country's ruling class concerns about the consequences for themselves and the nation.

By the first decades of the twenty-first century, the human consequences of playing out such an ideology were increasingly apparent to many Hondurans. An ideology that sees large sectors of the population and the land as disposable in the service of a neoliberal model of development can create consequences that the governing classes must somehow address—a growing sector of degraded land and broken communities, rising poverty, danger of losing sovereignty to international interests and to areas of increasing violence or ungovernability within the society itself. Such consequences and the question of how to address them still divide members of the Honduran political and economic elite. Individual responses are shaped in part by the degree to which individuals can access the wealth or benefits of economic development, but that is not the only consideration. The question of national sovereignty—the degree to which the resources of the country are in the hands of foreign interests—emerges as an issue of values and practicality about which members of the elite may differ somewhat, as does the question of what to do about growing poverty and discontent—ignore it, forcibly suppress the discontent of the poor, or address the most pressing needs in a reformist fashion.

In a rapidly evolving context that raises problems for the Honduran state and those who manage it, the dominant ideology requires those in control to redefine themselves and their role in relation to the rest of society. How do the powerful present themselves as guardians of national sovereignty while they are widely perceived as selling the country's land and resources to foreign interests? How do they refute the perception of widespread official corruption and impunity? How do they define themselves as protectors of security in a society that experiences a widespread sense of daily insecurity? In Honduras, these problems have been addressed in part by fashioning a complementary image of reality, an ideology of subordination that portrays the rest of society in ways that seem to justify control by the powerful.

An Ideology of Subordination

In contrast to the ideology and image they construct of themselves, the powerful and the institutions they control construct a set of images, assertions, and beliefs intended to define the reality in which most Hondurans live and the identities of ordinary Hondurans themselves. This ideology contains several messages. The first is that things are bad and getting worse. This idea is reinforced by much of the popular news media that presents a daily coverage of brutal criminal violence, by politicians' statements and speeches, and in some churches that present a picture of worsening violence and moral disintegration.[26] The second message is that things are going on normally—"Honduras is open for business," elections will be held, soccer games go on, and everything continues as usual. The messages seem contradictory. Taken together they suggest that the new normal is that things will keep getting worse. The power of this depiction of Honduran life lies in the fact that Hondurans actually do experience violence and insecurity at all levels of life. The ideology of subordination implies that this is natural and normal, or at least that it has become an integral part of daily life.

These messages were propagated even as the government expressed the need for stronger measures to curb crime and violence. Violence was now the new normal. Therefore, an increasing militarization of society was needed. Portrayed in various ways, including the rhetoric of the winning presidential candidate in the political campaign of 2013, this message had two effects. It promoted a level of distrust of all the major national institutions and a collective sense of depression and hopelessness that could undermine popular resistance.[27] It also justified the increased use of force (militarization) to control an unruly society. In the period before and after the 2013 presidential election, Hondurans and outside observers noted what seemed to be an increasing militarization of society, including deployment of soldiers in schools and on the streets, and the formation of a unit of several thousand "military police," in violation, some said, of the legal mandate barring the military from performing police duties (see chapter 3). Many Hondurans seemed to approve of this militarization policy. Were people just tired of the violence? Or was this a sign that this ideology of subordination was having an effect?

Such a set of apparently contradictory messages—things are getting worse but things are normal—has a social and psychological impact. A nationwide survey conducted in 2013 by a regional university and a private Honduran social research team discovered high levels of popular distrust and lack of confidence, as high as 75 percent in some cases, regarding eleven major national social institutions. Levels of distrust and lack of confidence in even the most trusted—churches, military, media—hovered around 50 percent.[28] An analysis and interpretation of these survey results by the director of the research team concluded that many Hondurans tended to see institutions and actors in the public sphere as adversaries or threats to family and self, while they saw the domestic sphere—home, household, and family—as their only security. This promoted a sense that individuals must depend only upon themselves and their immediate circle to survive by any means necessary (*salvese quien pueda*, "whoever can save himself, let him do so"). It also undermined attempts at collective, organized responses or resistance, and contributed to a profound national sense of depression, "*una sociedad hondamente deprimida*."[29]

In an early and controversial ethnographic study, Edward Banfield described what he called "amoral familism"—a situation in which there are no important or relevant public institutions mediating between the individuals and the state, so that the family becomes the only trusted social entity, and people cultivate loyalty to family before all else as the highest expression of morality. He showed how amoral familism in Italian society shaped values that contributed to the rise of the Mafia and its organization into crime syndicates known as "families" as a response to a society where nothing else was reliable and trusted.[30] In Honduras, the rise of both neighborhood gangs (*maras*) and other forms of organized crime or violence may be in part a response to the widespread sense of distrust in public institutions that seem to offer ordinary people no security or protection.

The 2013 survey showed that despite disillusionment or distrust with public institutions, people continued to express hope in or dependency on the same institutions. Many believed that partisan politics was itself part of the problem or that the political party system would not solve their problems, but they indicated they would continue to vote in elections. One interpretation of this apparent contradiction was that many Hondurans no longer believed in institutions, but they did believe in the values that institutions were supposed to uphold and promote.[31]

An example of this complex attitude is provided by Jordan Levy who described the problem facing teachers in communities in the Department of Valle in southern Honduras. Teachers indicated distrust in politicians and partisan politics, but they had to depend upon local politicians of the National or Liberal Parties and upon private businesses and corporations to fund school needs since the central government had begun to withdraw state aid.

Yet many teachers indicated that they might support Libre, an alternative political party in the 2013 national elections, hoping that a new government might return to funding the schools. The teachers passionately believed in the value of education for their poorer students especially, and they were willing to give the political electoral system another chance, even though they were critical and distrustful of both the political system to deliver support and an increasingly privatized school system that depended on the economic support and control of corporate interests that favored wealthier students rather than the poor.[32] So one response to the normalcy of expecting things to get worse was depression, and another was that people criticized institutions that did not function or functioned in violation of their primary mission, but they also wanted these institutions to function properly and they kept trying to shape them to their needs and purposes. The critique was usually expressed not in ideological but in concrete terms that touched the daily lives of people. For example, most of the teachers in Levy's study were also activists or supporters of the opposition party LIBRE in the hope that this party would be more responsive to the needs of teachers and public education.

The ideology of subordination contains another message—the people themselves are to blame. The worsening violence and failure of Honduran society is really the fault of the Honduran people themselves who are a violent people. This message appears in various ways, and seems intended to promote a popular internalization of a sense of moral inferiority among some Hondurans. Pine shows how some poorer Hondurans seem to accept a "culture of poverty" depiction of themselves—that their poverty and violence is in some way the result of their own lifestyle—and they embrace the message that they must work harder, embrace discipline, and gain an achievement mentality, as preached to them by pastors, government officials, and others.[33] This approach exonerates the elites and authorities from responsibility, and it implies that the problem and the solution are individual rather than societal or communitarian.

These two messages in this ideology of subordination suggested two ways for people to deal with reality—one promoted by the ideology, one not expressed. What was promoted was to pursue personal improvement. Some of the churches and other institutions emphasized this to the exclusion of societal transformation. People should turn to God, seek forgiveness, be saved individually, go to Alcoholics Anonymous, and pursue lives of individual virtue and piety, preferably as part of a chosen community that keeps itself separate from the evils of society. In his study of urban youth in the city of El Progreso in 2001, Jon Wolseth discusses this approach as one way that poor youth remove themselves from gang membership and violence by membership in an evangelical youth group and church.[34] Some religious institutions propagated a theology of providentialism.[35] God directs everything, and humans can only leave everything to God's plan in which everything has a purpose and should not be challenged (see chapter 9).

The other way to deal with the new normal of things getting worse was to seek self survival by any means possible (*salvase quien pueda*). These means included joining gangs (*maras*), hiring out for death squads (*sicarios*), emigration, or substance dependency. All of these served the needs of the powerful by deflecting and neutralizing resistance or by channeling hopelessness or discontent in ways that the managers of society could control, or thought they could control.

A tangible result of these messages of rising violence and hopelessness was seen in the emigration of thousands of Honduran children and youth who fled or were sent by desperate parents on perilous journeys to the relative safety of other countries—Costa Rica, Nicaragua, the United States. By the summer of 2014, the presence of thousands of young Central Americans seeking asylum at the southern border of the United States caused U.S. officials and media to characterize the situation as "the crisis at the border," while the real crisis was in countries like Honduras. Despite the assurances of Honduran President Hernandez that he wanted the country's youth to return home, children and youth in Honduras seemed to be special targets for elimination. According to some reports, at least four thousand children and youth were violently killed in Honduras between 2009 and 2014.[36]

SUCCESS AND FAILURE OF IDEOLOGIES

Ideologies are always closely related to actions, policies, strategies, or practices that they justify or promote. Together these constitute a system that attempts control. Ideology tries to "define what is realistic and what is not realistic." Actions, policies, practices try to "drive certain goals and aspirations into the realm of the impossible."[37] This chapter has articulated some salient features of ideologies of dominance and submission in Honduras. The next chapter will examine the actions, policies, and practices that accompany this ideological definition of reality.

But ideologies are not always effective and not always internalized to a significant degree. People can "see through" the contradiction between the reality posed by an ideology and the reality people live everyday. The ability to see this and move to action as a result may depend in part upon the positionality of individuals and other related factors that shape how people relate to the symbols, ideas, and values expressed in an ideology. There are boundaries and constraints on the deployment and efficacy of cultural resources for ideological uses and, consequently, the efficacy of ideologies to mobilize power in a society. People differ in their acceptance of ideologies. Social class, role, status, life experiences, changes in one's material conditions, the social groups and organizations one belongs or relates to, relative access to the means of communication, different local conditions, the framing of public discourse, and other factors can shape an individual's response to ideologies. There is also the possibility that, "the fewer the rewards a society offers to a particular group . . . the more autonomous that group will prove to be with reference to the norms of the society."[38]

People do not experience or interpret things in the same way. Religious symbols may have a different meaning and power for a believer and a nonbeliever, or even among believers. Even within the same social class, individuals may interpret and respond in different ways. In Honduras as elsewhere, people who have lived all their lives in poverty may embrace the promises of well-heeled politicians, or they may hear the same promises with cynical ears. Many cross-cutting forces shape how individuals respond to, embrace, or internalize the elements of an ideology or even use these to critique those who promulgate the ideology. In Honduras, it cannot even be assumed that the members of a social and economic "elite" all share the same level of belief and adherence to the very ideology of dominance that they propagate to the rest of society, despite forms of social control that elites exercise over their own would-be mavericks.

Other forces are at work, as well. As James Scott points out, "the nature of resistance is greatly influenced by the existing forms of labor control and by beliefs about the probability and severity of retaliation."[39] Collective action and what may be called a social movement may become possible with "the knowledge that the risk to any single resister is generally reduced to the extent that the whole community is involved."[40] The great banana strike of 1954 that seemed to signal the beginning of modern popular organizations and social movements in Honduras occurred in the historical context of changing labor control that emerged with the modern plantation system. The strike demonstrated the strength and relative safety of collective action, especially when other sectors of society began to support the strikers. As we shall see, this is a realization that has been put into abundant practice in the evolution of popular resistance in Honduras.

IDEOLOGY IN ACTION: MODEL CITIES (CHARTER CITIES) FOR HONDURAS

By 2010, the government of Porfirio Lobo began moving forward with plans to invite a Charter Cities (also known as Model Cities, the more common term in Honduras) development along the Caribbean coast. The move was seen as an important way to propel the government's plans for neoliberal foreign investment. Charter Cities also represented a way out of the economic difficulties and the rising violence in Honduran society. Essentially, the thinking was that "a crisis is a terrible thing to waste."[41] A preferred site was an area between the city of Trujillo and the Sico River, an area that was home to various Garifuna villages and was claimed by the Garifuna, one of the country's indigenous peoples. As an important part of the post-coup government's efforts to accelerate foreign investment and resource exploitation, the Honduran Congress passed a constitutional amendment and a statute in February 2011, to permit the creation of "Special Development Regions" (*Regiones Especiales de Desarrollo*, RED). These measures were intended specifically to pave the way (almost literally) for the establishment of Charter Cities. Some Hondurans criticized as traitors the Congress members who passed the legislation. Xiomara Castro, wife of the deposed president, Manuel Zelaya, said the legislation was so sweeping it should be brought to the people in a referendum. Leaders of some popular and indigenous organizations issued critical statements. Berta Cáceres, leader of the Lenca organization COPINH was quoted on the organization's website as saying, "a model city in a society in tatters is a contradiction." A group of lawyers, the country's attorney general, and others brought a legal complaint to the courts charging that the measures and the whole plan for Model Cities violated the country's sovereignty and the rights of its people to equality under the law, free circulation, public tutelage of labor relations, and the right of people not to be forced to change residence. In November 2012, the Honduran Constitutional Court declared the legislation unconstitutional and invalid. Members of Congress then summarily deposed four of the five judges who had issued the judgment, replacing them with others who duly declared that the law permitting REDs was constitutional. The plan was stalled when one of the major foreign architects of the plan withdrew and complained that the Honduran government was trying to exercise too much control over the development. When Juan Orlando Hernandez assumed the Honduran presidency in early 2014, plans for a Model City in Honduras were revived. Congress had passed a new law creating "special economic development zones" or *zonas especiales de desarrollo económico*, ZEDE. The preferred site was moved to the area near Zacate Grande on the Pacific Coast. From there, Honduran minerals and iron ore cold be shipped more easily to China and other Asian sites. Miguel Facussé, entrepreneur and author of the so-called Facussé Memorandum, held property in the area.[42]

Charter Cities or Model Cities is a movement to develop urban centers in poor countries that would function as virtually independent entities outside the laws and customs of the host country. A model city could be a center of manufacturing, commerce, processing and transshipment, finance, and more. It would be free to develop its own laws and rules, and would maintain a modern, efficient accounting system. It would act as a "development pole" for the country's extractive and other industry, its exports, and provide jobs, albeit under laws and rules determined by the investors and developers, not the host country. Essentially, a model city would be an independent enclave within a country, and would be tied to and responsive to the global market network, not the government or people of the host country, although the managers of a model city might adopt and adapt some laws and customs that were aligned with the intensive focus of the city upon neoliberal, globalized, economic development. For the Honduran government and some of the country's entrepreneurs, one of the advantages of a model city could be its functions as an outlet for extractive and other industries. A model city on the Honduran Pacific coast might include port facilities as a place to process and ship the thousands of tons of iron ore exported to China from Honduras each month. If processed in Honduras, the cargo would be less expensive to transport to China. Chinese companies like Sinohydro might get more Honduran contracts to build hydroelectric dams on Honduran rivers to supply energy and water for expanding mining, maquiladoras, and other industry.

But many Hondurans had serious questions about the assumptions and potential consequences of model cities development. A fundamental criticism of the model was its tendency to reduce and subordinate the fullness and complexity of human existence to purely economic consideration. Hondurans and foreign observers characterized the model as based on economic, cultural, and political assumptions or premises that together form a neocolonial ideology. These premises and assumptions include the following.

- *Identity economics*—The social and cultural norms that fashion a person's identity have a major impact upon the individual's behavior. Social and cultural norms can impede what might be the most rational and effective economic decisions and actions. The limits placed by culture and society on a people's identity and understanding of the world can be a crucial detriment to their economic well-being, shaping how people take risks, use time, see relationships, understand their environment. Poverty could be ended if the poor and nations let go of systems of bad laws and social mores that bind them to poverty.
- *Culture of poverty, again*—The social and cultural characteristics of a people or a nation may be a major reason for ongoing poverty or failure to develop. Thus, to promote development and overcome poverty, it may be necessary to change a society's norms, values, and laws. This assumption has several corollaries or implications. It implies that poverty is the fault of the poor themselves, their inefficient or disordered ways of living. There is no place here for an analysis of the power structures of a society or an analysis of who control what resources or how the powerful control the lives of the less powerful.
- *Replacement of offending culture*—Traditional cultures such as those of many indigenous peoples should be eliminated, changed, suppressed, and replaced with more economically efficient ways. This applies also to out-

dated national laws, such as agrarian reform laws that regard land as the patrimony of the entire nation, or that do not promote private ownership over collective ownership. Collective or community land ownership is economically inefficient and should be eliminated.
- *Democracy is not compatible with high economic efficiency and development*—To make the necessary changes in a people's way of life, it is necessary to have a firm authority. Left to themselves, ordinary people will not make the proper changes and will be tempted to cling to inefficient ways. Democracy is too vulnerable to non-economic rationality.
- *Complete and efficient accounting is crucial*—Wealth and poverty are about governance and especially about keeping track of wealth, productivity, taxes, and much more. The managers must have an accurate and complete knowledge of anything that relates to wealth generation and economic development. Business thrives on effective accounting. Privacy is sometimes a barrier to effective accounting. Life must be measured and accounted for.
- *Development implies or necessitates inequality*—Development necessitates accumulation of capital and control of resources within a relatively few managerial hands. Not everyone can or should participate. Resources may have to be taken away from the less economically efficient sectors of a population, such as indigenous or peasant communities.

It is not hard to see how these assumptions, this ideology of development could raise concerns in Honduran society over issues such as national sovereignty, local rights, indigenous rights, and much more. The Honduran government turned to the Charter/Model Cities solution in a context of poverty, social conflict, growing popular resistance, increasingly uncontrollable violence. Model Cities represented both a solution to the "failed state" and a means of advancing the development plans rooted in the so-called Facussé Memorandum and the Reaganomics for Honduras of the 1980s and the Washington Consensus, and above all its underlying assumptions and ideology seemed to articulate well with those prevalent among the country's ruling economic powers. Honduras was in crisis, and a crisis is a terrible thing to waste. In the next chapter, we shall examine further how this prevalent ideology was played out in practice. That will allow us to see more clearly what moved some Hondurans to adopt forms of resistance that are discussed in later chapters.

NOTES

1. James C. Scott, *Weapons of the Weak: Everyday Forms of Peasant Resistance* (New Haven, CT: Yale University Press, 1985), 236.
2. Elias Ruiz, *El Astillero: masacre y justicia* (Tegucigalpa: Editorial Guaymuras, 1992).

3. José Maria Tojeira, *Los hicaques de Yoro* (Tegucigalpa: Editorial Guaymuras, 1982).

4. In Bolivia, the hacienda system that legally kept indigenous workers bound to servitude on the land was not abolished until the revolution of 1952.

5. For the origins of this economic structure, see Darío Euraque, *Reinventing the Banana Republic: Region and State in Honduras, 1870–1972* (Chapel Hill, NC: University of North Carolina Press, 1996).

6. Steven Volk, "Land Pressures Lead to War between Honduras and El Salvador" (*NACLA Report on the Americas, XV*, No. 6, Decemner, 1981), 20, reprinted in Nancy Peckenham and Annie Street, eds., *Honduras: Portrait of a Captive Nation* (New York: Praeger, 1985), 149. See also, Rafael del Cid, "Las clases sociales y su dinámica en el agro Hondureño," *Estudios Sociales Centroamericanos* No 18 (1977): 154; Susan Stonich, "The Political Economy of Environmental Destruction: Food Security in Southern Honduras," *Harvest of Want: Hunger and Food Security in Central America and Mexico*, Scott Whiteford and Anne E. Ferguson, eds. (Boulder, CO: Westview Press, 1991).

7. Euraque, *Reinterpreting the Banana Republic*, chapter 3, esp. 30–35.

8. Marvin Barahona, *Honduras en el siglo XX: Una síntesis histórica* (Tegucigalpa: Editorial Guaymuras, 2005), 34–47, 73–82, 109–12, 152–54.

9. A sizeable literature has developed to describe and analyze such rural communities in parts of Latin America, owing much to the work of Eric Wolf, including, "Closed Corporate Peasant Communities in Mesoamerica and Central Java," *Southwestern Journal of Anthropology* vol. 13, no. 1 (1957): 1–18; *Peasants* (Upper Saddle River, NJ: Prentice Hall, 1966); "The Vicissitudes of the Closed Corporate Peasant Community," *American Ethnologist* vol. 13, no. 2 (1986): 325–29. Another early treatment of this appears in, W. B. Taylor, "Landed Society in New Spain: A View from the South," *Hispanic American Historical Review* vol. 54, no. 3 (1974): 387–413. Another formative example is the extended treatment given in James C. Scott, *Weapons of the Weak: Everyday Forms of Peasant Resistance* (New Haven, CT: Yale University Press, 1985).

10. See for example, W. G. Lovell, *Conquest and Survival in Colonial Guatemala: A Historical Geography of the Cuchumatan Highlands, 1500–1821* (Montreal: McGill-Queens University Press, 1992), 89; and S. J. Stern, *Peru's Indian Peoples and the Challenge to Spanish Conquest: Huamanga to 1640* (Madison: University of Wisconsin Press, 1982), 93.

11. Similar examples appear in Deborah Bryceson, Cristóbal Kay, and Jos Mooij, eds., *Disappearing Peasantries? Rural Labour in Africa, Asia, and Latin America* (London: Intermediate Technology Publications, 2000). The phenomenon of the peasant-rural worker in Caribbean plantation areas and the changing mentality and social networks of such a population were analyzed earlier by Sidney Mintz, "The Rural Proletariat and the Problem of Rural Proletarian Consciousness," *Journal of Peasant Studies* 1 (1974): 291–325.

12. Scott, *Weapons of the Weak*, 345.

13. Euraque, *Reinterpreting the Banana Republic*, 3.

14. Barahona, *Honduras en el siglo XX*, 2, 16–17, 34–47, 73–82, 193 ff.

15. Marvin Barahona, *Pueblos indígenas, Estado, y memoria colectiva en Honduras* (Tegucigalpa: Editorial Guaymuras, 2009), 193–95.

16. Mark Anderson, "When Afro Becomes (like) Indigenous: Garifuna and Afro-Indigenous Politics in Honduras," *The Journal of Latin American and Caribbean Anthropology* vol. 12. no. 2 (November 2007): 384–413.

17. Darío Euraque, *El golpe de estado del 28 de junio del 2009, el patrimonio cultural, y la Identidad Nacional de Honduras* (San Pedro Sula: Centro Editorial, 2010).

18. Scott, *Weapons of the Weak*, 336.

19. For a related discussion, see Eric Wolf, *Envisioning Power: Ideologies of Dominance and Crisis* (Berkeley: University of California Press, 1999).

20. Adrienne Pine, *Working Hard, Drinking Hard: On Violence and Survival in Honduras* (Berkeley: University of California Press, 2008).

21. Scott, *Weapons of the Weak*, 336.

22. Marilyn Mendez, "'Honduras Is Open for Business' cambiará la historia del país," *La Prensa* (April 10, 2011) illustrates the media promotion of this event and an underlying sense

of positive development. Tom Kavanagh, "Honduras is 'open for business,'" *New Statesman* (May 8, 2011) provides a more critical perspective.

23. Scott, *Weapons of the Weak*, 335.
24. Scott, *Weapons of the Weak*, 337.
25. Barahona, *Honduras en el siglo XX*, esp. pages 27–47.
26. Ismael Moreno, "Tercer sondeo de opinión del ERIC: Retrato de un país que va de mal a peor," *Envío Honduras* 11:37 (March 2013): 1–8.
27. Ismael Moreno, "Déficit de ciudadanía: Una interpretación del sondeo de opinión pública, UCA-Eric," *Envío Honduras* 8:28 (March 2011): 1–8.
28. Equipo de Reflexión, Investigación, y Comunicación (ERIC) y Universidad Centroamericana José Simeón Cañas, *Sondeo de opinión pública: Percepciones sobre la sitiación hondureña en el año 2012* (El Progreso: ERIC-SJ, 2013).
29. Moreno, "Tercer sondeo de opinión del ERIC," 1–2.
30. Edward C. Banfield, *The Moral Basis of a Backward Society* (New York: Free Press, 1958). Although Banfield's work generated criticism, in part for an ethnocentric and judgmental tone, some of its basic insights have been adapted to subsequent studies of gang life, the modern state, and more.
31. "¿Qué mentalidad y conciencia predominan en la sociedad hondureña, según los sondeos de opinión pública realizados por el ERIC?" *Envío Honduras* 12:41 (March 2014): 1–7.
32. Jordan Levy, *The Politics of Honduran School Teachers: State Agents Challenge the State* (University of Western Ontario, Electronic Thesis and Dissertation Repository, Paper 2142 (2014), http//:ir.lib.uwo.ca/edt/2142.
33. Pine, *Working Hard, Drinking Hard*, 13–15, 192–93.
34. Jon Wolseth, *Jesus and the Gang: Youth Violence and Christianity in Urban Honduras* (Tucson: University of Arizona Press, 2011), 102–28.
35. Andrés Pérez-Baltodano, *Entre el Estado Conquistador y el Estado Nación: Providencialismo, pensamiento politico y estructuras de poder en el desarrollo histórico de Nicaragua* (Managua: Instituto de Historia de Nicaragua y Centroamérica de la Universidad Centroamericana, 2008), 53–93, 243–57. Antonio Pedraz Gonzalez, SJ, "Sondeo de opinión pública y percepción religiosa," *Envío Honduras* 10:33 (March 2012): 30.
36. Telesur, "Almost 4000 Youth Killed in Honduras in Last Six Years," Telesur, http://www.telesurtv.net, posted November 20, 2014. Interamerican Commission on Human Rights (IACHR, Organization of American States), "IACHR Expresses Concern over Violent Deaths of Children, Adolescents, and Youth in Context of Citizen Insecurity in Honduras," press release (May 14, 2014) accessed on Organization of American States website, December 23, 2014.
37. Scott, *Weapons of the Weak*, 237.
38. Lee Rainwater, "Crucible of Identity: The Negro Lower-class Family," *Daedalus* 95 (1966): 212, quoted in Scott, *Weapons of the Weak*, 320 footnote.
39. Scott, *Weapons of the Weak*, 34.
40. Scott, *Weapons of the Weak*, 35.
41. Jack Rosenthal, "A Terrible Thing to Waste," *New York Times Magazine* (August 2, 2009): MM12.
42. Arthur Phillips, "Charter Cities in Honduras?" *Open Democracy* (January 7, 2014). Arthur Phillips, "Media Reports on Charter Cities Ignore the Larger Context," Center for Economic and Policy Research (February 27, 2014). Other reports of lawyers, judges, indigenous groups, student groups, and others opposing ZEDES and/or Charter Cities in Honduras, ConexiHon website (http://conexihon.hn/site/noticia/libertad-de-expresi%C3%B3n/hieren-en-honduras-comunicador-comunitario-de-radio-la-voz-de-zacate), and at other sites.

Chapter Three

Rituals of Control

The violence that Honduran society has experienced can be described and interpreted on at least two levels. One level includes the dramatic incidents of assassinations, disappearances, and mass killings. This provides a stream of separate snapshots of violence against individuals, and is often what the news media provide on a daily basis. At another level, there is the violence done to individuals and groups by the way the society is structured and the ways in which state and institutional laws, policies, and practices may harm or violate the lives of individuals and groups. This is more often the concern of the social scientist. Since the emergence of theories of dependency and concepts of underdevelopment in the 1960s and 1970s, many writers have identified this as "structural violence." It is violent because it permits only its own construction of reality. "These new engineers of power call themselves realists, but it is a hallmark of their realism that it admits no evidence and interpretation other than that which serves their purposes."[1] In reality, the stream of seemingly individual acts of personal or group violence and the policies and practices of social institutions and the state usually have a close causal relationship that may evolve over time. But the state and society's institutions, policies, and practices are the products of human decisions and actions taken by those who control such institutions and use them to perpetuate and increase their wealth, influence, or agendas for national development. In this regard, Honduran society is, unfortunately, a good example of the interplay between "street" violence and the structural violence of the state and social institutions. If we attribute a specific act of violence to narcotics traffickers or drug lords, we are also aware that the institutions of Honduran society—legal, judicial, military, economic, and such—have been used in ways that create or promote the conditions for narcotics violence to flourish.

Structural violence is often justified by ideologies of dominance and subordination such as we saw in the previous chapter. In this chapter, we examine some of the traditional and contemporary institutional practices of dominance and control that perpetuate structural violence and set conditions that may be conducive to increasing acts of violence in daily life. In the next and following chapters we describe some of the ways in which Hondurans began to question, challenge, and resist aspects of these institutions and the structural violence they enforced. There we see how popular resistance can arise in the space between the "false" reality painted by the ideologies of dominance and subordination and the actual daily experience of structural violence.

LORDS OF THE LAND: HISTORIC PATTERNS OF ECONOMIC DOMINANCE

Many of the patterns of control over land, labor, and resources we see today in Honduras and other areas of Latin America were first laid out during Spanish colonial times. Spain's control over its Latin American colonies in the centuries before independence was based largely upon systems for the control of land, labor, and whatever valuable resources—gold and silver—might be in or on the land. The *encomienda* system assigned to prominent Spanish colonists and their descendants control over an area of land and the rights to command the labor of the native people living in the area. In return, the colonist (*encomendero*) was supposed to protect the native people under his control, provide them with the means to feed themselves, represent them in legal and public business if necessary, and even punish them if they committed certain crimes. When this system became rife with the inevitable abuses of power, the colonial authorities instituted an alternative system (*repartimiento*) under which native peoples were grouped into villages or jurisdictions under the administration of a representative of the Spanish Crown.[2]

By the time Honduras gained independence from Spain in the early 1800s, the country had evolved a system of land and labor control that included modified versions of these earlier patterns. Large landowners continued to expect and command the labor of surrounding native populations and of poor rural non-Indian families in what became known as the *hacienda*—a term whose basic meaning denotes property, financial assets, or treasury. There were also communities designated as Indian or native, each with its own local authorities who were ultimately responsible to representatives of the national government, although the reach of the central government was usually weak in many areas of the country. But the haciendas of nineteenth-century Honduras, as elsewhere in much of Latin America, were not always engines of great wealth. Their owners could be described as land rich and capital poor.[3] Even if large landowners had been able to pour money into improving their haciendas, they had little economic incentive to do so, since markets for agricultural goods or ranch commodities outside of the local area were scarce, and transport and export systems were usually inferior or nonexistent. The native communities continued to produce for their own local communities and provide some labor (often conscripted) to large landowners. The basis of real wealth was mining. Throughout much of Latin America, the entire system depended on the labor of indigenous communities.

> Above all, it was access to an appropriation of labor that was the linchpin of the colonial economy and state. Yet coerced labor was also a key mechanism of political and economic control, and an intrinsic experience of the everyday lives of indigenous societies and African slaves on sugar plantations. Many coercive labor practices in different guises and contexts survived until well after the end of the colonial period and were a key grievance underlying popular revolts and rebellions up until recent times.[4]

With the development of the banana and fruit export industries in the early Twentieth Century, a second avenue to wealth in the emerging commercial center around San Pedro and the Ulua and Aguán Valleys was opened by a new class of entrepreneurs that included immigrants from the Middle East.[5]

During the 1960s and after, increasing demand in the "developed" countries of North America, Europe, Japan (and later China) for wood, paper products, minerals, and some agricultural products such as palm oil (used in making many processed and packaged foods) encouraged successive Honduran governments to grant concessions to foreign companies and Honduran entrepreneurs to extract these resources. These new enterprises and a developing international export market provided incentive for the wealthy and large landowners to expand into peasant and rural community lands. Environmental degradation resulting from some of these enterprises caused further loss of farmland for rural communities and small farmers. Population growth and the expansion of some urban centers added to the loss. These pressures resulted in declining production and rising prices of most of the basic grains consumed by local populations, affecting both peasant farmers and rural and urban workers. From 1952 to 1986 the number of kilograms of corn produced per person declined from 140 to 107, with similar declines in production of beans and sorghum. (see chapter 6)[6] The peasant organizations and unions that formed in the 1950s and 1960s pressured the government to address their need for land. To relieve mounting social pressures that might threaten its control, the government of General Osvaldo Lopez Arrellano passed the 1974 Agrarian Reform Law to administer the distribution of certain unused lands to peasants and small farmers. The law seems to have encouraged more land takeovers by peasant groups before and after its passage. Opposition came from some of the country's most powerful landowners and foreign companies. Lopez was forced from office the following year, and INA was not given the means to enforce the decreasing number of land titles it did award, although the law is often credited with providing some relief for landless peasants and for helping to avert the sorts of revolutionary activities that arose in neighboring countries such as El Salvador and Nicaragua.

RURAL AGENDAS, DIVISIONS, AND RESISTANCE

Until the 1970s, the majority of the Honduran population lived in rural communities and farmed the land to grow crops for their own consumption (corn, beans), to sell locally, and sometimes for export (especially coffee). The term peasant and its Spanish counterpart, *campesino*, are often used to refer to this rural population, although Hondurans occasionally use *campesino* to refer broadly to rural life in general. Wolf described peasants as a social class that produced for both internal family consumption and to meet the demands of a larger social and political system in the form of rents, taxes, tithes, tribute, as well as the need to maintain and replace inputs (tools, seed, animals) into the production process. Peasants were depicted as characteristically facing the need to balance internal family consumption against externals demands—what Wolf called the "peasant dilemma."[7] Despite a common impression that peasant life was traditional and unchanging, being a peasant was not a stable situation. Peasants might fall into debt and lose their land, becoming landless rural workers for wealthier neighbors or plantations or even seeking work in cities. Others might increase their resources and wealth, often at the expense of their poorer neighbors. Much depended upon the kinds of resources each controlled, the quality of their network of relationships with each other and with the powerful and well placed, the vagaries of the market, and other forces.

In Honduras, these processes were at work. Before the 1950s, demand for land was low enough to permit most peasant farmers to find enough land to meet their basic needs. By the 1960s, available land suitable for farming was becoming relatively scarce, just as prices for crops such as coffee were rising. These conditions provoked conflict over land, as farmers with the means tried to expand their production of export coffee and other crops. Some farmers faced threats to their access to land from both large landowners and their own better off neighbors. This promoted cycles of land conflict that have only increased in intensity since then, despite or perhaps because of the passage of the 1974 Agrarian Reform Law. These conditions also hastened the divisions within the rural farm population.

Jansen described a developing social stratification in the peasant population in Honduras beginning in the 1950s. Three different kinds of peasant farmers evolved as the acreage of land available to peasant farmers declined. "Family labor" farmers relied mostly on family but might hire a few local landless neighbors to work for them, as well. These farmers had relatively secure control of their land through inheritance or other legal means, and were not in much danger of losing it. They might produce a small amount of export crops such as coffee to be sold locally or to larger coffee producers. A second group were "petty commodity producers" who also had relatively secure hold over their land and focused increasingly on producing an export crop, most often coffee. Their total export production was not large, but was significant enough to ensure an income, backed up with some food production on their land. A third rural population that Jansen called "producer proletarians" consisted of people without land of their own who rented, sharecropped, squatted, or otherwise gained use of small plots of land that was not theirs, on which they produced crops for personal and family consumption (subsistence). The insecurity of their tenure, the smaller size of their plots, the inferiority of the land they could obtain, and other factors forced them to combine this kind of subsistence farming with working for others, often wealthier farmer neighbors or large corporate plantations.[8]

From the 1950s into the 1980s, many small farm producers organized into cooperatives that could provide access to land for their members and peasant communities. Their members were often "producer proletariat" who combined subsistence production with part time work on fruit company plantations, a pattern that had arisen when the fruit companies in the north and the Aguán Valley expanded into what had previously been peasant land, creating a large group of landless and land poor *campesinos*. As both peasant farmers and plantation wage laborers, the members of many of these peasant cooperatives joined to form peasant associations or unions. These unions played an important role in moving the government to pass the 1974 Agrarian Reform Law.

As Jansen points out, the family labor farmers and the petty commodity producers often improved their own situation at the expense of their poorer landless neighbors.[9] It could not be assumed that all *campesinos* were equal or had the same or even similar interests and agendas. These differences might shape quite different levels of acceptance or resistance to the ideologies and mechanisms of control imposed by the more powerful. These differences were partially reflected in the tendency of peasant organizations to splinter or multiply to represent different interests, and in their vulnerability to co-optation by powerful external interests.

Chapter 3
STRENGTHENING AND EXPANDING PATTERNS OF ECONOMIC CONTROL

The globalization of the world's economies and the trend toward neoliberal economic policy in Honduras since the 1980s served to reinforce and expand many of the earlier patterns of economic control. Eric Wolf's characterization of societies that provoked peasant rebellions in the past applies equally well to this modern neoliberal program in Honduras. "The guiding fiction of this kind of society—one of the key tenets of its ideology—is that land, labor, and wealth are commodities, that is, goods produced not for use but for sale."[10] In particular, large landowners who were engaged in producing agricultural export crops such as palm oil in the Aguán Valley had a strong incentive to expand production by annexing land, often taken by dubious legal means or by intimidation and force from surrounding rural communities and small farmers. Honduran governments began to award increasing numbers of concessions for mining and logging operations to wealthy Hondurans, foreign companies, or Honduran-foreign partnerships. In 1997, for example, the government concluded an agreement with Stone Container Corporation (then the world's largest producer of cardboard boxes) for the rights to log thousands of square kilometers in Olancho, a huge area that included indigenous and peasant lands and communities. When this deal became public, it prompted large popular protest demonstrations that brought together different popular organizations across Honduran society.[11] Beginning in 2006 the Zelaya government enforced a moratorium on mining concessions, but in early 2013 the post-coup government passed a mining law that ended the moratorium. In the following months, government awarded hundreds of mining concessions to Honduran and foreign interests. To accommodate this expansion of mining in Honduras and the expansion of the foreign factory (maquiladoras) sector of the economy, the government and foreign companies initiated a number of large hydroelectric dam building projects across rivers that happen to be central to the economies, cultural customs, and spirituality of several indigenous groups. The electrical energy and the water volume produced by these dam projects could be used in mining operations that require huge amounts of both water and energy. These plans affected the lives of Lenca peoples along the Gualquarque River in the southwest and Miskito, Pech, and Tawahka people along the Patuca River in eastern Honduras, among others (see chapter 5).

In general, the post-2009 governments used legislation as a means to strengthen control over the economy and promote further economic expansion along the same patterns as described above, trying to remove laws that seemed to hinder this expansion, and passing new laws to support it. The first major targets were agrarian reform and collective land ownership. Although the 1974 Agrarian Reform Law never seemed to provide enough land to poor peasants through legal transfer, it at least provided a standard to which peasant groups could appeal in their demands for land. The law represented the principle that the nation had a duty to try to provide access to land for those who needed it.[12] In addition, the 1982 Constitution contained sections that seemed to affirm the state's protection of land as a national resource, and access to land for Honduran citizens as a priority. Article 107 prohibited foreign ownership of land within forty kilometers of the northern Caribbean coast. Article 347 recognized a limited right of indigenous communities to their traditional lands.

In the early 1980s, the Association for Honduran Progress (*Asociación para el Progreso de Honduras*, APROH) prepared a national development plan that proposed important changes designed to bring Honduras fully into a neoliberal global economy. Authored primarily by the entrepreneur and APROH vice-president Miguel Facussé and sometimes referred to as the "Facussé Memorandum," APROH presented the document to incoming Honduran President Roberto Suazo Cordova (the first civilian government since the 1960s) at the start of his term in 1981. For Suazo, APROH became a virtual shadow Cabinet.[13] At the same time, the U.S. Embassy sent the government a letter outlining a very similar plan, popularly labeled "Reaganomics for Honduras."[14] These plans were on hold during the regional conflicts that disturbed Central America in 1980s when Honduras was also coping with a serious debt problem, but were revived when the Callejas government (1990–1994) and successive governments began to implement them. In 1992, the Honduran Congress approved passage of the Agricultural Modernization Law that created conditions for expanding the private entitlement of land, including land that was then community land or traditional indigenous land (see chapter 6). Immediately after Hurricane Mitch devastated the north coast of Honduras in November 1998, members of Congress with interests in attracting foreign tourist developers proposed to abolish or alter Article 107 to allow foreign ownership of land closer to the Caribbean coast, although popular resistance forced the temporary postponement of this move by arguing that the land belonged to the Honduran people, and that foreign owners would not be motivated to exercise the same care as Hondurans would over the land and environment, and that changing the law would facilitate the sale of land belonging to Garifuna communities along the north coast.[15]

In 2001, the Congress passed a forestry law (*Ley forestal de areas protegidas y de vida silvestre*) that transferred to government control areas of forested land that had long been in the territory and care of indigenous communities. This effectively weakened Article 347. The rationale for this move was that government could better protect and develop these forested areas. But the new law allowed Honduras to take commercial advantage of the country's still extensive forests. Large scale logging concessions were granted to foreign and Honduran companies, and illegal logging also increased dramatically, especially in eastern Honduras, prompting formation of popular and indigenous movements to protect the forests.[16] In 2004, Congress passed another property law and initiated a state program funded by the World Bank. PATH (*Proyecto de Administración de Tierras de Honduras*) promoted individual land entitlement as a basis for creating a free market in land. Communal landholding and cooperative land patterns that were traditional in indigenous and some peasant communities were seen as obstacles to the free commercial purchase and sale of land that was required to allow powerful Honduran and foreign economic interests to invest in development schemes within a neoliberal economic model. A coalition of popular organizations protested PATH on the grounds that it introduced a right of outside parties to obtain traditional communal lands, and it undermined the traditional role of land in indigenous and peasant communities.[17]

Government officials justified and promoted the drive to individualize and privatize land ownership and to eliminate cooperative and collective forms of land use as a means to promote security of individual title to farmers who had never before enjoyed secure title, and thus to promote economic prosperity. In reality, individual title made poor farmers more vulnerable to pressures from large landowners and corporate interests and eliminated the protection and support afforded by forms of collective ownership and association. Honduras was not alone in promoting this process. Shortly before approving its entry into the North American Free Trade Agreement (NAFTA) Mexico abolished Article 27 of its post-revolution constitution, thereby eliminating legal recognition of the traditional community lands (*ejidos*) that had provided access to land for poor farmers in many Mexican communities. In Honduras, the values of the Agrarian Reform Law of the 1970s were replaced with the values of the land market that gave advantage to those with the wealth and power to control the market.[18]

In 2006, the government of Manuel Zelaya announced a moratorium on the granting of mining concessions to Honduran and foreign entrepreneurs. The 2009 coup that removed Zelaya from power ushered in a temporary government until November, 2009, when presidential elections were held in a context of repression and popular resistance. The post-coup government of Porfirio Lobo ended the mining moratorium, by passing a new law promoting expansion of mining operations in different areas of the country but requiring concession holders to obtain the informed consent of local communities after obtaining the government concession but before undertaking mining operations. This last provision was recognition of obligations Honduras had as a signatory to international agreements. But mining concession holders, both Honduran and foreign entrepreneurs, found various ways to extract "consent." Interviewed in August 2013, Antonio, a small farmer and recognized leader in a community in southern Honduras said he was offered more than one million dollars if he would approve a mining operation in his area.

He refused, saying later that he knew the mining company was trying to have him persuade other community members, or would use his consent as evidence that the entire community approved when in fact most opposed the mine. In any case, he said, he did not believe the mine owners would ever pay him, a small farmer, such a large amount. Antonio and some of the older people in the community had been involved in successfully blocking lumber operations in the area during the 1970s. Antonio compared then to now and said the present situation was "very sad."

In some places, opponents of mining operations were killed. In August, 2013, in the small indigenous (Tolupan) farming village of Locomapa in Yoro, three members of a community group opposing a mining operation in the area were killed by what other local people identified as employees of the mine owner. Local police failed to prosecute perpetrators of these threats and killings. The alleged killers in Locomapa were reportedly still traveling freely in the community a year after the killings, even though everyone in the area seemed to know who they were (see chapter 5). Police said they had no vehicles or resources to pursue and take the alleged killers into custody. These and other examples illustrate how the mining law's technical requirement of consent from the affected communities could be annulled in practice through bribery, falsehood, or fear and violence directed by mining interests against local opponents of mining.

The degradation of environment caused by mining and logging activities had two devastating effects on local communities. Degraded environments often made small farming and even community life almost impossible. Pollution of water and land resources by logging or mining forced people to move. Often this meant the end of their traditional way of life, turning peasant farmers into displaced job seekers. Environmental destruction also undermined the spiritual values and morale of local communities where people derived pleasure and spiritual support from the place where they were rooted. In the peasant farming community of Nueva Esperanza, a large mango tree on a ridge overlooking the community became a symbol of the strength and rootedness of the people themselves. Receiving news in mid-2013 that a mining operation would begin in their area, community elders worried about the degradation it might cause, and the tree became a symbol of their determination to resist the mining. Elders said to sympathetic foreign and Honduran visitors that it would be a great sadness to lose the mango tree and that people would try to protect it and the ridge on which it stood. A few days later, the community awoke to find the tree gone and the ridge torn up in preparation for a mining road through the area.

The economic control that these sorts of incidents demonstrate goes beyond the imposition of extractive enterprises and the neutralization of local opposition. Faber argues that environmental deterioration from such developments in Central America is not simply an unfortunate side effect, but is an *intended* part of the economic control of society. Displacing rural people from their land creates a pool of cheap labor for the industries controlled by the economically powerful.[19] In Honduras, the growth of San Pedro Sula from fifty-five thousand inhabitants in the 1950s to over one million by 2010 partly reflects this rural to urban migration of the dispossessed.

Over the past century, but especially since the 1990s, the government practice of granting large concessions to foreign companies, allowing them to extract important natural resources with little restrictions and Honduran political and economic leaders to increase their bank accounts has seemed so entrenched in Honduran life that people invented (probably in the 1980s) a term for it—*vendepatria*, selling the nation or the national patrimony. Sometimes an individual may be referred to as a *vendepatria*. The term may imply lack of due patriotism, hypocrisy, or even treason. The economically powerful may deploy a self-professed image and ideology as the rightful leaders, managers, and guardians of the nation and its treasure, but this can be used by other Hondurans to fashion "the most damning critique" of the government and the economic elite for betraying that very identity.

MANIPULATING HISTORY AND MEMORY: REWRITING, ERASING, AND DISAPPEARING

In Honduras, mechanisms of control include the manipulation of memory, including attempts to erase collective memory or to rewrite history. After members of the political elite had successfully engineered the 2009 coup against an elected president, they were forced to deploy the military and the national police to repress massive popular demonstrations. In this disruptive and turbulent situation, the government and powerful business interests tried to portray a state of normalcy. By 2011, they were trying to implement a program to attract business and had adopted the slogan, "Honduras is open for business," so as to assuage the concerns of foreign investors that the country was safe, and to minimize the extent of popular outrage. The message was that there had been no convulsive national event worth recalling, no recent history as reference.

In the months after the 2009 coup, as the military and the national police applied increasingly repressive measures against popular resistance, Defense Minister Oscar Alvarez, appointed by the post-coup government, justified the need for such measures by likening the situation to that of the early 1980s. Just as his uncle military chief Gustavo Alvarez had in 1982, the younger Alvarez warned in the months after the 2009 coup that the Sandinista government, recently returned to power in neighboring Nicaragua, was training Hondurans as guerrilla fighters to infiltrate Honduras in order to topple the government and spread Nicaraguan socialism. Strong measures of control against popular unrest were required and justified by the imminent threat to national sovereignty posed by Nicaragua, and that in this time of national peril internal popular criticism and protest weakened the nation, and perhaps even amounted to treason or terrorism. But many Hondurans who had lived through the 1980s recalled that few people then believed in the dire warnings of a Nicaraguan threat, and that events simply did not support those warnings. Popular memory contradicted the Defense Minister's interpretation. Human rights defenders and leaders of popular organizations had a quite different interpretation of the "threat" and the force, based on what they remembered of the 1980s—the problem was the Honduran authorities, not the Nicaraguans.[20]

Reinterpretation of historic events was also an occupation of outside observers whose efforts to recast history were often aimed at a U.S. audience. In a January 3, 2014 op-ed piece in the *Washington Post*, Eliot Abrams described the events of the 2009 coup thus: "Zelaya forfeited power in 2009 after illegal attempts to rewrite the country's constitution." Zelaya was in fact removed at gunpoint by a military unit and forcibly put on a plane to exile. "Forfeited power" is a creative way to describe that history, as is describing Zelaya's proposed public opinion poll as "illegal attempts to rewrite the country's constitution." Abrams conveniently neglected to mention that this was only a first step in a long and complex process involving the wide participation of the Honduran people, the end of which would be anything but certain. Others strongly contested the characterization of Zelaya's action as "illegal."

Erasing memory also involves erasing the memory of people, especially those who are prominent critics of the powerful or are leaders of popular resistance. Assassinations and especially disappearances are the ultimate means of erasing a person's existence, first by physically removing the person, then by denying any knowledge of the person. Disappearing those who criticize or oppose the powerful is a practice reminiscent of the national security states of Argentina, Chile, and other military dictatorships in Latin America in the 1970s. Disappearances of activists and members or leaders of popular movements and organizations, and sometimes of children or youth became widespread in Honduras during the early 1980s. Most of the disappearances were allegedly perpetrated by police or military in Honduras at that time. They might arrest and detain an individual who was then held secretly and perhaps transferred to another location without the knowledge of family or friends. When human rights organizations or relatives and friends of the disappeared inquired, authorities could deny any knowledge of the disappeared person. Sometimes there was material or circumstantial evidence that the detained person had been tortured and killed. Often, however, there was only uncertainty about the person's fate. To be most effective, assassination or disappearance was often coupled with the insinuation or the story that the disappeared individual was really a criminal whom the authorities caught in some heinous crime, or a lowlife who really must have run off somewhere with a mistress or the labor union funds—that is, someone not worthy of a second thought.

Beginning in the early 1980s, the Committee of the Families of the Disappeared/Detained in Honduras (COFADEH) began to keep track of disappearances, to discover the fate of the disappeared and the identity and responsibility of the perpetrators. Their files contain at least 126 cases of disappeared persons from the 1980s and many more cases since then, as well as clandestine graves in rural areas or isolated "torture houses" where disappeared individuals were taken, tortured, and killed (interviews with COFADEH staff, 2012 and 2013). Such disappearances continued as a practice, although sometimes in lower numbers, through the succeeding years and became a part of the repression and violence that increased after the 2009 coup. The actual number of disappeared in Honduras since the 1980s is difficult to know with precision, in part because relatives, friends, or associates of a person who has disappeared may be too afraid to report the disappearance. By 2012, longtime Honduran social activists were commenting that the patterns of disappearance had changed in some ways since the 1980s. In the past, individuals were specifically targeted for disappearance because of their prominence as leaders of popular resistance or as critics of powerful members of the country's elite. While this pattern continued, it later broadened to include many other individuals. In addition, the badly dissected body parts of disappeared individuals stuffed into plastic bags began to appear in urban areas, as if to erase the physical image and integrity of the victim. This contributed to a generalized sense of randomness, insecurity, and chaotic violence in Honduran society. In this context, some human rights activists thought that youth seemed to be emerging as a special target of disappearances.[21]

In addition to physical disappearances, legal or policy disappearances seemed to "eliminate" certain social groups. Writing in 2011, anthropologist Jon Wolseth described the way in which recent Honduran governments wrote their policies in ways that eliminated consideration of the country's youth except as criminals and delinquents.

> Youths are effectively erased from political plans for human and economic development, experiencing social exclusion to the point of disappearance. This disappearance of youth from social programming combines with the more familiar form of disappearance in Latin America and Honduras—the disappearance of the physical body through kidnapping and murder. The coincidence is striking.[22]

Disappearances and erasure of memory are directed against memorial symbols as well as living persons. In 2012, COFADEH commissioned the construction of a metal sculpture of a human figure depicting freedom from captivity and commemorating all of the country's disappeared persons. The figure was located on a hillside beside the major road between Tegucigalpa and the southern city of Danlí. Within a few months, someone had shot bullets into the sculpture. Shortly after, the entire figure disappeared.

MANIPULATING LEGAL AND JUDICIAL SYSTEMS: IMPUNITY, BLAME, CRIMINALIZATION

The erasure of public memory of crimes and their victims is a most important defense of impunity for those who direct or perpetrate the crimes. Impunity—the ability to escape prosecution for illegal or criminal behavior—is one of the more salient and criticized features of Honduran daily reality and it is a necessary condition for the manipulation of the country's legal and judicial systems. It allows the powerful to evade, bend, remake, or ignore laws and to engage in various illegal activities without fear of being stopped. Impunity is achieved by several means. Some of these means have been practiced in Honduras for many years but became increasingly apparent, or at least increasingly troubling after the 2009 coup. The fact that the political leaders of the coup could stage what many thought of as an illegal and unconstitutional ouster of a duly elected president was seen as a major example of impunity. After the coup, the means of ensuring impunity included threatening or killing judges, lawyers, and others engaged in legal actions against powerful people or in support of any person or group that posed a challenge to the powerful. The killing in September 2013, of Antonio Trejo, a lawyer who had represented a peasant organization in a land claims case, and the noontime killing of Judge Mireya Mendoza in a busy street in El Progreso in July 2013, were two of many such killings. Mendoza had a reputation of integrity. Authorities or powerful individuals can arrange cover-ups of their illegal activities or crimes. Cover-ups became part of the protection of impunity. In January 2015, in a rare breach of impunity, public prosecutors in Tegucigalpa charged a lieutenant colonel and several lesser army officers with attempts to cover up the circumstances surrounding the killing of teenager Ebed Yanez (see chapter 1). Powerful figures continued to bribe members of the police and other law enforcement officials, and official corruption became a major accusation of popular organizations and human rights workers. Perpetrators of crimes were arrested and then mysteriously escaped or were released, while victims or other third parties were accused of perpetrating or inciting the crime—blaming the victim so as to deflect blame from the perpetrators. After the murder of a staff member of Radio Progreso in his home in El Progreso in October 2014, police quickly decided the murder was a crime of passion perpetrated by the slain man's male friend, despite any evidence to substantiate that theory. Victims were portrayed as deserving what they get, as if that justified their murder. Teens killed by police or the military were automatically guilty because they were teens, a social category prone to violent gang membership.

Violations of basic human rights were justified as measures to ensure national security or order. Police or the military were deployed to enforce actions such as illegal community evictions so as to provide an aura of legal law enforcement to what is essentially an act of violent land theft. In an example that gained some attention and notoriety in 2013, a foreign filmmaker who had come to talk with members of a peasant community in the Aguán Valley filmed the forcible eviction of the community, clearly showing police and military personnel carrying out the evictions on behalf of a powerful landowner who had claimed the land. Powerful people publicly accused of criminal behavior claim to be victims of persecution by public opinion, and may threaten legal action against their accusers. When the bishop of Copan accused one of the wealthiest large landowners in Honduras of involvement in criminal activity, the landowner threatened to bring libel charges against the bishop. He also complained that he was an honest victim of an international slander campaign.

The point of establishing mechanisms of impunity for some is to permit freer reign for the repression of others, especially those who offer a challenge to the dominant model of development. The judicial system can also be made to punish or immobilize those who seem to pose a threat. Delayed justice became a commonly used mechanism in dealing with leaders of popular resistance and popular organizations. This was often done with the explanation that the court system was overwhelmed, an explanation that in a country like Honduras is not easy to challenge. Pending hearings and trials, the accused activist was usually ordered to appear before an authority regularly, to remain in the country, perhaps to stay away from certain locations where public protest or demonstration has been occurring. Such was the case of Lenca indigenous activist leader Berta Cáceres in a case that extended through several hearings and changes through much of 2013 and 2014. Delaying hearings and trial for activists may have the intent of eroding public manifestations of support for them. But delay often seems to have an opposite effect. Public support for the accused grows over time, and in some cases may assume national or even international proportions. This was the situation with a man popularly known as Chabelo, a member of the peasant organization MCA (*Movimiento Guadalupe Carney*) who was accused of murder, almost entirely on the basis of contradictory testimonies in what many considered a political trial. He was imprisoned in 2008, and indications were that he would remain there indefinitely. As of mid-2014, he was still in prison and the legal process was not quite exhausted. A popular demonstration in Tegucigalpa in August, 2014, presented a request to Honduran President

Hernández to release Chabelo. Another form of delayed justice was the continuing government failure to investigate and prosecute incidents such as several large prison fires in which many people were killed or injured. (Many of the examples mentioned above are further discussed in chapter 7 in the context of popular resistance and efforts to redefine and transform Honduran judicial and penal systems.)

Constructing new legal definitions of crimes and categories of illegal behavior in such a way as to render illegal or criminal some of the actions of popular protest is another way of controlling dissent. In chapter 1, we saw that during periods of modern and recent Honduran history organized peasant land takeovers (*tomas de tierra*) have been considered as acts of terrorism. In examples during the years after the 2009 coup, activists and indigenous leaders who tried to stop or delay the building of a dam or the start of a mining or logging project were held responsible for costing the project owners money in delays—defied as a form of theft, property destruction, or any one of several other offenses. In 2013, Lenca activist leaders and their organization COPINH (Consejo Cívico de Organizaciones Populares e Indígenas de Honduras) that carried out protests against construction of a hydroelectric dam on the Gualcarque River were accused of costing significant income loss to the Chinese company Sinohydro that the government had contracted to build the dam. The Lenca were further charged with the patently illogical accusation of trespassing on land that their own Lenca people had legally claimed for generations (see chapter 5).

In addition to the judicial system, manipulation of the legislative process itself is another major arena in which law and justice become mechanisms of control for the powerful in Honduras. The 2009 coup occasioned considerable argument over the legality of the coup and the legitimacy of the accusations against President Zelaya that were a rationale for the coup. At the end of 2012, Congress summarily dismissed four of the five judges of the Constitutional Court after they declared unconstitutional a newly passed law opening the country to Charter Cities development. Congress then replaced them with other judges who approved a similar law. The Congressional removal of these judges was widely seen as an illegal overreach of the power of one branch of government into another, and was sometimes referred to as a "technical coup." (The coup and its "legality" are discussed in detail in chapter 7.)

Some older laws seemed to pose obstacles to the development plans of the country's economic elite but were symbolic of widely held popular values. Repealing such laws risked popular protest. In 1992, when the Congress passed a new law of agricultural modernization based on neoliberal policies that posed an alternative to the communitarian logic of the 1974 Agrarian Reform Law, the new law was promoted as an advance for individual land security and rights, even though it actually replaced the security of older patterns of communally held land, and even threatened to undermine the whole system of communal land. This sort of legislative (mis)representation might well be termed the "Trojan horse" stratagem, but this particular example of it did not seem to beguile many leaders of popular peasant and indigenous organizations such as the Garifuna Fraternal Black Organization of Honduras (OFRANEH) or the country's Catholic bishops who protested the new law shortly after it was promulgated (see chapter 6).

Sometimes new laws passed in order to facilitate greater control or exploitation of national resources must contain provisions that recognize other legal obligations of government that might restrict some of the major purposes of the new law. The Mining Law of January 2013 is an example. It required that mining entrepreneurs obtain full and informed consent from the people of local communities that might be affected by mining operations, and that they use legitimate means to purchase land from individuals and communities to locate mining operations. These provisions were required since Honduras is a signatory to several international treaties and conventions. But as we saw above, mining concession holders and government officials often used bribery, exaggerated promises, or threat to extract consent or the appearance of consent from local people. The unwanted provisions of the law could be effectively undermined with such practices.

In August 2013, a hearing was held in the city of La Esperanza in a criminal case that Honduran authorities had brought against Berta Cáceres, a leader of the indigenous popular organization, COPINH. COPINH members, others from the Lenca indigenous community, and Honduran and international supporters and observers formed a rally outside of the Justice Center (Palacio de Justicia) while the hearing was held inside. The center is a large, imposing building with exterior columns and the seal of the country and large gold-colored lettering over the entrance. The interior included a large open atrium connecting the building's two wings. The Justice Center is on the outskirts of the city in a large open area accessed by a short but rather poor dirt road. Its location in the middle of an open area makes it all the more imposing. A woman attending the rally outside the center said that the building was a symbol of what was wrong with the Honduran justice system. It was imposing so as to reinforce the message of control, authority, and official status. The money used for this symbol of dominance could have been directed instead to addressing more pressing needs. The building was supposed to symbolize justice but was the scene of injustice. It was large but also vacant in the sense of rampant impunity—most of the crimes committed went uncharged, untried, so what was the building for except to prosecute the victims and deter popular protest? Its location at a distance outside the city center meant that people arrived by taxi or other transport if they could afford it—symbolic perhaps of the difficulty or inaccessibility of justice for the poor.

THE WAR ON PROGRESSIVE CHRISTIANITY

On June 25, 1975, on a large farm (hacienda) known as Los Horcones, in the Department of Olancho, a group consisting of two ranking military officers, the owner of the Los Horcones hacienda, and several others reportedly murdered two Catholic priests and at least twelve peasant farmers. The peasants were leaders and members of the National Peasant Union (*Unión Nacional de Campesinos*, UNC). The killings included torture and mutilation. Several victims were burned in an oven on the hacienda. *Boletín Eclesial*, a bimonthly religious news publication, characterized this incident as "the gravest and cruelest confrontation in Honduran history between Church and State" (no. 54, May–June 1975). The incident was followed by the expulsion (deportation) of all the foreign priests and nuns in the Diocese of Olancho, leaving only a very few native clergy. The bishop, Nicolas D'Antoni, was relieved of his diocese.[23]

Commonly described in Honduras today as a "massacre," Los Horcones occurred in a context of peasant activism supported by sectors of the Catholic Church. UNC members had been influenced by the social doctrine of the Church (*doctrina socialcristiana*) that emphasized social justice, human rights, and a "preferential option for the poor," as well as social and political action.[24] After Los Horcones, many of the Catholic bishops and the official Church hierarchy began to retreat to less confrontational works that emphasized voluntary charity rather than demands for justice. Some Hondurans say the Catholic Church has never fully recovered its social justice momentum. There were continued divisions or disagreements within religious denominations, especially the Catholic Church, about involvement in social or political activism.[25]

In Honduras, the use of religion to control or dampen popular activism takes two major forms. The first is the active repression of those sectors of the religious communities that engage in, promote, or educate about questions of social justice, criticize the powerful, or offer support for popular organizations that engage in resistance. Los Horcones was an especially stark example, but it was not the last.

The second way in which religion may be deployed as a means of control is the advancement of theologies that undermine social activism. Theological systems can be understood as forms of ideology. Sometimes they can be aspects of an ideology of domination or submission. There are several commonly embraced types of theologies that can bolster the control of the powerful or undermine popular activism and resistance to perceived injustice. All of them are preached in Catholic and Protestant churches and religious institutions in Latin America, including Honduras. These theologies are discussed in chapter 9, along with the alternative offered by a "theology of liberation."

As in much of Latin America, division within Honduran religious institutions seems apparent. But the situation is more complex, and might better be characterized as a spectrum of thought and action that encompasses both Catholic and Protestant churches. In the 1960s and early 1970s, the years after the Second Vatican Council, the Honduran Catholic Church moved toward the *doctrina socialcristiana*, the option for the poor, and the promotion of human rights. When direct repression made clear the high cost of this turn and theological war was waged to discredit it, people in the Church responded in different ways. Some retreated to "safer" ministries and teachings, others tried to use accepted church works such as schools to promote some level of education about social justice, while some redoubled a more radical commitment to the agenda of Vatican II. This, too, is explored in greater detail in chapter 9.

MILITARIZATION AND THE NATIONAL SECURITY STATE

Honduras has had several periods of military rule, usually with the rationale of protecting the country from weak or corrupt civilian politicians. The most recent period ended in 1982, when the military handed over power to a civilian government but demanded in return that the military commander-in-chief be constitutionally independent of the president and the Congress. A further concession placed the National Police (then named the Public Security Forces or FUSEP) under the control of the military. This legal dual power structure lasted until the 1990s, when President Carlos Reina initiated his "moral revolution." Eventually, the police were separated from military control, and the control of the military was, at least on paper, returned to the civilian president.

In the 1980s, Honduran military and the police then under military control applied the national security doctrine. The military was said to be guarding society against internal communism and invasion from Nicaragua. The national security doctrine as received from the Argentine military that helped train the Hondurans in that period was based on an ideology that in its most developed form claimed the security of the state as the highest good, subordinating all individual rights and public institutions to that end. This ideology and doctrine supports the practice of impunity—the security forces are above the law when protecting the state from evil, or they are simply performing a legitimate exercise of force.[26]

The role of the Honduran military in national life is complex. The military has sometimes acted to enforce conditions of pacification and control to benefit the expansion of the business and economic interests and policies of the economic and political leaders. But the military is not simply the instrument of the civilian power structure. It pursues its own interests. High ranking officers, the colonels and generals, are often entrepreneurs and wealthy men themselves, part of the economic elite, who also have an interest in ensuring stable conditions for economic expansion. Military officers are involved in the expanding private security industry, and some are large landowners.

Within the military there is concern for what might be called national sovereignty. The military as a major institution of Honduran life is committed to the doctrine that it is supposed to be the guarantor and protector of national sovereignty. In addition, junior officers sometimes act in dramatic ways to ensure their own eventual advancement in the ranks. In 1984, junior officers staged the removal of the military chief, General Gustavo Alvarez, who had welcomed an increasing U.S. military presence in the country, and had implemented repressive "national security" measures against civilians. It is hard to know what mixture of self-interest, defense of national sovereignty, and qualms about their role in the heavy handed treatment of civilians drove military officers to engineer the removal of Alvarez. Nothing is simple in Honduras.

Increasing the complexity are social class differences. Ordinary soldiers and some junior officers are usually young and often come from poor families in both urban and rural areas. Their individual economic and social interests are different from those of the top ranks, and they may be socially and culturally closer to the communities from which they come. Joining the military has long been one of the few options for a "better" life open to many Honduran youth. If the military does not carefully and brutally train them to become part of a "special" unit, their social and emotional ties to the people may assert themselves in contradiction to the mentality of distant indifference that may be required of them to perform some of the more repressive and violent tasks in enforcing the control of the powerful against the more vulnerable.

The military itself shares the "enforcement and security" function with the national police and an expanding force of private security guards that in 2013 numbered as many as eighty thousand, twice the size of the military and national police combined.[27] Except perhaps for the 1980s and early 1990s, military duties have been traditionally separated from police duties. The police are to deal with ordinary daily law enforcement and anti-crime activities. The military are charged with protecting the safety and sovereignty of the country. Since at least the 2009 coup d'etat and the expansion of narcotics trade as a thriving economic and political force in Honduras, the anti-crime police function and the national security military function have been increasingly integrated. Embedded in the new ideologies of dominance is the rationale that the rising level of crime and violence is a threat to national security and political and economic stability, and ultimately national sovereignty, and therefore requires a joint police-military response. Ironically, this rationale also justified the expanding presence of U.S. enforcement agencies and military in the country to assist Honduran police and military in narcotics interdiction, especially in the Mosquitia.

The national police have a history of accusations that they employ deadly force in situations where it may seem excessive. But there is also evidence of popular support for harsh police measures to protect society from criminals and unwanted elements. During the 2013 election campaign, National Party presidential candidate Juan Orlando Hernandez made the pledge to increase police and military presence to counter crime on the streets a centerpiece of his platform. This approach, what Hondurans call the *mano duro*, is not entirely new in Honduras. Since at least the 1980s, media reports of extrajudicial killings of "criminals" and homeless street children have occurred with some frequency. Honduran human rights activists and some religious leaders lament that such killing seems to have become a routinely accepted way to deal with criminals and undesirables in Honduran society. Sometimes people ask whether there is collusion or even integration between death squad activity and police actions. Police are subject to many of the same conflicting forces and loyalties that may affect Honduran soldiers, and popular images of the police range from protectors to assassins.

Private security guards are not government agents but employees of private companies, corporations, or large landowners. They are not governed by a constitutional mandate but by the demands of their employers. Private security guards have long played a role in enforcing the control of wealthy individuals and businesses, large landowners, and foreign companies. Homes in wealthy urban neighborhoods, banks, and some businesses routinely employ hired guards. Large landowners have used armed security guards to remove—by threat and force—peasants and others from the land. As national and international criticism focused on human rights violations by the Honduran military and the police, the powerful turned increasingly to private guards to enforce their interests. This shift from the traditional reliance on the military to reliance on private individuals accountable only to their employer resulted in a large expansion of private security forces in the country. Honduran and international human rights organizations began to criticize some of these private "armies" for doing the work of "death squads."[28]

In 2013, the Honduran Congress changed the law to allow the integration of some police and military duties. The president of Congress was also a candidate for president in national elections later in the year. As we have seen, the keynote of his campaign speeches was a promise to put soldiers on every street corner or in every neighborhood to stem the rising violence. The outgoing post-coup government created and trained the first units of a new national military police (the Military Police for the Public Order, PMOP) to be deployed in urban areas. By then, soldiers were seen at road checkpoints in and near cities inspecting traffic, normally a police function. The new law seemed to return the country to the 1980s when the police were under military command, except that both were now at least nominally under civilian control. In January 2015, President Hernandez went on national television to announce his intention to amend the Honduran Constitution so as to make the new military police a permanent, constitutionally mandated institution. He said the country would hold a plebicite to have citizens vote on this proposal, and he implied that people who opposed it would be aiding criminal elements—an example of how criticism or legal opposition to government policy can be defined as a criminal act.[29] In a radio interview on Radio Progreso the following day, political analyst and former Honduran Congressman Efrain Diaz interpreted this intention to make the PMOP a permanent, constitutionally protected institution as a strategy to help ensure the reelection of Hernandez or another similar National Party candidate in the next election.

The internalization of the idea of Hondurans as a violent people—an idea built and encouraged by government, churches, media—contributes to the rationale for national security, this time against the people themselves. By 2013, some Hondurans began to see a clear pattern of increasing militarization of Honduran society in large and small ways.

This militarization seemed especially focused on the country's youth. In March 2014, the military announced a new program, "Guardians of the Fatherland" (*Guardianes de la Patria*). Military instructors at military bases would provide eight hours of training every weekend to a first group of 1,340 middle school and high school youth. The training was intended to "help [youth] to improve in ethical, moral, spiritual, and civic principles."[30] This announcement seemed to reflect an expansion of military influence into family life, education, and religious practice, since training in civic, moral, and spiritual principles was normally seen as the proper sphere of educational, religious, and family institutions. But the government was withdrawing public financial support from local school systems, and encouraging schools to seek private funding from corporations and others.[31] At the same time, children and youth were being killed at what seemed an accelerating pace, especially in the cities. Some Hondurans feared that this "war" against youth was intended to eliminate the next generation of social activists and popular resisters by killing some, keeping others in fear and poverty, and creating or doing nothing to change conditions that encouraged many young people to flee the country. Meanwhile, thousands of young people from Honduras, Guatemala, and El Salvador were arriving at the southern U.S. border seeking asylum.

The trend toward militarization had popular support but it also had many critics. There were small signs that some police and military were not happy with the level of militarization of society, that some police especially resented the feeling of being pushed aside by the increasingly important role of the military. Some human rights and religious leaders pointed out that the police and the military were supposed to uphold the law but sometimes they seemed to ignore it, giving bad example and inviting a general disregard for the rule of law, especially when judges and lawyers themselves are threatened or killed for doing their work. This reinforced the idea of the rule of the strongest. Some said that what was needed is not militarization but civilization. Critics pointed out that militarization and the entire national security ideology were based on the assumption and the perpetuation of fear, and that this had an isolating and paralyzing effect that undermines community and civic activity and promotes the rule of the powerful by force. There is a fundamental conflict of belief and perspective between believing that force creates security and believing that community and wellbeing create security. Fear as a mechanism to control popular activism was much more effective if ordinary people could be convinced that they themselves were the source of the violence they fear. For some Hondurans, civilization meant promotion of community, trust, mutual concern, and security based on meeting human needs and rights.[32]

THE U.S. ROLE IN THE CULTURE OF DOMINATION

The role of the United States in the militarization of Honduran society is important. The United States has a long history of both economic and military intervention in Latin America, usually to protect economic investments. The United States created its own apparatus of national security after World War II with the National Security Council and later the National Security Administration and other agencies of government, by implementing regional security aid agreements in Central America and elsewhere, and especially by establishing the School of the Americas (SOA) to train Latin American military officers. Graduates of SOA have been accused of a variety of assassinations, military dictatorships, and human rights violations over several decades. In the 1980s, the Reagan Administration moved to an emphasis on defense against communism and subversion, abandoning even the token emphasis on human rights that the Carter Administration had advanced. Central America was seen as a battleground for stopping communism in the Western Hemisphere, and Honduras was the linchpin in this strategy—the military base of operations for U.S. influence in Central America. Even before the 2009 coup, the focus of U.S. security aid in Central America had shifted to terrorism, gang violence, and narcotics trafficking.[33] Human rights activists in the United States and Honduras argued that continued aid to Honduran security forces through the Central American Regional Security Initiative (CARSI) and other means provided resources to those who have been accused of or implicated in human rights violations (SOA Watch website). In early 2015, an independent study by British researchers concluded:

It is too easy to say "counter-narcotics" operations are failing or misguided. Washington's policies in Central America may well have disastrous results for many, but through the maintenance of a certain status quo and the improvement of the climate for business and investment, they are undoubtedly a success for others.[34]

All of this took place even as the U.S. government elaborated programs of medical and other services to some rural Honduran communities, and programs to train Honduran security personnel and judicial officers in "professional" behavior and human rights (see chapter 10).

In the early 1980s, Honduran peasant organizer and leader Elvia Alvarado described how the peasant movements organized in response to the sorts of mechanisms of control that have been discussed in this chapter.

> We also learned to organize by watching the rich. They were the first to organize, and they're the best organized. They've got their private enterprise organizations, and then they have the government and army organized to protect them. They're super organized; so if we ever want to change anything in this country, we have to be even more organized than they are.[35]

NOTES

1. Eric Wolf, *Peasant Wars of the Twentieth Century* (New York: Harper and Row, 1969), 302. Johan Galtung, "Violence, Peace, and Peace Research," *Journal of Peace Research* 6:3 (1969): 167–91. Also Magaly Sanchez, "Insecurity and Violence as a New Power Relation in Latin America," *Annals of the American Academy of Political and Social Science* 606:1 (July 2006): 178–95.

2. Eric Wolf and E. C. Hansen, *The Human Condition in Latin America* (New York: Oxford University Press, 1972). W. G. Lovell, *Conquest and Survival in Colonial Guatemala: A Historical Geography of the Cuchumata Highlands, 1500–1821* (Montreal: McGill-Queen's University Press, 1992).

3. Mary J. Weismantel, *Food, Gender, and Poverty in the Ecuadorian Andes* (Long Grove, IL: Waveland Press, 1988), 65–66. Although Weismantel is especially describing haciendas in the Andes as land rich and capital poor, the conditions that produced this situation were widespread, including Honduras where not even the growth of the coffee export market reached most Honduran haciendas, at least not enough to make a financial difference as it seems to have in neighboring Guatemala, El Salvador, and Nicaragua. Darío Euraque provides an extended discussion of this point in *Reinventing the Banana Republic* (see below, note 5), 9–13.

4. Harry Sanabria, *The Anthropology of Latin America and the Caribbean* (Boston: Pearson, 2007), 8.

5. Darío Euraque, *Reinterpreting the Banana Republic: Region and State in Honduras, 1870–1972* (Chapel Hill, NC: University of North Carolina Press, 1996).

6. Susan Stonich, "The Political Economy of Environmental Destruction: Food Security in Southern Honduras," in *Harvest of Want: Hunger and Food Security in Central America and Mexico*, Scott Whiteford and Anne E, Ferguson, eds. (Boulder, CO: Westview Press, 1991), 43. Edmundo Valladares, "La miseria financiando el modelo de desarrollo," *El Tiempo*, January 5, 1981.

7. Eric R. Wolf, *Peasants* (Englewood Cliffs, NJ: Prentice-Hall, 1966).

8. Kees Jansen, "Structural Adjustment, Peasant Differentiation, and the Environment in Central America," in *Disappearing Peasantries? Rural Labour in Africa, Asia, and Latin*

America, Deborah Bryceson, Cristóbal Kay, and Jos Mooij, eds. (London: Intermediate Technology Publications, 2000), 195.

9. Jansen, "Structural Adjustment," 194–97.

10. Eric Wolf, *Peasant Wars of the Twentieth Century*, 277.

11. James Phillips, "Resource Access, Environmental Struggles, and Human Rights in Honduras," in *Life and Death Matters: Human Rights, Environment, and Social Justice*, second edition, Barbara Rose Johnston, ed. (Walnut Creek, CA: Left Coast Press, 2011), 215, and 219–20.

12. The usefulness of the 1974 Agrarian Reform Law for peasant groups is a theme in Elvia Alvarado, *Don't Be Afraid Gringo! A Honduran Woman Speaks from the Heart* (New York: Harper Perennial, 1989 [San Francisco: Institute for Food and Development Policy, 1987]).

13. Margarita Oseguera de Ochoa, *Honduras hoy: Sociedad y crisis política* (Tegucigalpa: Centro de Documentación de Honduras CEDOH, 1987), 24.

14. Nancy Peckenham and Annie Street, *Honduras: Portrait of a Captive Nation* (New York: Praeger Publishers, 1985), 45–49.

15. Mark Anderson, *Garifuna Kids: Blackness, Tradition, and Modernity in Honduras* (Austin: University of Texas Ph.D. Thesis, 2000), 234–39.

16. Maria Fiallos, "Honduran Indigenous Community in Standing Forest Area," *Honduras This Week*, June 9, 2003.

17. Phillips, "Resource Access," 220–21.

18. Jansen, "Structural Adjustment," 194. Phillips, "Resource Access," 219–21.

19. D. Faber, "Imperialism, Revolution, and the Ecological Crisis in Central America," *Latin American Perspectives* 19:1 (1992): 27.

20. An Amnesty International report on Honduras (December 4, 2009) quotes a leader of a popular organization (identity withheld). "All this accumulated impunity and the human rights abusers who are calmly walking the streets of Honduras, all this has to do with what is happening now."

21. In an interview in Tegucigalpa with a visiting delegation from the United States in September, 2013, Berta Oliva, director of the Committee of the Families of the Detained, Disappeared in Honduras (COFADEH) described a new kind of emergent violence that targeted youth in particular, who seemed to have no connection to resistance movements or popular organizations. Her interpretation was that this was an attempt to attack not only the leaders but the base of support of popular resistance which, she said, was the youth.

22. Jon Wolseth, *Jesus and the Gang: Youth Violence and Christianity in Urban Honduras* (Tucson: University of Arizona Press, 2011), 11.

23. The incident at Los Horcones is discussed in various places such as, Penny Lernoux, *Cry of the People* (New York: Penguin, 1982), 114 ff. Ismael Moreno SJ, "Dimensión social de la misión de la Iglesia Católica: Una mirada nacional desde la región noroccidental de Honduras" in *Religión, ideología, y sociedad: Una aproximación a las iglesias en Honduras* (El Progreso: Editorial San Ignacio, 2013), 103–4. Elvia Alvarado, *Don't Be Afraid Gringo: A Honduran Woman Speaks from the Heart*, trans. and ed. by Medea Benjamin (New York: Harper Perennial, 1989 [1987]), 82.

24. The so-called preferential option for the poor arose out of the deliberations of the world's Catholic bishops at the Second Vatican Council (1963–1964) as a reorientation of the Catholic Church's mission away from support for the status quo and toward a deliberate focus on supporting the poorest sectors of society and assisting them in changing their poverty and oppression.

25. Moreno, "Dimensión social," 103–4.

26. José Comblin, *The Church and the National Security State* (Maryknoll, NY: Orbis Books, 1984), 64–78.

27. Geneva Academy of International Humanitarian Law and Human Rights, "Honduras: Non-State Actors," Rule of Law in Armed Conflicts Project RULAC (University of Geneva, 2014). Estimates of numbers and role of private security guards also provided in discussion with Honduran human rights activists.

28. Geneva Academy, "Honduras: Non-State Actors," 2014.

29. Juan Orlando Hernandez, television address to the Honduran nation, January 14, 2015.

30. *El Heraldo*, 29 March 2014.

31. Jordan Levy, *The Politics of Honduran School Teachers: State Agents Challenging the State* (University of Western Ontario Electronic Thesis and Dissertation Repository, Paper 2142 (July, 2014), http://ir.lib.uwo.ca/edt/2142.

32. Ishmael Moreno SJ, Commentary on Radio Progreso, August 2013.

33. Peter J. Meyer and Clare Ribando Seelke, *Central American Regional Security Initiative: Background and Policy Issues for Congress* (Washington, DC: Congressional Research Service, May 6, 2014).

34. Ross Everton, "Justifying Militarization: 'Counter-narcotics' and 'Counter-narco terrorism,'" *Policy Report 3*, Global Drug Policy Observatory, Swansea University, UK (March, 2015).

35. Elvia Alvarado, *Don't be Afraid, Gringo*, 8.

Chapter Four

Evolution of a Culture of Resistance

In the previous two chapters, we examined the ideologies and practices of dominance that have characterized life in Honduras. Over many years, Hondurans have organized to critique, resist, undermine, and circumvent the control over their lives and living conditions that the powerful have tried to impose. To paraphrase the famous saying of Karl Marx, Hondurans organized to make their own history, but in conditions not of their making. These forms of resistance and transformation have become almost a way of life, a culture of resistance. In the present chapter we trace the evolution of this resistance through brief glimpses in time that do not pretend to offer a full history of Honduran popular movements. Instead, we shall see how the struggles of different sectors of Honduran society gradually converged onto an increasingly broad field or network of resistance and regeneration in Honduran life—a convergence that in some significant ways crossed social class and urban-rural lines and laid a foundation for the widespread movement of popular resistance that appeared after the 2009 coup. In following chapters, we examine some of the social and cultural aspects of this culture of resistance, resilience, and transformation.

In Honduran society, social activism—becoming actively involved in changing or improving conditions of life for oneself and one's community or society—often leads individuals to adopt forms of social critique or resistance. Here are two stories of how individuals became involved in both. Margarita and Manuel came to social activism and popular resistance in different ways—Margarita the practical-minded, Manuel the social and political critic. In Honduras there are many such stories, and many other different stories of how a culture of resistance evolves. Social activism and popular resistance movements are fundamentally about individual people, the lives they live, and the choices they make within the limitations and the sometime brutal demands of their historical context.

MARGARITA'S STORY

I interviewed Margarita (*pseudonym*) in El Progreso in August 2013. She had devoted her whole life to social activism, especially for women's rights. On the day I interviewed her, she had spoken at a rally to support a woman who was head of a regional peasant union and had been recently arrested for allegedly fomenting peasant land takeovers.

Margarita was born in a small town in the Department of Yoro. Her mother was poor. During much of her childhood, Margarita had to work and help at home rather than attend school. When she was in her teens, she began to take lessons through *Escuela Radiofonica*, a radio school sponsored by Caritas, an agency of the Catholic Church. Soon Margarita was working with Caritas in her area in social development (*promoción social*) helping local peasant women in their homes, educating about health care, economic and domestic issues, and rights. She also became active with women in labor unions. In the mid-1970s, she was arrested and detained for several days. The police charged her with being a communist. She told me she laughed when she heard the charge—the idea that promoting and educating about domestic improvement, health, and women's rights was somehow communist. In the mid-1980s, she was arrested again for her work with a national women's organization, the Visitación Padilla Honduran Women's Committee for Peace (*Comité Hondureño de Mujeres por la Paz "Visitación Padilla"*). The group is named in honor of an early twentieth-century Honduran activist, and many of its members have faced arrest, threats, and harassment for their involvement as women in "political" matters. Again, Margarita was released, and later joined the staff of another Honduran organization that promotes social-economic community development and popular education about human rights.

Margarita told me that Honduran women have always played a major role in trying to improve living and working conditions and even in promoting political change, but their role has often gone unrecognized.[1] She said that women comprised more than 60 percent of the active involvement in the national resistance movement (FNRP) that coalesced after the 2009 coup d'etat, but men controlled most of the planning and formal leadership in it and in the political party, Libre, that came out of the resistance movement. She said there were some prominent exceptions, mostly in independent organizations. As if to underscore Margarita's words, in the month that I interviewed her two prominent women—Berta Cáceres, leader of the indigenous Lenca organization COPINH, and Magdalena Morales, regional leader of a major peasant organization (CNTC)—faced criminal charges related to their activism. People said the arrests were essentially for leading their members in resisting international companies' exploitation of land and resources. A third, Berta Oliva, national director of the human rights organization CO-FADEH, had continued to receive threats, and later was publicly denounced on television and in the press for her criticism of the injustice of the Honduran justice system.

Social activism began for Margarita with receiving a concrete service—basic education—that opened possibilities for improving daily life for her and others. She said that the crucial basis of transformation is not ideology but concrete work to improve daily life, to promote a sense of empowerment, and to reduce a sense of dependency and insecurity in the basic matters of life. Women are especially important in this because they tend to have to deal most directly with everyday problems of living and family. An underlying subtext in this perspective that one encounters in Honduras is that the family is of great importance as a basic unit for transforming society.

Margarita said that the current period since the 2009 coup resembled in repression and violence the national security state of the early 1980s with one important difference. In the 1980s, the violence tended to target individuals who were seen as leaders of popular resistance. In the current context, there was still targeted violence against resistance leaders, but the violence had spread and become generalized, and it often appeared as random. The level of fear was higher.

Margarita's view of political parties, even "progressive" ones, was mixed. They tend to impede transformation, she said, because they offer people promises, provide a political identity, and promote loyalty, but they also promote dependency and the idea that the party leaders are the saviors, not the people. On the other hand, political parties need to be seen as welcoming to all sectors in order to gain broad support. This dynamic brings together people of differing social classes and interests, a situation that might provide training and context for a broad resistance movement that can cross social class lines and other social divisions and encourage people to see their particular interests in the context of a broader common purpose.

MANUEL'S STORY

I interviewed Manuel (*pseudonym*) a few weeks after my meeting with Margarita. My first question was "How did you become involved in social activism?" Now in his sixties, Manuel began by telling me that he had lived much of his life in urban areas of northern Honduras at or near the center of the foreign "banana empire." His father was active in the banana workers' historic strike against the U.S. fruit companies in 1954. Like many Latin

Americans, Manuel's father followed with interest the progress of the Cuban Revolution in the late 1950s, and nine-year-old Manuel began to read and hear about Cuba's revolution and to share his father's interest in social activism as a way of life.

Without pausing, Manuel continued his response to my question by talking about his own activities within the context of modern Honduran history from the 1870s to the present, providing a rather thorough "people's history" of the country—the difficulties, periods of repression, and the triumphs and successes of the popular movements in gaining political voice. Manuel spoke for nearly two hours without a break. He dwelt on periods that seemed to him particularly repressive—the dictatorship of Carias Andino in the 1930s and 1940s that his father had experienced, the military rule in the 1960s, and again the late 1970s, and especially the national security state of the early 1980s. All of these were periods of great repression when criticism and social and political activism were difficult and often dangerous. But there were also successes and the growth of popular organizations that promoted an increasing array of important rights—labor, peasants, women, indigenous communities, environmental concerns, and more.

Manuel concluded his two-hour people's history with an assessment of Honduras in the past decade. He said that he had never before seen the sort of popular enthusiasm that supported the presidency of Manuel Zelaya, not so much for the man himself but because his presidency seemed to be an opportunity, a brief political opening, for real social change. Manuel agreed with others that the period since the removal of Zelaya had been one of repression as great as any in the past. But to my surprise, he emphasized what he saw as positive changes that made the current situation different from past periods of repression. Now there was a broader and more organized popular resistance and even a political party, Libre, that had arisen out of popular activism and actually had a strong possibility of winning power in the upcoming elections. In fact, said Manuel, there were now many political parties. The historic dominance and political monopoly of the National and Liberal parties that represented the wealthy was threatened for perhaps the first time in Honduran history. The popular resistance, thanks largely to the young people who were part of it, now had become skilled in using popular cultural expression—art, music, theater, and radio—in promising ways.

With the historical perspective of his many years in social activism, Manuel tended to emphasize what he saw as progress in the popular struggles. But he thought that the violence and repression in which Hondurans live, especially the country's youth, was the big problem, not only because of the misery it caused but even more because it encouraged a high rate of youth emigration from the country, eliminating the future of resistance and transformation. His own father had first taught him about social activism and how people struggle for a better society, and this had helped set the course for

Manuel's own life. For Manuel, the real struggle of the resistance now had to do with the next generations. Because violence and lack of opportunity drove so many young people to leave the country, and because much of the violence seemed to target and engulf youth in particular, the country was losing a generation of young people. The struggle was for the hearts and minds, and quite literally for the bodies of the next generation of Hondurans. I recalled Manuel's concerns months later as thousands of young Hondurans were arriving at the U.S. border.

EARLY RESISTANCE AND RISING VOICES

We begin with the popular resistance of Honduran indigenous peoples. Their resistance and resilience runs like a counterpoint throughout modern Honduran history, first in the context of Spanish colonial rule (1524–1824), then in the modern independent state, down to the present in which indigenous communities are often seen as the frontline of resistance to the exploitation of the country's land and resources by foreign interests and other Hondurans. The collective resistance of indigenous people in recent years has become a point of inspiration for others, and it has contributed ancient practices to modern manifestations of resistance and transformation. Indigenous resistance deserves its own special attention and will be explored in detail in the next chapter.

In its earlier history as colony of Spain and then as independent nation, much of Honduras consisted of relatively isolated local communities. Popular resistance appeared primarily as local or community efforts to maintain local autonomy and control over land, resources, internal organization, and ways of life. In an effort to advance these agendas, communities sometimes sided with one or another faction of the ruling elite, although these factions also tried to manipulate this local support to serve their own purposes. These elite factions became the bases of political parties during the nineteenth century. But local communities could also mount their own subtle and overt forms of resistance to outside control ranging from selective non-enforcement of central government laws and demands to armed rebellion.[2] In their local communities, people had a place, a social identity, and a network of neighbors and relationships that formed a sort of "social security" net where forms of exploitation (by the local hacienda owner or others) were to some extend hidden or buffered by the closeness of daily relationships and interdependencies, by a community's isolation, and by the history of a community's struggles to keep outside exploitative forces at bay.

Gradually, and especially as Honduras tried to enter the world economy and its people took on specific roles in that economy, forms of resistance emerged that were not locally specific but rather tied to demands and needs that were more broadly shared. These were often expressed through forming popular organizations. Concentrations of workers brought together from different communities and areas to work in new economic projects or industries in the late 1800s provided a basis for the formation of organized labor activism that transcended localism. When people left their communities to join large work pools in distant locations as wage laborers, their employers and bosses were strangers, the exploitative nature of relationships was more apparent, and people sought identity and protection in joining with others in new kinds of collective identity and action. People entered into new social formations such as labor unions to advance collective agendas and to provide social networks of support. This shift in the forms and relations of production could entail a shift in attitudes toward a more critical and even militant perspective.[3]

RISE OF LABOR RESISTANCE: 1870–1960

In 1869, attempts to build an inter-oceanic railway across Honduras provided one of the first large concentrations of workers, both Honduran and foreign, in the country. There were many instances of conflict between workers and their contract employers because of poor working conditions and low wages.[4] With the failure of the project, the workers dispersed.

The expansion of United States economic interests in Honduras after 1880 provided additional reasons for resistance. The Rosario Mining Company's San Juancito mining operation became the largest employer in the country. But wages were low, working conditions in the mines were dangerous and difficult, and the management was considered harsh with workers. Labor unions were not legally recognized, but in March, 1909, workers at San Juancito began a strike. Paid by the company, the local police were called in and striking miners were beaten and injured. The army intervened on orders from the Honduran president to enforce a settlement. Several of the strike leaders were imprisoned.[5] At the time, silver, mined mostly by foreign companies, was perhaps the country's most important export.[6] Whatever interfered with mining operations was seen as a serious matter, especially if it interfered with the efforts of Honduran officials to attract foreign investment.

In urban areas, groups of artisans formed mutual societies or guilds whose purpose was to provide for their members in emergencies such as illness or death, or to provide educational funds—not to engage in more militant actions. With few exceptions, urban areas did not contain large concentrations of industrial workers until later.

Establishment of the large foreign-owned banana enterprises on the North Coast around 1900 was the context for a large and permanent concentration of workers in that area, along with the potential for conflict. Conditions for workers on the banana plantations were usually harsh and changed little over many years. Published in 1950, Ramón Amaya Amador's classic work, *Prisión Verde* (*Green Prison*), dramatically described these conditions. One of the first major labor actions in the banana plantations occurred in 1916, when workers at the Cuyamel Fruit Company reacted to what they considered unfair pricing at the company store by refusing to cut bananas or to load fruit. Cuyamel hired "scab" workers who cut several thousand bunches, but the striking workers destroyed the fruit with machetes before it could be transported to the wharves for export. Paid by Cuyamel, the army intervened and sent four hundred of the strikers to the prison fortress at Omoa. But the fortress commander refused to imprison the strikers because he thought their demands were justified.[7]

In the 1920s and 1930s, a series of strikes occurred over working conditions involving laborers at the large foreign banana plantations and their transport and docking facilities. By then, several trade unions had formed among the workers and were competing for membership and influence. Divisions among them arose about whether unions should be involved in partisan politics that some considered a betrayal of working class interests, and the degree of militancy appropriate for the unions.

In the early 1930s, the worldwide Depression affected Honduras. Some of the banana and fruit companies cut back operations and let go many workers, while reducing the hourly pay of others from twenty-five to seventeen cents. In response, strikes spread to several of the larger fruit companies along the North Coast during the first months of 1932. Striking workers even persuaded two hundred replacement workers to join them in the strike. This strike ended after five days when the companies agreed to most of the workers' demands for better working conditions and the workers agreed to have their hourly wage reduced to twenty cents. Ten days later, workers began another strike over pay, health care, and working conditions at another fruit company. This strike ended three weeks later, after negotiations mediated by two army generals secured an agreement for better working conditions but no pay raise for the workers.[8]

In April 1932, workers at United Fruit Company (UFCo) facilities near Trujillo and Puerto Castillo on the North Coast called a strike that lasted two weeks. A report from the U.S. diplomatic mission in Honduras to the State Department describes what happened and provides a good example of the collusion of company officials with the Honduran government and the army in suppressing the strike. UFCo's general manager went to the area to meet with an army general and troops sent by the Honduran president. The manager "bought off" the secretary of the strike committee, got the names of the strikers, and gave the list to the general who arrested the strikers and sent some of the leaders to prison in Tegucigalpa.[9]

While these incidents show the militancy and limited success of labor activism, they also exhibit patterns of repression that have continued to the present. Military and police personnel can still be found working for foreign companies in suppressing worker activism and popular protest. Foreign and Honduran government interests still work in concert, usually against the interests of workers, and may encourage divisions within the labor union movement that result in the establishment of rival or parallel unions more favorable to company or government control. The militancy and tenacity of the early Honduran labor movement seems all the more remarkable under these conditions. But worse was coming. In 1933, Tiburcio Carias Andino became Honduran president and ruled as dictator in all but name until 1949. The dictatorship repressed all forms of popular activism and protest. Labor leaders were arrested or executed and union activity went underground or ceased. UFCo's company lawyer became president of the Honduran Congress, and the government agreed to almost every demand of the company, often against the interests of rival fruit companies and the workers. But when Carias managed to alienate even members of his own National Party and many others, he had to relinquish power in 1949.[10]

THE 1954 BANANA STRIKE: ITS IMPORTANCE FOR POPULAR RESISTANCE

Carias was not the only dictator in Central America during this time. In Guatemala Jorge Ubico and in Nicaragua Anastasio Somoza also controlled brutally repressive regimes. But a military coup by progressive Guatemalan army officers forced Ubico into exile in 1944. Reformist governments came to power in Guatemala, enacting a new labor code in the late 1940s, and land reform legislation in the early 1950s that tried to rein in the economic and political power of United Fruit and other fruit companies. The second of these reformist governments, under Jacobo Arbenz, was deposed in a military and propaganda operation conceived and directed by the United States and carried out by dissident Guatemalans from a base in Honduras.[11] Dominated economically and influenced politically by United Fruit, the Honduran government allowed the use of Honduran territory as a staging ground for the coup against the Guatemalan president. United Fruit and powerful Honduran and U.S. government interests were clearly frightened by the possibility that Hondurans would get reformist or even revolutionary ideas from Guatemala's experience, especially since after fifteen years of the Carias regime Honduras itself was in need of major reforms that had long been suppressed.[12]

A series of grievances among banana workers in April, 1954, about overtime pay and suspension of individual workers triggered what seemed to be the accumulated indignation of workers who finally called a general strike on

May 3. The strike included workers from both major fruit companies, United Fruit and Standard Fruit. Daily life throughout the region was disrupted. Many workers, small business people, and peasants throughout the area and eventually the entire country expressed support in various ways for the strikers. Local people set up food committees and received donations from peasants, ranchers, and local businesses. They were able to provide enough food to sustain twenty-five thousand strikers for almost two months. The workers used the lessons of organization, efficiency, and discipline they had learned working on the plantations and port facilities. They effectively paralyzed not only the banana industry but also much of daily life and work in the banana region. They controlled most of the work centers and worker settlements in and around the vast plantations. The strike committee presented thirty demands that included higher wages, better medical treatment, decent worker housing, paid vacation, no arbitrary suspension or mistreatment of individual workers. At first the government and the companies delayed and refused to negotiate, hoping to wait out and "starve" the strikers, but this failed because the local population supported the strikers. While the workers were waiting for the company response, the area, including the urban centers of El Progreso and La Lima, were alive with marches and rallies in plazas and on soccer fields. People made music and songs and impromptu poets emerged. [13]

The companies began to negotiate, but they started separate negotiations with different local strike committees across the northern banana region in an effort to divide the strikers. Rumors circulated that Communists from Guatemala dominated the central strike committee. These measures were combined with police repression, imprisonment of strike leaders, and their replacement with others considered anti-communist and more compliant to company and government demands. Workers at Standard Fruit ended their strike in May. This seemed to weaken the movement, but the United Fruit strikers continued. The overthrow of the Arbenz reformist government in Guatemala on June 27 further emboldened United Fruit executives. They offered minimal concessions, ignoring most of the strikers' demands. After sixty-six days, the strike ended on July 9.

Most assessments of the 1954 banana strike emphasize that its importance went far beyond the modest concessions the strikers were finally able to obtain. Here are two examples:

> Hunger, police repression, intrigue and treachery finally managed to destroy the workers' ability to struggle. But even though they did not immediately achieve what they had set out to gain, their actions changed the course of Honduran history. The right to form unions was legalized, new social security laws were passed, collective bargaining was recognized in law in 1959, and above all, as a result of the strike the possibility of changing the structure of the ruling classes became more visible. [14]

> The most important historical significance of the banana strike of 1954 was that by its own efforts the working class (*la clase obrera*) emerged as a social and political actor that served as a model to the peasants and other social sectors, that they too start their own journey toward the recognition of their rights through popular organizing, public protest, and negotiation with the state.[15]

Barahona adds that the banana strike touched a deeply felt sense of nationalism and national sovereignty among Hondurans of all classes who were unhappy with the dominance of foreign fruit companies in their country, and that this contributed to the broad popular support given the strikers. It also promoted a nascent struggle for recognition of basic human rights. The first set of demands that the strike committee presented stated that they were inspired by the Universal Declaration of Human Rights that had been adopted and promulgated by the United Nations six years earlier, and by the InterAmerican Charter of Social Guarantees adopted the same year (1948) by the Organization of American States.[16] The charter outlines rights of the region's indigenous peoples, but it clearly touched the situation of many others, as well. It seemed as if the workers and labor unionists recognized a connection to indigenous communities and others through the international discourse of fundamental human rights.

The 1954 strike was already employing many of the resources that have characterized social protest and popular resistance to the present, including high levels of relatively democratic internal organization, popular support, appeals to national laws and international instruments of rights, and expressions of popular culture in music, poetry, and more.

PEASANT ACTIVISM AND AGRARIAN REFORM: 1955–1980

During the 1960s and 1970s, the labor agitation of the North Coast banana plantation workers was connected to the rise of peasant activism. After the 1954 strike, United Fruit reduced its production, allowed more of its lands to go uncultivated, and over the next five years laid off nineteen thousand workers, more than half of its workforce.[17] This created a situation of companies with extensive "idle" land and thousands of workers desperate for a way to ensure subsistence. United Fruit did allow some of the laid off workers to rent small portions of land for a time, but the company eventually evicted even these in order to turn some of the unused plantation acreage to ranching.[18] Some of these unemployed workers had originally come from peasant farming to the plantations to supplement the insufficient income they got from their small peasant plots. This was a population that understood the hardships of being both peasant and rural wage laborer. Population increase added to pressure on small farmers and peasants for land. During the same period, Honduras experienced an influx of peasant farmers from small and densely populated El Salvador seeking land in Honduras. These conditions—increasing population pressures on land, large companies and landowners with considerable unused acreage, thousands of unemployed workers who had experienced both peasant farming and labor activism in the 1950s, and an apparently shrinking land base available to small farmers—all combined to promote the rise of peasant activism in search of land.[19]

During the late 1950s, ex-workers-turned-peasants formed groups to press for land, and in 1961 they formed the Central Committee of Peasant Unity (CCUC). A year later this was reorganized as the Nation Federation of Honduran Peasants (FENACH). Disturbed by the militancy and the alleged Communist affiliations of some FENACH members, Honduran government and fruit company officials, large private landowners, and U.S. labor leaders promoted the formation of a rival peasant union that they could influence—the National Association of Honduran Peasants (ANACH). They combined this with harassment and repression against FENACH leaders that included imprisoning members and raiding and closing the organization's offices. The harassment prompted many FENACH members to defect to ANACH. These tactics illustrate a pattern used repeatedly to frustrate and undermine unionism as a form of resistance.[20]

The Catholic Church promoted a third current of organization among peasants based largely upon traditional Church teaching, going back at least to the time of Pope Leo XIII in the 1890s, that acknowledged the right of working people to organize to protect and improve their conditions. The Church had been promoting local community development in different parts of the country that resulted in cooperatives and community welfare projects and a sense of empowerment. In 1964, some of these communities in southern Honduras joined to form the Honduran Social Christian Peasant Association (ACASCH). Within five years, leaders reorganized this into a nationwide peasant organization, the National Peasant Union (UNC). Although its origins were in community development and welfare, UNC became increasingly militant during the 1960s as conflict over the need for land increased. UNC affiliates engaged in the first widespread land takeovers (*tomas de tierra*) in the south of the country. Because of their combination of religious social teaching and militant activism for land, UNC members later became prime targets of violence from large landowners and some government officials. The "massacre" at Los Horcones hacienda in 1975, in which eleven UNC members and two priests were killed, served as a stark example (described in chapter 3).[21]

In 1962, the reformist government of Ramon Villeda Morales responded to increasing pressure from peasant groups and the Kennedy Administration in Washington, D.C., that wanted to avert another Cuban-style revolution in Central America. After considerable opposition and weakening amendments, an agrarian reform law was passed, permitting the expropriation and redistribution of idle lands not serving a social purpose, although the interpretation of this made it virtually impossible to expropriate private land from large landowners. The National Agrarian Institute (INA) was established to administer the reform. The military coup of October, 1963, nearly stopped the work of INA, and the new military government directed its attention to destroying FENACH by raiding its offices, jailing its leaders, and killing other members who had mounted a limited armed resistance in rural areas. By 1967, however, the government was increasingly concerned about the possibilities of peasant resistance and shifted its priorities to promote economic development. A new INA director was allowed a free hand to redirect the agency's efforts toward the formation of peasant cooperatives as instruments to help "modernize" the agrarian sector. INA insisted that recipients of land be organized in groups or cooperatives. In communities throughout the banana country and the Aguán Valley of the north, people who were both peasants and sometime plantation workers formed local farming cooperatives. In 1970, cooperatives across the country formed FECORAH, the Federation of Honduran Agrarian Reform Cooperatives.[22]

The 1969 Soccer War with El Salvador resulted in the departure of many Salvadoran peasants from Honduras, so that more land became available. INA increased its activity. The war also showed the weakness of the Honduran military command and allowed a shift in power to more reform and modernization minded officers who returned General Osvaldo Lopez Arellano to the presidency in 1972. The new military government promoted a policy of state-sponsored modernization and national development. Agrarian reform became an important part of this policy, and passage of the 1974 Agrarian Reform Law became its major expression. Peasant cooperatives and unions, FECORAH, ANACH, and UNC generally cooperated with INA. But the replacement of Lopez Arellano by another military general in April, 1975, ushered in another period of repression against peasant organizations. In response, UNC leaders organized a series of peasant land takeovers across Honduras in an effort to advance and protect the agrarian reform. They believed they could not depend on INA or the government, but rather they themselves had to put into practice the purposes of the reform and carry it out. To dramatize the urgent need for land to feed rural families, they also sponsored a large hunger march from parts of the countryside to Tegucigalpa, but the military government tried to block the roads, closed UNC offices, and arrested some leaders and members.[23] The Los Horcones massacre involving the deaths of UNC members occurred the same day.

During the late 1970s, the Honduran government backed away from agrarian reform and from the support of peasant cooperatives. Land that was distributed by INA was often of poorer quality, while credit and technical assistance to cooperatives was reduced or lacking. In response, peasant organizations across the country formed the United National Peasant Front of Honduras (FUNACAMH) that soon organized a massive coordinated series of land takeovers totaling about six thousand hectares across several areas of the country. The peasant occupiers were removed from some areas, but some were able to remain and negotiate with government officials or landowners. By 1981 civilian government had returned, but the developing regional crisis that began to envelop all of Central America in the early 1980s only increased land conflict, peasant activism, and repression.

Labor and peasant unions suffered from attempts by large landowners and ranchers to limit their lands, and from Honduran and U.S. governments that engaged in divide-and-conquer tactics by setting up parallel unions under their control. The American Institute of Free labor Development (AIFLD) was active in Honduras and throughout much of Latin America in trying to discredit more militant unions and control more pliant unions.[24] AIFLD also had a hand in the destabilization of several "leftist" or "communist" governments in Guyana and elsewhere, but it worked closely with the Honduran government in trying to control the rising activism of workers and peasants. Labor and peasant activism continued despite these major hindrances.

The rise of labor and peasant activism before the 1980s was largely, though not entirely, directed to demands for better working conditions, better pay, or more land—demands that addressed immediate needs. These two currents of activism, labor and peasant, were largely based in the needs and realities of a Honduran working class that had gradually emerged as a new actor in Honduran public and political life. Events after 1980 began to draw these groups increasingly into situations of active resistance to encroaching agendas of globalization and national "development" imposed by a powerful Honduran elite and foreign corporate interests. Activism became increasingly resistant, directed not only to demands for improvement or land but also to the defense of the land and resources that peasant communities already had, sovereignty, environment, and basic human rights against perceived violations or threats. These largely working class organizations were also drawn into increasing collaboration with other groups arising out of the Honduran middle and professional class. Labor and peasant organizations became important components of the massive popular resistance and the National Popular Resistance Front (FNRP) after the 2009 coup.

RISE OF A MIDDLE CLASS, 1930–1980: AN INTELLECTUAL BASIS FOR RESISTANCE

By 1900, Honduras had a small but distinguishable middle class that consisted mostly of small business owners, estate managers, accountants, teachers, priests, and others whose livelihoods were often tied to servicing the large estates and the towns and communities that depended on agriculture, or a growing urban population and the state bureaucracy. With the rise of the banana and fruit industry in northern Honduras, more opportunities opened for the expansion of a middle class involved in the many commercial, industrial and professional skills required to service the growing industries in the area—breweries and soft drink, construction, cement, and local industries and businesses that catered to the needs of the growing population. Middle class people were diverse in their loyalties and political views, reflecting to some extent the different economic sectors on which their livelihoods depended. While some in the middle class lived, worked, and dealt daily primarily with other middle class or wealthier people, others, including some teachers and priests, did have sustained contact with the lives of the poor and the working class. By 1910, university students had formed an organization called Regeneration Honduras. Students organized sit-ins and demonstrations in support of unemployed urban workers and others, as well as for the right of autonomy for the university. By the 1920s, middle-class women were already organizing for the rights of women across social classes.[25]

During the Carias dictatorship (1936–1948) political and intellectual expression was severely constrained. That began to change by 1950, and Barahona characterizes the decade of the 1950s as a time of acute struggle between those Hondurans who wanted change and those who clung to the "liberal oligarchic state" that had dominated Honduran life since the 1870s.[26] The labor and peasant activism described in previous sections demonstrates how working class people engaged in organizing and direct action and emerged as a new voice in the social and political life of the country. What the rising middle class contributed was not so much organized action (though there was some of that) but reflection, analysis, and critique that began to build an intellectual basis for later resistance movements. Much of this was expressed in literary form. It is important to note that while some of the content of this analysis and critique dealt with issues of special concern to the middle class, such as political and intellectual freedom, some of it addressed the lives of poor and working class Hondurans. The 1950 publication of Amaya Amador's *Prisión Verde* (mentioned above) provided a critique of working conditions on banana plantations by someone who had been born into a working class family, worked on banana plantations in the Aguan Valley, and was also a powerful writer and journalist.

Weekly and monthly newspapers, journals, and reviews became important forms of expression, analysis, and critique, albeit not always overt. This literary output may seem misplaced in a country where only a small portion of the population actually reads. But the popular press reflected to some extent what middle class intellectuals thought were the problems of the emerging social groups of both middle and working classes, including unemployed and underemployed urban workers, university students, women, and intellectuals. The very names of some of the weeklies—*Voz Obrera, Alerta, Vanguardia Revolucionaria, Juventud Revolucionaria, El Machete*—reflected an attitude of militant critique and change that now seems surprisingly radical. This intellectual activity provides a glimpse of a middle class trying to give voice and interpretation to the concerns of the working class, albeit sometimes through a particular ideological lens that may or may not have reflected the attitudes of working class people.[27]

THE CRISIS OF THE 1980S: NEW FORMS OF DEFENSE AND RESISTANCE

In July 1979, Nicaraguans toppled the forty-five-year-long dictatorship of the Somoza family. Led by the Sandinista National Liberation Front (FSLN) the new revolutionary government introduced an agenda of national development based on a mixed economy of private enterprise and reform of the rural and agricultural sector to promote rural community life and peasant cooperatives. Large properties abandoned by the fleeing dictator and his associates were expropriated and given to peasant and small farm cooperatives or taken over as government-owned farms on which to grow major export crops such as tobacco. Some large and medium-sized family agricultural enterprises and ranches continued to operate. Basic freedoms of religion, press, assembly, and free speech were generally honored, and most Nicaraguans enjoyed more freedom than at any time under the Somoza dictatorship.[28]

Despite its mixed economy and freedoms, the new Nicaragua was seen and portrayed as a threat by many in the Honduran ruling classes and by the Reagan Administration in Washington that was already concerned about ongoing popular insurgencies in El Salvador and Guatemala. In Honduras, attitudes among the country's elite toward Nicaragua ranged from a desire to keep out of the internal affairs of a neighboring country to declarations that Honduras was in mortal danger of being invaded by a Nicaragua bent on imposing communism on its neighbors. The latter attitude fit conveniently with the concerns of the Reagan Administration that pressured the new civilian government of Roberto Suazo Cordova to allow a large buildup of U.S. military presence in Honduras. The country became the center of United States efforts to counter the Nicaraguan revolutionary government and the Salvadoran insurgency—in short, to defend Central America from communism and Soviet influence. A major part of that effort went into Washington's training and support on Honduran soil of a guerrilla force of Nicaraguans intent on toppling their government—the counterrevolutionaries or simply *la contra*, as many Nicaraguans and Hondurans called them. The Contras (as they came to be known in the United States) occupied extensive camps and training areas in southern Honduras along the Nicaraguan border and made forays into Nicaragua on campaigns of destruction against rural communities. Their tactics included killing peasants and burning their homes, crops, and any Nicaraguan government projects in the area—health clinics, agricultural extension projects, schools. Their purpose was to spread terror among the Nicaraguan rural population so that people would withdraw support from the Sandinista government. In 1986, the World Court condemned these tactics as violations of international law.[29]

Honduran peasants were among the first to feel the effects of the U.S. and Contra presence in their country. Some peasant groups began to complain that areas occupied by Contra training camps and new or enlarged military bases had taken land away from peasant communities. On the pretense of guarding against a possible invasion by Nicaragua, Honduran military chief Gustavo Alvarez Martinez adopted some of the most repressive measures of the so-called National Security Doctrine, rounding up many young male Hondurans, pressing some into military service, imprisoning others, suppressing most forms of dissent. The government issued Decree 33, setting a prison sentence of five to twenty years for crimes "against rural property," and followed this a year later with a law criminalizing all land invasions.[30] These actions made illegal the major strategy of peasants and peasant organizations for obtaining needed land. Labor union leaders were imprisoned, disappeared, and executed. The targets of special repression spread beyond the poor and the working classes to others, as well. Leaders and members of student organizations, teachers associations, newly formed environmentalist groups, and other associations with many middle-class and professional members, began to experience disappearances and assassinations.

As violations of basic human rights became more widespread, crossing social class lines, a new set of organizations arose in the first few years of the 1980s, most of them begun by professional and middle-class Hondurans who saw common cause with members of the older working-class popular organizations, labor unions, and peasant and indigenous groups, especially around the discourse of human rights.[31] The Committee for the Defense of Human Rights in Honduras (CODEH) was founded in 1981 with physician Ramón Custodio as its president. This was joined by the Committee of the Families of the Detained/Disappeared in Honduras (COFADEH), co-founded by professional women who had lost family members in the violent crackdown. These groups took the defense of the human rights of all Hondurans as their mandate, and COFADEH extended that to the legal defense and advocacy of victims of government repression. Both organizations were inevitably involved in documenting and denouncing government and military actions against Hondurans. The Honduran Documentation Center (CEDOH) was formed with Victor Meza as director and began detailed and painstaking daily documentation of events in Honduras and analysis of emerging patterns. CEDOH published a series of short but inexpensive and copiously referenced reports focused on important national issues such as U.S. military presence and influence, refugee populations, patterns of human rights violations, the plight of peasants and rural Hondurans, the Contra presence and its negative effects on Hondurans. Other groups began to organize around environmental issues, and began to describe threats to the natural environment posed by war games and U.S. and Contra military presence.

In 1980–1981, during the same period of repression, Jesuit priests in El Progreso started the Jesuit Reflection, Investigation, and Communication Team (ERIC-SJ). Honduran and other Central American, North American, and Spanish Jesuits had been active in the country for many years as parish priests in urban and rural areas especially in the Department of Yoro, and had developed an educational ministry among Honduran youth. In line with Catholic Church teachings, they promoted education around issues of social awareness and responsibility that eventually expanded to include the discourse of human rights and social justice. The people they ministered to were members of almost all of the country's social classes, from rural peasants to the sons of government officials. ERIC assembled a group of a few Jesuits and young, educated Hondurans. They began to study and reflect on the country's problems using the tools of social science and spiritual reflection, and supported programs to promote community awareness and development as an instrument of empowerment in rural areas.[32] ERIC began to publish analyses and studies through a journal (*Envío-Honduras*), a newspaper (*Mecate Corto*), and occasional monograph studies. ERIC also partnered with the staff of Radio Progreso, a major commercial radio station in the north that the Jesuits had acquired years earlier and envisioned as a forum for popular expression rather than a disseminator of corporate or government interests. ERIC's work involved both an ongoing critical assessment and public critique of oppression and an ongoing promotion through community development projects and media of models of a different society and future for Hondurans—building the better future in the present crisis.

These organizations continued in the tradition of middle-class analysis, advocacy, and communication, but in the context of crisis that marked the 1980s they also began to elaborate or join with others in programs of direct action on behalf of the poor, the vulnerable, and the victims of human rights abuses for people of all social classes. CODEH and especially COFADEH did not just analyze, chronicle, and critique human rights violations. They began to provide legal defense and advocacy for the victims of state repression. ERIC began to elaborate a program of community support that included helping groups of plantation workers secure access to land on which to locate settlements or communities, build houses, and provide essential services such as potable water and sewage—basic community development.

These groups did not include, or did not highlight, public demonstrations or popular organizing. But there were already popular organizations where social analysis and education about issues was integrated with direct popular actions, including protests. Women's organizations such as the *Comité Hondureño de Mujeres por la Paz "Visitación Padilla"* included both middle class and working class women and engaged in raising awareness of women's issues and broader societal problems through both popular education and direct action. University student groups, environmental organizations, and professional groups such as the Honduran Organization of Forestry Professionals added to the mix. University students organized around both ideological positions and practical problems, including academic freedom and concerns about national sovereignty and the future of the country's natural resources.

When peasants were evicted from their lands, or threatened or killed as they engaged in land takeovers, it went beyond the agenda of securing land for land-poor people and became even more clearly a fundamental human rights issue that involved CODEH or COFADEH as well as the peasant unions. During the 1980s, the pages of the periodic *CODEH Boletín*, for example, reported many incidents of torture, brutality, and other rights abuses against peasants, labor activists, and increasingly against indigenous rural communities. Out of daily experience, engagement, and analysis arose a sense that all the violations of rights and other forms of oppression were interrelated, and that human rights were somehow indivisible. One fruit of the Honduran situation throughout the 1980s was a clearer empirical recognition of this essential indivisibility that bound together different popular struggles.

HUMAN RIGHTS AND THE DISCOURSE OF RESISTANCE

The discourse of human rights provides a universal and generalized framework of words and concepts articulated in international documents the most salient of which is the United Nations Universal Declaration of Human Rights (1948). We have seen how the workers' strike committee that issued their set of demands in the 1954 banana strike began by invoking the UN Universal Declaration of Human Rights and the Inter-American Charter of Social Guarantees.[33] Rights became not simply the right of individuals to the means of livelihood, or even to have access to land, but the right of a specific peasant cooperative to continue without eviction on the land they had farmed for generations, or the rights of a particular indigenous group to decide whether to allow a hydroelectric dam on a sacred river. Human rights are adapted to a specific situation yet evoke a universal authority that underscores the justice of the demand. This appropriation of the discourse of human rights to specific situations became a feature of activism that could also draw together working class and middle class groups in a sense of common cause despite the social, economic, and cultural differences. Different groups could express a different specific critique of a situation but somehow realize that they were all connected by a larger sense of rights violated, demanded, protected.

This common rights discourse is illustrated by the widespread protest demonstrations that erupted in 1991 after the revelation that the Honduran government had entered into secret negotiations with Stone Container to award the Company forty years of logging rights to 320,000 hectares of tropical lowland pine forest in Olancho and the Mosquitia.[34] The area included the lands of several indigenous groups as well as various peasant communities. Large public protest demonstrations followed, with marches in several cities. These protests included peasants from the countryside, indigenous activists, professional foresters, university students, environmentalists, and many others.[35] What could have been essentially a concern only of the rural communities directly in the way of the logging rights became instead a nationwide concern for different groups in Honduran society, united in this instance by the discourse of human rights.

FORMS OF COLLABORATION: SEE, JUDGE, ACT

By the 1990s, resistance was bringing together people and organizations of different social classes, communities, and experiences and developing a framework of common discourse around human rights. There were several vehicles through which this collaboration was developed and nurtured.

In the early 1960s, the Catholic bishops of the world had gathered in Rome for the Second Vatican Council to deliberate and set the direction, priorities, and guidelines for the future of the Catholic Church. Bishops from Latin America carried with them the experiences of their priests, nuns, and lay leaders who lived with and ministered daily to poor and oppressed communities. The Church began to speak of a "preferential option for the poor." One of the early products of this shift was the formation of Christian base communities (*comunidades eclesiales de base*, CEBs) that formed throughout Honduras in the years after the Council. Small groups would gather with a lay leader or sometimes the local priest or nun and read the Gospels in the light of daily life. In this process, people began to engage in analysis of their current situation and the conditions of their country, and they found support from their faith and from each other to express criticism of the current reality and visions of the better life and world that they thought God intended. These groupings usually consisted of people of the same social class except, perhaps for the local priest. People of "humble" class and little education began to express their thoughts to each other.

The CEBs could be regarded as a form of democratization in a religious institution that was still essentially hierarchical. By empowering lay people to interpret and apply the scriptures, the CEBs also helped to address the scarcity of ordained priests that had plagued the Catholic Church for many years. The formation and spread of CEBs was facilitated in Honduras by the formation in 1966 of Delegates of the Word, a national network of local Catholic lay leaders and catechists from almost all social classes. The Delegates of the Word also responded to the scarcity of priests and trained local people to lead religious services, but they also began to provide—through religious training, practical education, and local leadership empowerment—an important system of support for local popular leaders and activists motivated by a desire for what they considered a more humane and equitable society (see chapter 9).[36]

The phrase, "see, judge, and act" (*ver, juzgar, y actuar*) summed up the method employed in most of these groups.[37] Seeing meant becoming aware and conscious not only of one's situation but especially of the larger forces that shaped that situation—constructing a sense of the larger reality. Judging meant evaluating and reflecting on what the larger reality meant, one's relationship to it, and what to do about it. Acting to change the reality could take different forms. The process of individual and group transformation that this promoted was similar to that elaborated in the 1970s by the Brazilian social thinker, Paulo Freire who called it "conscientization."[38] One of the fruits of this ferment was the formation in 1969 of a major Honduran peasant organization, the UNC (see above and chapter 9).

By the 1970s, workshops and conferences were becoming a vehicle for much of the collaboration that began to develop between working class popular organizations or communities and middle class organizations and individuals. This practice developed in part from the training offered to Delegates of the Word, but it also had roots especially in labor organizing in Honduras and elsewhere. Members of peasant communities or labor unions spent a day or two with priests, nuns, university professors, social and health workers, agriculture students to share their daily lives and learn from others. There was usually a mix of practical learning—a university agronomy student might demonstrate new farming and anti-erosion techniques, someone with legal knowledge might explain the basic rights of land tenure—together with conceptual learning about, for example, human rights. This model was also adapted for high school students who were brought together by organizations such as ERIC from different towns and rural areas and often different social classes for a weekend of presentations and discussion of human rights or social justice interspersed with singing, dancing, food, and socializing.

Dana Frank describes in some detail how by 1985 women workers in the banana and fruit companies were beginning to use the workshop as a vehicle to organize and campaign for a series of demands from wage equity to greater decision making within their labor unions, to eliminating domestic violence. She offers a glimpse into several workshops, and explains how the women learned the workshop form by attending a workshop in Costa Rica, and began to use it with some middle-class assistance:

> Through this early project the women refined their core educational method, the workshop, a form they learned in part from the ILO [International Labor Organization] workshop in Costa Rica, but more directly from middle-class Leftist men, often academics, who had helped them out in their earlier years.[39]

In a society where many people did not read or own a television, radio was a major vehicle of information and expression. Commercial radio was largely controlled by commercial and political interests and was often a medium for propagation of images of reality promoted by economic and political elites. But radio also developed as a form of popular education and expression. As we saw at the beginning of this chapter, Margarita began to learn about and become active in social causes through *Escuela Radiofónica*, a project sponsored by the Catholic charitable and social service agency Caritas especially for people who had little or no access to formal schooling, or as a supplement to public school. The Jesuits acquired Radio Progreso, a major commercial station in northern Honduras. It continued as a commercial station but developed programming that was a mix of popular culture, practical information of all sorts (health, agriculture) and social and political critique, often presented with humor. The young and largely middle-class men and women who joined the Radio Progreso staff investigated and reported developing news of importance about human rights and the struggles of popular organizations, such as some of the workshops organized by the women banana workers described by Frank (above), and popular protests throughout the country. Over nearly fifty years, the reporting and analysis sometimes drew reprisal from government officials. RP was closed and surrounded by police and military for a short time during the 2009 coup, but it later reported live from Tegucigalpa interviewing several judges who were holding a hunger strike to denounce what they considered the illegality of the coup. Radio Progreso's motto was, "*La voz que está con vos*" ([Radio Progreso is] the voice that is with you).[40] Such media outlets, few in number, reached a wide audience and promoted exchange of ideas, information, and discourse between Hondurans of different social classes who were involved in social protest and change and others who began to learn and think about these things. Community radio also began to appear in some towns.

Spurred especially by the oppressive conditions of the 1980s, a remarkable convergence of concerns and common efforts was taking place between middle class and working class organizations focused on basic rights and empowerment that continued in various forms through the 1990s and the first decade of the current century, and became a basis for a culture of resistance years before the 2009 coup.

HISTORICAL PRECEDENT: A TALE OF TWO COUPS

People in many of the popular organizations were enthusiastic about the presidency of Manuel Zelaya. The enthusiasm was sometimes mixed with some reservation because Honduran presidents have a long history of making and breaking promises and disappointing the hopes of people for change and a better life, and because Zelaya himself was a wealthy landowner whose father owned Los Horcones ranch at the time of the 1975 "massacre." But the president's actions seemed to reflect an agenda of change from old patterns. When popular organizations and social movements organized and held protests, as a politician he began to meet with and listen to their leaders and members, something few politicians did. He gave activists an impression that he was pragmatic and not driven by the same agendas and ideologies as others in the Honduran elite, although some of Zelaya's critics pointed to these same characteristics to label him an opportunist. During his presidency, a moratorium on concessions to foreign mining companies was accompanied by raising the minimum wage for workers and by overtures to the *Alianza Bolivariana* (Bolivarian Alliance) that Venezuelan President Hugo Chavez had formed with several Latin American countries as an alternative to the U.S.-sponsored Central American Free Trade Agreement (CAFTA). Zelaya seemed intent on strengthening Honduran national sovereignty. He did not demonstrate the requisite level of condemnation and disdain for the Nicaraguan Sandinistas who returned to power in Managua when Daniel Ortega won the Nicaraguan presidency in 2006. While such actions gained the support of many Hondurans, some in the ruling economic and political elite began to regard Zelaya as a traitor to his social class.

In early 2009, responding to an ongoing demand from popular organizations, Zelaya proposed a poll to determine if the people would support a question in the coming November elections on whether to hold a Constitutional Assembly that would be charged with revising, if appropriate, the Constitution and whether certain changes be made in order to broaden the avenues for popular participation beyond the virtual political power monopoly of the two major parties. But those who were accustomed to controlling state power accused Zelaya of trying to perpetuate his hold on the presidency, even though the proposed poll, no matter the result, could not lead to such an outcome. The November presidential election would occur before any Constitutional Assembly, and Zelaya was legally barred from seeking reelection.

On June 26, 2009, the day appointed for the poll, the military forcibly sent Zelaya into exile on orders from the Congress and the country's Supreme Court. Those who controlled these institutions of government claimed that Zelaya had violated the Constitution in attempting a power grab by trying to hold a popular poll. Independent legal experts in Honduras and elsewhere pointed out the Congress, not Zelaya, had violated the Constitution by the manner in which they removed the president from office.[41] Immediately after the coup, massive popular resistance formed. Thousands marched through the streets of major cities. The violent repression with which military and police met the protesters probably contributed to the growth of protest across the country and the formation of the National Popular Resistance Front (*Frente Nacional de Resistencia Popular,* FNRP). In the months and years since the coup, the culture of popular resistance that evolved over decades expanded in a variety of forms and expressions that will be the matter of the following chapters.

The historical continuity and change that underlies the evolution of popular resistance in Honduras is illustrated by reflecting on the 2009 coup in light of the popular resistance to the military coup of October 1963 when the army deposed the elected civilian and "reformist" government of Ramon Villeda Morales and soon consolidated its position by holding tightly controlled elections even as they imposed harsh measure of repression against popular resistance. The army's candidate, Colonel Osvaldo Lopez Arellano became president and repression continued. After the 1963 coup the broad popular resistance movement crossed social class and urban-rural divisions.

> The political opposition all agreed that the military coup was bloody and directed against the popular movement and the Liberal Party that were the bases of support of the deposed government. [There were] various attempts among the opposition to group its forces in resistance, including fleeting alliances between liberals and communists, and some professional associations or guilds (*gremios*) joined with these in order to create a united front against the *golpistas*. Among various resistance groups were the Integrated Liberation Movement, the Popular Action Front, the Patriotic Committee for the Defense of Popular Rights, ... the Honduran Revolutionary Party, the Constitutionalist Democratic Movement, and Liberationist Women. These attempts at resistance were suppressed (*sofocados*) by the military with a generalized repression in countryside and city. (*translation mine*)[42]

In a footnote to this passage, Barahona cites sources that make clear the multi-class composition of this resistance. For example, the Integrated Liberation Movement included both university student and peasant organizations. He also emphasizes that none of these broad resistance groups had much history or organization, and were largely ad hoc groupings that did not last long under severe military repression.

Some parallels to the 2009 coup are clear—deposing a president seen as "reformist," *golpistas* (those responsible for carrying out a coup d'etat) holding elections that conveniently elect their chosen candidate amid tight repression of broad popular resistance, a resistance movement that crosses social classes, urban-rural divisions, and even political ideologies. Many of the elements of current resistance in Honduras were already there in 1963, if only fleetingly. This earlier episode poses some haunting questions. What are the differences between then and now in both the forms of violence and repression and the forms and content of resistance? Will these differences determine the course of the current popular resistance? We may not be able to adequately answer such questions, but they may be worth keeping in mind as we explore some of the components of the current culture of resistance in Honduras.

In the context of the massive popular protests that followed the 2009 coup, Article 3 of the Honduran Constitution is relevant.

> *Nadie debe obediencia a un gobierno usurpador ni a quienes asuman funciones o empleos públicos por la fuerza de las armas o usando medios o procedimientos que quebranten o desconozcan lo que esta Constitución y las leyes establecen. Los actos verificados por tales autoridades son nulos. El pueblo tiene derecho a recurrir a la insurrección en defensa del orden constitucional.*

> [No one owes obedience to a usurper government, nor to those who assume public functions or employment by force of arms or by using means or procedures that violate or disregard what this Constitution and the laws establish. Acts certified by such authorities are null. The people have the right to resort to insurrection in defense of the constitutional order.][43]

NOTES

1. Alison Acker, *Honduras: The Making of a Banana Republic* (Boston: South End Press, 1988), 104–7.
2. Marvin Barahona, *Pueblos indígenas, Estado, y memoria colectiva en Honduras* (Tegucigalpa: Editorial Guaymuras, 2009), 108–9.
3. Sidney Mintz, *Caribbean Transformations* (New York: Aldine Publishing, 1974). The nature of this transformation from local to extra-local relationships and organization is a theme developed and inspired by the work of Karl Marx, in particular.
4. Longino Becerra, "The Early History of the Labor Movement," as translated excerpt reprinted in *Honduras: Portrait of a Captive Nation*, ed. Nancy Peckenham and Annie Street (New Tork: Praeger Publishers, 1985), 95. Original in Longino Becerra, *Evolución Histórica de Honduras* (Tegucigalpa, Editorial Baktun, 1983).
5. Becerra, "The Early History of the Labor Movement."
6. Darío Euraque, *Reinterpreting the Banana Republic: Region and State in Honduras, 1870–1972* (Chapel Hill, NC: University of North Carolina Press, 1996), 5.
7. Becerra, "The Early History of the Labor Movement," in eds. Peckenham and Street, *Honduras*, 95. Here and elsewhere Becerra cites Mario Posas, *Notas sobre las Sociedades*

Artesanales y los Origines del Movimiento Obrero Hondureño (Tegucigalpa: Esp Editorial, 1978).

8. Becerra, "The Early History of the Labor Movement," in Peckenham and Street, 98.

9. Becerra, "The Early History of the Labor Movement," 98.

10. See Victor Meza, *Historia del Movimiento Obrero Hondureño* (Tegucigalpa: Editorial Guaymuras, 1980).

11. Stephen Schlesinger and Stephen Kinzer, *Bitter Fruit: The Story of the American Coup in Guatemala* (New York: Doubleday, 1982). Marvin Barahona, *Honduras en el siglo XX: Una síntesis histórica* (Tegucigalpa: Editorial Guaymuras, 2005), 167–68.

12. Barahona, *Honduras en el siglo XX*, 168–69.

13. Acker, *Honduras; The Making of a Banana Republic*, 82–84. Barahona, *Honduras en el siglo XX*, 166–71.

14. Becerra, "The Early History of the Labor Movement," in Peckenham and Street, 101, translation in Peckenham and Street.

15. Barahona, *Honduras en el siglo XX*, 170–71, translation mine.

16. Barahona, *Honduras,* 170.

17. Peckenham and Street, 128–29.

18. Acker, *Honduras: The Making of a Banana Republic*, 90. Douglas Kincaid, "We Are the Agrarian Reform: Rural Politics and Agrarian Reform," in *Honduras: Portrait of a Captive Nation,* eds. Nancy Peckenham and Annie Street (New York: Praeger, 1988), 137.

19. Acker, 90. Peckenham and Street, 129.

20. Kincaid, "We are the Agrarian Reform," in Peckenham and Street, 137.

21. Ismael Moreno, "Dimensión social de la misión de la Iglesia Católica: Una Mirada nacional desde la región noroccidental de Honduras," in *Religión, ideología, y sociedad: Una aproximación a las iglesias en Honduras* (El Progreso: ERIC y Editorial San Ignacio, 2013) 103–4. Also Acker 97.

22. Kincaid, 138–39.

23. Kincaid, 133, 140–41.

24. See Acker, 84–86, for an additional description of the struggles of militant labor activists against infiltration by AIFLD and repression by the military government. For an extended description and analysis of AIFLD's anti-communist labor and political activities in another Latin American country, see Cheddi Jagan, *The West on Trial: My Fight for Guyana's Freedom* (London: Michael Joseph Ltd., 1966). In Guyana, AIFLD tried to turn labor unionism into a force to topple a government the United States considered "communist," a quite different political turn than the Honduran situation in which government and AIFLD worked in concert to undermine "communist" labor activism.

25. Acker, 100, 104–7. Barahona, *Honduras en el siglo XX*, 84–85.

26. Barahona, *Honduras en el siglo* XX, 157–59.

27. Some characteristics of the developing middle class in Honduras in the years after 1950 are described in Barahona, *Honduras en el siglo XX*, 148–53 and 173–76.

28. These observations about Nicaraguan life under the revolutionary government are based on my own observation, interviews, and conversations with many Nicaraguans in cities and rural communities. I lived in Nicaragua and researched the effects of the Contra War for almost two years (1985–1987) mostly in the northern departments of Estelí, eastern Leon, southern Madriz, and western Jinotega that were centers of military conflict during the Contra War throughout the 1980s. Some of this and the historical context is presented in, James Phillip, "Nicaraguan Peasants and the Search for Peace," *Human Peace*, publication of the Commission on Conflict and Peace of the International Union of Anthropological and Ethnological Sciences 10:2 (Winter, 1994): 11–16; and James Phillips, "When Governments Fail: Reparation, Solidarity, and Community in Nicaragua," in *Waging War, Making Peace: Reparations and Human Rights,* ed. Barbara Rose Johnston (Walnut Creek CA: Left Coast Press, 2009), 56–74.

29. Phillips, "When Governments Fail," 58–68. The World Court's formal declaration of finding is, International Court of Justice, *Case Concerning Military and Paramilitary Activities in and against Nicaragua, (Nicaragua v. United States of America) Jurisdiction and Admissibility 1984, ICJ Rep. 392 June, 1986* (New York: United Nations Press, 1986).

30. Acker, *Honduras*, 94.

31. Marvin Barahona, *Pueblos indígenas, Estado, y memoria colectiva en Honduras* (Tegucigalpa: Editorial Guaymuras, 2009), 233. James Phillips, "Resource Access," 216.

32. During the 1970s, Latin American Christian theologians and social activists had begun to turn to the social sciences as a starting point or method for basing reflection on the reality in which Latin Americans lived, rather than starting their reflection from philosophical universal principles where theological and pastoral reflection had always been grounded in the past. The significance of this shift for the development of Latin American liberation theology and social action is discussed in, Hugo Assmann, *Theology for a Nomad Church* (Maryknoll, NY: Orbis Books, 1976), 129; and in Gary MacEoin, *Unlikely Allies: The Christian-Socialist Convergence* (New York: Crossroads Publishing, 1990), 80–81, where Assmann is also quoted.

33. Barahona, *Honduras en el siglo XX*, 170.

34. Centro de Documentación de Honduras CEDOH, *Boletín 85* (February, 1992), 8. Hannah C. Riley and James K. Sebenius, "Stakeholder Negotiations over Third World Resource Projects," *Cultural Resource Quarterly* 19:3 (Fall 1993): 39–43.

35. Phillips, "Resource Access," 215.

36. I interviewed national and local leaders of the Delegates of the Word, with most interviews occurring in mid-2013.

37. Ismael Moreno, *"Dimensión social de la misión de la Iglesia Católica*, 103–4.

38. Paulo Freire, *Pedagogy of the Oppressed* (New York: Herder and herder, 1970). Also Freire, *Education for Critical Consciousness* (New York: Seabury, 1973).

39. Dana Frank, *Bananeras: Women Transforming the Banana Unions of Latin America*, English ed. (Cambridge, MA: Couth End Press, 2005), description of workshops 44–48, and note 27. Description of workshops here is supplemented by my own experiences as a participant in similar workshops in Central America.

40. Moreno, "Dimensión social," 108, footnote 111. For examples of the kinds of commentaries offered on Radio Progreso in the several years after the 2009 coup see, *Nuestra Palabra: Radio Progreso ERIC-SJ* (El Progreso: Editorial Casa San Ignacio, 2011).

41. Doug Cassel, "Honduras: Coup d'Etat in Constitutional Clothing?" *Insights* (American Society of International Law) 13:9 (October 15, 2009), 1–7.

42. Barahona, *Honduras en el siglo XX*, 205–6.

43. Quoted in Cassel, "Honduras: Coup d'Etat," 6, translation in original.

Chapter Five

Patterns of Indigenous Resistance

In February 2013, a group of popular organizations completed a two hundred–kilometer walk (*caminata*) from northern Honduras to Tegucigalpa, the capital to protest a new mining law. One of the participants noted especially the leading role of indigenous groups—Lenca, Tolupán, and Garifuna—in this walk. "The indigenous peoples were highly disciplined and resistant to all the hot sun, the rains, the winds, the pains, and the mosquitoes. They were the most firm on the journey. They have resources that the rest do not have: their long history of resistance."[1] With an apparently increasing series of threats to rights and resources, indigenous organizations have emerged as a leading force in the struggle over land, environmental preservation, and human rights in Honduras.

Honduran government agencies officially recognize eight major "ethnic" groups (*grupos étnicos*) within the national territory, with a total population of about 475,000 or perhaps 7 percent of the total Honduran population in 2001.[2] This number may not reflect the full extent of indigenous presence. The very process of defining ethnic and racial categories is always politicized. Official recognition and self-identification are not the same, and there are Hondurans who claim indigenous identity but are not counted in officially recognized groups. People of mixed indigenous and European ancestry in Honduras are generally considered *mestizo* (mixed), a designation that often obscures the extent of the indigenous ancestry and self-identity of individuals, especially since Honduras tends to identify its dominant national identity as *mestizo*. Ethnic group designation also includes about thirteen thousand inhabitants of the Bay Islands who are not considered indigenous and are designated as "Blacks who speak English" (*Negros de habla inglés*). The third largest group, the Garifuna (fifty thousand), trace a history and ancestry that combines both indigenous Caribbean and African origins. Today Garifuna communities are scattered across most of the Caribbean coastal area of northern Honduras. Unofficial estimates of the Garifuna population in Honduras vary, but tend to be higher than the official statistics, sometimes as high as eighty thousand or more.

The Lenca (around 300,000) comprise the largest recognized indigenous population. The largest concentration of Lenca today is found in the southwestern Departments of Intibuca, Lempira, and part of La Paz. Miskito groups (about fifty-six thousand) are scattered throughout Gracias a Dios (Mosquitia) in the east and along the border with Nicaragua. There are Miskito groups in Nicaragua, as well. Two groups smaller in numbers are also recognized in the Mosquitia, especially along the Rio Patuca. These are the Pech (four thousand) and Tawahka (2,600). Two other groups are among the ten largest. People of Chortí affiliation (thirty-seven thousand) are concentrated in the far western Department of Copan along the Guatemalan border. The Tolupán people (also known as Xicaque) number about ten thousand and occupy rural mountainous communities in much of the Department of Yoro in the geographical center of the country. All of these population numbers are "official" government estimates.

The current geographical distribution of indigenous groups in Honduras is a result of several historical processes. The entire region, as in fact most of Latin America, saw considerable interaction among different groups in trading patterns, warfare, linguistic influences, and at times the joining of several smaller groups. Before the arrival of European colonizers, Central America had been a cultural meeting ground for several different strands of civilization. It was a region where cultural and political influences from large and powerful chiefdoms of northwestern South America met the southern extension of dominant cultures and political entities from the north, primarily Mayan, but also from as far north as the Valley of Mexico. In what is now Honduras, Chortí and Lenca groups had a way of life shaped by the higher, mountainous regions in the west and southwest in which they lived and by Mesoamerican patterns of small farming of corn, beans, cocoa, cotton, and other crops, and settled village or community structure. These were people whom the Spanish invaders and colonizers regarded as more easily conquerable because of their more "civilized" way of life. The people who inhabited the central, northeastern, and eastern regions of Honduras—Tolupán, Miskito, Pech, Tawahka and others—had a way of life based largely upon hunting, fishing, and gathering combined with some cultivation, primarily of tubers or root crops rather than corn and beans, and their population density across a large area was lower than among the peoples of the west. The Spanish colonizers regarded them as more "savage" and more difficult to conquer and civilize.[3] The Garifuna along the Caribbean Coast arrived much later, around 1800, near the end of the Spanish colonial period.

SOME SPECIAL CHARACTERISTICS OF INDIGENOUS COMMUNITIES

Indigenous communities share some of the same characteristics and problems as other rural communities in Honduras, but they also have some historical and cultural characteristics that shape their understanding of the threats they face and the character of their resistance to those threats. In some ways these characteristics have contributed to forms of resistance that are now widely shared in the broader Honduran culture of resistance, and have also contributed to the acknowledged position of indigenous communities as the front line or the soul of much of the popular resistance in Honduras.

Indigenous communities have the longest history of resistance and resilience in Honduras. They have been in some form of resistance, at least sporadically, since the beginning of Spanish colonial occupation in the early 1500s. Indigenous communities often have a sense of their history and themselves as those who still survive, have never capitulated, and have never lost their special character and identity. Most peoples in resistance recall those who went before them in the struggle. In Honduras people tend to accord them the status of martyrs and saints, those who sacrificed for the people or the cause. Indigenous peoples do this as well, but they also draw from a longer history of great warriors in struggles for their freedom in resistance to colonial domination. In some ways, they are still struggling against what some see as an extension of colonial domination into the present. Their very identity as a people may be personified in these early warriors. The Lenca claim Lempira, who led a major resistance to Spanish conquest, as theirs. They sometimes chant, "Who are we? The blood of Lempira" (*¿Quienes somos? Sangre de Lempira*). The Garifuna have Chatouyer, the Carib chief who mounted a successful resistance for several years against British rule of the Carib islands in the eastern Caribbean. On a wall in a beachside restaurant in the Honduran Garifuna community of Triunfo de la Cruz is a brightly colored mural of this Carib leader. He has accompanied the Garifuna across space and time and is still with them in image and spirit, and they can claim to be his descendants.

Indigenous people in Honduras share with other communities the threat of resource extraction that takes their land and destroys the natural environment and resources on which they rely. But the roots of their resistance go deeper than the current particular issue, and are rooted in awareness that their existence and their way of life constitute a contradiction to the colonial and now the neoliberal ethos. Indigenous communities are often located in areas rich in natural resources that the dominant models of national development and the desires of powerful men have targeted for exploitation for mining, lumber, hydroelectric power, or tourism. Indigenous people often have a different and more complex and nuanced idea of what "natural resources" are that is not market driven and is deeply integrated with ancestral, historical, cultural, and spiritual significance that indigenous people have been able to reference consciously and use as added impetus to defend.

They know about international concepts of human rights for all people, but they also realize that they are people with particular cultural rights recognized in national agreements and treaties and in international declarations, conventions, and instruments such as the United Nations Declaration on the Rights of Indigenous Peoples and International Labor Organization Convention 169. This sometimes seems to give indigenous communities a special legal and moral standing in protecting environment under the rubric of defending their special rights. This has sometimes contributed to their recognition as the modern front line in the struggle over environmental and resources issues in Honduras and elsewhere.

With non-indigenous communities they share the reality of divisions within the community and the cooptation of some community members. But indigenous communities often have an added sense of unified identity as one people, and traditional, structured ways of common decision-making and action that have as their purpose resolving and healing differences and maintaining community. Many indigenous groups in Honduras have formal organizations that are identified by Honduran society as semi-official agents of the interests of those they claim to represent—COPINH for the Lenca, OFRANEH for the Garifuna, MASTA among the Miskito, and FETRIXY for the Tolupán/Xicaque. These organizations among indigenous peoples differ in at least one important aspect from other popular organizations. Indigenous communities sometimes see their organizations as forms of internal self-government or as supplemental to their traditional community leadership, in part because indigenous communities tend to emphasize their autonomy from the Honduran national government. They depend on their own organizations rather than on government officials. The organizations become in some ways an alternative government. This can pose a problem for indigenous communities when governments identify these organizations as the fomenters and organizers of indigenous resistance, and try, usually by using the criminal justice system, to remove organizational leaders from active resistance.

The level of unity between these organizations and the wider indigenous communities they represent cannot always be taken for granted. In their attempts to break down the resistance of indigenous communities, Honduran government officials and agencies and other interests sometimes try to coopt the leadership of indigenous organizations and to separate it from the expressed interests of the grass roots. According to members of Tolupán communities, such has been the difficult experience of FETRIXY since the 1970s.[4] Another tactic is the attempt to interfere with the functioning of the leadership of indigenous organizations, charging them with criminal behavior and forcing them to undergo legal processes and sometimes prison so as to hamper their leadership activities. This has been the case with COPINH leaders and the Lenca of Rio Blanco. Physical attacks and assassinations of organization leaders and active members is a frequent occurrence. Despite all of this, indigenous communities continue to mount forms of group resistance with or without the leadership or accompaniment of their organizations.

Indigenous communities can look back at their resistance through five centuries. It began as resistance to colonial domination and for indigenous people it has never ceased to be about colonial domination in its most literal sense. These are communities whose values and ways of life contradict the basic tenets of the modern Honduran state, just as they did those of the Spanish colonizers. Over the centuries, the modern nation builders have not really abandoned the colonial mentality of the Spanish conquerors who regarded the native peoples as inferior, dangerous, or obstacles in the way of progress. Those who rule the state have always demanded the submission of indigenous people to their agendas of "civilizing," exploiting, and "developing." It is not that indigenous communities have resisted all outside influence or change. Rather, the core of resistance has been their intent to appropriate such influences and change on their own terms and in their own way, to integrate these as they see fit into their traditional ways of life and to reject what they consider inappropriate or harmful. This is fundamentally an issue of autonomy that has contested the absolute dominion assumed first by the colonial conquerors and later by the modern state. It is also an issue of constructing and preserving a group identity in a modern nation. From this perspective of ongoing colonialism, the resistance of indigenous people is rooted somewhat differently from that of other sectors of Honduran society even as it shares much with the larger popular resistance. The issue of autonomy and identity raises a question that indigenous people and their organizations always deal with, that is when and to what extent to try to negotiate with Honduran governments and when to resist, or even what mixture of negotiation and resistance is most useful and possible in a particular issue or situation. Government officials regard some indigenous organizations as more accommodating, others as more confrontational.[5]

THE NEW COLONIALISM: EXTRACTION AND INDIGENOUS RESISTANCE

Colonialism is always fundamentally an economic system based on the exploitation of people, land, and resources for the benefit of others. Mining and logging have been important forms of such exploitation since colonial times. The Spanish conquerors and colonizers of Latin America were always looking for gold and silver, and they found it in small quantities in the Caribbean and huge quantities in Bolivia. In central Mexico, and parts of Central America including Honduras, the colonizers found areas rich in metal and mineral wealth. They forced indigenous communities to mine deposits of gold and silver. When Honduras became independent, the pattern continued as the Criollo elite replaced the Spanish authorities. By the 1870s, mining for gold and important metals had become the basis of wealth for the ruling class based in and around the mountain town and new capital at Tegucigalpa. Foreign interests such as Rosario Mining became prominent, and Honduran authorities and landowners made money selling mining rights and concessions to foreign interests.

Since at least the early 1800s, Honduras was known as a source of the highly prized wood, mahogany, one of the interests the British had in the northern part of the country. Logging became a source of wealth as mahogany and other precious woods were demanded for construction and fine furniture. Honduras had major stands of mahogany, a wood that was prized for its beauty and its resistance to termites and other insect infestations. British interests ignored Honduran state claims over the Caribbean coastal areas and engaged in logging and shipment of mahogany. Some Hondurans wealthy enough to capitalize logging crews and arrange foreign markets also began to exploit stands of mahogany in interior areas such as Yoro. Indigenous communities often claimed these logging areas as part of their own territory. When mahogany became too expensive to be used for construction and its market contracted, logging for cheaper furniture and paper products began to replace it, leading by the 1990s to large scale legal and especially illegal logging enterprises in areas such as Olancho where it often occurred in lands claimed by indigenous groups.[6]

With mining and logging enterprises throughout the twentieth century, indigenous communities suffered the pollution of their streams, rivers, and land, often forcing communities to move or even disband when they could no longer sustain farming or even daily life in such conditions. Some streams and water channels dried up entirely. It was estimated that one medium sized mining operation could use as much water in one hour as a middle-class Honduran family might use in twenty years. Similar patterns of exploitation and dislocation could be discerned in the great forest areas of Honduras, including parts of Olancho where foreign and Honduran interests engaged in both legal and illegal logging for precious mahogany and other woods, creating erosion and contamination of streams. Both mining and logging altered the natural setting that was crucial to traditional culture and ways of life for indigenous communities.[7]

Beginning with an economic crisis in Honduras in the early 1980s, the business Association for the Promotion of Honduras (APROH) and its so-called Facussé Memorandum, and the Reagan Administration's program for Honduran development, written by the U.S. Embassy in Tegucigalpa, provided the blueprint for Honduran governments to develop extractive industries as a way of relieving the country's ongoing debt crisis.[8] In addition to the mining and logging concessions, the government promoted plans for damming rivers in different areas, in part to provide water and energy for mining operations, but also for electricity for an expanding assembly factory (*maquiladora*) sector and for proposed tourism development along the Caribbean coast, home to many Garifuna communities.

Many of these extractive and exploitative projects targeted areas where indigenous communities lived or exercised legal ownership. The new exploitation prompted indigenous peoples such as the Lenca and the Garifuna to believe that their ability to resist exploitation demanded that they challenge the state's historic refusal to recognize the multiethnic reality of Honduran society. Indigenous people wanted recognition as active participants in a multiethnic society that recognized many voices in the political and public life of the country. By the 1990s, they were constructing ways to express their indigenous cultures while connecting these to the life of the nation and expressing resistance to neoliberal policies as a form of neocolonialism. Honduran historian Marvin Barahona affirms the importance of reclaiming the history of indigenous peoples from the colonial stereotypes of the past, and realizing that this reclamation of their own lived collective experience was a powerful source of strength in resistance for many indigenous people.[9] What follows here are brief sketches of the struggles of four major indigenous groups in Honduras.

TOLUPÁN GUARDIANS OF LAND AND ACCOUNTABILITY

The Tolupán struggle takes place in a context of old, intertwined, and overlapping interests. Among the indigenous peoples whom the Spanish colonizers considered less civilized and more difficult to conquer were the people they called Xicaque, now often referred to as Tolupanes. Before the Spanish conquest they occupied almost all of the current Department of Yoro, much of Atlantida and perhaps areas of Olancho, Colon and Cortes. But by the end of the 1500s, the Tolupán population was declining, mostly as a result of European diseases, and they were plagued by a variety of interlopers, including Spanish soldiers and missionaries, pirates, and foreigners wanting their land. Tolupanes responded by attacking plantations and European properties, conducting ambushes, and killing soldiers and colonists who tried to take their lands. The Spanish authorities attributed Tolupán militancy to their "savage" nature. José Maria Tojeira, a modern scholar of Tolupán history and culture, presents a different perspective.

> These claims [about the savagery of the people] when contemplated from the Xicaque perspective could mean the defense of their culture, a love of liberty

and free contact with nature, and a hatred for a "civil life" (*vida civil*) that implied definite levels of exploitation and subjugation to another culture.[10]

By the early 1600s, colonizers were settling in coastal valleys along the Caribbean coast, displacing Tolupán people from land they cultivated, and interfering with local traditional Tolupán subsistence patterns that depended heavily on sea turtles and canoe fishing. Gradually, Tolupán communities had to abandon these practices. Later, the British forcibly deported Garifuna people from the eastern Caribbean islands and exiled them to the islands off the Caribbean coast of Honduras. In the early 1800s, Garifuna communities occupied much of the coastal area of Atlantida and Colon formerly inhabited by Tolupanes. Tolupán communities had retreated from the coast into the rugged mountainous interior of Yoro to avoid European diseases, to escape living as mission Indians, and to preserve their culture as they wished. They continued to resist threats to their land and culture, and after 1821 they were able to take advantage of the weakness of the newly independent Honduran state and its inability to establish its control over all the national territory. The Tolupán were only finally integrated into the authority of the Honduran state in 1864 through the state's legal recognition of different Tolupán communities (*tribus*, tribes or bands) as rightful communal owners of sections of land in Yoro.

The global export market that attracted Honduran governments and large landowners in the latter half of the nineteenth century meant further problems for the Tolupanes. Landowners and the governor of Yoro tried to force Tolupán communities to grow sarsaparilla, the basic ingredient in drinks and tonics that became a fad in Europe and the United States. Then, by the 1870s, coffee became a major export crop, and the mountainous Tolupán lands were well suited for coffee cultivation. Large landowners tried to obtain Tolupán land through outright forcible takeover and extortion or sometimes through marriage to a Tolupán woman. Tolupanes who grew coffee for sale to exporters were often paid lower prices. Those who worked in coffee plantations for others were usually overworked and underpaid. By the 1920s the development of the foreign banana company plantations along the north coast meant jobs for Tolupanes, but they had to speak Spanish and gradually began to lose both their native language and aspects of their traditional culture.

There were twenty-eight Tolupán communities (*tribus*) by the latter half of the twentieth century, and in 1977 many of these joined in the new National Council of Indigenous Tribes (CONATRIN) that was affiliated with the peasant union ANACH. This was a time of increased peasant activism for land across Honduras, and the Tolupanes were peasant farmers trying to defend their lands. Peasant unionism seemed to be a supplementary way to do this, even though their concerns for the preservation of their particular cultural identity set them apart in some ways from non-indigenous peasants.

Soon after, Tolupanes became part of yet another new organization with the more militant and expansive title, National Federation of Tribes for the Liberation of the Honduran Indian (FENATRILINH).

None of these organizations was able to advance what became a prime objective of Tolupán communities—reclamation and use rights to extensive forest lands from foreign companies and Honduran landowners who resorted to threats and killings to frighten Tolupán communities and break their resistance. The land was desirable especially for its extensive stands of precious timber and good conditions for coffee growing. In addition, landless and desperate non-indigenous peasants from other areas began to encroach on Tolupán lands, and in at least one instance the government National Agrarian Institute (INA) awarded one of "the best regions" of Tolupán land to a peasant cooperative from elsewhere with the name *Los Invencibles* (The Unconquerables). At the same time, the government Honduran Forestry Development Corporation—basically a state company—began to take the place of the traditional Tolupán community leaders (*caciques*) in deciding whether to allow outsiders to use or harvest portions of community/tribe land, or simply bribing caciques for their assent. Some Tolupanes responded by forming the Federation of Xicaque Tribes of Yoro (FETRIXY) whose leaders gradually replaced the *cicaques* in defending and advocating for the rights of the Tolupán communities.[11]

These land struggles continued through the 1980s. From 1988 to mid-1993, at least five Tolupán community leaders were killed, including Vicente Matute, the president of FETRIXY and an outspoken advocate of Tolupán rights.[12] Tolupán resistance suffered from divisions within and among communities. Individuals in communities were sometimes paid to do the bidding of large landowners and other outsiders interested in trying to secure Tolupán land and resources. Sometimes disputes arose between Tolupanes themselves that outside interests saw as opportunities for division and exploitation. Almost since its beginnings, FETRIXY has had to struggle against interference from government officials. In recent years, members of some Tolupán communities have accused FETRIXY leaders of corruption and colluding with government and powerful outsiders instead of defending the collective interests of the Tolupán people.

In some areas, Tolupanes have experienced mining as yet another threat to their land and even their lives. In the small mountain community of Locomapa in Yoro, where three Tolupanes were killed in August of 2013 by men identified as working for the mine owner, people had erected barriers and carried out forms of nonviolent resistance against mining companies polluting their land and loggers trying to extract stands of mahogany that such communities defend. The killings raised the level of fear. The killers remained at large in the area. Members of the Tolupán community continued their resistance and began organizing new community elections to replace a local FETRIXY leadership. That leadership was accused of accepting money from mining and logging interests and government officials, and promoting divisions in the Tolupán community instead of protecting the resources and the people.

In July 2014, three hundred Tolupanes marched and rallied in the center of Yoro city to demand protection of their land rights, protection of their basic human rights and safety, and an end to official impunity and corruption. A month later, on August 25, people in Locomapa held a peaceful one-year remembrance of the killing of three of their community members. Hondurans from outside the community and international observers accompanied them. Local people said the killers were still at large in the area despite the nearly year-old arrest warrant against them. Elections for new tribal council leaders were scheduled for early September, and international observers were again invited to attend. The day before the scheduled election, the same men who had allegedly killed the three Tolupanes the year before arrived again in Locomapa, shooting their guns in the air and warning that they would kill anyone who participated in the election, including the international observers. The local community decided not to participate. They and some international observers turned their energy once again to demanding that the authorities execute the existing arrest warrant for the alleged killers.[13]

MISKITO AUTONOMY: RIVER, NARCOS, ANVIL, AND OIL

There are several quite different theories about the origins of the Miskito people and how long they have inhabited the eastern parts of Honduras and neighboring Nicaragua. The most accepted account is that the Miskito people have genetic and cultural roots in a very mixed population of many small native groups that met and mingled in this corner of Central America for centuries. They were joined in the 1600s and 1700s by people of African origin who were brought to the Caribbean region as slaves by Spanish, Portuguese, and English colonizers and escaped to or were shipwrecked along the Honduran/Nicaraguan coast.

The Spanish colonizers regarded the Miskito as among the peoples more "savage" and more difficult to "civilize." From the beginnings of colonial rule in the 1500s, almost to the first years of the twentieth century, those who claimed sovereignty over Honduras tried repeatedly to establish sovereignty over the Miskito, usually by force or by a combination of force and institutions of acculturation, especially church and school. Most attempts failed. Probably a major reason why the Spanish colonial governments regarded the Miskito as especially fierce opponents was that they did more than defend themselves from Spanish forays into their lands. Especially during the late 1600s and 1700s, they also engaged in what might today be called preemptive strikes against Spanish settlements and whatever represented Spanish influence over indigenous peoples, especially the missions.

> The most common mechanism of resistance of the Miskito in the face of threats to their area represented by the Spaniards was the preventive attack (*ataque preventivo*) against the Indian mission settlements (*reducciónes*) and Spanish towns in the territory of the Paya, Sumos, and Xicaque (*translation mine*).[14]

Miskito resistance also took the form of strategic alliance with Spain's enemies. Unlike most indigenous peoples in Honduras (except the Garifuna), the Miskito had historical connections to English colonizers. Throughout the 1600s especially, England challenged Spain for dominance over the Caribbean region, including the Caribbean side of Central America. In the Spaniards, the English and the Miskito had a common enemy. Miskito resistance prevented the Spanish colonial government and then the Honduran government from establishing firm control over the Mosquitia, and allowed England to establish a claim to hegemony over the area. In practice, English hegemony was not accompanied with the intent of English colonization of the area or an attempt to incorporate the Miskito into English culture. In the mid-1800s, the Honduran government continued to argue its claim to the Mosquitia in terms of its civilizing mission:

> The Constitution of the [Honduran] State prescribes the civilization and incorporation [of the Miskito] with the rest of the Honduran people, their brothers with whom they must form only one family, since they all come from the same origin, and for this only persuasion and convincing are employed.[15]

This language depicts the state's claim of hegemony over the Miskito as an act of nation building. It should be understood in the context of the other useful fiction deployed by the state, a concept of citizenship that subsumed and subordinated different ethnic and political differences and group identities under the cover of equal citizenship in the Honduran state.[16] The Miskito continued to resist this. The whole question of citizenship within the jurisdiction of the Honduran state posed a dilemma. It promised peace, at least theoretical equality, and needed services but at the price of surrendering independence and sovereignty that seemed crucial to protecting the Miskito way of life.

It is indicative of the Miskito resistance to the Honduran state that some of the most important outside influences entertained by Miskito communities came from a non-state source—Moravian missionaries who brought their form of Christianity to Miskito communities beginning around 1849. This evangelization was not enforced by a conquering state, and Miskito people could accept it on its own merits as it appealed to them and addressed their needs within the context of their culture. The Catholic missionary Manuel de Jesus Subirana baptized and preached among various indigenous peoples, including the Miskito, between 1846 and 1854, but Catholicism did not become an important influence among the Miskito as it did among other groups in Honduras. Perhaps for the Miskito Catholicism was too closely identified with Spanish colonial conquest, and the Catholic Church could not quite shed its burden as both a symbol and an instrument of the forces that had tried for three centuries to control the Miskito.

By the early 1900s, the Miskito had a long history of mixing with many other peoples, always wary of and resistant to government efforts to control them. By mid-century the Honduran government had changed its approach, temporarily deemphasizing legal and political claims, and instead highlighting the benefits and services the state could provide. In the early 1950s the government sent "Cultural Missions" (*Misiónes Culturales*) into Miskito communities. These were teams composed usually of a physician, a teacher, a woman who gave lessons in home management and domestic skills, and others. These teams established twenty-five schools in the region over a few years. Then in 1957 the government designated the region as the new Department of Gracias a Dios, and set up administrative centers in Puerto Lempira and Brus Laguna.[17]

The Contra War in the 1980s involved Miskito peoples in both Honduras and Nicaragua.[18] Miskito communities in eastern Nicaragua had a similar history of resistance to the central government in Managua and the culturally different influences of western Nicaragua. The Somoza dictatorship did not manage to exercise great control over Miskito peoples, concentrating its oppression instead in the more populous west of the country. The Sandinista revolutionary government that replaced Somoza began to pursue a mixed and seemingly contradictory approach, unsure whether to regard the Miskito as allies of the Contra and therefore enemies, or to court the goodwill of the Miskito with promises of internal autonomy.

For Miskito people on both sides of the Honduras-Nicaragua border, the situation was complex. Regarding themselves as one people, the Miskito were scattered across two countries that were deeply involved in a larger conflict neither wanted. While Miskito people in both Honduras and Nicaragua seemed less interested in pursuing the goals of the Contra forces, they did see the war as an occasion to reinforce their own autonomy, especially when government officials in both countries seemed to want them to support one side or the other in the Contra-Sandinista conflict. The Nicaraguan Miskito response was to emphasize their identity as an independent people ready to resist perceived threats to their autonomy from any direction. Some Miskito formed military forces to protect Nicaraguan communities from Sandinista Army attacks and to gain some control over the tendency of Contra forces to recruit Honduran Miskito youth. There were differences among the Nicaraguan Miskito leaders, however, that led to the formation of three different politico-military groups—MISURASATA, MISURA, and KISAN.

Miskito leaders of all these groups tried to protect Miskito control over the actions and policies of their groups as responsive to the interests and agendas of the Miskito people. This was undermined in Honduras by the presence of Honduran Army and U.S. CIA operatives in the Honduran Mosquitia whose primary intent was to use the Miskito to further the aims of the Contras and the Reagan Administration. From the Miskito perspective this posed two problems. Their objectives in resistance had to do with maintaining their autonomy from the central governments of both Nicaragua and Honduras and their national agendas, and with preserving their Miskito way of life as they decided. In contrast, Contra forces and the United States wanted the removal of the Nicaraguan Sandinista government and generally welcomed or acquiesced to U.S. influence. According to outside observers, CIA advisers and Honduran Army commanders used different forms of pressure such as imprisonment, deprivation of food supplies, and beatings to force the leaders and members of all three Miskito armed groups to unite and coordinate their activities with those of the Contra forces, effectively subordinating their own interests to those of the Contra and the Reagan Administration. Despite these pressures, Miskito leaders struggled to maintain their independence of action. Some even quit the Contra struggle and declared a truce with the Nicaraguan government. The Nicaraguan Congress had at least one outspoken Miskito representative during much of the 1980s.

Honduran Miskito communities felt the impact of an estimated thirty thousand Nicaraguan Miskito who fled to Honduras as refugees during the Contra war. These were people of the same ethnic identity, the same culture as the Honduran Miskito. This prompted some Honduran Miskito youth to try to join one of the Nicaraguan Miskito fighting units. The large influx of Miskito refugees from Nicaragua also caused environmental damage and disrupted life in some Honduran Miskito communities.[19] By the end of the 1980s, the Nicaraguan government had advanced a regional autonomy plan for the Miskito and other indigenous communities in eastern Nicaragua. This reinforced the intentions of Honduran Miskitos to achieve more autonomy from the Honduran government.

With the end of the Contra War in 1990, the Honduran government revived and expanded national economic development plans that emphasized foreign investment in mining and other extractive industries along with the expansion of the infrastructure and energy needed for development. Decades-old ideas for constructing hydroelectric dams along some of the country's major rivers were revisited. One of the largest rivers, the Patuca, runs through much of eastern Honduras from deep in Olancho Department to the Caribbean/Atlantic coast of the Mosquitia. In a region of few roads, the Patuca is a major transportation artery for many Tawahka and Miskito villages along its banks, and is crucial to the fishing, farming, and trading activities of these communities. In many ways, the river allows the Miskito and Tawahka to maintain their autonomy. In 2006, acknowledging years of protest from indigenous communities, the government of Manuel Zelaya placed a temporary moratorium on plans for construction of the dam project known as Patuca 3.

Despite this long history of protests from indigenous groups and Honduran and international environmental organizations, the post-coup government of Pepe Lobo (2010–2013) reversed the moratorium and contracted with the Chinese company Sinohydro to construct Patuca 3. Miskito and Tawahka people saw the dam project as both a direct threat to the ecosystems on which their ways of life depended, and as yet another chapter in the history of government trying to impose its own plans on indigenous communities. Resistance for these communities always came back to the defense and expansion of their autonomy and the rejection of government development plans. Autonomy was seen as the best defense of environment and natural resources and of the ways of life and values that depend on these. In the modern world, the defense of autonomy for people such as the Miskito and the Tawahka includes a call for international support for their resistance. In 2011, MASTA invited representatives of the U.S.-based organization Cultural Survival to attend the celebration of the thirty-fifth anniversary of the founding of MASTA as the governing body of the Miskito people. Cultural Survival also launched a worldwide letter writing campaign to demand that the Patuca 3 proposal be stopped.[20] In another area of Honduras, Lenca communities also resisted government plans for Sinohydro to build dams on their major rivers. Their resistance took particularly dramatic forms. (See below, this chapter.)

Beginning in the late 1990s, United States, Mexican, and Colombian anti-drug campaigns encouraged drug cartels in both Mexico and northern South America to use Central America as a new production and transshipment zone for narcotics intended for the United States market. Much of Honduras, and especially the Mosquitia became a major transshipment and production location for burgeoning narcotics traffic. By 2010, indigenous communities found themselves caught between the demands of drug traffickers and the periodic raids of Honduran military and police, U.S. Drug Enforcement Agency, and U.S. State Department units in an anti-drug campaign appropriately named Operation Anvil. The infiltration of drug traffickers in this region cast suspicion over Miskito people. People in communities throughout the region were forced to collaborate with drug traffickers while police, military, and U.S. anti-drug units were not disposed to employ much discretion or time to differentiate the guilty from local people simply trying to survive. Although some people were sometimes paid to load drugs onto boats for shipment down the river, it was clear that they or others risked harm or death if they did not comply. Around midnight on May 11, 2012, a U.S.-

Honduran anti-drug raiding force descended in helicopters near Ahuas, a largely indigenous community in the middle of the Mosquitia, looking for a boatload of narcotics that they thought had set off from the community. Instead, they fired on a boat full of Miskito people, killing four passengers including a pregnant woman, and seriously injuring others, including a fourteen-year-old boy who escaped by jumping into the river. Then the unit spent several hours raiding the community in search of traffickers. There are conflicting versions of this incident. At many points, the accounts of local people—including local officials and survivors of the attack and the raid—contradict versions from Honduran and U.S. government sources. The account presented here reflects some of the local testimony.[21] Reports began to circulate after this incident claiming that at least one of the survivors—the mother of a teenager killed in the raid—was being pressured by Honduran and U.S. agents to change her testimony.[22]

This raid was part of Operation Anvil that brought U.S. resources and advisers into collaboration with Honduran police and military. When this raid on Ahuas became an international story, Operation Anvil was temporarily suspended. Honduran observers and investigators said that Miskito and other indigenous communities throughout the Mosquitia were subjected to these pressures daily. Some Hondurans asked why the United States chooses to fight its drug war on Honduran soil, especially among indigenous people, rather than in the United States itself where the demand and the problem are rooted.

By 2012, some Hondurans thought that the search for oil was poised to become the most recent threat to Miskito and Tawahka autonomy and security. For years there was speculation and some initial indication that parts of the Mosquitia and the adjacent seabed might contain large oil deposits. In May, 2013, the Honduran government granted the British-based BG Group a four-year contract to explore for oil in the area, with a possible two-year extension. It also granted BG Group a twenty-year contract to develop and extract oil if found, with a possible five-year extension.[23] There seemed to be different attitudes toward the potential development of an oil industry in the Mosquitia. Many people were concerned that this could pose a threat to the environment that sustains the daily life and cultural values of Miskito and other indigenous communities, and might even force a mass exodus of indigenous people from the region. Another attitude sometimes encountered emphasized the possibility that local indigenous communities might benefit economically or politically.

GARIFUNA RESISTANCE: RACE, PALM OIL, TOURISM, AND CHARTER CITIES

The Garifuna whose communities today are scattered along the Caribbean coast of Honduras and Belize trace their ancestry to Carib Indian (Kalinagu) people of the eastern Caribbean islands of St. Vincent and Dominica, and marooned or runaway West African slaves in the Caribbean. These two populations became one people during the 1700s in the islands. Against English soldiers and colonists who called them Black Caribs they carried on a struggle for control of their islands. Garifuna historians today tell of some of their ancestors in St. Vincent jumping off cliffs to their deaths rather than surrender their freedom to the British. In 1797, the Garifuna on St. Vincent were forced to surrender to the British who packed 2,500 of them on ships and deported them to the island of Roatan off the Honduran coast. It is estimated that less than half survived the trip.[24] By choosing Roatan for the Garifuna exile, the British hoped to strengthen England's influence and claim to the Caribbean coasts of Honduras and Belize. By about 1800, Garifuna people had begun to settle in scattered villages along the Honduran coast. The number of Garifuna in Honduras in 1801 was estimated at around four thousand.[25] The timing is important because it would later become a basis on which the Honduran state recognized the Garifuna people as indigenous despite their mixed racial origins, since they were among the groups within the national territory before the founding of the independent Honduran state in 1824.

Garifuna culture became a mixture of Carib Indian and West African tribal practices, beliefs, and values. Over the years in Honduras, Garifuna people integrated Catholicism and other elements of Spanish Honduran life into Garifuna culture. People attended Mass and the Catholic sacraments and they still practiced the traditional *dugu* ceremony to honor their ancestors. Women still prepared and baked cassava bread but they added newer elements to the ancient ritual of preparation such as sprinkling the prepared roots with rum. Their way of life is in many ways still centered on the sea, the coastal lagoons, and the rivers from which they make a living. The core values of Garifuna life have persisted, such as reverence for ancestors, valuing autonomy and freedom, passing on a pride of identity and culture to their children, regarding the land as too sacred to be sold on the commercial market, and the cultivation of an identity as a resilient people with a history of resistance.

From their arrival on the Honduran coast, the Garifuna have had to interact with and often resist English and Spanish settlers and adventurers, mahogany loggers, pirates, and the Miskito and Tolupán peoples to their east and south. The independent but weak Honduran state that emerged after independence from Spain in the early 1800s was concerned about the Caribbean coast in part because of English influence there, but was unable or unwilling to greatly disturb Garifuna communities. Despite a history of warfare with the English and forced exile from their eastern Caribbean homeland, the Garifuna tended to abide English presence in northern Honduras, at least partly as a deterrent to Honduran state control. By the latter half of the nineteenth century, however, Honduran governments were engaged in nation building and were promoting a national identity as a *mestizo* nation of mixed indigenous and European race and culture. *Mestizaje*, the idea that a new people arose out of the mingling of Indian and European, became official or semi-official policy in various Latin American countries, including Honduras. This policy ignored the presence of people of African origin, and encouraged a context of discrimination against darker-skinned "African" peoples. Such a context forced the Garifuna to consider their mixed ethnic identity as a political issue, but also as a resource to be used in defending their rights and freedoms.[26]

Honduran authorities perceived the Garifuna as outsiders to Honduran citizenship for another reason as well. The Garifuna were considered one of the *pueblos selváticos* (savage peoples), along with their Miskito neighbors. In 1882, the governor of Trujillo formed a commission to study and prepare plans for "civilizing" these peoples. The commission report described the Garifuna as lazy, not given to work, "living in vagrancy, much affected by liquor, disobedient to authorities and inclined to disorder," and said that Garifuna religious beliefs were "indefinable and incomprehensible." The report concluded that granting such people citizenship would be useless until they had been subjected to a lengthy process of education, religious teaching, and other civilizing influences.[27] Garifuna people began to develop a response that emphasized their "civilized" qualities of community and "betterment" but also retained a willingness to activism and protest when necessary.

Garifuna people sometimes say that their ancestors whom the British deported to Honduras were the darker-skinned and seemingly more "African" Garifuna. During the first half of the twentieth century, the Garifuna had to deal with a climate of racial discrimination because of their perceived black (*negro*) characteristics. Some Garifuna who worked in the U.S.-owned banana plantations claimed they received less work or poorer working conditions from their American bosses. Garifuna workers were mistaken for or lumped together with black Jamaican and other West Indian immigrant workers. Other Hondurans sometimes regarded them as foreigners because it was thought that Black people could not be true Honduran citizens. This belief was likely a consequence of earlier official attitudes about the Garifuna as one of the *pueblos selváticos* or those too uncivilized for citizenship. Garifuna responded to this racism by drafting statements, petitions, and demands to the Honduran government for protection of their rights, and by public demonstrations. After an anti-racism march in La Ceiba in 1950, some

Garifuna formed the *Sociedad Cultural Abraham Lincoln* (Abraham Lincoln Cultural Society). The designation "cultural society" was used rather than something more militant-sounding. But the name also reflected the influence or inspiration of anti-racism struggles in the United States, a connection that grew stronger as the Civil Rights Movement developed in the United States in the late 1950s and 1960s. By then, the growing Honduran labor union movement that was born with the 1954 banana workers' strike became another arena for anti-racist activism, especially within the more militant unions. The dual emphasis on cultural, civilized development and anti-racist activism implied in name of this early Garifuna organization continued when Garifuna in Puerto Cortes founded the Black Fraternal Organization of Honduras (*Organización Fraternal Negra de Honduras*, OFRANEH) in 1977.[28]

In the 1980s, Garifuna activists and OFRANEH began to shift the focus of their protest from anti-racism to defending collective cultural, land, and resource rights—the same rights that had long been the primary concern of other indigenous organizations. In short, the Garifuna began to emphasize their "indigenous" identity as much as their African identity.[29] There were several reasons for this shift. By the early 1900s, Honduran governments were beginning to award land concessions along the Caribbean coast to U.S. banana companies, especially Standard Fruit, despite Garifuna traditional claims to the land. Gradually, more concessions were made to Honduran ranchers and agricultural entrepreneurs. Honduran law prohibited foreign ownership of land within twenty-five miles of the Caribbean coast, but this law was often violated. In the 1950s, when the fruit companies began to leave, much of their land came under the control of Honduran large landowners. Honduran governments at the beginning of the 1980s advanced a model of national development that emphasized expansion of extractive industries like mining and logging, and export agriculture in commodities such as sugar and palm oil, as well as tourism. The agricultural expansion of sugar and African palm production and the development of tourism along the Caribbean coast almost guaranteed conflict with Garifuna communities and their traditional way of life. A new emphasis on developing Honduras as a tourist destination included the promotion of the folkloric indigenous heritage of the country, but not so much its African heritage.

At least on paper, other indigenous communities enjoyed some legal protections to their lands and resources. Despite their presence in Honduras since before the country's independence, in practice government officials and many Hondurans considered Garifuna people African (*negro*) rather than indigenous, and they could be excluded from legal protections for their land and culture. This problem was brought home in the early 1980s by a dispute over land at Puerto Castillo near Trujillo. The Honduran government and the United States wanted to develop a training facility there for Honduran and Salvadoran military on land claimed by a U.S. citizen. It was land that Garifuna communities also claimed as theirs, and they argued that the U.S. citizen was not the owner (both because it was Garifuna land and because the alleged owner was not a Honduran citizen) and he could not legally sell to the government of Honduras. In the end, the government took over the land and established the training base, though it occasioned considerable controversy in Honduras and in the United States for several reasons (not least, the presence of Salvadoran soldiers training on Honduran soil).[30]

By the late 1980s, international and Honduran environmental and tourism interests began to support efforts to protect the Central American Coral Reef, second in size and importance only to Australia's Great Barrier Reef. Garifuna people who lived on the archipelago of small island keys (*cayos*) off the Honduran coast were affected. The Honduran Navy began to restrict traditional Garifuna fishing, turtle hunting, and other activities that the communities on these keys had practiced for generations without damage to the reef or the local environment. Garifuna reported that the navy sometimes confiscated their boats and simple equipment at sea, forcing some to swim to shore, and that some Garifuna went missing at sea. At the same time, sport and tourist fishing was allowed.[31]

To protect their land, resources, and way of life, it became clear that the Garifuna would have to resist the de facto denial of their indigenous status. OFRANEH activists sought to position the Garifuna as a people who shared the same problems and interests as other indigenous groups. In 1987 groups of Garifuna, Lenca, Miskito, Tolupán, Pech, and Tawahka people held the First Seminar Workshop with Ethnic Autochthonous Groups of Honduras (*Primer Seminario Taller con los Grupos Étnicos Autóctonos de Honduras*) and sent the government a proposal for the recuperation and collective titling of lands, recognition and preservation of languages and cultures, guarantees to allow continuation of traditional forms of organization (an issue related to autonomy), and the right of communities to export for commercial reasons.[32] The use of the term *grupos étnicos autóctonos* emphasized the unity of cause and interest among all these people rather than division by race or ethnicity. For a time, at least, Honduran governments began to lump the Garifuna together with other communities whose indigenous origins were uncontested.

In 1996 during the presidency of Carlos Roberto Reina, the Honduran government became a signatory to International Labor Organization Convention 169 that outlined some important rights for indigenous peoples, including the right to free, prior, and informed consent of indigenous communities that would be affected by proposed development or extractive projects such as mining operations, construction of hydroelectric dams, or facilities for tourism development. By 2000, the government had modified its older policies regarding indigenous communities from repressing their rights and claims to acknowledging some rights but trying to redefine and delimit them—a policy sometimes labeled "neoliberal multiculturalism."[33] An example was the government's initiatives in the early 2000s to convert community land claims into secure private titles to individuals. This offered the attraction of secure title but it also turned land into a private economically mobile commodity that could be more easily bought and sold—something necessary for neoliberal development but adverse to traditional Garifuna values. Another example of "neoliberal multiculturalism" in practice was the state's recognition of indigenous organizations even as it developed a policy of working with less militant organizations and marginalizing organizations that were more critical or resistant toward neoliberal policies.

In the 1990s several organizations claimed to represent at least sectors of the Garifuna population. The two most prominent were OFRANEH and the Organization for Ethnic Community Development (ODECO). Honduran government officials began to consider OFRANEH the more resistant to state development plans, so they tended to work with ODECO, whose leadership seemed more willing to negotiate and participate in government plans if these held potential benefit for Garifuna. OFRANEH leaders were seen as more ideological, and government agencies and outside interests tried different ways to isolate and undermine their leadership.[34]

In November 1998, Hurricane Mitch hit Central America causing loss of life and enormous damage to property, crops, and natural environment. Some estimates claimed as many as six thousand people died and perhaps 600,000 were left homeless—about 10 percent of the Honduran population at the time. Sixty percent of the country's infrastructure was damaged or destroyed, and three-quarters of basic food crops in the field were lost.[35] Mitch severely disrupted life in the fruit plantations and Garifuna communities along the Caribbean coast. In the aftermath, fruit companies used this opportunity to abandon fruit production and replant their lands with African palms, taking advantage of an emerging global market for palm oil. Or they sold land to wealthy Hondurans eager to establish their own palm oil enterprises. The Honduran government worked with tourism interests to develop plans to rebuild the devastated Caribbean coast as a prime tourist mecca, complete with hotel and resort compounds, golf courses, and ports. These plans targeted areas long inhabited by Garifuna communities. Some Garifuna saw the possibility of income and jobs in these plans, while others saw a threat to the Garifuna land base, cultural traditions, and community life.

After the 2009 coup, tourism development was reaffirmed as an important component of government plans to decrease the national debt as well as further national economic development. By 2013 enough foreign capital had been secured to build several tourist hotels and resorts on or near Garifuna communities. The names of some of these tourist developments—Honduras Shores Plantation, Banana Coast—evoke an imperialist nostalgia. While some Garifuna sold land or found work in tourist developments, OFRANEH and other Garifuna opposed the developments. But Honduran government plans to secure foreign investment for more tourist development on the Caribbean coast were hampered by the negative publicity Honduras began to suffer as a land of violence and corruption.[36]

Another component of the government's national development plans has involved the establishment of one or more Charter Cities (*ciudades modelos*) along the Caribbean coast. In 2013, the Honduran Congress passed legislation to permit the establishment of Zones of Employment and Economic and Social Development (*Zonas de Empleo y Desarrollo Económico y Social* ZEDES) designed to pave the way for the development of *ciudades modelos* in what was described as open and uninhabited or unused lands. But the proposed sites had to include coastal front for building port facilities, and most were on land where Garifuna communities were located or on land they traditionally used. The Charter Cities concept involve enclaves where entire cities are constructed and administered with foreign capital and in which the residents are exempt from Honduran (national) laws and institutions. Some government officials seemed to think Charter Cities would stimulate investment and development. But on the OFRANEH website and in protest marches the organization characterized Charter Cities as the ultimate expression of modern day neoliberal neocolonialism. Charter Cities plans met opposition not only from the Garifuna but also from environmentalists, popular organizations, and many others. The idea aggravated the already sensitive issues of *vendepatria* (selling the nation's patrimony, its natural resources and land) and national sovereignty on both local and national levels.

In the years after the 2009 coup d'état, Garifuna communities found themselves under pressure from government and private interests promoting tourist development and Charter Cities schemes, and from large landowners and Honduran entrepreneurs trying to expand palm plantations for production of palm oil for the global processed food market. Garifuna reported receiving threats from employees of large landowners, hearing gunfire near their communities during the night, attempts to poison lagoons where people fished and caught turtles, and the burning in 2012 of the house of a Garifuna woman who had just testified to members of an independent international truth commission (*Comisión de Verdad*).[37] There were ongoing attempts to further divide Garifuna communities with promises of jobs and money from an expanded tourist industry. Popular Belizean singer and world music songwriter Andy Palacios had earlier decried the threats to Garifuna lands and culture in his song, "Miami," named not for a Florida city but for a Honduran Garifuna coastal community.

Garifuna resistance also used appeals to international opinion and law. In 2003, frustrated with Honduran government violations of its own laws protecting Garifuna lands, OFRANEH filed a case with the Inter-American Human Rights Commission in Washington, D.C. The case was based in part on the demand that the Honduran government honor its obligations under international agreements such as International Labor Organization (ILO) Convention 169 that protects the rights of indigenous peoples. The commission found enough merit in the complaint to refer it to the Inter-American Court of Human Rights in Costa Rica in May, 2014, in the claims of two Garifuna communities—Punta Piedra and Triunfo de la Cruz. Garifuna activists used the OFRANEH website, more protest marches, and a campaign to educate Honduran popular organizations and international groups in a call for solidarity. They tried to keep alive a history of resistance going back to colonial times, and to educate their youth in this history and in Garifuna values. OFRANEH also continued its policy of supporting other resistance efforts, especially those of COPINH (*Consejo Cívico de Organizaciones Populares e Indígenas de Honduras*), the Lenca organization that seemed most closely aligned with OFRANEH's analyses and forms of resistance. Against the Garifuna case, the Honduran government argued that the Garifuna were not actually indigenous, in part because of their African origins. It will be recalled that earlier Honduran governments had accepted as "indigenous" those groups that resided in Honduran territory before independence from Spain in 1824, a definition that technically applied to the Garifuna who were already established along part of the Honduran Caribbean coast by 1800.

Although Garifuna communities and OFRANEH continued to resist most of these threats to their land and way of life, the gang and drug violence that afflicted Honduras did not spare Garifuna communities, and began to threaten Garifuna youth. By 2013, Garifuna parents were sending their children to seek asylum outside the country for safety, and asking what the future of the Garifuna communities in Honduras would be without their youth. Some of the young people who were part of the "crisis at the border' that United States news media reported in mid-2014 were Garifuna youth from Honduras.[38]

THE LENCA: BLOOD OF LEMPIRA

> The Lenca are believed to have been the most numerous and widespread indigenous population in Honduras in the period shortly before the arrival of the Spanish conquerors. Lenca people could be found from the southwest of the country into the Mosquitia in the east. Their remote cultural origins and affiliations have been the subject of differing scholarly interpretations. Under the leadership of Lempira, the Lenca and some of their allies put up a stiff military resistance to the Spanish conquerors, especially in the period of 1537–1539. When Lempira was killed, some managed to flee to more remote locations, but the rest were *reducidos*, placed in Indian settlements (*pueblos de indios*) and forced to pay tribute to their colonial rulers.[39]

During the colonial period, the Spanish colonial government considered the Lenca one of the more "civilized" or civilizable peoples, in part because they had long lived in settled communities and cultivated crops for their subsistence. These patterns continued under the independent Honduran state. The Lenca adopted aspects of European culture and shaped them alongside traditional beliefs and practices. For the most part, they embraced Catholicism and wove it together with their beliefs in the spirits of ancestors and in nature. Their way of life seemed similar to that of non-Lenca and non-indigenous peasant farmers. In the 1980s, one anthropologist characterized the Lenca as "peasant farmers of indigenous tradition."[40] This identification that seemed to subordinate indigenous identity to the primary identity of peasant farmer (*campesino*) was the product of almost two centuries in which the state and those who controlled its institutions had actively promoted the image of Honduras as a racially and culturally homogeneous society, and had ignored or repressed expressions of ethnic or indigenous difference. But for the Lenca and other indigenous people, such cultural syncretism—their selective cultural appropriation and blending with European and other traits—was more than a practical necessity in the face of a conquering force, and even more than a product of gradual acceptance. With the state's acceleration of a neoliberal development model of foreign investment and massive resource extraction in the 1990s, the syncretic cultural resources of the Lenca and other native peoples became a powerful source of strength, identity, and resistance.

In 1989, Lenca communities held the First Congress of the Lenca People. They adopted the slogan, "Lempira, Symbol of Sovereignty and Dignity." The Honduran state had adopted Lempira as a symbol of national history and identity as early as 1920, without fully recognizing the country's indigenous people. The Lenca claimed Lempira as their ancestor, but his figure became a symbol of resistance for other indigenous groups, as well. The Lenca appropriation of Lempira was a brilliant strategy for showing how the Lenca were both uniquely indigenous but also an integral part of Honduran society. The Lenca struggle could not be ignored or separated from the larger history and struggles of the Honduran people.[41] By adopting the historic memory of Lempira the Lenca also conflated time and united the past struggle with the present.

In 1989, a group of Lenca founded the Organización Nacional Indígena Lenca de Honduras (ONILH). From the beginning it remained committed to negotiating with government agencies to clarify and protect Lenca claims to land and resources, and it avoided more confrontational actions and public protests. But Lenca activism on behalf of their land and way of life was evolving, showing a more directly resistant character even as the official development policies of the government and the economic elite moved to implement a neoliberal development model for the country and its natural resources. In the early 1990s, Lenca people organized several direct actions in Intibuca, and in 1993 they joined with a variety of other popular organizations in the area to form the Comité de Organizaciones Populares e Indígenas de Intibuca (COPIN). Among its specific objectives was preservation of the forest cover. This ecological or conservation emphasis enhanced its appeal among non-indigenous popular organizations. COPIN included labor unions and peasant groups, teachers' associations, medical workers, human rights organizations, and environmentalist groups. Because of this, COPIN became a clear example of the convergence of interests and voices among traditional working class and newer middle class organizations. Barahona, points out that,

> the crisis in which the Central American people were living during 1980–1990, with its cycle of repression, authoritarianism, and insecurity stimulated the rise of organizations such as CODEH and COFADEH, a significant group of non-governmental organizations connected to popular organizations, and also environmental groups committed to the defense and conservation of natural resources. All these, together, gave life to new social movements. (*translation mine*)[42]

He makes the point that in this context, COPIN reflected this development, with indigenous people much involved. The Lenca and other indigenous people who formed part of COPIN were able to learn from the struggles of peasant unions and others defending land and resources, and in turn to share indigenous experience with these others. Thus COPIN represented a major advance in the formation of a broad culture of resistance in Honduras, and the realization that indigenous groups had been among the driving forces of this advance.

Within a year COPIN was reorganized as the Consejo Cívico de Organizaciones Populares e Indígenas de Honduras (COPINH). Lenca communities formed the core of this organization, and it adopted a more public and critical stance and forms of public witness and protest than the older Lenca organization, ONILH. Because of this, state agencies and government officials seemed to prefer to work with representatives of ONILH and to ignore or marginalize COPINH. Early in 1994, COPINH played a major role in organizing a series of marches from various indigenous communities, especially Lenca, that converged into a large march to Tegucigalpa to dramatize their demands for recognition of constitutional and other legal rights and protections of indigenous peoples. The government of Carlos Roberto Reina took notice and over the next few years adopted a series of piecemeal measures to address indigenous demands. Perhaps the most important of these was the Honduran state's adoption of International Labor Organization Convention 169 on the Rights of Indigenous Peoples. Among other measures, ILO 169 bound the Honduran state to seek free, full, and prior consent from indigenous communities before initiating projects or enterprises that might affect the welfare, lands, or resources of these communities. It became a benchmark to which indigenous organizations could appeal in the international community, especially when the Honduran legal system proved inadequate in defending the rights of the country's indigenous population.

The many marches in the 1990s organized and led by Lenca communities through COPINH with collaboration and support from other popular organizations, revived an old practice of communal pilgrimage (*peregrinación* or *romería,* sometimes *caminata*). Lenca leaders recalled the colonial practice of pilgrimage to locations where the Virgin Mary or other Catholic saints might have appeared or been present in spirit.[43] But the practice seems to have roots older and perhaps more universal than Spanish colonial Catholicism. The Lenca recognized ancient sacred places in their territory and knew that people or spirits might travel from one to the other. This is an idea found among many other indigenous peoples widely dispersed in the Western Hemisphere, each with its own specific sacred landscape and powerful or divine spirits. The sacred pilgrimage was known and practiced among ancient peoples in and around the Valley of Mexico with whom the Lenca may have some distant historical and cultural connection, the modern Huichol of western Mexico, the ancient Nazca in the coastal desert plans of Peru, and the Klamath, Modoc, and other native people of northern California, among others.[44]

Popular organizations in many parts of the world have long used marches as a form of popular protest, but usually these are limited in distance, often confined to a few city blocks, and may not evoke religious or spiritual aspects. Marches such as those resurrected by the Lenca from their past were usually longer, often many miles or hundreds of kilometers (including at least one from San Francisco Opalaca to Tegucigalpa) and quite often have at least an undercurrent of spiritual or religious as well as political meaning. In this sense they are pilgrimages. It is often the mixing of political statement with spiritual or religious symbolism and value that gives such pilgrimages added power as cultural resources of protest and resistance. During the Contra War in Nicaragua, thousands of people from cities, towns, and rural villages participated in the Via Crucis (Way of the Cross) that marched from the north of the country to Managua, the capital, to demonstrate against the war and to demand and pray for peace. The Christian symbolism of Christ's suffering and death represented in the Via Crucis evoked a powerful spiritual context for expressing the suffering of the Nicaraguan people as a result of the war. In Honduras, the Lenca drew on ancient traditional beliefs and more recent Catholic religious meaning and linked these to their demands for justice, protection of their lands, and the protection of basic rights.

In 2003, COPINH again demonstrated its ability to collaborate with other organizations and to cast the indigenous struggles within a wider context of popular concerns. The Lenca organization helped organize and hosted the Third Forum on Biological and Cultural Diversity in La Esperanza in the heartland of the Lenca communities. Eight hundred participants from many organizations across Central America and beyond attended, including members of indigenous, peasant, labor, youth, and women's organizations. The Third Forum addressed what it identified as threats that economic globalization posed to regional and global ecosystems and to many cultural traditions, and identified logging, mining, and tourist development as special threats to indigenous and local land rights. Later in 2003, the Lenca participated in another large congress, the Fourth Mesoamerican Forum against Plan Puebla-Panama (PPP). Held in Tegucigalpa, this meeting attracted almost 1,600 participants who drafted resolutions and plans of action to oppose the neoliberal model of development for Mexico and Central America proposed by PPP. This Forum rejected privatization of basic public services and utilities, which it saw as a violation of fundamental human rights. It also called for protection of labor rights, rejected bio piracy and aspects of free trade that harmed vulnerable populations, and called for the demilitarization of Central America and the closing of U.S. military bases in the region.[45] COPINH adopted several objectives for its work, including legalization of collective ownership of ancestral indigenous lands, development that was controlled and directed by local communities, and the general defense of the economic, political, social, and cultural rights of all people. The organization intended to conduct workshops with these themes in Lenca communities.

Near the end of 2012, representatives from different popular and human rights organizations across Honduras met to strategize how to strengthen resistance to a series of perceived threats to the natural environment and resources, human rights, national sovereignty, and people's dignity that seemed to intensify after the 2009 coup. Someone suggested a *caminata*. "Yes, like the *caminatas* of the indigenous people organized in COPINH," agreed another. "A *caminata* like those of indigenous people over the centuries," said a third person.[46] On February 25, 2013, two groups set out, one from the north of Honduras at the edge of Garifuna communities, the other from the heart of Lenca communities in the southwest. The northern group included people from a variety of different organizations, including people from Garifuna and Tolupán communities. Those coming from the southwest were led by a large group of Lenca. Their common destination was Tegucigalpa, the Honduran capital where they would present a limited set of demands to the Congress and the government. On the fourth day of the march the two groups met at Siguatepeque on the main north-south highway. There they celebrated a *guancasco*, a traditional Lenca festival of singing, dancing, and friendship between peoples. Then they went on to Tegucigalpa. This *caminata* included three hundred participants and covered two hundred kilometers in about ten days. People in communities along the way brought the marchers food, water, and even money. This march illustrates how an older indigenous (in this case Lenca) cultural form, the *romería* became a resource adopted by the larger popular resistance, and how various organizations and communities converged, literally and instrumentally, in an expression of popular resistance.

Since the early 1990s, but especially after 2000, Honduran government plans to develop hydroelectric power for mining, maquiladoras, and model cities involved the construction of a series of dams on some of the country's major rivers such as the Patuca (see section on Miskito Autonomy). The plans included the Gualcarque River that runs through the heart of Lenca communities in western Honduras. The river has both material and spiritual importance for the Lenca. In the years after the 2009 coup, the Honduran government gave a concession to DESA (*Desarrollos Energéticos*) to build a hydroelectric dam across the Gualcarque. DESA contracted with the Chinese company Sinohydro to build the Agua Zarca dam. The government also provided support that included the services of the Honduran Army's First Engineering Battalion to provide protection for the company compound by the dam site. The 2013 Mining Law, a revision of the 1998 Mining Law, imposed a 2 percent tax on mining companies that goes into a "security budget" administered by police and military. Some Hondurans interpreted this as an incentive to the security forces to take a special interest in protecting mining operations. People alleged that military units stationed at dam sites such as Agua Zarca received double pay—from the government and the company—making them effectively agents of the company. They also alluded to examples of companies offering bribes and incentives to local mayors, community leaders, and authorities whose support could ease the way for the companies. This tactic could result in a misleading appearance of local acceptance. Despite the requirement for full, free, and informed consent set forth in ILO Convention 169 and provisions in Honduran law, Lenca people and COPINH leaders claimed there was no such consultation about the Agua Zarca dam.[47]

On April 1, 2013, members of the local communities of Rio Blanco began blocking the road to the Agua Zarca dam project headquarters and the river, not allowing project machinery to pass. They also began nonviolent resistance. Members of the Lenca community maintained a constant presence at a roadblock they constructed on the road to the dam site, despite frequent evictions and threats by police who sometimes pointed their weapons at the Lenca gathered at the roadblock. Shots were sometimes heard in the vicinity of the roadblock. Occasionally international visitors and observers joined members of Lenca, Garifuna, and other indigenous communities and popular organizations in walking the road to the company plant. At times the walk was led with prayer and burning incense in traditional fashion. During their protest, the walkers were often faced with a contingent of the First Engineering Battalion guarding the company compound. During a walk on July 15, 2013, witnesses reported that a soldier opened fire on the protesters, shooting and killing COPINH member Tomás Garcia and seriously injuring his teenage son, Alan. A third Lenca man was also injured.

Several months before this incident, in May 2013, Berta Cáceres and another COPINH leader had been accused of illegal possession of a weapon. This case was dismissed for lack of evidence, but later reinstated in what seemed to some to be a politically motivated move. After the July incident, she and two other COPINH leaders involved in the Agua Zarca protest were accused of coercion, usurpation, and causing damages of over three million dollars as a result of the construction delay COPINH had allegedly cause. The three COPINH leaders were cited and ordered to appear at a court hearing scheduled for August 14 in La Esperanza.

La Esperanza is a city located in the southwestern highlands. The morning of the hearing was sunny and warm despite the city's elevated location. An hour before the hearing, people began arriving at a formation center about two kilometers from the courthouse. The gathered group included Lenca (some in colorful traditional dress), other Hondurans from popular organizations and communities as far away as the Caribbean coast in the north and Tegucigalpa in the south, and international observers from human rights organizations. The walls of rooms in the formation center were covered with brightly-colored murals that mixed depictions of Honduran indigenous people with international figures such as Martin Luther King, Gandhi, Ché Guevara, Nicaraguan Sandinista revolutionaries, and others such as the Fr. James Carney (Guadalupe) a Catholic priest from the United States who spent years among the peasants of Honduras and was killed apparently while in Honduran army custody in the early 1980s. Carney is still revered as a martyr for the poor in Honduras. Depicted alongside these more famous figures were deer with large soft eyes, an indigenous woman giving birth and a Lenca warrior standing guard over the birth, and motifs of corn plants. It seemed like an entire history of the Lenca in the context of and connected to other resistance struggles, portrayed in a form to educate and remind both the literate and the illiterate. The crowd gathered at the formation center finally set off with banners and signs in a march along dirt roads to the courthouse on the outskirts of La Esperanza. Some signs bore the names of organizations, others carried messages like "Stop the violence against the defenders," referring to those defending the environment and natural resources and the land and water of the Lenca. The entire group numbered perhaps 120 people, in addition to reporting crews from several news media.

At the courthouse, a truck with a loudspeaker system parked just outside the courtroom where the hearing for Cáceres was in progress. Representatives from organizations gave short speeches supporting Cáceres, denouncing injustices done to indigenous and other sectors of the Honduran population, and calling for defense of land, resources, national sovereignty, and human rights. Some speakers emphasized that the Lenca struggle against the dam was really a test case for the future of government policy and popular resistance. Others expressed gratitude for the show of international support. Under a blazing sun, the rally continued for two hours until the hearing inside ended and the lawyers came out to announce that another hearing was set for a date in September, and that meanwhile the three defendants were released in the custody of their lawyer who would be responsible for their "good behavior." They were enjoined from going near the company installations at Rio Blanco, and ordered to present themselves and sign in every two weeks at court. Shortly after the September court hearing, a judge ruled that Cáceres be imprisoned awaiting trial. The law mandates that an accused person who is freed pending one court case cannot be free pending a second case if the first is still active. The accused cannot be free on two different cases simultaneously. People thought that the first case against Cáceres for gun possession in May was deliberately reopened to ensure that she would be jailed awaiting trial on the second set of charges.

In the weeks that followed, Lenca people continued to maintain a presence at a small barricade they had erected on the road to the company compound. They allowed traffic that was not related to the company or the dam project. By September, Sinohydro had withdrawn from the project and left the compound. A small group of workers, foreign advisers, and Honduran soldiers remained. DESA contracted with the Spanish-Guatemalan company COPRECA to build the dam. There had been no police presence in the area before the start of the dam project. Now police operated out of the house of a non-Lenca family that had taken over some Lenca land years before and "sold' the land to DESA to build the dam. Police began to be sent from Tegucigalpa rather that drawn from the Rio Blanco area, and they were rotated out every month to ensure they did not develop relationships with the local Lenca community.

The Lenca resistance to the Agua Zarca dam assumed a special importance in Honduras. Many Hondurans in popular organizations and human rights groups began to regard this as a test case for the future of government policy and popular resistance. The Lenca and especially COPINH built on a history of placing the Lenca struggles within a larger context of the national reality, and portraying resistance to Agua Zarca in a way that touched other issues of major concern to Hondurans. It provided yet another case of trying to defend the country's resources from government and powerful people seen as selling out those resources to foreign interests for personal gain. It touched the sensitive issue of national sovereignty regarding foreign ownership and economic control. Lenca appeals to international agreements, laws, and conventions, and the fact that Lenca were killed during protests made this an example of the larger struggle to protect basic human rights and the rights of local communities, and turned it into a situation with international dimensions. The protest activities of Lenca and COPINH emphasized nonviolence and evoked spiritual and sometimes specifically religious beliefs and symbols. This appealed to many Hondurans who saw it as denouncing violence in a country where everyone was painfully aware of daily violence, and defending spiritual values in a context where everything in neoliberal commercialized society seemed to reward greed and violence. The indigenous core of the Lenca struggle also contributed to a sense of its importance, coming from a people with a long history of resistance and resilience who in fact claimed the national icon, Lempira, as their ancestor in resistance. For some Hondurans, what happened to the Lenca in this case became symbolic of what happens to Honduras.

ATTEMPTS TO WEAKEN INDIGENOUS RESISTANCE

Beginning in the 1990s, but especially after the 2009 coup d'état, the Honduran government and the economic and political elite employed various forms of control, force, and judicial maneuvering to build a neoliberal extractive model in indigenous lands. Integrated networks of control and interest between government and political officials, Honduran and foreign entrepreneurs and large landowners employed both state power—police, military, legal maneuvering—and private security guards to repress indigenous opposition and to weaken the power of indigenous organizations. Government officials and corporations engaged in mining and dam-building contracts justified these heavy handed measures by portraying indigenous resistance as a stubborn obstruction to economic advancement and national development of benefit to Hondurans. Indigenous resistance was portrayed as selfish insistence upon rights and privileges for a small part of the population, or even as a form of terrorism subverting the welfare and interests of the nation. This portrayal was elaborated even as indigenous people were simultaneously seen as an important part of the national heritage. Here is a brief summary of some of the ways in which indigenous resistance is subverted and weakened, as we have seen in the histories outlined in this chapter. Some of these measures are widespread in Honduras, while others specifically target indigenous peoples.

- Physical attack, killing, harassment, and community evictions in Tolupán, Miskito, Garifuna, and Lenca communities.
- Ignoring treaties and traditional land rights or obfuscating them with multiple claims, as in Tolupán communities where landlords advance dubious claims to lands claimed by tribe through previous government treaties.
- Co-opting or corrupting indigenous organizations such as FETRIXY, and dividing communities, as among the Tolupán people and to some extent

the Garifuna and the Lenca. Most major indigenous groups have at least two organizations that claim to represent them, one more accommodating to government and another seen as more critical of government policy. Government agencies tend to engage the one and try to exclude or marginalize the other. These divisions can promote or exacerbate internal conflict within indigenous communities, providing a further excuse for the state and security forces to intervene in indigenous communities, as happened among the Lenca;
- Catching indigenous communities between criminal drug trafficking and law enforcement authorities, as in the Mosquitia;
- Eliminating cooperative and collective land control. The principle and practice of cooperative and collective land ownership that is central to many indigenous communities has been under attack in Honduras since at least the early 1990s. Government officials and even some U.S. officials in Honduras expressed the idea that cooperative and collective lands were obstacles to "development" because they are largely outside the reach of the private, individualized, and commercialized land market promoted by the Honduran government. Laws gradually undermined the recognition of collective land ownership, and in many cases treaty rights and other claims were simply ignored with the rationale that the state has a prior economic interest for the greater good of national development;
- Erasing indigenous diversity, identity, voice—The government policy of promoting Mayan as the only real indigenous identity in Honduran cultural history ensures that other indigenous communities and voices are not legitimized or recognized in the nation's "official" history and cultural identity. Ostensibly promoted as part of a tourist policy, this policy grossly distorts history and anthropology in order to stifle or undermine the legitimacy of most indigenous voices. The nation is *mestizo* (Spanish and Indian mixture), and its Indian roots are Mayan—that is all. When Honduran historian Darío Euraque criticized the policy of mayanization, the post-coup government quickly removed him from directorship of the national museum of culture and history.[48]
- Blaming the victims—The state criminal justice system often ignores crimes against indigenous activists and communities while accusing indigenous activists of encouraging or engaging in criminal activity. The prosecution of COPINH leaders after the Lenca demonstrations against the Agua Zarca dam illustrates this tactic. In addition, lawyers who defend indigenous leaders may also be prosecuted on other charges;
- Attacking the defenders' defenders—Lawyers who defend indigenous defendants are themselves harassed or charged with crimes. This happened to the lead defense lawyer for accused COPINH leader Berta Cáceres;

- Justice delayed—Indigenous leaders charged with crimes may be imprisoned for months while their trials are postponed, or they may be forbidden to engage in activism while their cases are pending, sometimes for years;
- Unfamiliar legal systems—The Honduran legal and judicial system that tries indigenous people accused of crimes is often unfamiliar to them. Some indigenous leaders and non-indigenous lawyers who defend them complain about this cultural handicap. In addition, indigenous people do not usually have the resources to bribe or influence judges as the powerful might.

INDIGENOUS RESISTANCE AND NEOLIBERAL GLOBALIZATION

Indigenous resistance employs an array of cultural resources—nonviolence with an emphasis on a warrior past, a long history and a collective identity that gives strength of purpose, community organization often going back many generations, spiritual and religious values, ways of integrating indigenous resistance into larger national and international contexts that draw others to the struggle. Indigenous people also occupy a particularly conflictive place in resistance to the policies and actions of the Honduran state. The very existence and way of life that indigenous people such as the Lenca struggle to maintain seems to constitute a critique and a challenge to the basic tenets of the Honduran brand of neoliberal globalization.

- They defend place, location, environment, and a sacred geography that is their identity, and resist the tendency to turn place into space or commodity.
- They define resources as sustainers of life, and resist the tendency to turn environmental capital into financial capital.
- Their community and values resist privatization of the land and the river that flows across all manmade boundaries.
- They appeal to spiritual and social values that others value in a society where neoliberal globalization seems to ignore or commodify the spiritual.
- Globalization tends to conflate time—Everything mixes together in the current moment, and a sense of history and context is lost.[49] Indigenous communities in Honduras turn the conflation of time into a source of strength and defense—Lempira is alive today in their struggles.

As a result, indigenous people such as the Lenca are transformed, or transform themselves in the Honduran context from being seen as obstructionist relics of the past to being harbingers of a different future—a test case of what might be. Perhaps the attempt to construct an image of a different future is the core of indigenous resistance and perhaps the core of the larger culture of resistance in Honduras today.

NOTES

1. Ismael Moreno S.J., "Una caminata en repudio a la Ley de Minería," *Revista Envío Nicaragua* 32:373 (April, 2013), 28. Translation mine.
2. Instituto Nacional de Estadisticas, *XVI Censo Nacional de Población* (Tegicigalpa: Instituto Nacional de Estadistica, 2001.
3. See Marvin Barahona, *Pueblos indígenas, Estado, y memoria colectiva en Honduras* (Tegucigalpa: Editorial Guaymuras, 2009), 31–96.
4. For examples of repression against Tolupán FETRIXY leaders and attempts to coopt the organization see, Anthony Stock, "Land War," *Cultural Survival Quarterly* 16:4 (1992), 16–18; and Comité para la Defensa de los Derechos Humanos en Honduras CODEH, *Boletín* 80 (September 1991): 2–9. I discuss these also in, James Phillips, "Resource Access, Environmental Struggles, and Huan Rights in Honduras," in *Life and Death Matters: Human Rights, Environment, and Social Justice*, ed. by Barbara Rose Johnston (Walnut Creek, CA: Left Coast Press, 2011), 214–15.
5. Mark Anderson, "When Afro Becomes (like) Indigenous: Garifuna and Afro-Indigenous Politics in Honduras," *The Journal of Latin American and Caribbean Anthropology* 12:2 (November 2007): 401–4.
6. Maria Fiallos, "Honduran Indigenous Community in Standing Forest Area," *Honduras This Week*, June 9, 2003.
7. Fiallos 2003. See also Susan C. Stonich and Billie R. DeWalt, "The Political Ecology of Deforestation in Honduras," in *Tropical Deforestation: The Human Dimension*, eds. Leslie E. Sponsel, Thomas N. Headland, and Robert C. Bailey (New York: Columbia University Press, 1996), 187–215. The figures on water use in mining are mentioned often by anti-mining activists in Honduras and other Central American countries, for example, Caritas El Salvador, "Mitos y Realidades de la Minería de Oro en Centroamérica, http://www.stopesmining.org/j25/images/pdf/mitos%20y%20realidades, accessed August 2014.
8. Maria Oseguera de *Ochoa, Honduras hoy: Sociedad y crisis política* (Tegucigalpa: Centro de Documentación de Honduras, 1987), 23–24. Nancy Peckenham and Annie Street, eds., *Honduras: Portrait of a Captive Nation* (New York; Publishers, 1985), 245–47.
9. Barahona, *Pueblos indígenas*, 37–38.
10. José Maria Tojeira, *Los hicaques de Yoro* (Tegucigalpa: Editorial Guaymuras, 1982), 21, quoted in Barahona, *Pueblos indígenas*, 55, translation mine.
11. Much of the historical information in this section is based on Barahona, *Pueblos indígenas*, 49–61 and Tojeira, *Los Hicaques de Yoro*. Information on more recent Tolupán struggles over land and organization is based on Anthony Stock, "Land War," *Cultural Survival Quarterly* 16:4 (19992): 16–18; Comité para la Defensa de los Derechos Humanos en Honduras, *CODEH Boletín* 80 (September 1991); and *La Prensa*, March 3, 1988. Additional observations and information based on my interviews and discussions with informants in Yoro, August 2013.
12. Phillips, "Resource Access," 215. See also Stock, CEDOH, in previous note.
13. Information in this section obtained from Tolupán community members interviewed by international human rights workers, and from the international workers themselves who investigated these incidents in 2013 and 2014. There also several Honduran newspaper accounts of the killings at Locomapa. I also interviewed Catholic Church workers in Yoro.
14. Barahona, *Pueblos indígenas*, 68, translation mine.
15. Quoted in Barahona, *Pueblos iníigenas*, 77, translation mine.
16. Barahona, *Pueblos iníigenas*, 96–97.
17. Barahona, *Pueblos iníigenas*, 63–81.
18. Information on the Miskito people during the Contra War (1981–1990) based on the author's fieldwork in Honduras and Nicaragua at that time, some of this appears in James

Phillips, "Repatriation and Social Class in Nicaragua," in *Coming Home? Refugees, Migrants, and Those Who Stayed Behind*, eds. Lynellyn D, Long and Ellen Oxfeld (Philadelphia: University of Pennsylvania Press, 2004), 150–69. Also S. James Anaya, "The CIA with the Honduran Army in the Mosquitia: Taking the Freedom out of the Fight in the Name of Accountability, Report on a Visit to the Honduran Mosquitia during April, 1987," unpublished manuscript. Anaya was staff attorney for the U.S. National Indian Youth Council.

19. Barahona, *Pueblos indígenas*, 231–32.

20. Danielle DeLuca, "In Pursuit of Autonomy: Indigenous Peoples Oppose Dam Construction on the Patuca River in Honduras," *Cultural Survival Quarterly* 35:4 (December 2011), 12–15. Also Kendra McSwenney, Zoe Pearson, Sara Santiago, and Ana Gabriela Domínguez, "A River Tale: Protecting a Tawahka Way of Life," *Cultural Survival Quarterly* 35:4 (December 2011): 16–20.

21. For a detailed account and analysis of this incident see Annie Bird and Alexander Main with Karen Spring, "Collateral Damage of a Drug War: The May 11 Killings in Ahuas and the U.S. War on Drugs in La Moskitia, Honduras" (Washington, DC: Rights Action and the Center for Economic and Policy Research, August 2012).

22. Karen Spring, "Evidence the DEA Attempted to Alter Testimony on Drug War Massacre in Honduras," Center for International Policy Americas Program, http://www.cipamericas.org, January 30, 2015, retrieved January 30, 2015.

23. Available from *La Prensa* website, http://www.laprensa.hn/inicio/443116–96/bg-group-iniciara-exploracion-petrolera-en-la-mosquitia-de-honduras, accessed August 2014.

24. The film, *Garifuna Journey*, (filmmaker Andrea Leland, New Day Films, 1998) describes these events from the perspective of modern Garifuna historians in Belize. The film also describes some traditional Garifuna cultural customs.

25. Barahona, citing other sources, *Pueblos indígenas*, 101.

26. Mark Anderson, "When Afro Becomes (like) Indigenous: Garifuna and Afro-Indigenous Politics in Honduras," *The Journal of Latin American and Caribbean Studies* 12: 2 (November, 2007): 390–91. Much of the information relating to Garifuna ethnic politics and identity in this section is derived from Anderson's article and chapter.

27. Barahona, *Pueblos indígenas*, 158.

28. Anderson, "When Afro Becomes (like) Indigenous," 392–93.

29. Anderson, "When Afro Becomes (like) Indigenous," 392–93.

30. Allan Nairn, "The United States Militarizes Honduras," in *Honduras: Portrait of a Captive Nation*, edited by Nancy Peckenham and Annie Street (New York: Praeger, 1985), 296, reprinted from "End Game," *NACLA Report on the Americas* 18:3 (May/June, 1984): 30, 39–41. Alison Acker, *Honduras: The Making of a Banana Republic* (Boston: South End Press, 1988), 117.

31. Sandra Cuffe, "Militarization of the Mesoamerican Barrier Reef Harms Indigenous Communities," Truthout (Truth-out.org) website, May 12, 2014, accessed August, 2014, http://www.truth-out.org/news/item/23729-militarizatin-of-the-mesoamerican-barrier-reef-harms-indigenous-communities. For an extended discussion of "green neoliberalism" and gender in Garifuna communities see Keri Vacanti Brondo, *Land Grab: Green Neoliberalism, Gender, and Garifuna Resistance in Honduras* (Tucson: University of Arizona Press, 2013).

32. Anderson, "When Afro Becomes (like) Indigenous," 393–94.

33. Anderson, 398, citing Charles R. Hale, "Does Multiculturalism Menace?" Cultural Rights and the Policy of Identity in Guatemala," *Journal of Latin American Studies* 34 (2002): 485–524.

34. Anderson, 403–4.

35. Paul Jeffries, personal communication based on information provided by the Honduran Christian Commission for Development.

36. Mark Anderson, "Garifuna Activism and the Corporatist Honduran State Since the 2009 Coup" in *Black Social Movements in Latin America: From Monocultural Mestizaje to Multiculturalism*, Jean Muteba Rahier, ed. (New York: Palgrave MacMillan, 2012), 53–73.

37. Personal communication from a member of the support team that accompanied the Comisión de Verdad.

38. Tim Smyth, "Garifuna People Are Risking Everything to Flee their Ancestral Homeland," VICE News website, https://news.vice.com/contributor/tim-smyth, posted August 21, 2014.

39. Barahona, *Pueblos indígenas*, 86.

40. The phrase is from Anne Chapman, *Los hijos del copal y la candela* (Mexico: Universidad Nacional Autonoma de Mexico, 1986), vol. I, page 13, cited in Barahona, *Pueblos indígenas*, 87.

41. Barahona, *Pueblos indígenas*, 234.

42. Barahona, *idem,* 233.

43. Barahona, *Pueblo indígena*, 234, provides an example of this use of spiritual symbolism and the practice of *caminata*.

44. Archaeological evidence in the Valley of Mexico suggests a theory that what later became great ancient city-states such as Teotihuacan began as small pilgrimage centers. Similar interpretations are offered for ancient sites in the Andes, including an interpretation of the famous Nazca lines as pilgrimage routes on the dry Pacific desert coast of Peru. Until at least the 1960s, some groups of Huichol continued to make pilgrimages to sacred places for community healing and to collect sacred peyote. In 1996, Modoc elders in southern Oregon told the author about ancient beliefs of the sacred journeys of the spirits between the major mountains of the region. There is also a body of literature about indigenous walks and pilgrimages in colonial Latin America. Pilgrimages for religious or sacred purposes could also take on a political character of popular protest or resistance, combining sacred and political character.

45. Suzanne York discusses both of these meetings in, "Honduras and Resistance to Globalization," International Forum on Globalization website http://.ifg.org/analysis/globalization/Hoonduras.htm (Winter, 2003).

46. Ismael Moreno, "Una caminata en repudio a la Ley de Minería," *Envío Nicaragua* Año 11 no. 32 (April 2013): 25, translation mine.

47. For two discussions of mining and its impact on Honduran rural communities, including examples of water usage, see, Javier Suazo, "¿Una minería benigna para Honduras?" *Envío Honduras* 10:36 (December, 2012): 36–40. And Jennifer Avila, "La explotación minera, tan dura como la dictadura," *Envío Honduras* 11:38 (June 2013): 28–34.

48. Darío Euraque, *El golpe de Estado del 28 de junio del 2009, el patrimonio cultural, y la Identidad Nacional de Honduras* (San Pedro Sula: Centro Editorial, 2010);

49. Arjun Appadurai, "Disjuncture and Difference in the Global Cultural Economy," *Theory, Culture, and Society* vol 7 (1990): 295–310.

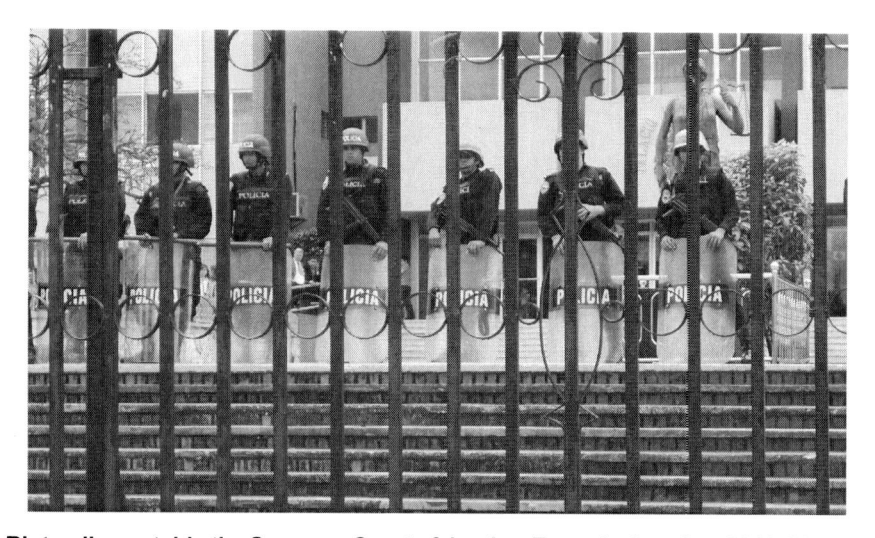

Riot police outside the Supreme Court of Justice, Tegucigalpa. Jan. 2010. Photo by Lucy Josselyn Edwards.

Indigenous Lenca walk to protest a dam project on their sacred river. Rio Blanco, Intibucá, May 2013. Photo by Lucy Josselyn Edwards.

A show of determination at the roadblock where indigenous Lenca halted traffic. Photo by Lucy Josselyn Edwards.

Honduran military arrive at civilian protest, Rio Blanco, Intibucá, May 2013. Photo by Lucy Josselyn Edwards.

Private guards detain two men on the highway south of the capital, Tegucigalpa. Private security outnumber Honduran police and military combined. Photo by Noah Phillips-Edwards.

Three Tolupán elders are murdered while peacefully protesting mining and illegal logging in their community, August 25, 2013. Photo by Lucy Josselyn Edwards.

Remembering the dead and missing. Monthly vigil of COFADEH, the Committee of Families of the Disappeared Detained in Honduras. Tegucigalpa, September, 2014. Photo by Lucy Josselyn Edwards.

Hundreds of *campesinos* have been murdered in the northern Bajo Aguan Valley since the 2009 coup d'état. Tocoa, Feb. 2012. Photo by Lucy Josselyn Edwards.

Evening vigil at gates of Comayagua prison demanding justice and commemorating the 362 people who perished in a fire there in Feb. 2012. Photo by Lucy Josselyn Edwards.

Graffiti in Tegucigalpa mixing culture and resistance. Photo by Lucy Josselyn Edwards.

Solidarity in the United States, annual protest vigil at School of the Americas, Ft. Benning, GA, where Latin American officers are trained. Photo by Lucy Josselyn Edwards.

Chapter Six

Nourishing Resilience

Food, Environment, Community

I was traveling with the parish priest in the Aguan Valley of northern Honduras on a day in 1988. We drove to the end of a rutted, dirt road, left the vehicle, and walked up the hilly path for an hour to a small farming community of scattered houses. There was no electricity, no refrigeration, no piped running water except for a couple of public faucets, and no road traffic—no road. There was one small *pulpería*, a tiny shop that was no more than the side room of a private house. You could go up to the window and buy a few essentials like cooking oil, matches, soap, maybe candles or kerosene, and *chicle* (chewing gum). As I sat resting outside the small chapel, I saw a local man coming up the steep path leading a donkey. The poor beast was laden with four cases of bottled Coca Cola. The scene seemed incongruous, even surreal. That was 1988. Today, it seems normal.

In almost any larger city in Honduras today, one can find bakeries, pizza shops, and supermarkets selling bread, flour tortillas, and pasta. It was not always so. Although the Spanish colonists introduced wheat to Latin America to make Communion bread and satisfy their craving for Mediterranean foods in this new world, wheat did not become an integral part of most people's diets or the national cuisine until later. By the latter half of the twentieth century, countries like Honduras were importing wheat from the United States or receiving it as part of foreign food aid. Government policy driven by a high national debt, weak economy, and private interests increasingly promoted large-scale export agriculture at the expense of local peasant and small farm production for local market. Food at cheaper prices was imported to feed urban populations.

The changes are part and reflection of a profound transformation in Honduran society that has promoted both dependency and resistance. In a private interview in 1989, Ramon Velasquez, director of the Honduran Institute for Social and Economic Investigation, warned that, "Bread has a profound impact in Honduras, but until now nobody seems to be paying any attention." In recent decades, policies and practices related to food and agriculture have seemed to some like threats that could undermine the entire peasant sector as a social class, the food security of both urban and rural poor, the health of many Hondurans, and the relative food independence of the country. The emerging movement of resistance recognized food, agricultural policy, and related environmental issues as crucial aspects of the effort to construct a more resilient future. Community development also emerged as a locus of struggle, resistance, and resilience insofar as it presented examples of processes of emergent self-reliance, local autonomy, and empowerment.

FOOD AS HISTORY, IDENTITY, AND POWER

In all human societies, food is history, identity, symbolic communication, and power.[1] Food communicates as well as nourishes. The cuisine of a people reflects and literally embodies their past. A fairly typical meal for a peasant family in Central America today might consist of corn tortillas, beans, homemade cheese, and black coffee. The corn for tortillas and the beans have been cultivated in the region for thousands of years, but the cheese comes from cattle whose ancestors were originally introduced by Spanish colonizers in the 1500s, and coffee reflects the development of an international export economy out of Central America as recently as the late 1800s. If the peasant family goes down the road to the local *pulperia* (corner store) and buys a bottle of Coke, they have entered the late twentieth century and the global marketplace.

Because food reflects a people's history, it also contributes to the construction of identity. Patterns of food consumption can especially reflect ethnicity and social class. While the indigenous peasant family is eating its corn tortillas and beans, the urban middle class family might be consuming flour tortillas or bread with chicken, rice, and vegetables. In Central America, corn (maize) in particular is a marker of the indigenous basis of the region's cultural identity, even though not all indigenous peoples in Central America consume corn as the basis of their diet (for example, the traditional Garifuna food was cassava). For many, corn has come to symbolize indigenous. This identity is seen as more than historic or symbolic. It is also physical. To say as some Mayan and other indigenous Central Americans have, "We are people of the corn" is to claim identity, but it also means, "We have eaten so much corn as so central to our diet for so many generations that our bodies are literally made of the nutrients of corn."

Food is power in at least three ways. It provides calories and nutrition to fuel the human body and provide the power needed to function adequately in one's society. This is survival for the individual but also for the community or the society because it seems to guarantee the continuation of the basic functions of life and human reproduction. Because food is essential to human life, food itself or the means to produce or obtain food can be manipulated so as to control others or make them dependent, to gain power over them. Food can be used as a commodity, something to gain wealth, especially in a market economy. On a national or international scale, food as commodity—its value and trade in a global marketplace—can deeply affect the futures of many people. Food is also powerful when it becomes symbolic of power, for example spiritual power. Food has long been a part of religious ritual and spiritual symbol in many societies—the Passover meal of Judaism, the Communion service of Christianity, Thanksgiving, or the sharing of a meal between former enemies or new allied groups. Food has power to unite people to something spiritual or divine or simply to unite people with each other.

For all these reasons, food and the resources needed to produce and consume food—land, natural resources, tools or technology, policies, practices, and values that determine distribution—are critical to survival, freedom, community, but also to control and hegemony. The evolution of a culture of resistance and resilience has included the gradual evolution of the struggle over food and food resources—land, natural resources, and environment.

LAND CONFLICT AND FOOD INSECURITY: BEGINNINGS OF CRISIS AND RESISTANCE

In colonial Honduras and throughout the nineteenth century, land for small farming was relatively abundant but, as we have seen, by the 1950s peasants and small farmers in many parts of Honduras were experiencing a gradually shrinking arable land base. Large fruit company plantations and commercial agricultural production, commercial cotton growing, and mining and logging operations had taken over large areas of arable land or had contaminated areas making them unable to sustain small farming communities. The fertility of some areas of arable land was declining. Population increase and the in-migration of peasant farmers from land-poor El Salvador further increased pressure for land.[2] These pressures promoted the rise of peasant activism for land in the 1960s and 1970s that led to the agrarian reform law of 1974. But that law did not adequately address the land problem. Production of the basic grains consumed by the majority of the population began to decline. Between

1952 and 1986, the number of kilograms of corn produced per person declined from 140 to 107, with a similar decline in beans and other grains. The number of hectares planted in these crops also declined, even as the Honduran population increased.[3] Meanwhile, plantation-style export agriculture expanded, moving gradually from bananas to other fruits to sugar, palm oil, coffee, and other crops. Lowered production of basic grains meant a rise in the price of locally produced grains. The local price of corn (maize) increased by 107 percent and beans by 117 percent in the short period between 1972 and 1979, as economist Edmundo Valladares reported in *El Tiempo*, January 5, 1981. Food insecurity increased.

In the 1980s, an expanding U.S. military presence, along with a Contra army in southern regions of Honduras took more land. A series of environmental disasters pushed the situation further. Peasants in Yoro endured a drought that hindered corn farming and pushed many into accepting U.S. food aid, much of it in the form of wheat—substituting wheat in place of corn. Floods in 1988 in Choluteca and in 1990 in the Aguán Valley, both important agricultural areas, destroyed farms and homesteads. Increasing scarcity of arable land contributed to the differentiation of rural small farmers into a more stable and secure group of producers and a less secure and increasingly landless rural population. At the end of the 1980s, anthropologist Susan Stonich noted, "despite thirty years of economic growth, a majority of Hondurans find themselves less able now than in the mid-1960s to obtain their basic food requirements."[4] For years, Honduran economic and social analysts and some government officials had identified the evolving government policy of export expansion at the cost of local food production as a major reason for food insecurity and land conflict. Some linked it directly to widening poverty and human suffering. When Honduran Central Bank economist Edmundo Valladares was quoted in the front pages of the daily, *El Tiempo* in January 1981, the headline characterizing his statements read, "The misery financing the model of development" (*La miseria financiando el modelo de desarrollo*).

At the end of the Central American wars in 1990, the Callejas government (1990–1993) implemented a program of "structural adjustment" (known commonly as *el paquetazo*, the package) in order to obtain loans and aid from international financial institutions and to orient the country's economic and agrarian policies firmly in the direction of neoliberal development. The Agricultural Modernization Law passed in 1992 was part of the adjustment. The law reduced export taxes, increased sales taxes, eliminated agricultural credit especially for smaller farmers, and eliminated price controls on agricultural products. All of these measures favored large agricultural export enterprises at the expense of smaller producers. Even the rising prices of agricultural products did not put money into the pockets of peasants and small farmers, but meant that the urban poor ate less or found cheaper and less nutritious food substitutes. Individual property rights were promoted to replace collectively held land. "The propagation of individual property rights over land put an end to the redistributive approach of land reform and redirected state intervention to land titling and the development of a land market."[5]

With the land scarcity crisis described above, the Agricultural Modernization Law almost guaranteed an intensification of division and resistance in sectors of Honduran society throughout the 1990s. The various peasant unions were divided about the benefits and evils of the law. The UNC (National Peasant Union) preferred to see the law as a partial step forward because of its emphasis on providing land titles and land security. The union demanded that critics of the law offer acceptable alternatives for modernizing Honduran agriculture.[6] At the same time, the Catholic Church's National Commission on the Social Ministry (*Pastoral Social*) convened a workshop of clergy and experts in agrarian policy. The resulting statement endorsed by the Catholic Bishops' Conference was a strong critique of the law. The bishops said the law was dehumanizing. They expressed concern over individualizing land ownership since this threatened to divide the land among large landowners and foreign enterprises while squeezing out peasants and small farmers, and to turn land into a mere market commodity for the few instead of a source of life and community for all. The bishops said this policy would increase rural poverty and unemployment leading also to a migration of rural poor to the cities and aggravating urban problems of crime, inadequate public services, and family disintegration, as well as environmental problems in both urban and rural areas. The statement warned that the policy embodied in the law would increase the level of food dependency and insecurity for the country and especially for the poor.[7] Predictably, government officials characterized the Church's position as biased, one-sided, and even ideological—a coded way of saying "socialist."[8] Some peasant and indigenous organizations staged hunger walks and protests against the Agricultural Modernization Law during and shortly after its passage. To some extent, at least, the subsequent history of intensifying land conflict and urban and rural violence throughout the 1990s and into the next century showed the validity of the bishops' warning.

FOOD AID AS SALVATION AND DAMNATION

At the time of the Nicaraguan Revolution (1979), the United States began increasing its food aid to other countries in Central America, in part to strengthen U.S. influence in the region and to counter the influence of revolutionary Nicaragua. Foreign food aid to Honduras began to play a major role in shaping food and agricultural policy for the Honduran state. Under U.S.

Public Law 480 (PL 480), the U.S. Agency for International Development (AID) oversaw the transfer of food aid to Honduran government agencies. During the 1980s, food aid to Honduras increased annually on average, and was quite substantial by 1990. For the Honduran government and those who controlled its policies, increasing U.S. food aid could not have come at a more opportune time. The country continued to face a severe economic crisis and hunger and discontent were rising. U.S. food aid came with conditions that included Honduran adoption of an agricultural policy that almost exactly coincided with the neoliberal trend of the Callejas government. The Agricultural Modernization Law of 1992 embodied this policy. The essential outlines of this approach had been proposed a decade before in both the so-called Facussé Memorandum through APROH, and the so-called "Reaganomics for Honduras" statement of the U.S. Embassy to the Suazo Cordova government in 1981 (chapter 3).

To understand the impact of U.S. food aid on Honduran society, it is useful to trace its impact at the household and at the national level. Two-thirds of the aid by volume was in the form of wheat or wheat flour. Most of this aid was not channeled directly to households, but was routed through Honduran government agencies to private entrepreneurs and businesses who expanded their production and sale of wheat-based foods such as flour tortillas, bread, pasta, and pizza that became popular in the cities where pizza shops, bakeries, and supermarkets multiplied. Wheat obtained in this way could be sold more cheaply than locally grown corn, and it began to replace corn as a central element of daily diet in urban areas. In rural communities, the country's peasants and small farmers could not grow corn for sale on the local market at prices competitive with the low price of wheat coming from foreign food aid. Farmers who depended on sale of their corn for their income were forced out of the market, and some lost their land. The number of landless peasants and farmers continued to grow. The results of food aid on many Honduran households were a shift in diet, a weakening of a traditional way of peasant and small farm life, and a blow to personal identity that was built on being productive corn farmers with a modicum of food security.[9] All of this created or enlarged markets in Honduras for U.S. food producers, and augmented a pool of landless, unemployed people in Honduras who could form a cheap labor force in maquiladoras, plantations, and elsewhere.

Beyond the household level, U.S. food aid also influenced Honduran government policy and the state in at least three ways. First, food aid came with pressure to implement certain agricultural and land policies, in particular the promotion of private individual titles to land. This meant attempts to reverse earlier policies of promoting or allowing peasant cooperatives and indigenous or community collective lands. Before he was removed from power in the 2009 coup, President Zelaya was considering the expansion of title to peasant cooperatives in some regions of Honduras, a move that would have strengthened the government's commitment to the continuation of the principle of cooperative and collective land ownership. After the coup, Honduran and U.S. officials returned to praising the virtues of individual titles and de-emphasizing the importance of cooperative and collective land ownership.[10]

U.S. food that came to Honduras through much of the 1980s and 1990s came with pressures on the Honduran government to continue promoting agricultural export expansion and curtailing or eliminating what was considered an unproductive peasant economy. The substitution of cheap wheat for local corn in the Honduran diet helped toward this end, and specific measures such as the Agricultural Modernization Law also favored export businesses at the expense of local food production.

Finally, both U.S. and Honduran officials regarded food aid as a form of indirect economic aid. Aid was redirected to private entrepreneurs and stimulated a processed food industry in Honduras. Some aid was in the form of grains intended for animal consumption that would benefit a growing ranching and cattle sector. The Honduran government received food aid as a free gift or at low prices and could then sell aid to private business at higher prices to be made into products sold at still higher prices in middle and upper class markets in Honduran cities.

Popular resistance to these developments took several forms. After the passage of the Agricultural Modernization Law, the annual *tomas de tierras* (land takeovers) by peasant groups that normally occurred before planting time continued, to protect peasant small farming communities and to gain back some of the land taken by powerful interests, but especially to reaffirm the now-challenged concept of land as a right belonging to all the people in the spirit of the 1974 Agrarian Reform Law. Popular organizations and coalitions staged marches and demonstrations to criticize a set of government policies that made it harder for people to afford basic food items and increased hunger and food insecurity. In November 1990, ten thousand people marched in Tegucigalpa to protest the set of structural adjustment policies (*el paquetazo*) declared by the Callejas government that made it harder for people to afford to feed their families. They marched through the streets chanting, "Transparent, transparent is the hunger of our people" (*Transparente, transparente es el hambre de nuestra gente*).[11] This was before the passage of the Agricultural Modernization Law, and there was already much hunger and mounting popular protest. Although some came to see the Law as a positive response to their concerns, others denounced it as exacerbating the problem of hunger.

Some of the early resistance to these trends came in the form of critical analyses, studies, and statements. In May 1989, the Honduran Documentation Center (CEDOH) reprinted an eight-page advance summary of a study by the Inter-Hemispheric Education Resource Center based in New Mexico.

The summary was highly critical of U.S. food aid. That CEDOH published the summary in Spanish and in an inexpensive format for circulation in Honduras might itself be interpreted as a form of protest, especially in the context of CEDOH's long list of publications and reports that employed critical analysis of policies and trends in the country and the role of the United States in Honduras (see chapter 4). The Catholic bishops' critical statement on the Agricultural Modernization Law, released in August, 1992, after passage of the law was another example of the sort of protest that originated in largely middle-class educated circles. It took place on paper and in the realm of ideas and policy, although the bishops' statement claimed a certain moral authority. As the 1990s progressed, popular organizations began to protest some of the consequences of both the Agricultural Modernization Law and U.S. food aid. Marches with the themes of hunger and landlessness occurred. Protest included policy critique and street action.

In July of 2000, popular organizations held an "International Meeting of the Landless" in San Pedro Sula. Representatives from an estimated eighty-four groups from different countries in the region attended. The meeting's declaration specifically condemned the attempt to do away with even a token commitment to the principle of land reform in favor of the mechanism of the land market and the privatization of land ownership.[12] In an interview in 2003, a director of the Association for Honduran Development (ANDROH) echoed a widespread concern among popular organizations and some business and government people, as well. "The situation for the landless peasant is worsening every day in Honduras. These peasants constitute 95 percent of the peasants and farmers in the country, making the situation complicated and increasing the necessity to put the situation on the agenda."[13] Concern and protest was fueled by many incidents that seemed to illustrate how government agrarian policies of promoting export agriculture at the expense of peasants and small farmers was contributing to landlessness and hunger. One example occurred at a community called Los Limones where peasant families had lived and farmed for at least a generation on land that United Fruit Company allowed peasants to use as it was reducing its acreage of bananas in the previous decades. But when the global market demand for palm oil increased, the company wanted the land to plant African palms. In July of 2007, the company ordered the eviction of seventy-four peasant families—178 individuals, including forty-five children—members of the *Tierra Nuestra* (Our Land) Peasant Movement.[14] In such cases, the Honduran government seldom intervened to stop the evictions; rather, it frequently authorized military or police units to carry out or oversee evictions along with company agents.

FARMING, ENVIRONMENT, AND SUSTAINABILITY

As the number of landless peasants and farmers continued to increase during the 1990s and into the new century, peasant organizations and cooperatives continued to engage in *tomas de tierra* (land taking) for growing crops, protests against the seizure of peasant community and cooperative land by large landowners and companies, and attempts to call attention to widespread hunger and food insecurity. The many examples of rural peasant and indigenous people and organizations engaged in forms of direct resistance to mining and logging operations near their communities were attempts to protect natural resources of land, air, and water as the physical bases of both farming and local community life. Peasant and indigenous communities found allies among middle-class Hondurans, environmental groups, and non-governmental organizations interested in rural community development, such as the Association of Non-Governmental Organizations (ASONOG). In 2001, some of these groups joined to launch an anti-mining campaign with the slogan, "Honduras is worth more than gold."[15]

What seemed like defensive and short-term survival efforts often had another dimension. Peasant land takeovers reflected crucial short-term needs to ensure food for the present, but they also reflected a realization that peasants could not depend on government to make good on the old promises of the agrarian reform.[16] Forms of proactive resistance began to emerge that emphasized environmental and sustainable farming, appropriate agricultural technology, developing small farming and community regimes that cared for both present need and future resources, a shift in thinking about food and nutrition, and an emphasis on holistic or integral rural community development. All were elements in an emerging movement of resilience. Resistance meant building an alternative future, although it cannot be said with confidence that everyone engaged in these activities with that larger "revolutionary" objective consciously in mind beyond an immediate and personal or local need to find more practical solutions to daily problems. For some, the idea that their activities might be a form of resistance was a gradual realization.

An important element in the development of farming as resilient resistance was recognition that traditional forms of peasant and small farming in Honduras were not always ecologically sound or sustainable.[17] Sustainability is a relative term whose meaning depends in part upon the external context in which one lives and functions. In Honduras in the 1990s and after, that external context included the many threats to rural communities and the natural environment that have already been mentioned, government policies that did not favor peasants and small farmers, and an apparently constricting access to land and good natural resources. For individuals these trends could be perceived as an increasing sense of insecurity, and a loss of independence and self-reliance tied to a loss of land, resources, and community.[18] Threats to sustaining a good way of life came in the form of loss of independence and increasing dependency.

The meaning of sustainability also depends upon differing personal or internal goals and measures such as the standard of living, level of food consumption, and length of existence a peasant family regards as acceptable or desirable. These personal or family standards may be influenced by comparison to others and may change over time. Peasant and rural families may want a better life for their children in a growing national economy; or they may try to convince themselves in the face of seemingly overwhelming limitations to be satisfied with a standard not much above bare survival. Social scientists have thought that peasants tend to be wary of change and innovation. Those who feel at the edges of survival want to avoid risk, especially in the form of new technologies or social revolutions, while those who think they are doing relatively well by the status quo may be hesitant to disrupt it. Sustainability can mean that one's way of life is or can be good enough that one wants to continue it, hand it on to one's children, and take measures to strengthen, not fundamentally change it. To keep a younger generation in rural farming communities in Central America instead of migrating to cities or foreign countries means developing and sustaining a rural quality of life that is seen as desirable. One is willing to consider changing some things to preserve or sustain more important things. Such a concept of sustainability seems to be important to different forms of activism among peasants and small farmers in Honduras. The next three sections describe three examples of such activism—critique and rejection of resettlement schemes, lessening reliance on external market inputs into local farming, and promotion of a balance between short-term cultivation and long-term resource development.

CRITIQUE OF MARGINAL DISPLACEMENT AND RESETTLEMENT SCHEMES

One way in which peasant farmers and rural communities displaced by large landowners, government schemes, or natural disasters tried to sustain a way of life was to move to other locations, often on marginal lands where farming was not sustainable. Typical results were soil erosion, diminishing soil fertility, environmental degradation, and after a few years the failure of the land to sustain a family. If displaced peasants were lucky enough to find arable land with a promise of long-term agricultural sustainability and they actually cleared and prepared the land for cultivation, they were often pushed off the prepared fields by large landowners or other powerful interests. At least as early as the 1970s, some peasant groups began to criticize and reject practices of moving to "new" areas as a solution to land hunger. They were aware of the potential for environmental degradation, and they also argued that these "solutions" merely allowed government officials to avoid the responsibility of taking the land reform law seriously. Why should peasants have to settle for inferior land while large landowners and companies were allowed to appropriate even more good land? Some peasant activists seemed to prefer to fight for what they believed was theirs rather than simply move to marginal areas.[19]

There were other reasons for concern about resettlement since it had the potential of bringing different peasant and indigenous communities into conflict. An earlier example of what could happen occurred in 1988 when the Tolupán organization FETRIXY formally complained to the National Agrarian Institute that had permitted a group of non-Tolupán peasants calling themselves *Los Invencibles* (The Invincibles) to occupy one of the "best regions" of Tolupán land in Yoro (*La Prensa*, March 3, 1988). Peasants were accused of killing Tolupán in land disputes (see chapter 5). The reality and the possibility of this continued to be both an obstacle to and a motivation for the development of solidarity and the search for ways to keep people on their land in a sustainable manner that included security of possession but also appropriate farming methods and technology to sustain the land without increasing the external dependency of farming communities.

APPROPRIATE TECHNOLOGY AND SELF-RELIANT COMMUNITY

In the 1960s, building on a history of peasant studies, anthropologist Eric Wolf described what he called the peasant dilemma.[20] Increasing external demands upon a peasant or small farming family in the form of higher taxes or fees, higher rent, lower prices for crops or higher prices for input such as fertilizer, pesticides, or household needs may push cultivators into trying to get more out of their land than it can ecologically sustain. The result is decreasing soil fertility, erosion, or other conditions that undermine the long-term sustainability of the resources and the peasant household. Family labor may be increased to ensure more production, but that is not sustainable beyond very tight limits dictated by human work capacity and health. A potentially important mitigation of this dilemma is to avoid the necessity of buying commercial inputs of fertilizer or pesticide, and instead to develop alternatives that address cultivation problems without dependency upon expensive external commercial agricultural inputs that often require increasing levels of application or use in order to sustain an acceptable level of effectiveness over time.

One day in the middle of the rainy season in 2013, I accompanied a Honduran friend on a tour of some of the rural communities near where he lived in the southern Department of El Paraíso. Some of the small farm communities in this lush valley were concerned about plans to develop gold mining on the mountain ridge at the end of the valley. In other places high in the hills, we passed the remnants of older mining operations of the 1950s and crossed a couple of streams where the trickle that still ran was a dark color, water contaminated beyond use by mining fifty years earlier. Almost no one still lived in these hills. In another area, we came to peasant communities where people still farmed and life seemed to continue. My friend knew the people in one of these communities, so we stopped there and spent a few hours. At the house of a farm family, the mother proudly showed how she made the classic Central American version of laundry soap—the bar of scented soap that is rubbed on wet clothes to become lather as the clothes are rubbed and kneaded in the *pila*, the stone washboard and sink. Normally Hondurans buy such soap in shops and supermarkets if they do not buy imported detergents. This woman made laundry soap from some very simple ingredients that she obtained locally at cheap prices. She used the soap herself and sold it to her neighbors. For them, it was cheaper than the store-bought kind and available without traveling a distance. At first, this seemed to me a very simple and almost insignificant example of home economics and cottage industry.

But then we went over to the adjoining field. With a broad smile, my friend announced, "They are building a *casa malla* [mesh or screen house] here." What I saw was a plot of land the size of an American football field, entirely surrounded by a simple but apparently sturdy wooden frame, with a white cloth mesh covering the entire frame. The result was to form a tent over the field that let in sunlight, rain, and air but kept out insects and other pests, stray seeds, and other airborne contaminants. I had seen similar structures near my home town in the United States. Two men were working in the unplanted field, laying soft piping for ground drip irrigation along furrows between raised ridges running the length of the field. They stopped their sweaty labor long enough to greet us with broad smiles and explain to me the advantages of this *casa malla*. Most important, this construction eliminated the need for pesticides and most pest control measures. It also prevented other biological contaminants from invading the crops and it helped to dissuade hungry animals. The lesson emerged that this kind of technology helped to eliminate dependency on certain forms of inputs such as pesticides that otherwise had to be bought at significant price in town. The *casa* and the irrigation piping were technology that the local people could construct and control themselves, moving them a step away from dependency on the large agricultural chemical companies. The technology seemed simple, but a woman standing near the field told me that making the large mesh covering in several pieces required the labor of many people in the community over about three months. The men built the frame and prepared the field, the women laboriously sewed together the covering—a painstaking task that demanded skill and had to be done just right. So this little project brought together members of this community to make something that could lessen their dependency on the larger corporate world beyond. Cottage industry soap making was another little piece of this strategy. The price to be paid for this relative independence was long, hard work by many members of the community.

Outside help did contribute to this project. The Catholic diocese donated the land for the experiment. An international nonprofit organization contributed a small sum to obtain some of the materials. The local Catholic lay leaders (Delegates of the Word) also helped to promote the idea among other community members. But these inputs did not tie the community to a perpetual dependency on chemicals or a bank loan. People understand and appreciate this aspect, since the price of external inputs such as pesticides can be significant and commercial pesticides often create an increasing need for more inputs. Decreasing external dependency provides a kind of security and freedom and a space for further empowerment. Introduction of new ways may at first seem to divide a community but may also provide increased opportunities for working together and for taking pride in an important group accomplishment, as the beaming faces and apparent pride of the *casa* builders and the soap makers seemed to illustrate. Simple innovation implemented by local community members around potential benefits people can easily appreciate opens the possibility of improvement in the future. This is especially important in conditions where people have little margin for failure and where there is suspicion and distrust. The real benefit of this for the evolution of resistance and resilience is as much the strengthening of community as the actual material changes. Both are important.[21]

COMMUNITY DEVELOPMENT AND THE DEVELOPMENT OF COMMUNITY

In December 1999, almost ten thousand peasants and rural dwellers engaged in a *toma de carterra* (road takeover). They blocked traffic on a major highway in the northwest of Honduras near the city of Santa Barbara. They had been petitioning the local and national governments for more than a year to upgrade and repair roads leading to their communities. They were also demanding schools closer to or in their small communities and electricity and health services in the communities.[22] They were tired of being ignored by government and they wanted some of the basic institutions of functional community life. They served notice that peasants, small farmers, and rural people were not isolated and downtrodden cultivators concerned only with daily survival. They wanted the basic elements of a civilized society.

Honduran and international organizations have promoted projects in rural communities for many years. Typically these projects have addressed material needs such as providing a permanent potable water supply, building a schoolhouse, constructing latrines. Some groups, such as the Honduran Christian Commission for Development (*Comisión Cristiana de Desarrollo, CCD*) also promoted basic information and education about health, literacy, human relations, and more. The Catholic organization Caritas began an elementary education program by radio to reach rural communities where many people lacked opportunities for schooling. The deeper dimensions of community development implied the development of community—building a sense of solidarity, trust, and empowerment among community members. Over time, community solidarity and trust was recognized as one of the major defenses that rural people had against external exploitation. Creating distrust or division was a way that outsiders tried to overcome local resistance. Building trust and empowerment was important in advancing the interests of the community in the face of outside agendas. Local sustainability was always another aspect of this, but it began to emerge as a conscious idea and goal as conditions for Honduran peasants and rural communities became increasingly difficult after the 1960s as state policies seemed to favor resource extraction at the expense of environmental integrity. Sustainable community development has become a recognizable part of popular resistance in Honduras inasmuch as it sets out an alternative model for the present and the future that challenges the dominant state policies of neoliberal export oriented development. Resistance in this sense is an ongoing conflict between two quite different understandings of "development"—the one that measures development in terms of global economic goals and wealth production, the other that measures development in terms of human relationships, identity, and sufficiency.

La Unidad (pseudonym) is an example of a kind of community development that emphasizes the development of community, combining material improvements with strengthening social relationships.[23] La Unidad began as one of more than forty workers' compounds scattered across a vast United Fruit plantation. The workers' compounds included rows of very simple housing, often barracks, a raised water tank, a large garage or storeroom for company machinery and equipment, and sometimes a small store owned by the company. Children of workers might attend a small elementary school somewhere on or near the plantation. A health clinic was located at or near a central compound elsewhere on the plantation that included the plantation or company office, more garages and storehouses, and nicer housing for management staff. There might be a soccer field. Some plantations also had small dirt or paved runways for small company planes. Most of the plantation workers living in the compounds were landless peasants from the countryside, others had too little land to sustain their families and so they took additional work on the plantation. Some had been members of peasant cooperatives or unions.

When United Fruit began to transfer much of its banana production from Honduras to South America, the company entered into agreements to lease or sell a few of the compounds and surrounding lands to the workers. La Unidad was one of these. Today some former compounds are sizeable *pueblos* with different kinds of housing—traditional *campesino* adobe or mud houses, small modest cement or brick houses, and a few large more imposing houses. Shops and stores have appeared. The roads in some places have been widened, but they are still of dirt that is dust in the dry season and mud in rainy times. Over the years since the 1970s, La Unidad has gained ownership of its lands and has expanded into what is now almost a small town of more than 1700 residents. There is now an elementary school, a community center, a health clinic, and at least two churches—Catholic and Pentecostal. The construction quality of housing varies from sturdy and colorful adobe, brick and tile, to simple wooden framed structures needing paint. The people of La Unidad have organized their community into ten or more neighborhoods (they call them *barrios*) and people seem very clear about the boundary markers between barrios—this street, that side of the river, the blocks behind the Catholic church. Barrios have names—Santa Tecla, San Antonio, La Cuenca—and people seem to feel it important for their barrios to maintain a sense of identity. Each barrio chooses a barrio leader, and the whole pueblo seems to be governed by a mayor and a council of barrio leaders. The people work in various employments in local shops, transportation, machine mechanics, or on the African palm plantations nearby that have partially replaced bananas.

In 2008, some La Unidad barrio leaders invited staff members of ERIC's Social Promotion section to help them develop and finance plans to meet long-term community needs. ERIC saw this as an opportunity to assist the community's willing leaders in establishing a process of community participation, decision-making, and implementation that Unidad could continue to adapt and use after ERIC withdrew—a sustainable process. The process was slow because it depended upon the timetable and decision-making of the community and their process of arriving at shared priorities. The process ERIC proposed broadly reflected and adapted the model of social activism that included reflection or analysis of the situation, gathering and assessing information, and communicating the findings that would permit decisions about what was to be done, what projects undertaken. Then followed the next round of reflection on the previous experience, and so on.

By 2013, La Unidad had completed several successful projects to improve some bridges and the community's water supply. An ERIC staff member had worked with barrio leaders for many months on a new round of reflection and information gathering. Barrio leaders and other community members had conducted a community survey in the different barrios. The ERIC staff member returned once more to La Unidad in late August of 2013 to present the barrio leaders with a document that would outline some long-range plans for the future of the community. The idea to develop this plan had already been approved by the leaders, but now came the hard work of gathering more information, reflecting on needs, and outlining priorities. Barrio leaders at this meeting mentioned a few needs that people often expressed, in particular security concerns when traveling on the roads to and from the community. There was gang activity in the area, and while La Unidad had managed to keep most of it out of the pueblo, there were concerns about travel along the roads beyond. Two related concerns were general improvement of the roads, and more work in protecting some barrios near the river from flooding during the rainy season. A few comments expressed concern about keeping La Unidad's youth out of gang activity, but that discussion was relegated to another time. Before the meeting ended, the ERIC staffer repeated the list of criteria for projects, a list that the community leaders had helped develop. Any project should:

- benefit many people, at least an entire barrio, not just a few individuals,
- be able to be completed in manageable pieces that can be accomplished in a day or a few days so as to promote a sense of immediate accomplishment,
- be able to be financially supported by a variety of external donors, not government,
- contribute in recognizable ways to a long term vision or strategy of development for the entire community.

This example of community development in La Unidad illustrates some important points about community development as a form of resistance to external control and exploitation, and about that much maligned word, empowerment. La Unidad still sees a need to rely on external sources of funding for some of its larger projects. The community first went through the slow and often difficult process of developing community priorities first and funding afterward. They insisted on broad community agreement, although perfect consensus seemed impossible. Some of the leaders, at least, recognized the need to balance present needs with future visions. Every project had to relate somehow to such a larger vision. The community faced pressures from local and national politicians and officials who tried to exercise control over community development projects in at least four ways—influencing community members against ERIC or its staff, trying to change community proposals, placing legal requirements or restrictions on proposals to make implementation more difficult, or simply claiming credit themselves for successful projects. Community development projects in Honduras have experienced all of these kinds of interventions, making them fields of struggle and sites of resistance.[24]

MILPA Y CAOBA: INTEGRATING PRESENT AND FUTURE

Because most peasants and small farmers face the ongoing challenge of providing enough food and surplus each year to feed their own families and to meet their obligations such as taxes, replacement of tools, household needs, and rents, they may be tempted or forced to devote all of their resources to yearly survival. The insecurity of both food supply and land tenure in a country of agrarian conflict only adds to the urgency of the present. Sometimes, small farmers in Central American countries try to increase their income by channeling limited resources into the production of the latest export crop fad. The region has experienced historic boom and bust cycles in which everyone plants an export crop such as coffee that is in high demand today but loses its high price in the world market tomorrow, driving both large and small producers toward economic ruin. Those especially who have no long-term resources are at the mercy of external forces.[25]

The August 2013, edition of the newspaper *aMecate Corto* carried a small article with the title, "Milpa y Caoba."[26] *Milpa* has several meanings in Spanish. In a narrow sense, it denotes a field where a peasant farmer plants corn. More broadly, *milpa* is used to signify the resources and farming done to sustain a peasant family for the present and the immediate future. *Caoba* can signify the mahogany tree or its wood or a grove of mahogany trees. Although mahogany was extensively logged and exported in the past as a precious wood, its characteristics make it a symbol of great value, durability, and resistance (to pests, rot, etc.). The article stressed the need for a balance between working to meet present and short-term need (*milpa*) and cultivating long-term valuable and durable resources for the future (*caoba*) as a measure of resistance to the vagaries of day-to-day survival. This exhortation was in fact exemplified by Tolupán communities in Yoro that actively resisted and blocked the efforts of large landowners and logging enterprises that wanted access to some of the remaining extensive stands of mahogany in the mountains (see chapter 5). Resistance in this community and others like it seemed to be animated by a realization that the threat to the mahogany represented a threat to the life and future of the community itself. The threat was not only the loss of the mahogany. It was also the economic model of short term gain exemplified by cutting down and turning great and ancient trees into lumber for export for the profit of powerful interests that may undermine the sustainability of the local community. Peasants have sometimes been portrayed as fatalistic.[27] This and other examples of how such communities try to protect their long-term resources belie some of that characterization.

The "Milpa y Caoba" article went on to apply the lesson to popular organizations and popular resistance movements in general, that it is important to avoid becoming so engaged in the immediate struggle that the larger context and the future goal is obscured, or that action is not supported by analysis and reflection. It is also essential to avoid developing long-range strategies and analyses without connection to the everyday, immediate struggle. This counsel reflected a model of praxis that is consciously engaged by some Honduran organizations and the editors of *aMecate Corto*, and is summarized in the words, *reflect, act, and communicate*.

PROMOTING NATURAL FOODS, TRANSFORMING WAYS OF THINKING

By at least the time of the 2009 coup d'état, it had become clear to some Hondurans that the state policies of promoting export agriculture, reducing or eliminating peasant food production, inviting foreign food aid, and supporting the expansion of a national processed food industry posed certain threats to Hondurans at several levels, including physical health, self-reliance, and even identity and sense of place. I learned about this (to me) surprising aspect of popular resistance in Honduras while interviewing members of popular organizations, rural peasants, musicians, and religious leaders, and by observing how they provided their daily diets and cuisine. What follows is some of what I learned.[28] Some people borrowed inspiration and moral support from the natural foods movement in the United States and Europe. This movement promoted the development of a consumer market for food that was locally produced, organic or without large chemical inputs, and environmentally friendly. Activists said that this had the potential for empowerment in several ways. Natural foods give nutrition, strength, and health, and a sense of wellbeing to the body, in contrast to artificial foods that contribute nothing or are even harmful to health. Natural foods empower the body. They also imply self-reliance, since they are largely produced and consumed closer to home and local community without reliance on outside corporations or distributors. Their price may sometimes be higher, but the producers and distributors tend to be part of the local community, and may be known to the consumer, so flexibility in pricing is possible, reflecting community relationships. The money returns to the local community. Natural foods imply a rejection or a sense of control over the penetration of external economic and cultural forces (wheat bread, Coca Cola) into the local community and the nation. They imply a critique of corporate power. Finally, natural foods depend on an understanding and close connection to place, land and a more intimate relationship with the natural environment. This is sometimes understood or experienced as a sense of identity, security, and belonging, thus empowerment.

In Honduras, all of these considerations are especially relevant to challenging the power of an economic elite. For example, a large food corporation owned by one of the leading landowners and entrepreneurs in the country produced a variety of processed foods and snacks, soaps and oils for the national and the international market, including palm oil that was also exported and widely used as an ingredient in processed foods. The owner and the corporation faced various accusations that they were responsible over two decades for the violent evictions of peasant communities and the seizing of community land in an effort to expand palm oil production. Promoting natural foods was a way of withdrawing customer support for the processed food market, its owners, and some of the violence and injustice that seemed to support it.

CONCLUSION

The natural foods strand of resistance was not so much a stand-alone campaign as a motif in the larger resistance efforts, and it appeared appropriate in the context of other struggles. As one labor union activist commented in a conversation about natural foods, "Transformation is most of all about changing people's ways of thinking, and that takes time." He described some of the difficulties in trying to get people, especially in the cities, to rely on natural and local rather than processed supermarket foods. State policies favor export crops over locally grown food crops. Even if small farmers managed to produce food crops for the internal market in major towns and cities, getting the crops to markets was often beyond the means of the farmers without the use of middlemen. Urban people had no land and often no garden spaces. Natural foods could be more expensive than processed or even imported foods in the markets. Customers were concerned with price and convenience. Perhaps most powerful and subtle of all the obstacles was the acculturation of Hondurans to supermarkets with processed and imported products that symbolized convenience, modernity, and status. Changing people's ways of thinking about food became the subject of songs and other expressions of popular culture and popular education. Changing the policies and agrarian structures that hindered production and marketing of natural foods was tied to the development of local self-reliance and a thriving rural small farming sector. All of these aspects of daily subsistence served in different ways to advance a sense of empowerment and to lessen a sense of dependency upon larger economic forces beyond the control of local communities.

Chapter 6

NOTES

1. See, for example, Sidney W. Mintz, *Sweetness and Power: The Place of Sugar in Modern History* (New York: Viking Penguin, 1985) and *Tasting Food, Tasting Freedom: Excursions into Eating, Culture, and the Past* (Boston: Beacon Press, 1996). Also Sidney W. Mintz and Christine M. DuBois, "The Anthropology of Food and Eating," *Annual Review of Anthropology* 31 (2002): 99–117.

2. Tim Merrill, *Honduras: A Country Study* (Washington, DC: Government Printing Office for Library of Congress, 1995). Steven Volk, "Land Pressures Lead to War between Honduras and El Salvador," *NACLA Report on the Americas* 15:6 (December, 1981): 20–22, reprinted in *Honduras: Portrait of a Captive Nation,* eds. Nancy Peckenham and Annie Street (New York: Praeger Publishing, 1985), 148–51.

3. Susan Stonich, "The Political Economy of Environmental Destruction: Food Security in Southern Honduras," in *Harvest of Want: Hunger and Food Security in Central America and Mexico*, eds. Scott Whiteford and Anne E. Ferguson (Boulder, CO: Westview Press, 1991), 52.

4. Stonich, 43.

5. Kees Jansen, "Structural Adjustment, Peasant Differentiation, and the Environment in Central America," in *Disappearing Peasantries? Rural Labour in Africa, Asia, and Latin America,* eds. Deborah Bryceson, Cristóbal Kay, and Jos Mooij (London: Intermediate Technology Publications, 2000), 194.

6. *El Heraldo*, 26 August, 1992: 43.

7. Conferencia Episcopal de Honduras (Honduran Catholic Bishops' Conference), "A la opinión pública nacional," unpublished official copy.

8. *El Heraldo*, August 26, 1992: 43; *La Prensa*, 26 August, 1992: 41.

9. Much of this analysis is contained in, Centro de Documentación de Honduras (CEDOH), "La ayuda alimentaria estadounidiense en Honduras," *CEDOH Boletín, Numero Especial 41* (May 1989). Here CEDOH reprints part of an advance copy of a study by the Inter-Hemispheric Education Resource Center (Albuquerque, NM: IERC, 1990).

10. For a detailed discussion of Honduran government land policy to 2003 see the report by Richard T. Nelson, "Honduras Country Brief: Property Rights and Land Markets," (Madison, WI: Land Tenure Center, University of Wisconsin (June 2003).

11. Comité para la Defensa de los Derechos Humanos en Honduras CODEH, *Boletín* 70 (November 1990): 7.

12. Intercontinental Cry, "Declaration of the International Meeting of the Landless in San Pedro Sula, July 24–26, 2000," retrieved from Intercontinental Cry website, July 14, 2007, intercotinentalcry.org.

13. Intercontinental Cry, "Declaration of the International Meeting of the Landless in San Pedro Sula, July 24–26, 2000," retrieved from Intercontinental Cry website, July 14, 2007, intercotinentalcry.org.

14. Intercontinental Cry, "Declaration of the International Meeting of the Landless in San Pedro Sula, July 24–26, 2000," retrieved from Intercontinental Cry website, July 14, 2007, intercotinentalcry.org.

15. Michael Marsh, "Honduras Is Worth More than Gold," (Tegucigalpa: Asociación de Organismos No Gobernamentales ASONOG, retrieved from asonog@hondudata.com, 2002.

16. See Douglas Kincaid, "We Are the Agrarian Reform: Rural Politics and Agrarian Reform," in Nancy Peckenham and Annie Street eds., *Honduras: Portrait of a Captive Nation* (New York: Praeger Publishers, 1985), 135–147. Kincaid outlines the evolving sense of criticism among peasant groups toward the failure of the Agrarian Reform Law and government to fully implement the promise of the reform, and the realization that peasants must do it themselves and compel the government into action.

17. James Phillips, "Resource Access, Environmental Struggles, and Human Rights in Honduras," in Barbara Rose Johnston ed., *Life and Death Matters: Human Rights, Environment, and Social Justice,* Second edition (Walnut Creek, CA: Left Coast Press, 2011), 210–211. Jorge Arevalo Cárcamo (Honduran daily, *El Tiempo*, September 7, 1988) detailed some of the conditions that forced peasants to practice unsustainable farming methods. A more recent treatment of this in the context of national land policy and agrarian economy is found in

Richard T. Nelson, "Honduras Country Brief: Property Rights and Land Markets" (Madison WI: Land Tenure Center, University of Wisconsin, June, 2003).

18. Phillips, "Resource Access, Environmental Struggles, and Human Rights in Honduras," 210.

19. Elvia Alvarado, *Don't Be Afraid, Gringo: A Honduran Woman Speaks from the Heart* (San Francisco: Institute for Food and Development Policy, 1987; reprint, New York: Harper Perennial, 1987). Alvarado expresses this attitude of some Honduran peasant groups to insist that government officials meet the obligations of the 1974 Agrarian Reform Law to redistribute portions of large unused agricultural properties and to return lands "stolen" from peasant communities by large landowners instead of making peasants move to marginal lands. This attitude remained strong after the 2009 coup, for example, in the activities of the CNTC (National Confederation of Rural Workers) and other groups in the northern areas of Honduras. Also Phillips, "Resource Access," 213.

20. Eric R. Wolf, *Peasants* (Englewood Cliffs, NJ: Prentice-Hall, 1966).

21. For discussion of issues involved in such development see for example, Tom Greaves, Ralph Bolton, and Florencia Zapata, eds., *Vicos and Beyond: A Half-Century of Applying Anthropology in Peru* (Lanham, MD: Altamira Press, 2011).

22. From the author's notes, December, 1999.

23. Information about Unidad community is based on interviews with staff members of the Equipo de Reflexión, Investigación, y Communicación (ERIC) in El Progreso, and field visits to the community.

24. Similar interference by politicians into local community institutions is described by Jordan Levy, *The Politics of Honduran School Teachers: State Agents Challenge the State* (University of Western Ontario Electronic Thesis and Dissertation Repository. Paper 2142 (2014), http://ir.lib.uwo.ca/edt/2142. Levy describes how Honduran school teachers try to minimize the influence and control of politicians over local schools, funding, work accountability, and curriculum. Local big business leaders may also become involved. The dynamic of minimizing this influence is integral to trust and lessening conflict within the local community.

25. An example of this phenomenon is discussed in T. Christian Miller and Davan Majaraj, "Coffee's Bitter Harvest," *Los Angeles Times* (October 5, 2002). Scholars such as Peter Rosset have been analyzing the effects of agricultural commodity boom and bust cycles in Latin America for many years—for example, Peter Rosset, "Food Security and the Contemporary Food Crisis," *Development* 51:4 (December, 2008): 460–63.

26. *A Mecate Corto* ("by a short rope") is published monthly in Honduras by the Jesuit organizations Radio Progreso and ERIC (Reflection, Investigation, and Communication Team) in El Progreso.

27. An extreme example is the depiction of a Zapotec peasant community in Oaxaca, Mexico, depicted by Michael Kearney, *The Winds of Ixtepeji: World View and Society in a Zapotec Town* (New York: Holt, Rinehart, Winston, 1972; reissued in 1986 by Waveland Press).

28. Information and analysis in this section are based on interviews with members of popular organizations, artists and musicians, and religious leaders and their families, and personal observation of daily life among some of these informants, especially in the Departments of Yoro and El Paraíso in 2013. While their perspective may be shared by many other Hondurans, it is likely that the majority of those involved in popular resistance do not engage in the same "natural" food practices, nor even share a consciously developed analysis of food as resistance.

Chapter Seven

The Legal Order

Challenging Judicial and Political Systems

On February 14, 2012, a massive fire killed 361 inmates and a visitor (a pregnant woman) at the general prison in Comayagua, Honduras. Many of the inmates who died had been in the prison for months or years awaiting trial when they perished. As news of the fire went international, rumors spread in Honduras that the prisoners had been locked down during the fire, and that the prison guards or the police did not allow the fire brigade into the prison until it was too late to save most of the inmates. Six months later, on August 14, several hundred family members and friends of the victims led a candlelight procession from the center of Comayagua to the prison gates where they held a vigil with photos and recollections of the victims. Family members of those who died in the fire gave short, emotional speeches demanding official accountability. People punctuated the procession and the vigil with chants of *"Justicia!"*[1]

Many Hondurans seem to have little faith in the integrity of the country's penal and judicial systems. In the opinion of some lawyers and judges the penal system is corrupt, while the judicial system has nearly collapsed at the local level and has lost its political independence at the national level.[2] These systems are widely seen as being at the service of the powerful to be used to stifle popular protest and resistance. Without fair and functional penal and judicial systems, popular resistance becomes much more difficult and dangerous, but it may seem all the more necessary. In chapter 3 we saw how the legal and judicial systems are manipulated through criminalizing acts of legal protest and resistance, blaming the victims, delaying justice, ignoring laws, threatening and eliminating judges and lawyers, promoting impunity, and corruption of judicial and political functionaries. This chapter examines some of the ways in which Hondurans engage in efforts to transform the administration of justice into something they believe will be more just and equitable. Hondurans are also concerned about a re-founding or remaking (*refundación*) of the constitutional order and the political system to make them more open to broader democratic participation and less easily controlled by a few. This is seen as a bulwark against further corruption of the legal and judicial systems and a way of reducing conflict in Honduran society.

DEFENDING THE ACCUSED

In Honduras, accusations of criminal behavior have become a standard way to discredit and weaken individuals and popular organizations that challenge or resist the policy and practice of the powerful. When leaders or members of popular organizations are accused of crimes or detained for nonviolent protest or resistance, other organizations often mobilize their members and alert international solidarity and human rights groups. A public statement or press release may be disseminated to denounce the accusations or detentions. If hearings or trials are held in the case of the accused, organizations often form rallies or vigils around the courthouse at the same time. These can become quite loud with fiery speeches and popular chants to be heard inside the courthouse. The rally of support held at the August 2013 hearing of COPINH leader Berta Cáceres was an example (described in chapter 5).

Another example of this sort of popular defense involved the case of Magdalena Morales, Regional Secretary of the National Confederation of Farm Workers (CNTC) who was arrested in July 2013, in El Progreso. Morales was a leader in a campaign that included CNTC members and members of ADCP (Association for Campesino Development of El Progreso) who had engaged in an occupation of land claimed by the sugar company AZUNOSA. The land issues involved in this case are worth describing briefly as an illustration of the complex politics of land conflict in Honduras. The government National Agrarian Institute (INA) had ruled that AZUNOSA was occupying far more than the 250 hectares allowed by Honduran law, and had been illegally operating on the land for more than twenty years. INA ordered the expropriation of over three thousand hectares of the land claimed by AZUNOSA, and allotted ten million dollars in compensation to AZUNOSA. INA set aside the expropriated land for landless peasant families to live on and grow crops. AZUNOSA, owned by the British multinational company SAB Miller, refused to relinquish the land, and warned that Honduras would have to answer to the European Union for violating an investment protection covenant between Honduras and Britain. Near the end of 2012, the Honduran government annulled INA's expropriation and confirmed AZUNOSA's claim. Honduran peasant groups claimed that the investment protection covenant had expired in 2005, and they appealed. The case went to the Honduran Supreme Court. In this context, peasant organizations did what they had done for years in many similar situations—they tried to be proactive in their claim to the land by occupying it ("we are the agrarian reform"). During months of working on the land, as many as 1,600 peasant families had built simple houses and grown crops of corn, squash, beans, yucca, and plantains, according to one informant. On June 10, 2013, soldiers, police, and company security guards arrived and began evicting the peasants. According to informants, company guards also destroyed hundreds of acres of crops and the houses that peasants had built.[3]

On July 26, Morales was at a meeting of CNTC leaders in El Progeso when a truckload of police arrived and arrested her. By some accounts, an AZUNOSA employee was driving the truck. Morales was charged with usurpation—illegally taking and using what belongs to others—and a preliminary hearing was set for the next day. A second hearing was set for the morning of August 22 at the municipal courthouse in El Progreso. On that morning a crowd of about one hundred people gathered in front of the courthouse. Representatives of popular and professional organizations delivered short speeches. CNTC and ADCP members emphasized the need for actively defending their right to land and the agrarian reform, and they denounced the government's apparent criminalization of peasants and agricultural workers. Members of women's organizations declared that the government and the powerful were especially targeting important women leaders of popular organizations, including Cáceres, Morales, and Berta Oliva, director of the human rights organization COFADEH. Morales's lawyer emerged from the hearing long enough to report the status of the legal case against his client, and to emphasize that he and other lawyers who defended popular resistance leaders would continue to do so. Morales herself did not appear, raising speculation that the authorities did not want her appearance to heighten the zeal of the demonstrators.[4]

Sometimes authorities accuse activists of various kinds of criminal charges that may seem unlikely, illogical, or even absurd, such as charging indigenous activists with trespassing on lands they have claimed for generations (chapter 5). Defending against such charges includes pointing out the illogic of the accusations, pointing out that people had engaged in the same activities for generations without incurring criminal charges, or constructing a counter identity that challenged the accusations. Thus, peasants engaged in occupying land were not criminal trespassers but were merely putting into practice the intent of the Agrarian Reform Law and helping INA, the National Agrarian Institute to do its work. In some cases, peasant organizers and leaders could point out that INA had already granted them collective title to the land they were occupying. Lenca activists portrayed themselves as defending the land they held legally under treaties and agreements with previous governments for generations, and protecting the country's natural resources against foreign exploitation. Far from being law-breakers, these people cast themselves as law upholders in the face of authorities and foreign companies who ignored the law. The more the authorities accused the popular activists, the more the activists cast the authorities as the real law violators. The popular resistance found ways to turn the myth of law enforcement into the "most damning critique" of the accusers. In these cases, the underlying conflict goes beyond the incident at hand and concerns a struggle to establish a positive collective identity that contradicts the negative.[5]

Sometimes the level of violence used in the arrest of an accused person seemed far beyond the nature of the accusation. On October 13, 2013, Luis Galdamez, a journalist for Radio Globo (known for its investigative reporting) was stopped by two policemen who dragged him from his car, beat him severely, and tried to force him into a police vehicle, allegedly for a minor traffic violation. Passersby intervened to stop this. Galdamez was also a LIBRE Party (*Partido de Liberación y Refundación*) candidate for Congress. He said he had received death threats during his regular Radio Globo program *Tras la Verdad* (Behind the Truth). He and his family were supposed to be protected by the general precautionary measures mandated by the Inter-American Commission on Human Rights, obliging the Honduran government to provide protection. In this case, other journalists and human rights organizations publicized and denounced the incident, pointing out that such a brutal police response was an example of harassment of an honest journalist and member of the political opposition.[6]

DEFENDING THE DEFENDERS

Antonio Trejo Cabrera was the lead lawyer in a lawsuit brought by the peasant organization MARCA, representing some peasant communities in the Bajo Aguán region of northern Honduras. MARCA claimed that the peasants had a legal right to certain lands. In a rare victory for the peasants, the court upheld MARCA's claim and awarded ownership to the peasant group. Trejo was also the pastor of an evangelical church. On the evening of September 22, 2012, a few weeks after the MARCA legal victory, Trejo presided at a wedding in his church. After the wedding, he went outside to the parking lot to retrieve the wedding documents from his car (some accounts say he received a call on his cell phone and went out to his car).[7] There he was shot multiple times and died. On July 23, 2013, municipal judge Mireya Mendoza Peña was shot and killed by two gunmen on a motorcycle while driving her car at noon in downtown El Progreso. She had a reputation for integrity, and was thought to be about to pronounce a stiff prison sentence in the case of a convicted gang member. One shooter was apprehended, but the motorcycle driver and the "intellectual author" of the crime (popularly thought to be the powerful gang leader) were not identified or charged.[8] Both of these killings were publicly denounced by both Honduran and a variety of international organizations, including among others the Council on Hemispheric Affairs, the Washington Office on Latin America, Lawyers for Lawyers, the Law Society of Upper Canada, the Inter-American Commission for Human Rights (an agency of the Organization of American States), and even the U.S. State Department. Such international attention is among the weapons used to call the Honduran legal system to account.

Lawyers who defended activists, and judges with reputations for integrity became targets of threats and assassinations. The Honduran National Human Rights Commission (CONADEH, a government agency) reported that seventy-two lawyers were killed in the four years of the Lobo presidency (2010–2013). In addition, the behavior of the country's Supreme Court, especially its Constitutional Chamber (*Sala Constitucional*) and its top legal authorities during and after the 2009 coup undermined their legitimacy among many Hondurans, and contributed to a sense that any semblance of "justice" in the justice system was in grave danger.[9] The defenders of justice found some limited protection in organizing or being part of organizations that could command public awareness. The Broad Movement for Democracy and Justice (*Movimiento Amplio por la Democracia y Justicia,* MADJ) and the Association of Judges for Democracy (*Asociación de Jueces por la Democracia,* AJD) provided some support for lawyers and judges. AJD included judges who had been dismissed or removed from office because of their opposition to what they considered the illegal and unconstitutional nature of the 2009 coup, as well as others who publicly opposed government practices that seemed designed to weaken the country's judicial system.

The administration of justice in Honduras, however, and the attacks against it did not follow a simple pattern. The protection of lawyers and judges, and the ways in which courts resisted or succumbed to bribery or threat were shaped in part by local political and social conditions. Local courts in some areas were relatively free of control by local landowners or other powerful interests, while in other areas this was not so. Courts at a regional or national level could overturn local court decisions that favored peasants or popular activists, or they could impose constraints on the lower court decisions so as to render them useless.[10] It was clear to some Hondurans that partial legal victories were important but never secure without also addressing the impunity and corruption that seemed to infect the entire society.

Chapter 7
CHALLENGING IMPUNITY

One of the most frequent and ongoing demands and objectives of popular resistance in Honduras is the elimination of a "culture of impunity." Impunity, understood as the unaccountable abuse of authority and force by a powerful elite, is a linchpin of the whole system of repressive control. Increasingly, the culture of impunity also raises for some Hondurans the fear of a society in which, sooner or later, random violence will grow out of the control even of the powerful who might have been using violence for their own ends—leading to pervasive and random violence as the new normal. In Honduras, the ideology that supports impunity incorporates two fundamental beliefs or illusions—liberal oligarchy is the normal and natural order of Honduran society, and the doctrine of national security is in the best interest of all citizens of the state. The ideology of liberal oligarchy accords primacy of control and management of society to a few who are entitled to use whatever means necessary to maintain their control and to "manage" the state (see chapter 2). The doctrine of national security posits the survival and welfare of the state or nation as the highest priority and permits, even requires, the managers of the state and especially the security forces to do whatever is necessary to guarantee the survival of the state or nation. National security ideology can make this imperative a replacement for the demands of ordinary morality, and can justify the use of force and violence to attain certain ends.[11] Such a justification replaces the ideal of the rule of law with the rule of the strong. Violence becomes the normal resource of the state and those who control the state. There are at least three broad strategies to challenge this—with counter violence that may itself become corrupt, with nonviolent resistance that demands considerable risk and sacrifice, and by ending the monopoly of control over the state and government exercised by the few, replacing it with a broader popular participation. This last seems to challenge one of the major historical characteristics of the Honduran political system, but the National Popular Resistance Front (*Frente Nacional de Resistencia Popular*, FNRP) and the Liberty and Re-foundation Party (*Partido de Libertad y Refundación*, LIBRE) made this democratic transformation one of their major objectives, as we shall see.

Impunity cannot be fully understood in the abstract. It is felt through its effects in people's lives—how does the free rein of the powerful threaten ordinary people's lives? Popular challenges to impunity link the practice of impunity to the daily violence, killings, community displacements, land conflicts, disappearances, and crime that people in both urban and rural areas experience. Hondurans have developed various practical ways to challenge impunity, through demanding legal accountability in individual cases, promoting popular education about impunity and rights, engaging in "memory work," and conducting vigils that are partly forms of public protest. Impunity can be challenged from within the judicial system or by extrajudicial means such as popular protests or Truth Commissions.

Organizations and individuals demand accountability from officials. Human rights organizations such as CODEH and COFADEH and popular organizations such as labor and peasant unions regularly issue public denunciations of killings along with demands for prompt and thorough investigations and, as for example in the assassinations of Antonio Trejo and Mireya Mendoza, discussed above. COFADEH, MADJ, and some other human rights groups also work with legal teams or individual lawyers to defend accused individuals or to present legal complaints and lawsuits. Demands for accountability were usually directed at the police, the military, or government officials. The 2012 killing of Ebed Yanes (described at the start of chapter 1) was followed by what seemed a cover-up by military officers in charge of the unit that killed Yanes. The boy's father was a businessman with professional training and was determined to find justice in his son's death. At some risk to himself, he gathered some information and gained support from COFADEH to build a case that began to receive some recognition and did bring to light what seemed to be the military cover-up. People of humbler background and fewer resources may not have even these small victories. Such victories were relatively rare, and legal action faced enormous obstacles in a context where victims, their families, witnesses, lawyers, and judges were all afraid and corruption seemed widespread. So popular protests and public demands were directed against impunity and for accountability, as in the vigil and the cries for "justice" after the 2012 Comayagua prison fire. There was some safety in numbers in these mass public demonstrations, and they could bring wider attention to a societal problem in a way that individual legal cases might not.

Impunity is also challenged through popular education. Many of the workshops conducted by popular organizations provide some basic information about impunity as part of a larger discussion of basic rights. Early in 2013, Radio Progreso and ERIC published a fifty-two-page booklet with text and cartoon illustrations entitled, *Impunity: Law of the Strong that Crushes the Victims (Impunidad: la ley de los fuertes que aplasta a las victimas)*. Despite the intense title, the text, in question and answer format, is strewn with colorful cartoons that drive home their message in a lighter medium.[12] Impunity is also highlighted in articles in non-mainstream newspapers and periodicals such as *aMecate Corto, Vida Laboral*, and others that reach a relatively small readership.

In Honduras, "memory work" is a particularly expressive and powerful way of challenging impunity. Conversely, erasure of memory is one of the most powerful defenses of impunity, as we saw in chapter 3. Memory work challenges impunity by constructing or strengthening a sense of community with a shared reality, a connection to past generations, and a common purpose.[13] Humans engage individual and collective memory in histories, folklore, and mythology to construct or negotiate group identity, for adaptive survival, and in conflicts that arise around social change. People speak of "bitter memories" that help to perpetuate cycles of retributive violence that serve the interests of various actors. Memory is conjured to portray a people as victims, or as people who try to claim the moral high ground and sometimes legal and other rights. Memories should also be understood as "weapons of the weak." They are ways of tapping the power of past struggles and victories or as forms of resistance to the "official story."[14]

Popular organizations especially practice memory as an almost sacred duty. They often begin their conferences or workshops with an entrance ceremony that features remembering their dead or disappeared members. One large gathering of several popular organizations in the Department of Valle in 2011 began with members forming a large circle along the walls of the meeting hall. Members called out the names of assassinated or disappeared members as family or friends carried lighted candles and photos of the victims into the hall. When a name was called, the assembly shouted, "*Presente!*" The strengths and virtues of each named victim were recounted briefly, along with a few words about how they were killed or disappeared. People responded with calls for justice or a shout of, "Who is responsible?" In this and other gatherings, popular organizations often referred to their assassinated members as "our martyrs." as if the act of collective remembrance takes on an almost sacred aura reminiscent of the Christian concept of the "communion of saints." The strength of this kind of remembrance lies especially in its emphasis on making the name, face, and strength of the individual and the nature of the violence against the person a part of the collective memory of the group, and in grounding memory in the actual lived experience of those who knew the victim as a live human being and part of their community. It also lends an almost sacred aura to the sacrifice that the individual made in the struggle. Such collective remembering challenges the tendency of impunity to justify itself by isolating individuals, defining political repression as combating criminal activity, and creating "false" memories and accounts not grounded in actual lived experience. In response, popular memory constructs or strengthens an awareness of community that transcends both time and individual grief and provides a power to challenge oppression and impunity.

In the judicial context, impunity rests also upon the use of force and corruption. Corruption can mean the bribing of officials. Judges and prosecutors are bribed to ensure that they do not prosecute or sentence powerful individuals. If bribery does not work, threats are employed. Some Honduran public prosecutors (*fiscales*) and judges have focused specifically on the dangerous work of exposing and trying to prosecute corruption and corrupt officials.[15]

APPEALS TO HONDURAN AND INTERNATIONAL LAW

Hondurans keep trying to make their leaders and institutions obey the country's laws. This involves a complex logic because not all laws are seen as beneficial to the majority of people. We have seen how peasant organizations engaged in land takeovers and other actions to ensure that the 1974 Agrarian Reform Law was implemented. Rather than passively wait for the National Agrarian Institute to implement the law, the people do it themselves, thereby also "encouraging" INA to do its duty. One of the purposes of many popular protests and demonstrations is to denounce instances in which government officials and security forces ignore the country's laws or fail to apply the laws equally to all citizens, allowing the powerful to operate "above the law." It may be a testament to the resilience of the Honduran people that despite the skepticism of many years of official illegality, people continued to call their leaders to account to obey and enforce laws (see end of chapter 4). The 2013 Mining Law presented a more complicated situation. Rural communities, peasant organizations, and indigenous groups invoked that part of the Law that mandates consultation with the local community and its full, free, and informed consent before a mining project can begin. This provision was especially invoked in those too-frequent cases when companies and government officials seemed to be ignoring it.[16] But the same communities did not always appreciate other provisions of the Mining Law that threatened harm to their interests, such as the end of the moratorium on issuing new mining concessions, granting priority water rights to mining companies instead of local communities, and permitting what may be environmentally destructive practices. In dealing with complex laws, resistance often consisted in demanding that some parts be honored and observed and other parts be repealed.

The frequent failure of officials to enforce laws or to enforce them equitably meant that organizations sometimes turned to international law and international covenants and declarations for support. Honduras is a member of various international organizations and a signatory to international covenants to which the country legally binds itself. Indigenous groups such as the Lenca and COPINH invoke the United Nations Declaration on the Rights of Indigenous People and the International Labor Organization's Convention 169 on the rights of indigenous people (see chapter 5). If the Honduran justice system was not open to legal claims and demands for protection, recognized organizations could try to utilize regional or international judicial structures. In chapter 3 we saw how the modification of laws or the creation of new laws was one way in which the powerful eliminated older legal barriers to the expansion of their control. This transformed the law itself into a problem for others. After exhausting the possibilities of Honduran law without relief, organizations could in some cases turn to international laws and jurisdictions for help. Early in 2014, the country's Constitutional Court (*Sala Constitucional*) rejected the argument of a group of indigenous and popular organizations (primarily OFRANEH and Garifuna communities) to block the development of Charter Cities. The petitioners' argument was that the law that permitted such development violated the country's sovereignty and was unconstitutional because it abrogated the state's authority and laws within the precincts of the proposed Charter Cities. The petition argued that the state had no right to abrogate its own authority of any part of the national territory. Seasoned by past experience with the country's judicial system in denying or ignoring Garifuna claims, the Garifuna and OFRANEH had also presented a legal petition to the Inter-American Human Rights Commission (an arm of the Organization of American States) in Washington. The petition asked for international legal recognition of the territorial claims of the Garifuna over at least two important Garifuna communities near the Caribbean coast. The Commission found enough merit in the petition to refer it to the Inter-American Court for Human Rights, based in Costa Rica. The Honduran government's counterargument claimed that the Garifuna were not really an indigenous people of Honduras, and were therefore not protected by the international treaties and covenants for indigenous people. This position seemed to contradict an earlier historic policy of the government.[17]

Honduras has also been the object of several international commissions studying the human rights situation and the functioning of the Honduran judicial system. In the months after the 2009 coup, the Inter-American Commission on Human Rights sent an international fact-finding delegation to Honduras. The delegation issued a report detailing numerous violations of legal process, incidents of violence by security forces, and much more.[18] The Commission extended legal "protective measures" to various Hondurans who were receiving death threats because of their work in popular organizations or human rights. This obliged the Honduran government to provide special protection to guarantee the safety of the protected individuals. But there were complaints that the government was lax about extending protective measures to the designated individuals. The government failed to extend protection to Carlos Mejia, a member of the Radio Progreso staff whom the IACHR had designated for "protective measures." In April 2014, he was killed in his home. The police at first declared the killing a common crime, but some of his co-workers saw his murder as a deliberate blow to the work of Radio Progreso and a warning to the Radio's staff. Among the many Honduran and international statements deploring his murder was a statement by U.S. Senator Tim Kaine that said in part, "Honduran police failed to protect Carlos, despite repeated requests to do so from the Inter-American Commission on Human Rights. The police need to take immediate steps to protect Carlos's surviving colleagues at Radio Progreso and its research arm, ERIC, who also live under constant threat."[19] International laws and commissions do not guarantee that Honduran officials or institutions will uphold either Honduran or international law, but these international instruments do provide a way for Hondurans to gain wider attention for their struggles, and to invite the world's scrutiny. This notoriety can have an economic impact if international lenders and investors begin to question the country's political and social stability, or if governments begin questioning how their foreign aid to the Honduran state is being used.

EMPLOYING THE DISCOURSE OF HUMAN RIGHTS

The modern Western concept of human rights was finally articulated internationally after World War II. The fascist regimes of Europe and the war made it obvious that individuals needed protection from the violence of their own and other governments and states.

The United Nations Declaration of Universal Human Rights (1948) developed a concept of human rights that had four basic characteristics. Human rights were seen as residing in individuals, not governments, states, or groups. Human rights were inalienable. Humans had certain rights by virtue of being human. This meant that neither king nor parliament nor pope could give individuals their rights, nor could they take them away. Human rights were also seen as universal, applying equally to every human being regardless of age, nationality, gender, race, or any other particular characteristic. Finally, human rights were indivisible. Having certain basic rights implied other rights. The right to life implied a right to those things that support life. Each of these characteristics came with certain difficulties or ambiguities. If rights are individual, can groups have rights? If rights are inalienable, how can governments claim to be giving people their rights? If rights are universal, what happens when such rights seem to conflict with the cultural traditions and norms of a particular group? If rights are indivisible, where does this stop, practically? Do all people have a right to land or a job to guarantee they can feed themselves? Do they have a right to a clean environment with clean water so they can live? Moreover, two kinds of rights, essentially complementary, were understood. There were rights that guaranteed freedoms from certain evils and violations of the individual. And there were rights that posited freedoms for something good, such as life, liberty, freedom of expression, or clean water.

In the years since the UN declaration, an ongoing international dialogue has gradually extended the concept of rights in several directions—to refugees and displaced people, to indigenous peoples, to environmental and ecological concerns, to especially "vulnerable" populations such as women and children. Anthropologists and others began to notice that people everywhere were employing the discourse of human rights by invoking international concepts, but adapting and applying them to the particular political, social, and cultural contexts in which they engaged in various struggles.[20] A concept of rights began to emerge that was processual rather than essentialist. Rights were not something to be stated and defined once and for all in a document. Rights were defined in the daily struggles of people for what they thought most important and worth the struggle. Through local leaders such as the leaders of social movements or popular organizations who bring the discourse of human rights to local or national struggles, people adapt this discourse to local struggles and defined their rights in particular situations by exercising them and demanding them.[21] This processual nature of rights is akin to Honduran peasants saying, "We are the agrarian reform," we define the reform by acting for what we believe is right and necessary.

In Honduras, people engage concepts of human rights as a form of defense—to gain a modicum of protection from the incursions and violence of the powerful, or at least to lay bare destructive situations—and as a claim to a better life—to claim a greater share of what sustains life and basic humanity. While human rights organizations such as CODEH and COFADEH specifically used the more universal and abstract term human rights (*derechos humanos*) regularly in their work, much of the demand for rights in Honduran society is couched in the particulars of a concrete situation—the right to this parcel of ancestral land, the right not to have the community water supply contaminated by mining operations, the right to use the legal and judicial systems for redress of grievances without fearing for one's life, or the right simply to walk down a street without fear. If pressed, the Hondurans who struggle for these concrete demands could probably connect most of them to more abstract or universally framed rights such as a right to life, to association, or to physical safety and integrity.

Honduran society since at least the 1980s has seen a convergence of concerns and even collaboration between popular organizations, human rights groups, and others. One of the fruits of this connection has been to increase the ability of people, or at least the leaders and activists of popular organizations, to invoke the more abstract and universal discourse of human rights to define the particular struggle in which they are engaged, thus wedding the particular to the universal. This has often taken the form of appeals to international statements such as the UN Declaration on Universal Human Rights or the ILO Convention 169—documents couched in more abstract terms but often mentioned by Lenca and other indigenous activists as support for their own struggles with the powerful. People in protest marches in Tegucigalpa and other cities carry signs invoking human rights. The April 2010 issue of the magazine *Vida Laboral* contained a cover photo of a large protest march with a marcher carrying a sign that read, "We demand punishment for these violators of human rights." In a direct sense, this appeal to universal human rights discourse is another way of inviting international attention to the particular concerns with which Honduran groups are engaged—in this case countering official impunity.

Major human rights organizations in Honduras have operated under conditions of threat and danger to their staff members and clients. COFADEH director Berta Oliva has faced death threats and surveillance for most of the thirty years of the organization's existence. The COFADEH office was under surveillance at various times, and staff members received threats to themselves or family members. Through all of this, COFADEH continued to engage in several major human rights functions. The staff documented reports of human rights violations from many parts of the country. The organization helped victims or survivors bring lawsuits defending individual and group rights. COFADEH engaged memory work through keeping the photos and stories of many disappeared Hondurans prominent in its work and through public projects of memory such as its project to complete a *Ruta de la Memoria Histórica* (see chapter 8).

Religion has been an aspect of Honduran life in which the concept of human rights is expounded, usually embedded within a more theologically grounded discourse that emphasizes the sacredness of each person as a "child of God." Because such religious discourse with its symbolism has become so integrated into Honduran culture and life, it has become a vehicle for familiar expressions of what human rights can mean, and it gives human rights the added power or legitimacy of a divinely ordained mandate. This may partially explain why leaders in some Honduran churches have had a "problematic" relationship with some members of the country's powerful elite since at least the 1960s, even as other churches continued to support the elite.

With international obligations as a signatory to various human rights documents, increasing activity by Honduran and international human rights groups, the human rights related activities of some sectors of religious institutions, and even the increased scrutiny the country endured as the center of U.S. military deployment in Central America during the 1980s, the Honduran government came under pressure to display some interest in guarding the human rights of its citizens. During the presidency of Rafael Callejas (1990–1994) the office of National Human Rights Commissioner was created, and Leo Valladares was named commissioner. In 1996, the Honduran Congress extended his term until 2002. His mandate was to collect and document known or probable cases of human rights violations and to refer these to the country's attorney general for possible prosecution. Valladares himself had no prosecutorial powers. But he took his work seriously. He began the major task of trying to document the many cases of disappearances of activists that had occurred in Honduras during the 1980s. His "interim" report, *The Facts Speak for Themselves* (1993), detailed what was known about 184 disappearances from the previous decade. Throughout most of his term, he was engaged in trying to locate and access documents that might shed light on many apparent cases of human rights violations during the 1980s and into the 1990s. He met opposition at each step. The Honduran military claimed they destroyed records more than five years old in order to save storage space. Argentine military had helped train and work with Honduran forces in the 1980s, but Argentina released only a small amount of information. When Valladares published *In Search of Hidden Truths* (1998), a report detailing how his attempts to access information were hindered, he testified before a U.S. Congressional committee. Soon after, the United States released some information to his office. When his term ended in 2002, Valladares continued to work for human rights and wider popular participation in government as director of the non-governmental Association for an Active Citizenry. He was a public critic of the 2009 coup. In 2011, unknown men in a taxi began following him, parking outside his house. His family received a series of anonymous phone calls from someone asking for his son, who had been killed two years earlier. Valladares reported these incidents to the police who told him and his family to take extra security measures and consider leaving the country.

Valladares served much of his term during the presidency of Carlos Roberto Reina (1994–1998). Reina himself had been imprisoned three times under former military dictatorships for his criticism of those regimes. This gave him a lifelong interest in human rights. As president, Reina declared a "moral revolution" to combat corruption and curb the power of the military. He achieved some success in both, but it was temporary. Like other reformers, he had to maneuver around the interests of a powerful elite. The National Commission for Human Rights in Honduras (CONADEH) continued to function as a government entity with regional offices in several areas of the country. Their work was limited to documentation and referral of individual complaints and cases for possible prosecution or protection. The limited size and mandate of the staff and the climate of fear surrounding most cases of human rights abuse hindered CONADEH's effectiveness.

THE CONSTITUTIONAL ORDER, THE COUP, AND *REFUNDACIÓN*

Honduras has endured a history of political and constitutional instability. During the nineteenth and early twentieth centuries, political factions, most of them controlled by the wealthy and powerful, vied for power and even engaged in brief armed civil conflicts. From the 1930s until 1980, military governments deposed civilian presidents several times and the country alternated between military and civilian rule. The Honduran military was a major political actor, and military governments ruled the country continuously from 1963 until 1980, when the army returned the country to civilian rule, but kept a special status for itself that made it effectively independent of civilian control The return to civilian government in 1980 coincided with a period of economic crisis and the harsh application of national security measures. In this context, the country drafted a new constitution in keeping with the return of civilian rule. The military insisted on keeping a special status for itself essentially independent of civilian control, a condition that continued until the Reina government (1994–1998) reasserted civilian constitutional control over the military. The 1982 Honduran Constitution was born in a time of repression and crisis. Although it contained many provisions that seemed to guarantee certain rights, it did not open the government or the political process to the broad public participation that some had hoped. The problem resided partly in the way the Constitution structured the government and partly in the way that a small elite seemed able to dominate the political system.

The acceleration of neoliberal development policies and projects in the 1990s and thereafter, coupled with a rising level of violence due to political repression, criminal gangs, and narcotics trafficking highlighted for some Hondurans the problems of impunity and corruption. The two major political parties—National and Liberal—largely controlled the electoral process through local bosses and patronage systems that rewarded the faithful and withheld from the independent and the critics. All of this encouraged some Hondurans to think that a major restructuring of the Honduran constitutional and political systems was necessary as a condition for the success of other kinds of popular struggles. President Zelaya finally proposed to hold a popular opinion poll in June, 2009 to assess public support for adding the question of constitutional reform to the November elections. If the coup had not intervened on the very day of the proposed poll, and the poll results had been favorable, Hondurans would have been able to vote in November for or against forming a constituent assembly to write a new national constitution. If people voted yes in November, a constituent assembly would have been elected to write the new constitution. This would have occurred sometime after the national elections in November 2009, in which Zelaya could not be a candidate.

The coup that stopped the proposed poll on June 28, 2009, and removed Zelaya seemed to underscore for some Hondurans the need to restructure the government and construct a constitutional order that would be more inclusive and participatory.[22] One of the major themes that emerged from the massive popular protests in the months after the coup was expressed in the term *refundación*. This term, roughly translated as "refounding," came to mean both a general sense to doing away with older structures of repression and the very particular objective of writing a new national constitution. This became a specific goal of the conglomeration of organizations and individuals that called themselves the National Popular Resistance Front (FNRP). Some within the Front saw electoral partisan politics as a way to achieve *refundación*. If they had a popular party that could prevail in the national elections of November 2013, they would have the means to effect direct change in the constitutional order, and address other serious issues of impunity, corruption, and political oppression. The party that emerged from this bore the name *Partido de Libertad y Refundación* (LIBRE). It did contest the 2014 elections, and its candidates won a number of mayoral and Congressional positions. Its presidential candidate, Xiomara Castro, gained the second highest number of votes, showing perhaps that LIBRE was a political force to challenge the monopoly of the two major traditional parties. Many accounts and charges of fraud, threat, and the assassination of candidates marred the political campaign leading to the election, and the election itself (see the case of Luis Galdamez, above, this chapter). In this context, it is unclear whether Castro might have won in a "clean" election as many of her supporters thought. In any case, Castro's and LIBRE's second-place finish was seen as an important event for Honduras. Some saw this as a sea change in Honduran political life, with LIBRE as a political force to challenge the monopoly of the two traditional parties. Others cautioned that the popular resistance was not well served by becoming too attached to the fortunes of any political party, even an apparently progressive party such as LIBRE. Many Hondurans did vote for LIBRE because it represented something better, but they cautioned against letting LIBRE become synonymous with a broad popular resistance.[23]

For some Hondurans, especially those concerned with the rights of women in Honduran society, the importance of the goal of refounding the state (*refundación*) by promulgating a new and more democratic constitution had an anti-patriarchal aspect. At its root, patriarchy connotes the power of men over women, husband over wife and children. Patriarchal power is expressed in both punitive and patronizing attitudes and actions. Men must keep women and children under control in the domestic sphere and act as their agents and protectors in the public sphere. This idea of patriarchy was an inherent part of the colonial and post-colonial rural society of much of Latin America, not only in the household but also throughout society's institutions. On haciendas, for example, the relationship of the owner (*patrón*) to his workers (*peónes*) was conceived as that of a father to his children. In the colonial church, the authority of the priest (father, *padre*) was to both admonish and give penance but also to encourage and safeguard the morals of his congregants, his "children in the faith." Patriarchy shapes relations of ethnicity (*mestizo* over *indio*), social class (owner over worker), and especially gender. Historian Elizabeth Dore traces the close relationship between the subordination of women in all spheres of life and the political power of *caudillos* (strong men) and dictators in post-colonial Nicaragua. She writes of the "little patriarchy" of the household and the "big patriarchy" of the dictatorship or the presidency, and shows how the two were related in daily life.[24] In Latin America, the *caudillo*—the powerful military ruler or dictator—was the "Father" of the nation who had to both punish and protect the citizens. The citizens were like children, to be seen and not heard. The big patriarchy need not be embodied in a single powerful ruler or dictator. A group, an oligarchy, or a powerful elite can embody a sort of big patriarchy in its ideology and practice, as we saw in chapters 2 and 3. If it is an elite rather than a single dictatorial figure, popular resistance may lack the galvanizing symbol, the single figure that embodies everything that is to be resisted. From this perspective, the need to refound the Honduran state in ways that increased popular participation in and control of the political life of the country was a way to curb the power of an elite that seemed to treat the rest of society as children to be bribed and punished but not treated as equals.

One of the many effects of the 2009 coup was to further weaken the public image and legitimacy of the Honduran judicial system, and especially the Supreme Court that had acquiesced in a coup that many considered a major violation of the Honduran constitution. The Association of Judges for Democracy (AJD) lamented this weakening of judicial legitimacy that seemed to make a mockery of the rule of law at the highest levels of the state, and might make it harder for honest judges to function.[25] The image of an independent and impartial Supreme Constitutional Court (*Sala Constitucional*) was furthered weakened by the "technical coup," the summary dismissal by Congress of four Constitutional Court judges who had declared unconstitutional the statute permitting Charter Cities that the Congress wanted (see chapter 2). The irony in all of this—for example, having those who disregarded the most basic legal procedures prosecute those who criticized the illegality—became part of the case for resistance. Who were the real upholders of the law? Who were the real scoff-laws? Some judges protested the "technical coup" and other illegalities at the highest levels by engaging in a hunger strike for days in front of the Supreme Court in Tegucigalpa. Radio Progreso staff came down to Tegucigalpa to cover this news story of protesting judges. Radio Progreso's director later reflected that the radio staff started by considering this just another potentially important news story, but soon began to feel a great respect and connection to the hungry jurists and the importance of the rule of law and the principles and practices they were trying to defend by risking their own bodies when the legal system to which they had devoted their lives seemed in grave danger.

THE COMMISSION OF TRUTH AND THE TRUE COMMISSION

Countries such as Guatemala and South Africa that have experienced internal civil conflicts, wars, repressive regimes, or genocides have instituted "truth and reconciliation" commissions. These commissions are usually formed some time after the end of conflict during a relatively stable period. The mandate may vary, but it usually includes trying to find out the facts of what happened during the conflict, and especially who was responsible for what acts of violence, atrocities, or violations of human rights. Usually, these commissions hear testimony from many victims as well as alleged perpetrators, including government officials. Ordinarily, commissions do not have prosecutorial powers, but state prosecutors or organizations of citizens may use their reports as a basis for criminal or civil lawsuits against alleged perpetrators. Commissions may also be used to support popular demands for accountability and an end to impunity.[26]

The 2009 coup d'etat and the protests and repression that followed it were a traumatic event in Honduran society. After the removal of Zelaya, an interim government was installed with the president of the Congress, Roberto Micheletti as interim president until the regularly scheduled elections of November, 2009. Those elections were held while popular protest and repression of protest were ongoing. One of the first acts of the new president, Porfirio Lobo, was to declare an amnesty for those who might have committed illegal acts during the coup. Internal protests continued and foreign governments, especially in Latin America, withheld formal recognition of the "post-coup" Lobo government. Foreign investors hesitated. In an effort to improve its image of legitimacy, the Lobo government named a *Comisión de la Verdad y Reconciliación* (CVR, Truth and Reconciliation Commission). Its mandate was to investigate and determine the facts of what happened before, during, and shortly after the coup and to identify responsibility for some of the acts of illegality that occurred in the executive branch of the Honduran government. It was not mandated to talk to ordinary citizens, alleged victims of abuses, or leaders of popular organizations. Nor was it mandated to investigate violations and illegalities that the Congress and the courts might have perpetrated, although these legislative and judicial branches were encouraged to cooperate with the commission's investigations.

Not long after the CVR began its work, leaders and activists in popular organizations and human rights groups, and even some international organizations denounced it. The CVR, "makes the victims invisible and gives a mantle of protection to the victimizers," said a prominent Honduran human rights activist. Criticism focused especially on the fact that the CVR was appointed by a government that was not at all impartial since many of its functionaries were involved in the coup and/or benefited from the removal of Zelaya; and the fact that the CVR did not collect the testimonies of victims. One year after the coup, some Hondurans and international organizations formed an alternative *Comisión de Verdad* (CDV). The name was deliberately chosen since the Spanish phrase "*de verdad*" is used to emphasize that something is genuine or real. This was the *true* independent Commission as opposed to the government's showcase commission. The term reconciliation was not part of the name. Reconciliation implied getting on with the future, but this was seen as another form of official erasure of memory and promotion of impunity unless the victims received some form of justice. The conscious mandate was to give voice to the victims and to make the case for prosecution of official abuses.[27]

The organizers of this alternative *Comisión de Verdad* attracted some prominent Honduran and international figures as commissioners. Among prominent international commissioners were Nobel Peace Prize winner Adolfo Perez Esquivel; co-founder of the Mothers of the Plaza de Mayo in Argentina, Nora Cortinas; and a former judge of the El Salvador Supreme Court who was also a victim of political repression during the 1970s and 1980s. The CDV commissioners were aided by a staff from Honduran and international agencies. They traveled to different areas of Honduras and collected almost two thousand testimonies from people who claimed to be victims of political repression. Some of those who gave testimony knew they were taking risks in doing so. A day after testifying to the CDV, a Garifuna woman saw her house burned.[28] Others were threatened or attacked. A driver for the support staff of the Commission was attacked and nearly killed.[29] Despite these risks, people chose to give testimony or to be associated with the work of the CDV.

In July 2011, the government's "official" *Comisión de la Verdad y Reconciliación* issued its report. It admitted that violations and illegalities had occurred, and made recommendations for the future, but did not name or implicate government officials or government entities in unconstitutional or illegal activity in relation to the events of and following the coup of 2009. With this, the Commission's mandate and its work ended. The alternative *Comisión de Verdad* continued its work, issuing a report in October 2012 that covered a longer period of time and a much wider variety of testimonies. The report's title summarizes its focus and purpose, *La voz más autorizada es la de las víctimas* (*The Most Authoritative Voice Is the Victims'*). The report ended the formal work of this Commission, but its findings and the whole idea of an ongoing search for truth that highlights the people's experience and expression became an integral part of the resistance. When the report was issued, a Honduran Commission member told the public that although the Commission's work was done, "now there is a new Truth Commission that is all the Honduran people, with the mission of demanding the fulfillment of the recommendations from our Commission."[30]

Chapter 7
WEAK STATE, STRONG ELITE, POPULAR RESISTANCE

This chapter has discussed some of the ways in which Hondurans confront the state in its legal, judicial, and political aspects. The examples have also shown, perhaps, that the state is not monolithic and does not always act and react with one accord. Many diverse forces, relationships, and conditions—personal, local, and national—affect how agents of the state act officially at any particular time and place, and how they interpret policies and laws. Hansen and Stepputat argue that it is useful to conceive of the state as, "a multitude of discrete operations, procedures, and representations in which it appears in the everyday life of ordinary people . . . a dispersed ensemble of institutional practices and techniques."[31] That people experience the Honduran state as a complex and often contradictory reality makes individual and group acts of resistance both more and less difficult. Resistance is more difficult because the consequences cannot always be predicted. What will this judge rule? Who will the police or the soldiers at this checkpoint stop and detain? Will this protest march be permitted to pass or will it be met with tear gas? Will authorities accede to international pressure and release this person from detention? Will the rivalry between police and military act in our favor or make an example of us? Resistance is easier inasmuch as state authority is embodied in human beings who are vulnerable to the emotions, social and political pressures, sacred cultural norms, and internalized morality that can at times humanize the execution of inhuman policies. Detained at a checkpoint on a rural road in western Honduras by police one evening, a church group was ordered to surrender its identification documents. As time passed and they sat in their van waiting and wondering what would happen, they began to sing a hymn. As they sang, the police sergeant removed his hat, and the lines on his face softened. Within a few minutes, the police returned the identification papers and sent the group on its way with a wish for a good trip home.

Honduras is often characterized as a country with weak state institutions and a weak central government. In the country's history, government control has not always extended to all regions of the country, and state institutions are chronically unable to carry out basic functions of governance. This situation, it is argued, has bred corruption and a tendency to substitute coercive force for law and functioning bureaucracy. But Honduras is also a country with a small elite that seems extraordinarily powerful and in control. At first this seems paradoxical—weak state, strong ruling class. Yet one could argue that the ruling class is able to become powerful and to maintain its exclusive monopoly of political and economic power in part because state institutions are weak. A major theme of resistance in this chapter has been the popular effort to strengthen the institutions of state power precisely by making them more democratic and inclusive.

NOTES

1. From the author's field notes, August, 2013.
2. Asociación de Jueces por la Democracia, "Administración de justicia y persistente fragilidad institucional," Statement of the Association of Judges for Democracy for Public Hearing 147, Human Rights Situation in Honduras, Washington, DC, March 2013, published in *Revista Justicia* 6:12 (July, 2013): 39–67.
3. Author's field notes and interviews with journalists present at a court hearing for Morales, August, 2013 and with an official of CNTC, September, 2013.
4. Author's field notes and interviews with journalists present at a court hearing for Morales, August, 2013 and with an official of CNTC, September, 2013.
5. In an illegal land occupation that the author studied during fieldwork in Jamaica in 1974, the occupiers, all landless plantation workers who had occupied a small portion of corporate sugar plantation land, declared that they were not "squatters" but rather Jamaican citizens putting into practice the mandate expressed by the prime minister, Michael Manley, that growing food to feed the country was a necessary and patriotic act. Most of the occupiers were supporters of Manley's People's National Party.
6. Proyecto de Acompaniemiento de Honduras PROAH, "Summary of Human Rights Issues and Events in Honduras for October-December 2013," PROAH website http://honduranaccompanimentproject.wordpress.com (English) or http://proah.wordpress.com (Spanish).
7. Honduran daily *El Heraldo* (23 September, 2012). Almost a year later, *El Heraldo* (August 15, 2013) reported that the police were maintaining an official silence in the investigation of Trejo's murder.
8. *El Heraldo*, July 24, 2013.
9. *El Heraldo*, July 24, 2013.
10. Asociación de Jueces por la Democracia, *Revista Justicia* 6:12 (July, 2013).
11. José Comblin, *The Church and the National Security State* (Maryknoll, NY: Maryknoll Books, 1984), 64–78.
12. *Impunidad: La ley de los fuertes que aplasta a las víctimas* (El Progreso: Radio Progreso y Equipo de Reflexión, Investigación, y Comunicación, ERIC-SJ, 2013).
13. James Phillips, "Challenging Impunity with Memory in Today's Honduras," paper read at American Anthropological Association Annual Meeting, San Francisco, (November, 2012).
14. Marvin Barahona, *Pueblos indígenas, Estado y memoria colectiva en Honduras* (El Progreso y Tegucigalpa: Editorial Casa San Ignacio y Editorial Guaymuras, 2009), 259–70.
15. A newspaper interview with public prosecutor Luis Xavier Santos provides an example. "Quiero poner un granito de arena en la lucha contra la corrupción," *aMecate Corto* (August, 2013), 5.
16. It is instructive that the most "popular" provision in the Mining Law—that government and companies obtain full, prior, and informed consent before initiating mining operations—is a provision enshrined in various international covenants, including the 1969 International labor Organization Convention 169, to which Honduras is a signatory. Some Hondurans thought the government included that provision in the Mining Law in order to signal "lip service" compliance with its international obligations.
17. Mark Anderson, "Garifuna Activism and the Corporatist Honduran State Since the 2009 Coup," in *Black Social Movements in Latin America: From Monocultural Mestizaje to Multiculturalism*, ed. Jean Muteba Rahier (New York: Palgrave MacMillan, 2012), 53–73. An earlier phase of the Garifuna appeal to international law and justice is reflected in a 2007 finding of the Inter-American Commission on Human Rights (IACHR), *Report No. 39/07, Petition 1118–03, Admissibility: Garifuna Community of Cayos Cochinos and Its Members, Honduras* (July 24, 2007).
18. Inter-American Commission on Human Rights (IACHR), *Honduras: Human Rights and the Coup d'Etat* (English version, original in Spanish), OEA/Ser.L?V/II, Doc. 55 (30 December, 2009). The IACHR also conducted follow-up visits to Honduras in 2011 and 2013. Inter-American Commission on Human Rights, "Preliminary Observations of the IACHR on Its

Visit to Honduras on May 15–18, 2010," Organization of American States, OEA/Ser L/V/II, Doc. 68 (3 June, 2010), English version.

19. Senator Tim Kaine, "Statement on the Murder of Carlos Mejia Orellana" (April 18, 2014), http://www.wola.org/.../kaine_statement_on_the_murder_of_carlos_mejia_orellana_in_honduras. Honduras Accompaniment Project, "Reflection on the Murder of Carlos Mejia, Radio Progreso: Was Carlos Mejia a Target?" (May 15, 2014), https://hondurasaccompanimentproject.wordpress.com/.../reflection-on-the-murder-of-carlos-mejia-radio-progreso.

20. Mark Goodale, ed., *Human Rights at the Crossroads* (New York: Oxford University Press, 2013). Taken together, many of the chapters in this volume illustrate how the idea of human rights has evolved in complex ways and is applied in different ways in different contexts, including conflict and change.

21. Sally Engel Merry, "Transnational Human Rights and Local Activism: Mapping the Middle," *American Anthropologist* 108:1 (June, 2006): 38–51.

22. Doug Cassel, "Honduras: Coup d'Etat in Constitutional Clothing?" *Insights* (American Society of International Law) 13:9 (October 15, 2009). There is a sizeable body of critical analysis from both Honduran and international sources, much of it arguing that Zelaya was acting within his constitutional mandate, and that the process of his summary removal from office was itself unconstitutional. For more about the events of the 2009 coup and Zelaya's version, see, for example, http://www.cnn.com/2009/WORLD/americas/06/28/honduras.president.arrested/index.html.

23. Ismael Moreno SJ, "Déficit de ciudadania: Una interpretación del sondeo de opinion pública UCA-ERIC," *Envío Honduras* 8:28 (March 2011): 1–8. Some of the irregularities reported or alleged in the 2013 election included death threats against LIBRE candidates, armed men removing LIBRE election workers from polling places, dead people voting, and vote buying by the National Party. Several LIBRE candidates in local and Congressional elections were assassinated. Several who did win local races were killed in the months after the 2013 election.

24. Elizabeth Dore, *Myths of Modernity: Peonage and Patriarchy in Nicaragua* (Durham, NC: University of North Carolina Press, 2006).

25. Asociación de Jueces por la Democracia AJD, "Administración de Justicia."

26. Marcie Mersky, "Las Comisiones de Verdad como herramientas no judiciales de lucha contra la impunidad," *Envío Honduras* 9:31 (December, 2011): 22–25.

27. For a discussion and comparative analysis of the two commissions, see Francisco José Aguilar Urbina, "Justicia transicional y comisiones de esclarescimiento de la verdad," Envío Honduras 9:31 (December, 2011): 16–21. Aguilar was a member of the Comisión de Verdad and a former president and secretary of the United Nations Human Rights Commission.

28. Personal communication from support staff of the Comisión de Verdad.

29. Personal communication from support staff of the Comisión de Verdad.

30. This quote and a summary version of the report of the independent CDV are contained in, Proyecto de Acompanimiento Internacional de Honduas PROAH, "La Comisión de Verdad presenta su informe, 'La voz más autorizada es la de las victimas'" PROAH website, http://proah.wordpress.com(Spanish), posted October 22, 2012.

31. Thomas Blom Hansen and Finn Stepputat, eds., *States of Imagination: Ethnographic Explorations of the Postcolonial State* (Durham, NC: Duke University Press, 2001), 14, quoted in Jordan Levy, *The Politics of Honduran School Teachers: State Agents Challenge the State* (Doctoral dissertation, University of Western Ontario, 2014).

Chapter Eight

Ancient Weapon of the People

Popular Culture

Esteli, in northern Nicaragua, is a city of many colorful public wall murals. The message on one mural reads, "Art, weapon of the people" (*El arte, arma del pueblo*). Art and popular culture play an important role in popular resistance. How some forms of popular culture are integral to Honduran resistance is the subject of this chapter.

In the 1950s, anthropologist Robert Redfield coined the terms "Little Tradition" and "Great Tradition."[1] The Little Tradition was the tradition of the people that was rooted in a long history and was the collective product or popular expression of community. The Great Tradition was the cultural expression extant among a particular social elite, and it was sometimes the creation of specific individuals. The two "traditions" influenced each other in various ways. The symphonies of Brahms are full of traditional peasant folk melodies and dances. Much modern rock music draws heavily from the classical music of Bach. In reality all artistic expression is integrated and capable of almost endless permutation and borrowing. Human thought, emotion, and experience are sources of seemingly endless creativity not always bound by differences of social class, time, or ethnic heritage. As a result, in an oppressive political and social context that stifles and dehumanizes life, almost any artistic expression that stirs emotions and visions and reminds people of their humanity might be considered resistance. Popular culture may be seen in this larger context.

In all societies in the world, people express their daily experiences, hopes, troubles, and struggles in ways that can be communicated and shared with others. They use the known symbols of their own and sometimes other cultural traditions and they rework these in certain structured forms. We know these forms as music, art, language, storytelling, playacting, public festival, and more. Popular culture is the work of people creating expressions of their world and their experience, and freely adapting and changing older expressions to reflect new situations. In the early 1980s, revolutionary Nicaragua became an example of the idea that revolutionary change and artistic expression, especially poetry, were closely linked.[2] Particular expressions of popular culture are always a work of collaboration inasmuch as individuals rework what the community—often unknown and anonymous others—have created over years, transforming this in ways that speak to current realities. People express the wide range of human emotions and experiences in popular culture—the "blues" music of Mississippi's black elders, the sensual eroticism of some Cuban peasant folk songs or Brazilian *carnaval*, the images of life and struggle depicted in Latin American street murals. Latin American poets from Nicaragua's Ruben Darío to Chile's Pablo Neruda have woven the images of the popular culture of their land and people into their poetry, and have fashioned critiques of what is and visions of what might be.

People use popular culture in many ways to promote resistance to undesirable situations through some form of criticism, constructing an image of a better reality, or calling people to construct aspects of that reality. Expressions of popular culture can become in themselves acts of resistance. Sometimes these acts are done in such a way as to hide their significance from authorities or those who embody what is being resisted. Slaves in colonial North and Latin American societies used popular fiestas to express acts of criticism, mockery, or defiance, sometimes in the guise of fun-loving or innocuous figures. Oppressed people discovered that they could "get away with" considerable criticism of their oppressors if they presented these as the actions of buffoons, clowns, or comedians. The oppressors would ignore it, laugh at it or interpret it as another proof of the inferiority of the oppressed. But for the oppressed, such expressions represented at the least emotional release, keeping hope or a spirit of defiant resistance alive.[3]

At other times, popular culture as resistance is meant to be public, open, and declared, deriving much of its power from its very public expression. In 2002, Eric Canin described how the people of Managua, Nicaragua, celebrate the fiesta of the city's patron, Saint Dominic (*Santo Domingo* or *"Mingüito"*) each August. The saint's statue is carried in procession from the Santo Domingo church in a wealthy neighborhood down to the other church of Santo Domingo in one of the poorest neighborhoods of the city. There, the statue is installed in the small church and several days of popular street celebrations follow that are entirely the domain of the people. Civil and religious authorities generally do not interfere. For these three days, the streets belong to the people and the saint is theirs. This is the one time of the year when these people of the poorer areas are really in charge in this limited context. Then parishioners from the wealthier church reclaim the statue and return it to its "home." One year, the people of the poor parish refused to relinquish the saint at the end of the fiesta. They locked Saint Dominic in their church until the authorities intervened and negotiated the transfer thereby recognizing the power of the people as a force to be reckoned with.[4]

Forms of artistic expression derive power from symbolic ambiguity, the ability to evoke a variety of interpretations and responses from individuals. When integrated into acts or movements of popular resistance, part of the artistry is in the selection and framing of popular cultural expressions so as to convey messages, emotions, or ideas without the need or intent to deliver an explicit message. In this way, popular culture provides emotional and imaginative context, support, and perhaps nuance to explicit acts or demands that may be current in popular resistance. Popular culture enlivens resistance, provides emotional focus, complements the pragmatic nature of resistance with visions and dreams, and connects particular struggles to larger expressions that can be understood or embraced by others. Popular culture is or becomes the shared heritage of an entire community or a people, and it can promote solidarity in resistance. In Honduras, forms and expressions of popular culture are integrated into expressions of resistance, and themes of resistance are expressed in popular culture in many ways, as this chapter will demonstrate with a few examples. The purpose of these examples is not to provide a survey of popular culture in Honduras, but to suggest how forms of popular culture can express popular resistance as critique and as alternative vision. An ethnographic or grassroots perspective of popular culture in Honduras can reveal currents of popular resistance expressed therein.[5] Some aspects of what is sometimes considered popular culture—television, sports—are not explored here, nor is Honduran literature examined.

MUSIC: PORTABLE RESISTANCE

Of all the forms of popular culture, music and song may be the most widely accessible and replicable and the most often created. People can see a mural but most cannot reproduce it easily. Almost anyone who can hear can sing a song repeatedly and in many contexts. Music is portable. In Honduras, people sometimes make up songs to commemorate events in popular struggles. Songs commemorating the 1991 El Astillero massacre (described at the start of chapter 2) are examples. "The life of a peasant is worth the same as a rich man's." These songs may never become the stuff of stage performance. They are meant as expressions of popular criticism and as reminders, attempts to record the history of struggle, especially among peasants and rural people who remain largely anonymous and collective, and who may rely on oral rather than written tradition to remember their history. The "incidents" that the perpetrators of violence and injustice would prefer to forget and erase are not forgotten in the songs. At another level, musicians and singers with some local, national, or even international recognition compose songs that point out oppressive situations or highlight the struggles of ordinary people.

One of the most famous exemplars of the music of popular resistance in Honduras since the 2009 coup was Café Guancasco. The group began around 2006 when two Hondurans formed a duo with the idea of making music in the modern Latin American tradition of *trova experimental*. *Trova* can refer to music composed by troubadours or traveling musicians. The *nueva trova* music that became popular in Cuba after the revolution had its roots in groups of neighborhood and other musicians getting together in a house or local club (*casa de la trova*) to experiment in making and sharing music together—much of it celebrating life in revolutionary, liberated Cuba. In Honduras, the duo that became the core of Café Guancasco began to perform in local bars, festivals, and on television and radio. They were influenced by a variety of international musical groups and individuals from the Beatles to the Chilean Victor Jara and the Cuban Silvio Rodriguez, but they fashioned their own music and lyrics from the context of Honduran daily life. They soon gathered other musicians, most of them with a history of political activism, and named the group Café Guancasco. The name intentionally invoked two aspects of Honduran culture. The Lenca term *guancasco* refers to the indigenous custom of holding a celebration that unites two groups of people in friendship, communication, and sharing (chapter 5). The café is a place where people of diverse backgrounds meet and share conversation and ideas. So Café Guancasco is the meeting and sharing that builds community. Their productions soon caught national and international attention and the group began to appear in the world music scene. Their musical influences were global, but the content of their songs expressed realities of Honduran life, and they became perhaps the most famous musical group in Honduras.

On the day of the 2009 coup that removed President Zelaya from office, Café Guancasco performed for a large crowd of anti-coup protesters that had gathered in front of the exiled president's home. They were eventually dispersed by military and police units. Their public performances inspired others to write and perform music of resistance. In the weeks after the coup, Café Guancasco became identified for some Hondurans with the newly forming FNRP (*Frente Nacional de Resistencia Popular*). They were sometimes called *la banda de la Resistencia*. A protest march organized by the FNRP and allied groups for the national independence day (September 15) in 2010 ended with a gathering and outdoor concert in the main plaza in the center of San Pedro Sula. Café Guancasco was featured in the concert, but soon after it began a large contingent of well-armed police assaulted the band and the audience. One person was killed, several injured, others detained, and musical instruments and sound equipment were destroyed or confiscated. At least one account of the incident claimed that the police used tear gas and water cannon against the audience. One report pointed out that, "the concert was a family affair with a big presence of youth and children, boys and girls."[6] Some Hondurans interpreted this as the beginning of a major repression against the arts in resistance after the coup. Shortly after this incident, Café Guancasco and others in the FNRP decided to rededicate October 21 (the traditional Honduran Armed Forces Day) as *Dia del Arte y la Cultura en Resistencia*. The individual members of Café Guancasco began to experience harassment and threats. Their response was to continue their style of performing at popular resistance events and staging impromptu concerts in poor neighborhoods and places where people seemed to need hope, as well as on television and recordings. For the members of Café Guancasco, support for popular resistance was expressed both in their music and in their choice of audience and place, their affiliations.

The singer Karla Lara is well known and beloved in Honduras for her songs that portray the efforts and aspirations of many Hondurans for the future of their society. Her performances of the national anthem (*himno nacional*) began to take on a new meaning after the coup because of how she rendered it and because of a very few word changes to reflect the post-coup situation. She sang what became known as the *himno nacional de resistencia*. On tours, Lara has also brought her music to international audiences in the United States and elsewhere to convey the image of a Honduras where people are constructing something positive in the midst of the negative.

These are only a very few examples of the way in which music expresses the experience of people in resistance and envisioning a better life.

ARTS AND CRAFTS WITH A DIFFERENCE

Much, perhaps most popular artistic expression appears in the fashioning of material culture that serves quite utilitarian or mundane purposes. In the warm climate of Honduras, T-shirts are a clothing item of choice for many, and a way to carry a message or a symbol that can express individual values, sympathies, and identities. Tourists can buy T-shirts with colorful designs loosely imitating traditional or indigenous forms. Designs, symbols, and messages on T-shirts can also be a means of publicizing organizations, causes, and events. In the aftermath of the 2009 coup, T-shirts began to appear in El Progreso and elsewhere for the group of Artists in Resistance that formed in affiliation with the FNRP. Black T-shirts with red and white lettering (black and red, the recognized colors of revolution) carried the words, "21 October, Day of the Artist in Resistance. All voices, armed with culture against barbarism." Below this was the image of a crowd with raised clenched fists at what could have been either a protest or a concert, or both. On the back of the shirt was the message in large white letters, "Our art is combative and irreducible action" (*Nuestro arte es acción combative e irreducible*). That the image could have been either protest or concert was appropriate inasmuch as protest rallies at this time began to feature musical groups, and some musical concerts included many expressions of protest.

T-shirt art become an easily accessible form of popular expression in resistance and in celebrating and publicizing popular organizations or important events. COFADEH commissioned T-shirts of red with white design to commemorate or publicize its development of a "Historic Memory Route" (*Ruta de la Memoria Histórica*) that would lead groups as if on a short pilgrimage to several historic and notorious places where people had been detained, tortured, disappeared in the 1980s and since. The effort was to keep alive the memory of the victims and the crimes against them. The front of the shirts depicted in simple, small line drawings the places on the route, each with a place label, and the bus at the start to carry people along the route—from the *Hogar contra el Olvido* (Home against Forgetting, a park that COFADEH was planning in Tegucigalpa), to *Nueva Tatumbla, La Montañita, Plaza de la Merced* (also labeled, Plaza of the Disappeared), *Museo de Memorias Vivas* (Museum of Living Memories), *Casa del Terror*, and ending at the memorial sculpture that was placed along the highway between Tegucigalpa and Danlí but was later disappeared. A sign bore the message, *Vivos los queremos!* (We want them back alive!). Putting so much detail on the front of a T-shirt meant that everything was very small, inviting people to take time to look more closely and absorb the significance of the entire route. The cartoon-like line drawings contrasted with the horror of what was remembered, providing an almost haunting effect. The right sleeve bore the logo of COFADEH—a globe highlighting the outline of Latin America with a dove flying over it—a traditional symbol of peace and freedom.

MURALS: OLD FORM, NEW MEANINGS

Murals are usually large and very public forms of expression. Mural art has a long history in Latin America. Ancient Mayan, Aztec, and other civilizations that predated the arrival of Europeans often had spectacular and richly colored murals adorning the inner and sometimes the outer walls of important public temples or palaces, and depicting fantastic scenes and figures. Their context was historical, religious, and political. In the twentieth century the famous muralists of Mexico such as Diego Rivera and Clemente Orozco created murals that often formed a collage of daily life, social classes, and historic events and struggles. This type of "proletarian" mural art seemed to dissolve the difference between Great and Little Tradition. In many Central American cities today one finds brightly colored and creatively designed murals, some intentionally educational (e.g., on the side of the regional hospital in Estelí, Nicaragua, promoting breastfeeding), others more abstract interpretations of social or political life.

Sometimes murals are meant to commemorate and inspire a group of people or to portray and remind them of their identity. The murals on the interior walls of a Lenca training center near La Esperanza, Honduras, (described briefly in chapter 5) do all of that, and also place Lenca identity within a larger global and historical context of resistance and struggles for social justice. A mural covering one entire outside wall of the Radio Progreso station in El Progreso is done in small bits of brightly colored glass of blue, red, green, orange, yellow—the colors of nature and earth. They depict a dove in flight, musical notations, the Radio Progreso logo of two men smiling at each other across a microphone, green hills rising from the sidewalk line, a rainbow colored banner fluttering across a blue sky, small human figures in a little community at one corner of the mural, a woman's large head and wide eyes gazing out over the scene, and a banner with the message, "Break the silence, express yourself." At the other end of the mural is an "SJ" in red (abbreviation of the Jesuit Catholic religious order that owns Radio Progreso). Down in the lower right corner, a large gray spider seems to crawl slowly up the wall. This mural bears no negative or critical message. Everything is positive, joyful, upbeat, colorful, sunny, and liberating. The wall provides an image of a happy world on a street in a city where people are assassinated on streets daily. The mural encourages, supports, offers visions of something better, and in some ways depicts what Radio Progreso aspired to promote in its daily broadcasting. Creating a public mural is often a work of community, with many different people contributing a little to a final product that takes time to complete. It can also become an act of resistance, a form of very public expression in a society where expression must often be guarded and fear is pervasive.

THE PRIVATE LIFE OF GRAFFITI: GANGS AS RESISTANCE?

Graffiti are another form of expression and they are abundant in cities and towns in Honduras, and are sometimes seen even on the sides of schools, shops, or bridges in small communities. They are usually the work of individuals who create them quickly so as not to be interrupted by police or others who would object. Political graffiti have been present in Honduras since at least the 1980s, and there are two kinds—partisan graffiti that highlight a particular political party, and critical graffiti that offer a critical or ironic commentary (often symbolic and wordless) of political or social conditions. After the 1980s, political graffiti were quickly outnumbered by graffiti produced by members of youth gangs (*maras*). Gang graffiti are not simply statements of territorial claim for a particular gang. In his ethnographic study of youth gangs in a neighborhood in El Progreso in 2001, anthropologist Jon Wolseth comments about gang graffiti that, "there is little proprietary interest and few claims of ownership on the part of the gang. Rather, neighborhood spaces become the billboards for gangs to advertise their presence to others in the neighborhood."[7] Wolseth found that gang graffiti sometimes contain lists of nicknames of active gang members, and he concluded that, "this is a visual reinforcement of the idea that the gang is a collective made of individual members who are themselves tied through historic relationships."[8] Wolseth also cites other studies by anthropologists Susan Phillips and DiegoVigil in explaining that gang nicknames (*apodos*) are an act of love between gang members that ties a member to a network of relationships of those who demand from each other and take care of each other.[9]

Because they are identified with "criminal" or violent groups, gang graffiti may be dismissed as non-art. But many graffiti display a sense of design and even symbolism that is in some sense creative, at least as an expression of a desired or imagined identity. This identity is collective and individual, a sort of imagined and yet partially realized community. In the context of modern Honduras, gangs, especially youth gangs can be interpreted as another form of resistance to the authority, norms, and rules of a state or a society that is experienced as dangerous, repressive, exploitative, dehumanizing, and hypocritical. Insofar as gangs provide a sense of belonging, community, loyalty, and fierce accountability, they offer an experience of something different. Yet their forms of resistance make them in some ways instruments of the very forces of fear and oppression they resist. The alternative world that gangs offer and try to create may address the most basic needs of its members but it is exclusive. It does not usually offer a larger alternative for a better life (where violence would be unnecessary) either for its members or for the whole of Honduran society. The resistance to social norms that Honduran gangs seem to present may also be diluted by police collusion, control, or involvement in gang activities, and by the fact that the largest Honduran gangs are at least loosely related to the larger international networks of the Mara Salvatrucha (MS) and the 18th Street (M-18).[10]

It is almost as if there is a graffiti war in Honduras today that reflects two different alternative realities or futures. Will Honduras be the locus of the "war of all against all" or the locus of a more politicized, democratic, peaceful, and just society? In Honduras, most graffiti of both kinds are created by young people who are at the center of tension between these alternative visions. This is why many people in Honduran resistance movements say the most important challenge is to integrate all of Honduran society, especially its youth, into the construction of a better society.

THEATER TO STIR THE CONSCIENCE

There is a history of theatrical expression in Honduras. For example, during the 1954 banana strike (see chapter 4) the strikers, their families and supporters took over public places in El Progreso with music, poetry, marches, and skits.[11] Popular theater in Honduras takes several forms. Fiestas and public celebrations often include skits or even short plays prepared and performed by local groups to depict aspects of the history of a people, social problems, occasionally political critique. The actors are often amateurs, members of a local community, and the story line is often the product of various influences woven together into a whole by one or a few people. Costumes are makeshift, but often imaginative. Characters are sometimes conscious stereotypes that are "overacted" to make clear a moral or other contrast and drive home an image or an impression. Such theater has ancient roots and is a form of education and remembrance that is especially geared to a population with relatively little formal education but much folk wisdom. Plays and skits are performed by schoolchildren on the national holiday (September 15) and on other special occasions. They are also a feature of celebrations marking particular ethnic or indigenous holidays. The content of much of this popular theater is not particularly or consciously critical, and past resistance struggles may be depicted in simplified or packaged form devoid of critical edge. Sometimes, however, popular theater can convey biting criticism of social conditions or political figures under the guise of traditional story lines or comedy.

Out of this tradition of local popular theatrical expressions came *Teatro La Fragua* (Theater of the Forge), perhaps the best-known "amateur" or semi-professional theater group in Honduras. La Fragua was the name of a former United Fruit Company compound in El Progreso that was later a Jesuit residence, but the name also conveys how the young people who produce *Teatro La Fragua* hammer out or fashion visions, critiques, and images in the heat of Honduran reality. Since it began in Olanchito in 1979, *Teatro La Fragua* has been a training ground for several generations of young Hondurans in acting and in the exploration of critical social themes. Not all the young actors remain in theater, but they are all trained to take the critical skills of their acting into their future lives. In 2013 *Teatro la Fragua's* motto was, "Season of artistic expression for a Honduras at peace" (*Temporada de expressión artística por una Honduras en paz*).

Based in El Progreso, the group performs also in other cities and rural areas in Honduras, and sometimes in other countries in Central America, and it has toured in Spain and the United States. It has become an established part of the local and Honduran scene, and counts among its financial patrons and supporters the city of El Progreso, *El Tiempo* (a major national newspaper), and several large Honduran businesses, including one of the largest supermarket chains in the country. In 2015, the group's website described its mission.

> Teatro la fragua actualmente define su labor en la sociedad hondureña como despertar la creatividad del pueblo a través del teatro para encontrar soluciones a los problemas actuales, convirtiendo al teatro en una alternativa educativa que exprese al mismo pueblo y al mundo la riqueza, la belleza, y el poder de los valores culturales hondureños y centroamericanos, en un momento histórico caracterizado por el fenómeno de la globalización económica y cultural que margina y excluye a aquellas culturas consideradas como inferiors.

> (Teatro la Fragua defines its work in Honduran society as awakening the creativity of people through theater to find solutions to current problems, using theater as an alternative education that expresses to Hondurans and the world the richness, beauty, and power of Honduran and Central American cultural values. in a historic moment characterized by economic and cultural globalization that marginalizes and excludes those cultures it considers inferior. *Trans. mine.*)[12]

This is theater that addresses the traditional functions of theater to entertain, educate, and raise and explore questions, moral dilemmas, and social issues. It does not always take clear positions on particular issues, but approaches indirectly or radically in the sense of exploring an underlying cultural, moral, spiritual, psychological, or social basis or context. Some of the plays presented are written by Hondurans, others by well-established foreign writers. One of the plays the group presented in 2013 was *Frontera sin Fin* (*Frontier Without End*). The play was adapted from a work of a well-known dramaturge in California. It explores the hopes and tragedies of Central Americans trying to make the trek to emigrate to the United States—the hopes for a better life, the sadness of leaving family, the uncertainty for the future, the robbery, assault, and other dangers on the way, and the many bureaucratic and other frustrations and confusions that can divide friends and strain old relationships. The decision to emigrate is never condemned or approved, but its complexity becomes apparent. The play also suggests a critique of U.S. immigration and border policy or bureaucracy. The topic and its complexity are highly relevant to Honduran life. After presenting the play, the director and the actors usually spent an hour fielding audience questions and comments about the play and its themes.

RECLAIMING PUBLIC SPACES AND BRINGING PROTEST TO THE STREETS

On page 11 of the August 2013 issue of the newspaper *aMecate Corto*, Honduran journalist and writer Manuel Torres Calderón described how his sadness and frustration over the loss of public spaces in Tegucigalpa to gang and political violence moved him to take a long stroll with his wife one Monday afternoon from his neighborhood into some of the central areas of the city. It was a stroll of defiance, but also a form of healing—deliberative and deliberately impractical. The only plan was to enjoy the city again. Torres explained that what troubled him most about the shrinking sense of safety in public spaces was that it destroyed society. "If there is anything that I resist it is the abandonment of public spaces. Every meter conceded to isolation is a loss of society."

He referenced the Polish sociologist Zygmunt Bauman for whom the greatest social evil of our time was precisely the loss of society itself, the loss of civic community. For a few hours Torres and his wife wandered the streets enjoying the great public buildings, shops, cafés, parks and bridges. Near the end of their walk, they saw birds take flight from the branch of a tree and soar above the streets. Torres concluded:

> *¡Que cosa! Una bandada de pericos errantes convertida en símbolo de humanidad, libres de competencia entre ellos. Ajenos a ese campo de batalla urbano sobre el que sobrevuelvan sin pedir permiso.*
>
> What a thing! A band of errant parakeets converted into a symbol of humanity, free of competition among themselves. Far from the urban battlefield, they fly high above it without asking permission. (*Trans. mine*).[13]

In Honduras today, murders and abductions occur in public places, on streets and highways. Fear prevents many Hondurans from lingering in public parks or taking leisurely walks in neighborhoods. Local gangs (*maras*), hired drive-by assassins (*sicarios*), and even police and military checkpoints and patrols make the streets and highways seem dangerous. Public spaces important to the promotion of civic life and community become increasingly places to be avoided or used as little as possible. The public sphere shrinks, isolation increases, the quality of life decreases. This may reinforce the control of a few powerful individuals and groups, but it is a life of anxiety for parents sending their children to school each day, or husbands and wives wondering if their partner will return from work. Much of popular culture is set in public spaces—street murals, people playing music in the park, athletic events, outdoor skits, parades and fiestas, even the simple enjoyment of strolling one's city or community and sharing that with others. The abandonment of public spaces undermines community life and restricts the creation and expression of popular culture.

Hondurans have often responded to these threats to public space by making a very big show of filling public space. Despite the dangers, Hondurans continue essential daily routines that may require being in or passing through public places. But in cities, at least, parents do not usually allow children to play in the streets. In wealthier neighborhoods, many homes are like compounds, surrounded by walls or fences and patrolled by private security guards and dogs. In poor neighborhoods, where gangs regularly demand "protection" money from residents, parents find ways to leave the area, or they send their children off on the long and dangerous journey out of the country to find safe asylum in the United States or elsewhere.

Occasionally, people have participated in organized walks over long distances along some of the major public highways in the country. Many such *caminatas*, organized by popular organizations and often led or accompanied by indigenous groups, have occurred in recent Honduran history (chapter 5). These *caminatas* are often several hundred kilometers in length, and tend to have the aura of a pilgrimage or a spiritual journey or quest, appropriate to the ancient origins of this form of public expression.[14] Their spiritual undertone and their length make these *caminatas* different in character but not always in ultimate purpose from the many protest marches that Hondurans have staged in their recent history, especially after the 2009 coup. Protest marches (*marchas*) are perhaps the most apparent and even stereotypic displays of popular resistance. These marches tend to be limited in distance and duration, often within the confines of city blocks. There have been many protest marches involving many thousands of Hondurans in the decades since the great banana strike of 1954 filled the streets of El Progreso and other northern towns. Some marches combine elements of protest with a spiritual dimension. In August 2013, when people walked through the streets of Comayagua with lighted candles to the prison where many of their loved ones had been burned six months earlier, the walk and the vigil at the prison gates became a place to remember, to grieve, and also to denounce and protest the lack of accountability of the authorities (see chapter 7).

As public spaces have in recent years seemed increasingly under the control of the violent, protest marches have also become occasions to take back popular control of public spaces. People who participate in protest marches in the current context of Honduran life are aware that participation involves certain risks. Police and military units may try to break up marches and arrest protesters. Marchers have been shot. Sometimes provocateurs appear, often feigning drunkenness and acting in violent ways so as to provoke the nonviolent marchers into a violent response.[15] But protest marches are usually organized carefully by popular organizations that also deploy some of their members along the route and train them in procedures to follow for security and to defuse potentially violent situations. There may be safety in numbers. What an individual would not express in public might be more safely and powerfully expressed in company with many others. So to participate in a nonviolent protest march in Honduras involves, at some more or less conscious level, a sense of taking back the streets and public spaces. We can understand this decision and the significance of protest marches within a wider context, as Scott suggested in an earlier study in another area of the world:

> Seen in the light of a supportive subculture and the knowledge that the risk to any single resister is generally reduced to the extent that the whole community is involved, it becomes plausible to speak of a social movement.[16]

Honduran protest marches provide the structure of a "supportive subculture" (the groups or coalitions organizing the march, such as the FNRP and others) in order to create and display the involvement of what should appear as "the whole community" (marchers in their thousands) in an act of public protest. Involving "the whole community" is a gradual and problematic process, although the 2009 coup provided a great impetus toward galvanizing "the whole community" in protest—part of the evolution of a "social movement" of resistance and rebuilding.

Protest marches are often occasions that bring out popular creativity in expressing protest. Sometimes a few people clad in bright clown-like colors or stereotypic characters march on stilts, swaying as they walk with their bodies appearing above the heads of other marchers, taking on an almost comic character as they bob and weave among the other marchers in displays of great stilt coordination almost as if they were dancing down the street. Stilt figures are a tradition in popular and some religious fiestas, and the custom is here adapted to a demonstration of collective protest. The appearance seems to counter the daily fear and terror of public spaces with a display of comic lightness with just an edge of menace (masked figures towering over the scene), as if to say, "We the marchers own this place." Even the protest signs that marchers carry often display creativity in conveying their message, sometimes with biting sarcasm. One sigh bears the image of a devil with a facial photo of a political leader involved in the coup. Another sign depicts President Lobo as a wolf—*el lobo*. A third sign depicts the Cardinal, widely believed to be supportive of the coup, as a wolf in sheep's clothing.[17] Critical of the news coverage of the mainstream Honduran press, marchers in one large protest march in San Pedro Sula on August 11, 2009, bore a sign reading, "Become stupid in only five days! Read *La Prensa!* Satisfaction guaranteed or your money back!"[18] *La Prensa* is a major national newspaper owned by members of the elite.

One Friday afternoon in 2013, as I stood at the doorway of a building in El Progreso waiting for the ride that would take me to the neighborhood where I was living, a large crowd of people, most in white blouses or T-shirts, came running down the street, many smiling broadly, others chatting with nearby runners or walkers. Spread out in small groups, they ran, jogged, and walked by in the heat and humidity. The crowd took a full ten minutes to pass. Many shouted or signaled invitations to bystanders to join them. When I asked, I was told they were following a predetermined route through the streets of downtown to one of the public parks where they would spend another half-hour or hour before dark, congregating, playing games and making music. At the front of this crowd of movers were students from a city high school who had decided to do a run through the city streets en masse every Friday afternoon at about five in order to "take back the streets," as someone told me. These students had learned that students in San Salvador (El Salvador) had begun a similar weekly action to take back their streets from gangs and violence in that city. For those of us who are addicted runners, this action was more than symbolic. Running involves a very physical here-and-now commitment of body and soul, and every run becomes a leap of faith in oneself and one's environment. Here, the young runners had enlivened the older folks to join them at any pace—jogging, walking—they could manage.

THE COMPLEXITY OF A POPULAR FIESTA: GUADALUPE CARNEY DAY

As in most of Latin America, popular and religious fiestas have long been a regular feature of life in cities and in some rural areas of Honduras. Fiestas perform a complex set of functions—providing sociability and entertainment for rural and poor communities with few other opportunities for these, offering occasional moments of popular education about many aspects of daily life, offering occasions for people to expand or strengthen social networks, and more. Fiestas can also be opportunities for politicians and local power brokers to make a public appearance, advertise their public generosity, campaign for office, or simply convey messages that may reinforce aspects of a dominant ideology. Fiestas can be social spaces in which many cultural symbols are in play at once, and conflicting interpretations and messages can be conveyed. At some fiestas celebrating the national holiday or the national day of indigenous people, schoolchildren and some adults wear costumes and recite lines that reinforce the official version of Honduran indigeneity as entirely Mayan, to the exclusion of other native groups (see chapter 5). So fiestas may provide opportunity for both dominant and alternative stories and realities to be presented and even juxtaposed. Religious fiestas honoring a saint or commemorating a moment in the Catholic liturgical year may bring together traditional colonial rituals and hierarchies of control with messages about social justice and love for others.

In Central America, honoring as saints and martyrs those who gave their lives in the service of others is an important practice. In Honduras, one of these honored dead is James Francis Carney, a U.S. citizen and Jesuit priest who lived from 1961 to 1979 among peasant farmers in some of the rural areas of the country. Known universally as Padre Guadalupe, Carney was beloved among the peasants and the poor with whom he lived and worked because of his passionate support for their struggles and their resistance to the exploitation of their lives. In his posthumously published autobiography he wrote, "Why are the campesinos so poor in this rich valley? They are farmers who do not have any land! We rebel against that, even if they call us communists, even if they kill us. We have to wake our people up, tell them to get organized, help them to change the situation."[19] With such a perspective, Carney ran afoul of some powerful people. The Honduran government exiled him to Nicaragua in 1979. He returned to Honduras in 1983 as the chaplain of a band of armed Honduran revolutionaries who were quickly killed or captured by units of the Honduran army. One version of Carney's death claims that he was killed in a battle with the military. Others believe he was killed while in military custody. His body was never produced. No one was prosecuted for his death, and thirty years later his family in the United States and friends in Central America were still seeking facts. He became a revered figure throughout Central America, most of all in Honduras, where many people emphasize his practice in love and devotion to the poor and are indifferent to ideological criticisms of his alleged "Marxism."

Several Honduran organizations joined to sponsor a day of commemoration of Padre Guadalupe on Saturday, September 14, 2013, the thirtieth anniversary year of his death. The organizers conceived the occasion in the form of a traditional *campesino* popular fiesta. For weeks before the day, radio and other announcements emphasized both the memory of Carney and the elements of food, music, skits, and celebration that were hallmarks of traditional fiesta. An underlying (and sometimes explicit) message was that Padre Guadalupe was for and of the Honduran people, especially the poor, the peasants, and anyone who struggles for justice in the country. The fiesta would be held in El Progreso on the grounds of the Jesuit-run *Instituto Técnico Loyola* high school. Radio announcements invited people to come for the day from outlying communities, and many came from outside El Progreso. The day started with a march under a hot sun through some of the main streets of the city. Hundreds participated, some in organized groups wearing their brightly colored T-shirts from popular organizations, others as individuals or small groups of friends, families, work companions, or people from other communities. As the march proceeded over the next hour or more, the tone could be described as a mixture of celebration and determination. A troupe of young people in costume on stilts danced their way through the ranks of marchers. People chatted, others shouted demands for justice for various causes, especially an end to violence, respect for the country's land and resources, and accountability from authorities. Many marchers simply walk silently along with what seemed a focused forward gaze, as if determined to reach a goal. The day was hot and humid, as usual in El Progreso, and some marchers may simply have wanted to reach the destination at the *Instituto*.

One of the young men holding a large banner for the human rights organization COFADEH was sixteen-year-old William (pseudonym). His hand had been severely injured on May 11, 2012, as he rode in a boat at night on the Patuca, going to visit his grandmother for Mother's Day, when the boat was attacked and fired on by U.S. and Honduran drug enforcement agents in helicopters.[20] His friend died in the same attack, and William heard his cries but could not help him. William managed to swim to shore. He was brought to Tegucigalpa for treatment, and later hand surgery, and received ongoing support from COFADEH. Learning about this attack and the lack of any official U.S. compensation to the survivors, a church congregation in Oregon later raised the four thousand U.S. dollars for a surgery to repair William's hand. Now, here he was smiling broadly and marching in the Guadalupe Carney Day parade in El Progreso, holding up part of the large COFADEH banner with his hands. This festival brought together people with a wide variety of experiences and stories.

Soon after most of the marchers had arrived at the *Instituto* grounds, a Catholic Mass was celebrated outdoors to begin the festivities on a serious spiritual note. Several of the priests had personally known Padre Guadalupe. At least one had been deeply influenced to enter the priesthood and devote his own life to the work of justice and mercy for which Carney was known. The large crowd included many who seemed to participate intently in the Mass, and others around the periphery who chatted, sat looking distracted, or continued to prepare the large pots of food nearby. During the offering of gifts that is a traditional part of the Catholic Mass, people representing different organizations and different communities presented symbolic tokens in front of the altar.

The end of the Mass signaled the start of the eating. People in long lines waited more or less patiently in the hot sunlight for the traditional tamales, beans, rice, and smaller amounts of some local specialties from different communities. No alcoholic drinks were visible, on the *Instituto* grounds, nor did anyone seem "under the influence" as the day progressed. This apparently universal sobriety was unusual in a popular fiesta. Following eating came the music and the skits, performed by local groups and amateur talents. A youth group presented a skit depicting a bit of indigenous life, possibly Lenca, but it was not easy to tell by the costume or the script. While some watched, others mingled and wandered about talking with friends and acquaintances. By about three in the afternoon, the festivities began to wind down, and the crown diminished. Three young staff members of Radio Progreso, neatly dressed for the fiesta, sauntered off to a market down the street. Padre Juan, a white-bearded older priest in T-shirt, shorts, and sandals left the grounds pedaling his bicycle with a broad smile and shouting farewell to the small groups of peasants and rural people also leaving to trek home. People who had come from outlying communities began the trip home, probably anxious to arrive before dark. The realities of a violent country were never far away, even at the edges of such a festive day.

Guadalupe Carney Day brings together the forms of a traditional Honduran religious folk fiesta, typically held in honor of a patron saint, to honor the memory and spirit of one whom many Hondurans consider a modern saint. Carney is portrayed in two complementary ways—as one who accompanied and ministered to the ordinary people and loved to be with them, and as one fiercely committed to social justice, especially on their behalf and in their company. Choosing to honor him appeals to the interests, concerns, and emotions of poor *campesinos*, working class poor people, and middle-class urban people who for various reasons are dedicated to what they understand as social justice—priests and nuns, students and youth, lay church leaders, human rights advocates and popular organizations. The crowd that marched and participated included people from all of these social groups and more. The fiesta brought together people with quite varied and vivid experiences of injustice, oppression, or glimpses of a better reality. The fiesta recreated in a delimited space and time, a small experience of what a better life might be, or for some, perhaps, the memory of a better past that may or may not have happened but is, in any case, now seemingly gone. It was almost a civic and religious ritual of renewal. A brief experience of something better that is actually created by ordinary people in the present time and place, this fiesta combines spiritual reflection, enough good food to eat, singing, dancing, skits, conviviality, the free mixing of social classes and backgrounds on a field of equality and in relative freedom from fear and violence—an enjoyable and fleeting experience of a better reality that is a reminder in the middle of an unsatisfactory world that ordinary people are not alone and together can build the better future. The absence of alcoholic drink helped to eliminate the occasion for fighting and violence, and it also banned what some consider one of the primary instruments of control and oppression in some Latin American societies.[21] This momentary creation and enjoyment of life seemed to contradict the violence and oppression of much of daily life in Honduras, or to make it seem all the more heinous and unnecessary. In this sense, the fiesta was an act of resistance and a subtle critique of what Honduras seemed to have become. The popular "saint" honored by the event was a modern symbol of resistance to many.

Chapter 8
LAUGHTER: ANCIENT WEAPON OF THE PEOPLE

Laughter can be a powerful support for a people trying to resist and survive what oppresses them. Laughter can be related to critique of oppression—mocking, exaggerating, or "making fun of" the ideology and practices of oppression and the oppressor. The power of this lies in unmasking the false and hinting at the truth, the demystification of the ideology and practice of oppressive control. Laughter generated in this way can also provide a small example of risk and freedom in speaking truth to power in dangerous times, and in dismantling a bit of the fear that often acts as an instrument of control. In another context, laughter that comes from enjoyment of a happy moment can provide a fleeting glimpse of a better life in dangerous times. Hondurans employ laughter in all these ways.

The March 1990 issue of the *Bulletin of the Committee for the Defense of Human Rights in Honduras* (CODEH) was replete with the "usual" accounts of peasant dislocations, political assassinations, and human rights violations, and the all too frequent photos of people showing the wounds of torture. But on the front page was a photo of a certain Doña Edelmira, a mother from a small community in the Department of Santa Barbara, who farmed and made straw hats for a living. Here in this front-page photo, Doña Edelmira was smiling broadly as she made a hat with one of her children. Her message was, "*Es tiempo de desenterrar el arma antigua del pueblo—la risa—y empuñarla en las luchas por una Honduras digna.*" (It is time to resurrect the ancient weapon of the people—laughter—and to brandish it in the struggles for a dignified Honduras. *Translation mine.*)[22]

Outsiders who visit or become acquainted with Honduras express surprise at the way Hondurans seem to be able to laugh and joke about many things in their daily lives. Outsiders sometimes (but not often) misinterpret such laughter, thinking that it reflects happiness or contentedness about the conditions of life and Honduran society. But in Honduras, as in so many places, laughter can be a very old and powerful weapon of resistance and resilience—resistance because it is used to reveal and disarm the absurdity of oppressive situations, falsehoods, or dominant ideologies, and resilience because laughter arms people for the long struggle by reminding them of their essential humanity. The smile, the laugh, and humor are deployed to disarm many potentially tense or oppressive situations. Hondurans stopped at a military or police checkpoint may appeal with a smile to the humanity of the police sergeant or the soldier. Popular culture is a major context for humor. *NotiNada*, is a radio program aired regularly on Radio Progreso and produced by several young people who often project disguised "cartoon" voices to point out, even mimic the absurdity and contradiction in some of the events of the week and the conditions of society. Cartoons in publications reveal the absurdity, falsehood, or irony of a policy, a statement, or a situation, and Honduras is replete with such cartoons in popular media. What cannot be said in serious discourse can be implied in humor. Musical lyrics, skits in folk festivals, scenes in plays about the most serious issues, and radio programs employ humor that both disarms and relieves fear and stress through evoking a smile or a laugh. People laugh at the thing instead of cowering before it. Laughter and humor can even seem empowering and can reveal the humanity of the "oppressor" who, like the fabled emperor, really wears no clothes. Humor is difficult to repress because of its ambiguous and contagious nature—it can critique and humanize at once.[23]

PHYSICALITY, POPULAR CULTURE, AND RESISTANCE

Popular culture and popular resistance are woven together in many ways in Honduras. Popular culture can critique what people experience as oppressive and can provide glimpses of an alternative reality. One of the salient features of popular culture is its tendency to evoke physicality, the involvement of the body. Even radio, television, and literature engage the ear, the eye, as well as the mind. Music, clothing, claiming public spaces, theater, murals, marches, fiestas are all forms of expression that engage bodies in their creation and enjoyment. It is as if ideas, reflection, ideology are not enough to create and sustain popular resistance. The engagement of people's bodily experience is integral to resistance because people know oppression and violence first of all as physical experiences—bodily harm, poverty and hunger, anxiety, physical detention and imprisonment, even fear that restricts physical freedom (one cannot walk freely in public spaces). Resistance seems to require a response that reasserts physicality as a human trait, a human "right." If humans are integral beings, this makes sense. Praxis requires both thought and action, and action implies engaging one's body. Another way to see this is that resistance requires struggle or at least exertion. Popular culture provides channels of bodily engagement that also touch the mind and the emotions. Forms of popular culture appeal to human, shared experience, but also encourage individual expression. Resistance movements are composed of individuals with many different stories and experiences of life that are rooted in individual bodies. The body remembers and knows what oppressive conditions are in different ways. It also remembers what is enjoyable, freeing, and pleasurable. Popular culture helps these disparate bodies, these individuals to relate their own experience to that of others and even to a sense of common humanity.

The importance of the physicality of resistance should not be underestimated. The tendency to separate individual existence into mind and body, to alienate mind from body, has been one of the fundamental justifications for various forms of oppression and violence in the modern world. Saying that the "soul" is more important than the "body" has condoned the most heinous crimes against human populations, as many of the indigenous peoples of Latin America discovered when the Europeans arrived with the cross in one hand and the sword in the other. This may be why students and advocates of social revolution and "liberation" have condemned this fundamental alienation within the human being. Resistance engages body memory and may be the struggle to regain the full exercise and enjoyment of our humanity. Popular culture humanizes resistance, reminds us of the humanizing goal of resistance, and nourishes our resilience. Ironically, understanding the physicality of resistance will be important as we explore the spirituality of resistance in the next chapter.

NOTES

1. Robert Redfield, *Peasant Society and Culture: An Anthropological Approach to Civilization* (Chicago: University of Chicago Press, 1956).

2. One of the first acts of the Sandinista revolutionary government in Nicaragua in 1979 was to plan and carry out a literacy campaign that increased the country's literacy rate by over thirty percent in six months. Government ministers and revolutionary leaders spoke of building a "nation of poets." There were several recognized poets in the higher offices of the revolutionary government, including Vice-President Sergio Ramirez and Culture Minister Ernesto Cardenal. Cardenal began organizing poetry workshops in towns and rural areas around Nicaragua when the revolutionary government took power and the literacy campaign developed. It was commonly said that revolutionaries are poets at heart, and that liberation from dictatorship includes the empowerment of ordinary people to express their feelings, experiences, and visions in poetry and other forms of free expression.

3. See for example, William H. Beezley et al. editors, *Rituals of Rule, Rituals of Resistance: Public Celebrations and Popular Culture in Mexico* (Wilmington, DE: Scholarly Resources Inc., 1994), xxiv–xxvi.

4. Eric Canin, "Mingüito, Managua's Little Saint: Christian base Communities and Popular Religion in Urban Nicaragua," in *Contemporary Cultures and Societies of Latin America: A Reader in the Social Anthropology of Middle and South America*, Third Edition, ed. Dwight B. Heath (Long Grove, IL: Waveland Press, 2002), 467–79.

5. R. Handler, "Romancing the Low: Anthropology vis-à-vis Cultural Studies vis-à-vis Popular Culture," *Political and Legal Anthropology Review* 17:2 (1994): 1–6. Handler writes, "In the absence of ethnographic fieldwork—or some other method to engage directly with the people 'out there' who are creating and consuming the cultural products being analyzed by scholars—the discourse of cultural studies on resistance remains profoundly elitist" (4).

6. *Vida Laboral*, September, 2010, 4–5.

7. Jon Wolseth, *Jesus and the Gang: Youth Violence and Christianity in Urban Honduras*. (Tucson: University of Arizona Press, 2011), 66.

8. Wolseth, *Jesus and the Gang*, 67.

9. Susan Phillips, *Wallbangin': Graffiti and Gangs in L.A.* (Chicago: University of Chicago Press, 1999). James Diego Vigil, "Group Processes and Street Identity: Adolescent Chicano Gang Members." *Ethos* 16:4 (1988): 421–45.

10. Jon Horne Carter, "Gothic Sovereignty: Gangs and Criminal Community in a Honduran Prison," *The South-Atlantic Quarterly* 113:3 (Summer, 2014): 475–502.

11. Marvin Barahona, *Honduras en el siglo XX: Una síntesis histórica* (Tegucigalpa: Editorial Guaymuras, 2005), 168–69.

12. Teatro la Fragua website, www.fragua.org/INDICE.HTM (April 25, 2015).

13. Manuel Torres Calderón, "Visita guiada por Tegicigalpa," *aMecate Corto* (August, 2013), 11. Zigmunt Bauman, whom Torres references, developed a critique of a world in which human society is endangered by attempts to measure, account for, and predict everything, to control every human movement—a world where authority fears the stranger and the unpredictable. He argued, in effect, that this undermines the spontaneity, fundamental trust, and human interaction that are the basis of human society. Torres implies that such is the present danger for Honduran society.

14. Long treks and pilgrimages are noted in the Bible, ancient Greece, Medieval Europe, the Islamic Middle East, Asia, and pre-colonial and colonial Latin America. Most of these are primarily religious expressions, but could sometimes be regarded by participants and authorities as acts of protest or resistance. They differ from simple travel or movements of exile or diaspora.

15. All of these dangerous possibilities actually occurred during the peaceful demonstrations conducted by COPINH and Lenca activists in the area of Rio Blanco in their ongoing protests against the damming of the Gualcarque River in 2013 (see chapter 5).

16. James C. Scott, *Weapons of the Weak: Everyday Forms of Peasant Resistance* (New Haven, CT: Yale University Press, 1985), 35.

17. *Vida Laboral*, "Resistencia Popular," Edition 43 Especial (September, 2009): 5. This entire special edition is devoted to reporting a variety of street and public protest demonstrations in the aftermath of the June, 2009, coup d'état. The entire front and back cover of this edition is filled with a panoramic color photo of a massive protest march held in San Pedro Sula on August 11, 2009 in the central park in front of the cathedral.

18. *Vida Laboral*, September, 2009, front cover photo.

19. James Francis Carney, *To Be a Revolutionary* (New York: Harper-Collins, 1985).

20. A detailed report of this incident is provided in, Annie Bird and Alexander Main with Karen Spring, "Collateral Damage of a Drug War: The May 11 Killings in Ahuas and the U.S. War on Drugs in La Moskitia, Honduras" (Washington, DC: Rights Action and the Center for Economic and Policy Research, August, 2012).

21. Adrienne Pine, *Working Hard, Drinking Hard: On Violence and Survival in Honduras* (Berkeley, CA: University of California Press, 2008), 85–134, especially 90–93.

22. Comité para la Defensa de los Derechos Humanos en Honduras (CODEH), *Boletín 62* (March, 1990): 1.

23. William H. Beezley et al., "Introduction: Constructing Consent, Inciting Conflict," *Rituals of Rule, Rituals of Resistance*, William H. Beezley et al eds. (Wilmington, DE: Scholarly Resources, Inc., 1994), xxv–xxvi.

Chapter Nine

A Spiritual Struggle

What could be more authoritative as a critique of violence and oppression than a divine commandment? On July 3, 2009, one week after the 2009 coup d'etat in Honduras, the bishop and the leaders of the Catholic diocese of Santa Rosa de Copan issued a public statement that included this injunction:

> We want to remind everyone, and especially the Armed Forces and the national Police, about the fifth commandment that says: You shall not kill (Exodus 20:13). This commandment also forbids blows (*golpes*), injuries, and every humiliation against the human being who was created in the image and likeness of God and is a temple of the Holy Spirit. (*Translation mine.*)

Religion—both in its organized, institutional form and as a more spiritual, internalized sense—often invokes divine authority. But how effective is this if one's purpose is to change not only individuals but also an entire society? This chapter examines some aspects of the role of religion and non-material ("spiritual") approaches in relation to popular resistance and societal transformation in Honduras. Most of what we have seen in previous chapters might lead us to conclude that Hondurans who are involved in resistance that is manifest in so many different ways are convinced that their actions and their strengths can actually engage and subdue the very real material forces that oppress their lives. Whether individuals act in resistance out of a positive and optimistic sense of what can be accomplished or are driven by desperation with uncertainty about the outcome is not always easy to discern. When we try to understand the systems of domination and violence that resistance engages in Honduras, our interpretation tends toward social scientific description and explanation of the economic, political, social and military contexts as shapers of human behavior and policy. This is enormously useful, and it is clear that Hondurans who engage in big and small acts of resistance to violence and oppression are analyzing and interpreting economic, political, social, and military realities. But many people go beyond these contexts and forces in trying to understand a reality that seems to them so enormous, inhuman, and entrenched.

One day in 2013, I was traveling with a Honduran Catholic priest who had spent many years accompanying his people and often acting as a spokesperson for the victims of human rights violations. We began talking about why there was such violence in the country and how to address it without feeling overwhelmed. This priest knew something about mass psychology, sociology, and politics, how economic structures can oppress people, and many other social scientific analyses of the situation, and how people in groups in power can lose sight of the morality that might once have guided them. He knew that people all over Honduras were trying to build a better society, and he himself had devoted his life to this. But for him there was more, another level of reality that was somehow integrated with and acted upon the visible, material world. He confided that he thought the struggle for Honduras was fundamentally a spiritual and moral struggle.

The remnants of the former seminarian in me thought that somehow this was true, but the social scientist in me was uneasy about invoking a spiritual realm. I knew that the way social scientists normally approach such a "spiritual" question is within the category we label "religion," and *that* category could lead to some quite complex and apparently contradictory realities. Religion is generally observed, studied, and interpreted in its social and cultural manifestations as *organized religion* or the social and cultural institutions and external practices of religion that play a visible and traceable role in the history and life of a society such as Honduras. Engaging the complex and contradictory category of "religion" requires an examination of how what is understood as religion or religious faith in Honduras today helps or hinders people's efforts to transform their actual material conditions of life, especially oppression and violence. But how does this engage the "spiritual struggle?"

I was also uneasy because I knew that the discourse of the spirit is not easily understood or expressed in words, nor is it easily interpreted to others who do not share a belief in this "spiritual realm." This concern I could partially assuage with the standard anthropological approach that, whether or not there is an "objective" reality, people act on what they believe to be real. To understand others we need to realize that their beliefs are very real for them, though they may be mingled with much doubt. In turn, people's sense of reality is shaped in many ways by their experience of life and the material conditions in which they live. The material or external conditions of life and the internal ideas that people have are in a dynamic relationship.[1] What people believe may move them to address the conditions in which they actually live. What if we were to take seriously the idea that for some Hondurans a spiritual struggle is at the root of their resistance and resilience? What would "spiritual" really mean? How would this struggle be manifest and observable in Honduran life in these times?

Since colonial times, Honduras has been a largely Christian, mostly Catholic country. The truth of this characterization is apparent in daily life. Churches are numerous, crosses and symbols of religion and especially Catholicism abound, and the political and cultural prominence of the Church and its appointed leaders soon becomes apparent in the newspapers and in political and policy discussions. Beside Catholicism, there has been a small Protestant presence in Honduras since at least the latter part of the eighteenth century brought, in part, by the incursions of the British in the north of the country. This presence remained small until the 1960s, when evangelical, Pentecostal, and neo-Pentecostal churches especially began to grown rapidly in Honduras, adding other forms of Christianity that today rival Catholicism in numbers of adherents.[2] But this omnipresence of Christianity belies a more complex reality if one asks exactly how the most fundamental beliefs and teachings of the faith penetrate and inform the lives and actions of individuals and especially institutions. Hondurans and outside observers are driven to ask, if the country and its people are supposed to be guided by Christian values and beliefs, why are Honduras and its people experiencing such a time of great violence, violation of basic rights, greed, and other evils? Is it the fault of individuals who do not live according to "spiritual" values? Or is the country in the grip of some terrible evil or madness beyond normal human failing and wrongdoing? Hondurans do ask themselves such questions. We have seen that some of the answers lead either to self-blame—we are sinners who create our own misery—or to relinquishing any responsibility—it is all God's plan and not for us to question. These may be strategies of psychological survival, but they do not support a sense of resistance and change.

As a result of these concerns and observations, this chapter approaches the realm of the spiritual on two levels—first, an examination of organized religion as an observable institution in Honduran history and life; and then an attempt to describe, understand, and interpret what Hondurans mean by the "spiritual struggle" at a deeper, more broadly human level. This division is not simply a convenient analytical strategy. It acknowledges that in everyday life in Honduras the elements of organized religion and the "spiritual struggle" (or at least the way people understand and interpret this) engage each other in constant tension—sometimes destructive, sometimes creative. First we trace some aspects of the historical institutional churches—primarily Catholic but also Protestant—and their role in popular resistance and resilience. Then we examine some widespread theological ideas as forms of ideology that have undermined or supported popular activism and resistance.

We conclude by exploring more specifically what some Hondurans seem to mean by the deeper spiritual struggle.

RELIGIOUS SYNCRETISM, ACCOMMODATION, AND RESISTANCE

Fresh from the "reconquest" *(Reconquista)* of the Iberian Peninsula from the Moslems at the end of the fifteenth century, Spanish conquerors arrived in Central America in the early 1520s with the cross in one hand, the sword in the other, and a militant and triumphal belief in Christian conquest. Much has been written about the resistance that native people displayed in the face of Spanish methods of religious conversion.[3] Religious syncretism, the blending of Christianity with indigenous religion, was an apparent result. Syncretism has generally been interpreted as a way in which native people accepted the outer forms of Catholic Christianity and hid their older beliefs and practices under the guise of the new religion.[4] This syncretism was made easier by some apparent similarities between European Medieval Catholicism and the religions of various (but not all) indigenous peoples of Latin America—a situation that Mary Lee Nolan termed "the permissibility of the familiar."[5] These included the necessity of human sacrifice and the redemptive death of Jesus; the importance of ritual, ceremony, and even sacraments; belief in an afterlife; penance and self-inflicted disciplines; a three-tiered concept of the architecture of the universe into underworld, earth, and heavens; prophecy as witness and social critique; a pantheon of lesser gods and a pantheon of saints who intercede and help humans; priesthoods, sacred virgins, and nuns; even the idea of virgin birth was not entirely unknown in some indigenous theologies. These characteristics and many more eased the process of blending religious forms of Catholicism and some indigenous religious beliefs in ways that the later arrival of Protestant Christianity did not. But syncretism is not unique to Latin America; most religious traditions have been deeply shaped by syncretism. What is important is not the fact of syncretism but the politics of why syncretism exists and how it is used as a form of resistance or accommodation in relations of often unequal power.[6]

Another characteristic of the appropriation of religion to empower a group was the appropriation of Catholic religious symbols and figures by different groups as a part of their collective identity. Today one can see graphic examples of how the Catholic reverence for the Virgin Mary, mother of Jesus, has been translated, adapted, and expressed in ways that make her one with the people, one of theirs, reflecting their identity or their idealized identity. The classic portrayal of the *Virgen de Altagracia*, patron saint of the Dominican Republic, shows her wearing the crown, jewelry, and fine robes of a queen, and the physical features identified as white or "European," as

Dominican society emphasizes its European (Spanish) heritage. The Virgin of Guadalupe (*la Guadalupana*), patron saint of Mexico, is really the patron of the indigenous poor of that country, depicted in simple garb, darker complexion, and an expression and stance that signals help and support rather than conquest and triumph. Religious syncretism, and to some extent symbolic appropriation, were the result of a process of survival that entailed both accommodation and resistance, but a resistance that used the cultural forms and even the beliefs of the conquering religion of the colonizers in ways that preserved older beliefs or encouraged empowerment.

As we saw in chapter 2, oppressed people can sometimes invoke the basic elements of an ideology of domination to form the most damning critique of the gap between ideology and reality, turning the ideology of domination into an instrument of liberation. Sometimes others provide a voice for this that the oppressors cannot ignore. The European conquerors of Latin America preached a Christian Gospel to the conquered native people, but their brutal actions and oppressive policies often seemed to contradict the morality of the Gospel. To the Spanish Catholic colonists who flocked to church on Sunday in sixteenth-century Santo Domingo, Spanish priest Antonio Montecinos preached his (in)famous sermon the week before Christmas, 1511, invoking basic Christian moral teachings and symbols to condemn the ways in which his hearers were oppressing the remaining native peoples of Hispaniola. He pointed out the gap between their professed religion and their actions. Bartolomé de las Casas describes this scene in his *History of the Indies*:

> Antonio de Montesinos ascended the pulpit and took as the text and foundation of his sermon, which he carried written out and signed by the other friars: "I am the voice of one crying in the desert." After he completed his introduction and said something concerning the subject of Advent, he began to emphasize the aridity in the desert of Spanish consciences in this island, and the ignorance in which they lived; also, in what danger of eternal damnation they were, from taking no notice of the grave sins in which, with such apathy, they were immersed and dying. "I have ascended here to cause you to know those sins, I who am the voice of Christ in the desert of this island. Tell me; by what right or justice do you hold these Indians in such a cruel and horrible servitude? On what authority have you waged such detestable wars against these peoples, who dwelt quietly and peacefully on their own land? Wars in which you have destroyed such infinite numbers of them by homicides and slaughters never before heard of? Why do you keep them so oppressed and exhausted, without giving them enough to eat or curing them of the sicknesses they incur from the excessive labor you give them, and they die, or rather, you kill them, in order to extract and acquire gold every day? Are these not men? Do they not have rational souls? Are you not bound to love them as you love yourselves? Don't you understand this? Don't you feel this?"[7]

For this sermon, Montecinos received death threats and demands for his deportation back to Spain. But note, as Las Casas reports, that the other friars in Santo Domingo also signed this sermon. A modern and symbolic denunciation of Christianity's entwinement with colonial oppression occurred when Pope John Paul II visited Peru in the 1980s. Indigenous people took the occasion to send him a copy of the Bible, saying they were returning to him the Bible since it had brought them neither peace or justice, and the Christians who oppressed them evidently needed the Bible's teachings more than they did. Since colonial times and into the present, Christianity has served as a two-edged sword—an instrument of domination, but also of critique and even liberation.[8]

In Honduras today religious forms and beliefs remain important resources for expressing resistance. But religious faith is not just its forms; it also *informs* resistance and animates it. Some people are driven to resistance because their religious faith leads them to condemn the fear, violence, oppression, and human degradation they see or experience, and presents to them the vision of a better human life and society.[9] The mixing of Christian and indigenous religious beliefs that some Lenca people in resistance have expressed may be seen not as a dilution but as a strengthening of the power of religious belief in these conditions of stress and resistance.

CHURCH, STATE, AND RESISTANCE: 1824–1950

Throughout the colonial period (1524–1824) the Catholic Church was present in Honduran territory primarily through the missionary activities of a few priests among indigenous peoples and serving the small numbers of colonizers. Honduras was part of the larger province that included most of Central America. The church's authority and the colonial political authority were closely related and supposedly complementary. In significant colonial towns, the administrative center and the church faced each other across the central plaza or park. In the largest centers of colonial power such as Mexico City, the governor's palace and the cathedral faced each other. The church was supportive of the major purposes of the colonial state—conversion and "civilizing" of indigenous peoples and maintenance of social order achieved through inculcating Christian morality and obedience to proper authority. Originally, the Spanish monarchs seemed to think of the church as a moral counterforce against the excesses of Spanish colonists and governors, and at times priests and bishops took this role seriously, sometimes at a cost to their own positions or safety. But the church as a social institution was a partner with the colonial state in maintaining an often oppressive and exploitative order even as it offered a promise of something better in the next world to people who experienced oppression.

The independence movements that swept Central America in the early 1820s were informed by an ideology of liberalism, reform, and modernization. The kind of political and social liberalism that energized the desire for independence tended to see the church as an arm of a backward, repressive colonial order fueled by superstition and corruption. In areas of Central America where a more conservative political ideology dominated, the church was seen in its historic role as an instrument of the state, to be used (and misused) as the rulers of the newly independent Central American states saw fit.[10] One tragedy of the Catholic Church in this era was that it let its identity be reduced to the role of servant to the political authorities, so that the new governments either rejected it as a relic of the past or regarded it as subservient and faithful to the state. To many of the new leaders of the newly independent countries, the church's power and land wealth seemed a potential threat and/or a source of wealth to new and fragile independent governments.

After almost fifty years of political turmoil and very weak central authority, Honduras came under the rule of a Liberal government in 1876 that vigorously promoted the modernization and development of a Honduran state, economy, and society. The Catholic Church had to contend with a somewhat subdued but still present strain of anticlericalism in successive governments well into the twentieth century. By the early 1900s, it had to contend also with several major institutional problems. The state controlled the educational system, depriving the church of one of its major avenues of influence among the middle and upper classes—private schools that would educate upper and middle-class youth. There was no functioning Catholic seminary to train Hondurans for the priesthood, in part because of government anticlerical policies. This deprived the church of a local clergy, forcing it to rely on foreign missionary clergy from Europe, the United States, and other Latin American countries. This may have weakened the image of Catholicism as a cultural institution rooted in the history and cultural identity of Honduras.[11] In 1933, this foreign reliance provoked a conflict with the Carias dictatorship when the German-born archbishop of Tegucigalpa died. Normal church procedure would have been for the pope and the Vatican to appoint a successor, but the Carias government tried to exert control over the process and to nationalize it, proposing a Honduran priest in Tegucigalpa as the new archbishop. Vatican authorities rejected this, and the post of archbishop—head of the Catholic Church in Honduras—was vacant until the end of the Carias regime in 1947.[12]

Chapter 9

RISE OF EVANGELICAL PROTESTANTISM AS A SOCIAL AND POLITICAL FORCE

Although there had been a small if sporadic presence of Protestants in northern Honduras since the late eighteenth century, some of the earliest Protestant missionaries and congregations became established in the latter half of the nineteenth century. Their entry was eased by the liberal anticlericalism that restrained somewhat the political influence of the Catholic Church, and perhaps by the influence of the United States in Honduras. By 1940, Protestant churches were active and slowly expanding, and Pentecostal churches were working especially among marginalized populations in poor urban neighborhoods. The new wave of Pentecostal, neo-Pentecostal, and Evangelical denominations tended to be more theologically fundamentalist and politically and socially conservative, although their character often reflected the realities of the social classes in which they were based or to which they mainly appealed. Some Pentecostal churches attracted and identified with people in poor urban neighborhoods and were more likely to support the struggles of poor people. Others, such as some of the Evangelical and neo-Pentecostal churches had many adherents and much appeal among middle class and wealthier Hondurans, and reflected the political and social views of their members.[13]

THE CHURCHES AND THE RISING POPULAR ORGANIZATIONS: 1950–1965

By the 1950s, Catholic and Protestant churches in Honduras were confronted with and had to find ways to engage a society in which popular organizations were beginning to find voice as a force in the political and social life of the country. Catholic and Protestant churches began to address the needs of these emerging social groups, devoting more attention to addressing basic needs such as literacy and primary education, family life, simple household economics, prenatal and postnatal support and information, and basic preventive medicine. Trained teams visited rural communities or were based in church facilities in poor urban neighborhoods to fill some of the gaps in the basic services that longtime government neglect had helped create. International Christian aid organizations such as Caritas (Catholic) began to have a presence in Honduras.

During the 1950s, the Catholic hierarchy tried to reassert a stronger church presence in Honduras by increased attention to social needs, by preaching and prayer campaigns open to the general public in different parts of the country, and by instituting *Acción Católica* (Catholic Action), a training program for lay church leaders who could act in areas where the scarcity of priests was especially acute. The bishops also thought of *Acción Católica* as a means to bind ordinary faithful Catholics more closely to the bishops and their agendas for the church.[14] This initiative and its concept may have been an antecedent of the Delegates of the Word movement that developed in Honduras in the 1960s and 1970s after the reforms of the Second Vatican Council.

In 1957, the Liberal government of Ramon Villeda Morales came to an accord with the Catholic hierarchy. The government's agenda of liberal reforms was meant to engage the rising popular organizations, to incorporate their voices into Honduran society and political life, and to address some of their primary needs without making them voices of opposition or resistance. In its accord with the Catholic Church, the government acknowledged the church as an important voice in society, and it set aside the official anticlericalism that had characterized earlier Liberal governments. But in 1963 a military regime replaced the Villeda government and unleashed repressive forms of control over popular organizations, especially the peasants and the labor unions. Catholic Church support for the legitimate right of labor to form unions and engage in collective bargaining was well established, at least in theory, since the end of the nineteenth century. The Honduran church found itself trying to argue for such rights in a context of government repression of labor and peasant unions. At the same time, the convening of the Second Vatican Council (1962–1964) called the world's Catholic bishops to Rome to engage in the extensive overhaul of Catholic theology and pastoral outreach that in the following decades deeply affected the church in Honduras and elsewhere and its relations to popular resistance and the state.

Since colonial times, the Catholic Church had been an integral part of Honduran society and culture, and an important source or provider of comfort, solace, hope, and community for many Hondurans, but it was not a source of or a support for movements of social change, major reform, or popular resistance. When mass popular organization did enter Honduran life, especially with the banana strikes of the 1950s, the Honduran Catholic church was confronted with the question of how to respond to this evolution of popular power. For many years, the church had operated within the confines of a liberal state and with a theology and a pastoral plan that would soon seem inadequate to address both the rise of popular need and organization on one side and the rise of the neoliberal state on the other. Despite its entrenched place in Honduran life, the Catholic Church depended heavily on foreign priests and suffered a constant shortage of priests that seemed a crisis but gradually became for some an opportunity for church reform, especially after the Second Vatican Council. According to some analysts, the longstanding patterns of the Catholic Church had difficulty adapting to the needs of a society of increasing social complexity.[15]

Chapter 9
THE CATHOLIC CHURCH AND THE LEGACY OF THE VATICAN II COUNCIL (1960–1990)

When the Catholic bishops of Honduras and the rest of Latin America, Africa, and Asia went to Rome for the Second Vatican Council, they brought with them what they had learned from their priests and nuns who lived among and ministered daily to people in city slums, small towns, peasant villages, and banana workers' compounds, as well as in private schools and wealthy protected neighborhoods. What the bishops brought was an ethnography of poverty, lack of basic services, oppressive working conditions, and human rights violations directed especially against the poor—societies marked by enormous gaps between great wealth and profound poverty where political structures favored a few and effectively shut out participation by the many. The bishops were aware that these were societies where popular organization was emerging and people were looking for avenues of participation and change. Coming three years after the triumph of the Cuban Revolution (1959), the Second Vatican Council convened in a world still assessing the significance of the Cuban experience and what it meant for alternative visions of society for the poor and oppressed—and, indeed, for the wealthy and powerful. It became clear to some that these societal conditions were not in keeping with the deepest moral teachings of the Catholic Church, and that such a situation might drive desperate people to seek alternative visions of human life offered by communism or fascism. Reflection on all of this also raised more disturbing questions about capitalism itself and its apparent excesses, and caused some church leaders to consciously adopt a more neutral, skeptical, even critical attitude toward capitalism so as to avoid endorsing capitalism "by default." Some at the Council also wanted to reaffirm that the primary concern of the Catholic Church should be people, especially people in crisis, more than doctrine or ideology.[16]

In the aftermath of the Second Vatican Council, the Catholic Church in Latin America adopted the "preferential option for the poor." This term was open to different nuances of interpretation. It could be simply an affirmation that the church had always taught charity and concern for the poor and now wanted especially to emphasize this—although this seems not to have been the intent of the Council. It could mean that the church should minister to all, but have a special concern for the poor and vulnerable. It could be interpreted as a rebuff to the rich and powerful with the church now taking the side of the poor in some form of class conflict. But it could also be interpreted to mean that the church should take a proactive stance to support and defend the poor and to promote their empowerment and organization even to the point of popular resistance to oppressive and inhuman conditions. People of all social classes and economic conditions in Latin America saw different mandates, threats, or promises in this preferential option for the poor that reflected tensions within the Catholic Church and potential for conflict between church and state.

Garrard-Burnett and Stoll argue that the "option for the poor" and the rise of liberation theology that provided the theological context for this approach undermined the Church's traditional patronage role as a broker between poor and wealthy, between the state and the people, and removed the Church as a buffer or protection for the vulnerable.[17] Instead of patron and protector, the Church now supported the direct empowerment of the poor and vulnerable, and thereby undermined its own "neutral" intermediary position. It allowed those with a vested interest in the old status quo to accuse the Church of promoting class conflict and betraying the traditional alliance of Church and state (or Church hierarchy and wealthy) in maintaining stable social order. The transition was dangerous for both the poor and the Church as long as it was not successfully completed. This soon became abundantly clear in Honduras and elsewhere.

The emergence of *comunidades eclesiales de base* (CEBs, basic church communities) in Latin America was a concrete legacy of the Second Vatican Council. In Honduras, CEBs developed in the 1960s, earlier than in some other regions of Latin America. People in their different groups and communities—peasants and laborers, teachers, housewives, office workers—met to read and reflect on the Gospels in the light of their individual and collective everyday reality and the national context. What does the story of Jesus driving the moneychangers from the temple really mean for the lives of day laborers now in Honduras? How does the daily experience of the Honduran people in these small communities compare with a vision of life and humanity that Jesus presented in the Gospels? CEBs had potential for empowering people to challenge what they saw as unjust or oppressive in their lives. Although it may not have been their particular intent, the CEBs promoted four processes that were crucial for popular organizing and resistance. They brought together people to share experiences and broke the isolation of individuals, giving courage to people in groups to express their reality. They gave each person—theologian or peasant farmer—an equal space and legitimacy, undermining the hierarchical model that allowed a few to dominate others (a major change in the traditional practice of the Catholic Church). The CEBs encouraged thoughtful reflection and critical analysis of the shared reality that people were living, starting not from abstract moral principles but from concrete examples and lived experiences. They provided religious, scriptural bases for people's critique and resistance, thereby joining religious faith to popular resistance.

The new model of church evolving out of Vatican II allowed the Latin American Catholic Church to make virtue out of necessity. Chronically plagued by a scarcity of trained priests and the dominance of foreigners in the Honduran priesthood, and with a sense of the attraction that the model of lay leadership in the proliferating Protestant churches had for many people, the Catholic hierarchy promoted the development of a major program for training individuals in local communities to lead religious services and CEB sessions in the absence of a priest, and in general to act as leaders in the religious and civic life of local communities. These individuals were Delegates of the Word (*Delegados de la Palabra*). Founded in Honduras in 1966, regional networks of Delegates of the Word gradually developed among communities, and at a national level, holding periodic assemblies for prayer, practical training in leadership, and reflection. By 1985, Honduras had over ten thousand Delegates of the Word.[18] In some communities, Delegates of the Word became leaders of local initiatives for change. Some Delegates became recognized community leaders of resistance to various mining or other development projects that seemed to threaten local environments and people's livelihoods, health, or security. These patterns of community leadership continued into the present, as the example of Antonio shows. A Delegate of the Word in his local community in southern Honduras, he had been a leader in organizing his community's opposition to the operations of a foreign lumber company in their area in the 1970s, and he was again a leader in organizing community opposition to foreign mining operations in the area in the years after the 2009 coup d'etat (see chapter 3). A woman who was a Delegate of the Word in her urban community was also a leader in her municipal workers union in denouncing what the members saw as corruption in the city government. She continued her role even after she and her family received anonymous threats.

Delegates of the Word embodied, to a greater or lesser degree, a theology that saw spiritual and material life as a single inseparable reality, and the attempt to construct conditions worthy of the "dignity of the children of God" as an unavoidable task of believers.[19] Delegates might not speak much of how their religious faith inspired them, in part because they saw their very activity for the community as an expression of their faith. In some communities, Delegates of the Word and local Protestant lay leaders worked together to organize and effect change, transcending doctrinal or sectarian differences to find common cause. The evolution of a culture of resistance in Honduras also had the effect of encouraging, even demanding that people of different and no religious beliefs work together, not always an easy accomplishment, given a long history of religious competition and distrust among believers themselves and between believers and social activists wary of all religion as a form of reaction and a traditional instrument of oppression. The evolution of the culture of resistance in Honduras seemed to demand a change of mind and perspective about traditional religion and religious differences for both believers and non-believers.[20]

Hondurans who became Delegates of the Word or engaged in regular CEBs were also people with jobs and material lives such as plantation workers or peasant farmers. Some of these Delegates and lay church leaders became leaders in the popular organizations that arose in the 1960s and early 1970s, especially the labor and peasant unions. The National Peasant Union (UNC) was formed largely as a progressive Christian alternative to other major unions that were seen as either too conservative, controlled by elite interests (ANACH), or too influenced by Marxist ideology (FENACH, see chapter 4). In the eyes of some, at least, the church was now linked directly of progressive popular organizing. Opponents in the Honduran government and ruling class began to see the UNC as a popular organization most resistant to their plans for the country, and the Catholic Church as a potential threat to the social and political order that supported the ruling classes, especially after the Latin American bishops reaffirmed this new direction for the Catholic church at a major conference held in Medellin, Colombia, in 1968. The Document on Peace drafted at Medellin warned:

> This situation [of poverty and dependency in much of Latin America] demands all-embracing, courageous, urgent, and profoundly renovating transformations. We should not be surprised, therefore, that the temptation to violence is surfacing in Latin America. One should not abuse the patience of a people that for years has borne a situation that would not be acceptable to anyone with any degree of awareness of human rights.[21]

The massacre of Los Horcones (1975) and several similar incidents—threats to clergy and Delegates of the Word, the expulsion of foreign priests, the virtual closure of the entire diocese of Olancho for a time—served stark notice to church people that their involvement in or support for popular organizations that offered resistance to the interests of the powerful would trigger brutal, violent responses (see chapter 4). After 1975, Honduran Catholic bishops began to retreat from their support for direct popular resistance in the face of such brutal responses. More traditional "church" activities were promoted instead. In part, the bishops feared for the safety of their priests and nuns, and even their very ability to function as a church if their actions invited a brutal response.[22] In 1979, however, events in neighboring Nicaragua caught the attention of anyone who thought that religion and revolution could not mix. Many Nicaraguan Catholic priests, Protestant ministers, Delegates of the Word, or lay leaders in the churches joined the revolution that overthrew the Somoza dictatorship by arms and nonviolent means. Some, such as Jesuit priest Fernando Cardenal, had to struggle with uncertainties and fears and to reconcile their traditional ideas of religious faith with the necessity of a revolution.[23] For some members of the powerful Honduran elite, the Nicaraguan example only confirmed their sense that the Catholic Church was infiltrated with communists and corrupted by Marxist ideas.

Throughout the early 1980s, Honduran governments, powerful individuals, and the security forces continued a campaign of assassinations, kidnappings, surveillance, and harassment of Catholic priests, lay leaders and some Protestant ministers. The government expelled several more foreign-born priests, including James Carney (Padre Guadalupe), and the military enforced the temporary closure of Radio Progreso in 1979.[24] Carney's expulsion occasioned a popular petition in his defense that gained twenty-five thousand signatures. Similar conflicts between the Catholic Church and powerful interests were also brewing in other Latin American countries.

While church members participated in popular organizations and continued to engage in land takeovers, demands for better working conditions, or respect for human rights, Honduran Catholic bishops tried to express a more narrowly focused criticism of the national security regime but also issued statements that seemed to contradict their own criticisms. When the Suazo Cordova government tried to stop a delegation of two hundred Catholic nuns from the United States from entering Honduras to pray and demand an end to U.S. intervention in Honduras, the spokesperson for the Honduran bishops declared the bishops' disapproval of the nuns visit, but affirmed approval of the presence of U.S. soldiers in Honduras. This and similar incidents led some people to speak of an apparent division in Honduran Catholicism between a conservative "institutional church" and a progressive "popular church," although many people thought this idea was an exaggeration of the real tensions that seemed to exist, and was counterproductive to the dialogue of mutual love and respect that should characterize all sectors of the church.[25] Meanwhile, the bishops focused attention on the corruption and lack of transparency that seemed to characterize both major political parties. This critical focus could also serve as a vehicle for some critique of the repression of justice and human rights. Commenting on Honduran politicians, Bishop Raul Corriveau of Choluteca said: "Many of those who could change the situation exhaust themselves in partisan struggles or in shady manipulations of public funds, branding as communists all those who cry for social justice or defend human rights."[26] Church officials made denunciations of the way in which public officials removed themselves and the political process from the control of the citizens.

THE CHURCHES IN NATIONAL AND LOCAL STRUGGLES: 1990–2014

In the years from 1990 to 2014, the Christian churches, Catholic and Protestant, were actors, albeit in different ways, in the evolution of resistance at both national and local levels. Nationally, the presence of the institutional Christian churches was apparent in the statements and actions (or inaction) of the Catholic bishops and mainline Protestant organizations, and in the general orientation of the major Catholic religious orders, especially the Jesuits and the Franciscans. The Franciscans supported the work of the national Delegates of the Word and the strengthening of family and parish life that tended to express the orientation of the church toward serving the poor and provided a basis for local social activism. The Jesuits maintained their presence in secondary education, training youth in social consciousness, basic human rights, and democratic principles, as well as the active involvement of youth in projects of social action and community development. Jesuits also maintained Radio Progreso as a voice for independent and often critical news reporting, opinion, and community events. They supported the work of ERIC in conducting critical social analysis of Honduran society and issues, and in community development and empowerment. Some Protestant churches, including at least one Evangelical congregation, did become involved in engaging the social and political ferment. The pastor of the Agape Church in Tegucigalpa led prayers for peasants fasting outside the National Assembly demanding a new land reform law. He also included reflection of major social issues in his sermons. But other national religious leaders, both Catholic and Protestant, publicly supported the policies and practices of the government, the military and police. Some observers detected a pattern in the different responses and relationships of churches to the government and the country's elite.[27]

At a local level, church engagement with popular struggles became more urgent and costly. In Central America, parish priests in rural areas usually served many small rural communities, traveling to these periodically from a base in a centrally located town. During the years from 1990 to 2014, many rural parish priests (and some urban parish priests) found themselves serving communities that were actively engaged in struggles with mining companies, large landowners, drug lords, or corrupt local police—sometimes with all of these. Many people in the rural communities drew moral and emotional support from their strong religious and spiritual beliefs. In this context, serving the religious and spiritual needs of a people involved in a struggle for survival and accompanying them in their struggle might make any attempt to separate religious and secular or religious and political almost meaningless. With almost every action or choice, priests became involved—willing or hesitant—in the very political yet also "spiritual" struggles of their people. For some priests, this accompaniment meant accepting danger and risk. For example, in 2001, Jesuit Peter (Pedro) Marchetti's apparent support for peasant organizations engaged in land struggles with local large landowners in the Aguán Valley made him a target of the landowners who offered a reward of 500,000 *lempiras* (about US$32,000 at that time) for his assassination.[28] Marchetti was forced to leave the area. In September, 2012, lawyer and Protestant minister Antonio Trejo Cabrera was killed in the parking lot of a church where he had just conducted a wedding. Trejo was the lawyer for a peasant group involved in a land dispute with large landowners in the Aguán

Valley. He had been receiving death threats since at least June, 2012. In August of that year he was detained briefly for participating in a protest related to the land case. In September, shortly before he was killed, he had joined other lawyers in presenting a constitutional challenge to the law establishing "special development zones" (ZEDES) supported by the government.[29] Local priests who seemed to support the struggles of one social class—the peasants, the rural poor, laborers—sometimes found themselves branded as traitors or bad priests by other sectors of their parish—the elites who had traditionally regarded the church as their ally or servant, or by middle-class parishioners who thought their priests or ministers should not be so involved in secular causes.

Incidents of direct violence and brutality against socially active religious people sent at least two messages. One was obvious—religious involvement in social activism has strict limits that are defined by the interests of the economically and politically powerful. The other message was that a religious institution that turns toward social activism and a "preferential option for the poor" has lost its way and abandoned its traditional role as defender of hierarchy and the social order, and must be brought back to that role. The proper role of religion was as dispenser of personal discipline, spiritual comfort, and charity. Food and clothing distribution to the poor and needy was proper church work. Asking *why* people were poor and needy, or supporting peasant demands for land, were not.

ADDRESSING THE COUP: THE STATEMENT OF THE DIOCESE OF SANTA ROSA

The 2009 coup presented the churches with the need to address a major trauma in the life of Honduran society. The constitutional legal order, weak and oligarchic as it was, was now broken, despite the face-saving gestures of those in Congress who had engineered the coup. An already insecure society became more insecure, since no one knew exactly what would follow. The cardinal's apparent support for the coup angered and scandalized some Hondurans. In the days after the coup, he publicly urged Zelaya not to return to Honduras or there might be bloodshed.[30] When Zelaya did try to land at the airport amid a crowd of supporters, the military fired on the crowd, killing teenager Obed Murillo. Some thought the cardinal knew the military would unleash a violent repression on the demonstrators. Major Evangelical church leaders also publicly supported the coup. Many Hondurans in resistance movements formed the conclusion that church leaders and the hierarchy in general supported the coup. A few church leaders chose to denounce openly the coup and to express what they thought were the demands and yearnings of most Hondurans. Led by their bishop, Luis Santos, priests and lay leaders of the diocese of Santa Rosa de Copan issued a joint statement within a week after the coup (*Mensaje de la Diócesis de Santa Rosa de Copan*, July 3, 2009). The statement is remarkable and instructive in several ways. It specifically denounces (*repudiamos*) the "substance, form, and style" of the coup which it describes as the illegal imposition of a new executive power. It provides a list of specific rights that it claims are violated or threatened by the "state of exception" (similar to martial law) declared by the Congress, and it provides a list of demands in the name of the Honduran people. Among the threatened rights:

> the rights to associate freely and demonstrate publicly, the inviolability of the home and household, the right to private property, freedom of the press, diffusion of ideas and opinions, personal liberty including the right not to be detained without cause or indefinitely by the police. . . . We especially denounce the violent form in which Radio Progreso and other communications media were silenced, the illegal detentions, the disappearances of some of our citizens, and the bloody beatings. . . . The immense majority of Hondurans do not want street confrontations, civil wars, or wars with other countries. . . .We Hondurans want peace. We don't want lies. We want to be told the truth. No more injustices. We want respect for the integrity of the person and for human rights. We want to live in freedom. We don't want repression. (*Trans. mine*)[31]

It is worth noting that Bishop Santos had long been known for speaking publicly against the abuses of successive governments since the national security state of the early 1980s. This post-coup statement brings to light a church that openly denounces the actions of the political powers as illegal and in violation of the basic rights of Hondurans. The list of these rights included especially those that seemed most necessary for a people in a democratic society to express their criticism and even to engage in active resistance, and rights most threatened by the repressive response of the state security forces against the public demonstrations and expressions of popular resistance to the coup. The statement also echoes the demand for truth from public officials. The gap between the legal maneuvers and public pronouncements of the *golpistas* and the realities that people saw unfolding revealed the lies. The church leaders of Santa Rosa expressed this in the context of the Jesus of the Christian Gospels who often spoke of truth.

Coupled with these denunciations, however, are passages that seem to affirm a human connection with those whose actions deserve condemnation, and exhortations to believers to address the perpetrators of violence and evil in loving and redemptive ways. Fear is specifically identified as a factor in creating and sustaining contexts of violence and oppression. The statement implies that denunciation of evil and resistance to oppression are really acts of love and healing for the entire society—a complex and perhaps controversial message to many.

Chapter 9
THEOLOGY AS WEAPON

Religious beliefs or theologies offer to believers different ways of interpreting and understanding not only a spiritual reality but also, and perhaps especially, a worldly reality. The kinds of religious or theological beliefs one accepts have consequences for one's involvement in transforming one's society. In Honduras, as in much of Latin America, there are different kinds of widely preached and accepted "theological" beliefs that can undermine people's efforts to resist and transform an oppressive reality. These beliefs are worth review because all of them were extant in Honduras in the first decades of the twenty-first century as potential obstacles to personal engagement in popular resistance and social transformation.

Dualism

Since the Spaniards arrived in Latin America in the early 1500s, bearing the cross in one hand and the sword in the other, a theology of dualism has been one of the most enduring and consequential ideas in the arsenal of domination, justifying some of the most heinous violence and oppression against the poor and vulnerable. Dualism conceives of humans as formed of body and soul—a physical body of earthbound material, and a non-material, spiritual, and free soul that does not die—and teaches that the soul is more important than the body. What happens to the body is not really important as long as the soul is pure and intact. Oppressed people could be told that as a matter of faith they should care more about their souls than the material conditions in which their bodies lived, because their souls are what mattered in the afterlife in paradise or hell. This idea not only justified the theft of land and resources from native peoples or the poor; it could also divert attention away from people's efforts to improve their material conditions. This dualistic body-versus-soul perspective encouraged divisions in human life that further weakened collective resistance or the building of a new community—separating body and spirit, the good from the bad, spiritual from earthly, man from woman, the saved from the damned. Ideas like this drove Marx to elaborate his critical concept of human alienation and the characterization of religion as an opiate. Dualism can deaden the conscience of people in a way that, according to one Honduran religious observer, was apparent in the recent political life of the country, especially the events around the 2009 coup.[32]

Spiritualism

Closely related to dualism is spiritualism, the belief that one should devote oneself to spiritual things and avoid the affairs and problems of the world, including involvement in political activism.[33] One implication is that the way to address the problems of this earthly life is by prayer and avoidance. The church should not be involved in "political" or social issues or causes, and definitely should not promote popular resistance.

Providentialism

A theology of providentialism teaches that everything in history and life is decided and arranged by God, and everything that happens furthers the plan of God. Humans should learn to accept and accommodate themselves to God's plan as it unfolds, for somehow God is taking care of everything. The implication is that resistance to "God's plan" is a form of rebellion against God. Combined with a hierarchical theology that sees political and religious authorities as unquestionable agents of God's plan, providentialism exhorts people to assent to the policies and actions of authorities without resistance or even serious questioning. In his major study of the political and social effects of this belief in revolutionary Nicaragua, Perez Baltodano asserts that providentialism is widely preached in churches and invoked with some frequency by public figures in Nicaragua, to support neoliberal policies.[34] A similar observation can be made about Honduras.

Hierarchy of Being

The idea that there is an ordained hierarchy of being—God, religious and political rulers, society ranked with each one in one's proper place—has pervaded much religious and political thought in the Western world. The German theologians who developed the school of "political theology" in Europe in the 1960s and 1970s identified this belief that rulers were God's instruments as one of the major reasons why Hitler gained legitimacy among many religiously observant Germans, and why many German Christians did not resist Nazism. It is a belief that can serve well the needs of a political dictatorship or a powerful oligarchy.

Dispensationalism

Dispensationalism is the theology that teaches that Jesus will come again at the end of the world to judge everyone. The good will be taken up into heaven, but the evil will be damned with the destruction of the earth. This end times may come quickly, and good and faithful Christians do nothing to postpone the second coming of Jesus and the end of the world. Some of the signs that this end is near are increasing natural disasters and especially increasing evils in human society. Such a theology has an appeal in a society such as Honduras where daily violence, insecurity, fear, and oppression may seem rampant. There is no need to engage in efforts to challenge and transform the evils plaguing society because these evils only hasten the Second

Coming that the Christian awaits. Striving for a better earthly society may be blasphemous because it interferes with the plan and timing of God for human life. One should dedicate oneself to keeping apart from the evils of society, not engaging them.

One of the offshoots of this theology was the so-called satanization of the struggles for change in Central America in the 1980s, especially the Nicaraguan Revolution. The Reagan Administration in Washington, D.C., and the government in power in Honduras characterized the revolutionary movements of that decade as "communist" and therefore atheistic efforts to fundamentally change human society. Such efforts were the work of Satan.[35] Dispensationalism became a major strand of the theology preached especially in some of the more fundamentalist evangelical churches in Honduras and elsewhere in Central America.

Gospel of Individual Prosperity

The gospel of prosperity teaches that material wealth and prosperity are signs of God's blessing and favor, whereas poverty and individual crisis are signs of sin, lack of faith, or a disordered personal life. Although this belief could encourage individual efforts at personal material and spiritual betterment, it was also a rationale for enormous differences in wealth and resources among social classes, and neglect of measures to better the lives of the poor and address social injustices. Embracing this theology, the wealthy and powerful in a very poor country such as Honduras could maintain the status quo of inequity with an easy conscience, even convincing themselves that they were fulfilling God's will by amassing wealth and ignoring or even exploiting others. Aside from rationalizing economic injustice, the gospel of individual prosperity emphasized individual effort to better one's own situation, thereby undercutting group or community efforts and the need to struggle for community or societal improvement. While the other beliefs discussed above are forms of theology that can dissuade the oppressed from mounting collective resistance, the gospel of prosperity is a theology for the wealthy and powerful or for a rising middle class that justifies their position and actions with a divine blessing.

National Security: The State as God

National security is primarily a political doctrine that has very significant religious, spiritual, and moral implications. The doctrine claims that the security and welfare of the state is the highest good, and all individual lives, rights, and liberties must be subordinate to the security of the state. The military are the ultimate arbiters and guarantors of state security. The doctrine has roots in European nationalism of the late nineteenth century and the fascist regimes of the 1930s, and was adopted by Latin American military dictatorships in Argentina, Brazil, and Chile in the mid-twentieth century and in the early 1980s in Honduras where the doctrine resulted in national security states. The United States was also influenced by the doctrine of national security during the Cold War, and instituted the National Security Agency and a gradually increasing and secretive bureaucracy of intelligence. The U.S. Patriot Act that came out of the events of September 11, 2001, seemed to further legitimize the national security doctrine in the United States.

The Catholic Belgian/Brazilian theologian José Comblin wrote extensively about the implications of the national security doctrine and state for both religious belief (theology) and for the activities of religious institutions in Latin America. This doctrine is often sold to people through the discourse of nationalism. To illustrate this, Comblin quotes the work of a major Latin American proponent of national security:

> To be nationalist is to be always ready to give up any theory, any ideology, feelings, passions, ideals, and values as soon as they appear as incompatible with the supreme loyalty which is due to the Nation above everything else. Nationalism is, must be, and cannot possibly be other than an Absolute One in itself, and its purpose is as well an Absolute End—at least as long as the Nation continues as such.[36]

Comblin concludes critically, "Consequently, the nation takes the place of God. What happens then to the God whom the elites claim they want to worship by establishing a Christian society? This Christian God is only a cultural symbol."[37]

In Honduras this doctrine was invoked to justify the repressive conditions of the early 1980s and since, and was useful in justifying the 2009 coup against the Zelaya government. In modified form, it appeared again in the political campaign rhetoric of presidential candidate Juan Orlando Hernandez in 2013, and in the expanded militarization of Honduran society in the first months of Hernandez's presidency in 2014. National security appeals to a society experiencing daily violence and insecurities of all sorts. But the doctrine of national security tends to regard all dissent, all popular resistance, all criticism, and most critical education as threats to national security. The role of religion is to be a support for obedience, hierarchy, and social order, not to support popular resistance or alternative visions of society. Religious institutions are a support for the power of the elite and the state as long as the religion they offer does not go much deeper than "only a cultural symbol."

Religion as a Collection of Cultural Symbols

Religious symbols, ritual, and symbolic gestures are cultural resources. They are meant to express what words may be unable to say, and they are often more powerfully evocative of emotion than are words. Such symbols can help lead people to deeper "spiritual" or human experiences, but the symbols are not the experiences. Cultural symbols can be used in various contexts for various reasons, since they carry meaning at multiple levels of human consciousness and experience. The depth of meaning in a religious symbol depends in part upon the depth of experience of the beholder. A crucifix, an image of Jesus nailed to a cross may carry a different emotional meaning for a person who has suffered or who carries a weight of guilt than for someone who has experienced neither of these. Religious symbols can be debased by overuse, being deployed in many contexts throughout everyday life in ways that may even seem contradictory to some of the deeper meanings the symbols might carry.

At the inauguration of Porfirio Lobo as Honduran President in January 2010, the cardinal archbishop of Tegucigalpa attended the ceremonies and presided over a public Mass for the new president. Symbolizing the church's blessing of the political regime, such a gesture was nothing new in Honduras and the rest of Latin America. But many Hondurans had refused to participate in the elections that chose Lobo in November, 2009, in a context of ongoing popular protest and repression of protest, only five months after the coup. They considered the elections as illegitimate, and they saw the new regime as a product of those who had planned and executed the coup against President Zelaya and were now pretending to normalize their usurpation of power with a show of elections and an inauguration ceremony. In this situation, many hoped that the cardinal, the chief visible authority of the Catholic Church in Honduras, might withhold his blessing and his presence from the inauguration as a symbolic critique of the usurpation and illegality of the new regime and its violent methods. They hoped that by withdrawing his blessing, the cardinal would use the occasion as a symbol of religious resistance. The cardinal's presence, however, signaled the opposite. It was a sign of contradiction, confusion, and even scandal for some Hondurans. For others, it confirmed their skepticism or cynicism about organized religion and its corruption. There were some who thought that perhaps the cardinal was simply being pragmatic, wanting to maintain a relationship with the political powers that would keep open opportunities for the church's influence on public policy. For still others, the cardinal's behavior highlighted the shallowness of the religious symbol and the need for a deeper spirituality that would not sell the church to the political powers of the day.

A THEOLOGY OF LIBERATION AND SPIRITUAL STRUGGLE

In contrast to the theological teachings describe in previous sections, in the 1960s, throughout Latin America a different kind of theology was emerging.

Catholic and Protestant theologians began to distill this new approach in books with titles such as *A Theology of Liberation*, by Peruvian theologian Gustavo Gutierrez (1973).[38] The new theology started not from abstract philosophical principles but from reflection on the lived experience of people, and so it relied on the social sciences for "*analisis de la realidad.*" It emphasized the voice of God in every member of the community, not just church authorities. It went beyond charity and saw commitment to social justice as an integral part of faith. And it emphasized the need for people to be able to live in material conditions that were, "worthy of the dignity of humans as children of God."[39] The theology of liberation that was part of this kind of religious faith provided a basis for regarding social activism and even popular resistance as an expression of faith, both as resistance to oppression and injustice and as constructive efforts to build more human and just alternatives in society.[40] For some, this opened the possibility of a dialogue with secular philosophies that also emphasized social justice—socialism and even Marxism. For others, the imperative of restoring justice and human dignity in situations of massive tyranny could lead to the necessity of armed resistance. In Honduras, a few embraced these possibilities, while others affirmed that a theology of liberation unlocked for them an even more radical nonviolent path of asserting the humanity of their oppressors and the possibility of liberating themselves by liberating their oppressors of the burden of having to oppress others.

A Honduran friend and devout Catholic told me this story. He was driving home late one night in 2010 in the rain when he saw a man in a parked car by the side of the road. Such situations are often considered dangerous in Honduras. My friend stopped, went over to the other car and recognized the man inside as a prominent official in the national security forces. He had been implicated in or accused of the killings of many Hondurans, but he enjoyed impunity. When he saw my friend, he took out his gun and was clearly frightened, but his attitude seemed to soften a bit when my friend asked what the problem was and whether he could help. The problem was a car breakdown. The man agreed to go to my friend's house and use his phone until the problem was fixed. My friend, who years before had been detained and tortured by the security forces, said it was a very odd experience having a man of such violent reputation in his house. He said this man seemed more like a frightened animal than the author of so much violence. "He has no soul," my friend said sadly. He said he thought this man was driven by fear because he has so many possible enemies, and that he is a captive to this burden of the legacy of his actions, a burden that only gets heavier the more he reacts in fear.

Honduran newspapers and television news are often filled with stories of brutal killings, replete with graphic photos. Most of the victims are poor, or sometimes middle-class, people of all ages. This sort of crime reporting seemed almost a stock in trade for some of the mainline news media. People such as Berta Oliva, longtime director of the Committee of the Families of the Detained/Disappeared in Honduras (COFADEH), worried that Honduran society was rapidly becoming desensitized to such dehumanizing brutality.[41] In the years after the 2009 coup, the violence seemed to increase in scope and take on a different character. Now there were almost daily reports of finding plastic trash bags filled with the hacked body parts of children, some a young as six or seven. There were reports of people being assassinated, sometimes shot dozens of times. In at least one case, the body of a man was found shot at least three hundred times in the face. This sort of brutality seemed beyond any rational explanation. Assassinations were utilitarian—they eliminated opponents or leaders of resistance movements. Killing the victim was enough. Or if frightening others was also the purpose, a few additional bullets or a few moments of torture of the victim would be enough to spread that fear. But some of this brutality went beyond any such "utilitarian" ends. It seemed as if there was a form of madness or evil beyond normal human rational self-interest that possessed and dehumanized the perpetrators as they commited acts that dehumanized others.

It is in such a context that some Honduran religious and human rights leaders and activists occasionally speak of a spiritual struggle, but what they mean by that is not always easy to identify. People speak of many components (weapons?) of such a struggle—hope, freedom from fear, freedom for openness and love, happiness or joy, a sense of the uniqueness and value of others, priorities that place people before things, a sense that the individual is not the center of everything, a connectedness to all of creation, a deep sense of peace and much more. What this discourse describes are internal dispositions that are realized always in relationship to others and to constructing some sort of community in external action.

But then there is this other violent reality that seems hard to explain in the scale and dimensions of human life. Some people such as the man my friend met on the road one night seemed to be burdened by a heavy load that does not allow them to be free of the cycle of violence and injustice. One day in August 2013, I joined a group of eight people in a base Christian community (CEB) reflection in El Progreso. The text was the story of the resurrection of Jesus from the dead. The group related this to the current situation in Honduras. They said that in a time of death and insecurity for his followers, Jesus rose from death, and that this was a challenge to the oppressive powers of the state that crucified him but also a challenge to all of the violence, fear, and insecurity the people were experiencing. For them, the story of the resurrection signified hope, the power of love, and a repudiation of fear. I was surprised that almost everyone in our reflection circle spoke not of poverty and inequity but of violence, fear, and insecurity as the things that the spiritual struggle primarily engages. Perhaps this is what discerning the spiritual struggle means—not struggling against the person but against whatever makes people turn to violence and oppression, to evil acts.

There are many everyday incidents in which Hondurans manage to engage the inherent humanity of those who threaten or oppress them. It can be as dramatic as the post-coup public statement of the Diocese of Santa Rosa or as small as a smile or a kind word at a military checkpoint. The enormity of violence and oppression is reduced, brought down to human dimensions, and dispelled by reminding people of their human goodness and their connection to others. Liberation, as in the theology of liberation, seems to have these two related meanings. One is the liberation of oppressed people from the structural violence of human institutions and oppressive systems. The other is the liberation of others from the burden of being instruments of evil. It should be apparent that the two are closely related.

NOTES

1. Here we engage the old dispute between idealism and materialism by posing a dialectic between ideas and material conditions, a daily dynamic between how the world shoves against us and how we interpret those shoves. This issue is not confined to the question of the role of religion, but is a central question in any form of human resistance and social transformation, and has given rise to a large philosophical, political, and theological literature spanning centuries and devoted to understanding and interpreting this. Paulo Freire's early work on literacy and the culture of silence is a more recent example of how this question is interpreted in the context of popular critique and social transformation, Paulo Freire, *Pedagogy of the Oppressed* (New York: Herder and Herder, 1970), and *Education for Critical Consciousness* (New York: Seabury, 1973).

2. In 1986, Protestants were reported as 11.7 percent of the Honduran population. See, Latin American Socio-Religious Studies Program (PROLADES) and Visión Mundial Internacional-Honduras, *Estudio Socio-Religioso de Honduras* (Tegucigalpa: Vision Mundial Internacional-Honduras, 1986). PROLADES regularly publishes studies on the growth of Protestant and other religious groups in Central American countries. A CID-Gallup poll in 1997 reported Protestant membership at 21 percent and Catholic membership at 63 percent of the Honduran population. By 2007, CID-Gallup reported that Evangelical Protestantism had grown to 36 percent of the population, while Catholicism was at 47 percent.

3. See, for example, Leonardo Boff and Virgil Elizondo, eds., *1492–1992: The Voices of the Victims* (London: Concilium-SCM Press, 1991).

4. Charles Stewart and Rosalind Shaw, eds., *Syncretism/Anti-Syncretism: The Politics of Religious Synthesis* (London: Routledge, 1994).

5. Mary Lee Nolan, "The European Roots of Latin American Pilgrimage," in N. Ross Crumrine and Alan Morinis, eds., *Pilgrimage in Latin America* (New York and London: Greenwood Press, 1991), 44.

6. Stewart and Shaw, *Syncretism/Anti-Syncretism*, 7.

7. Excerpt from Bartolome de Las Casas, *History of the Indies*, reprint in Kevin Reilly, ed., *Worlds of History,* First Edition (Boston: Bedford St. Martins, 1999), 504–505. English translation in Reilly.

8. Pablo Richard, "The Violence of God and the Future of Christianity," in Boff and Elizondo, *1492–1992: The Voices of the Victims*.

9. In Nicaragua during and after the successful revolution that overthrew the brutal Somoza dictatorship, many Catholics and Protestants said they came to join the revolutionary movements because of their religious beliefs. Miguel d'Escoto, Nicaraguan priest and Foreign Minister in the revolutionary government said that Nicaraguan Christians realized they had to end

the dictatorship because the oppression had robbed the people of their dignity "as children of God." James Phillips, "Body and Soul: Faith, Development, Community, and Social Science in Nicaragua," National Association for the Practice of Anthropology, *NAPA Bulletin* 33 (2010): 14.

10. An example of such a conservative (reactionary) leader was Rafael Carrera who ruled in Guatemala during the era of independence struggles in the 1820s. Edelberto Torres, "Francisco Morazan and the Struggle for a Central American Union," *Ariel XXI* Number 233 (June 1971), reprinted in Nancy Peckenham and Annie Street eds., *Honduras: Portrait of a Captive Nation* (New York: Praeger, 1985), 15–16.

11. Marvin Barahona, "El contexto histórico de las iglesias Cristianas en Honduras en el Valle de Sula," in *Religión, ideología, y sociedad: Una aproximación a las iglesias en Honduras,* Equipo de Reflexión, Investigación, y Comunicación (El Progreso: Editorial Casa San Ignacio, 2013), 65.

12. Barahona, "El contexto histórico," 66.

13. While it is useful for some purposes to separate Protestant and Catholic activity and appeal among social classes in much of Latin America, lived religious identity and practice among many Latin Americans may seem more complex and murky as people combine forms of Catholicism and Protestantism into new religious practices, such as the Catholic charismatic movement. See, for example, Virginia Garrard-Burnett and David Stoll eds., *Rethinking Protestantism in Latin America* (Philadelphia: Temple University Press, 1993), 8–9.

14. Barahona, El contexto histórico," 67–68.

15. Garrard-Burnett and Stoll, *Rethinking Protestantism,* 5–6.

16. An extended discussion of the ways in which these ideas entered Catholic social teaching is provided in, Gary MacEoin, *Unlikely Allies: The Christian-Socialist Convergence* (New York: Crossroads Publishing, 1990).

17. Garrard-Burnett and Stoll, *Rethinking Protestantism,* 4–7.

18. At the same time, Catholic bishops also established eight training centers (*centros de capacitación*) to provide opportunities for rural people to study and reflect. Some lay leaders and Delegates of the Word also formed the Honduran Christian Democratic Movement that later became the Christian Democratic Party. Peckenham and Street, *Honduras: Portrait of a Captive Nation,* 168. Alison Acker, *Honduras: The Making of a Banana Republic* (Boston: South End Press, 1988), 96. Moreno, "Dimensión social," 104–5.

19. Phillips, "Body and Soul," 14.

20. There were some prominent examples of this change of perspective about the role of religious belief in transforming society as opposed to promoting reaction to change. The meetings between Brazilian Catholic theologian Fray Beto and Fidel Castro in the 1980s, and Castro's interest in the role of Christians in the Nicaraguan Revolution of the 1980s open the Cuban leader to a different reality than he had experienced with Cuba's own religious hierarchy in the years after the Cuban Revolution. Frei Beto, *Fidel and Religion: Castro Talks on Revolution and Religion with Frei Beto* (New York: Simon and Schuster, 1988).

21. I reproduce this quote from the Medellin Document for Peace as it appears in English translation in MacEoin, *Unlikely Allies,* 55.

22. Ismael Moreno, "Dimensión social de la misión de la iglesia católica: Una Mirada nacional desde la región noroccidental de Honduras," Equipo de Reflexión, Investigación, y Comunicación ERIC, *Religión, ideología, y sociedad: Una aproximación a las iglesias en Honduras* (El Progreso, Editorial San Ignacio, 2013), 103–4. Acker, 96–97. Peckenham and Street, 169.

23. Fernando Cardenal, *Sacerdote en la Revolución: Memorias, Tomo 1* (Managua: Anama Ediciones, 2008).

24. Equipo de Reflexión, Investigación, y Comunicación ERIC, *Religión, ideología, y sociedad,* 73–74. Acker, 97.

25. Equipo de Reflexión, 74–75.

26. This quote is taken from the writings of James (Guadalupe) Carney describing Bishop Corriveau's statements. Reproduced in Equipo de Reflexión, 75–76.

27. Support for the 2009 coup among some Evangelical pastors is reflected in, for example, the following: http://www.christianitytoday.com/gleanings/2009/july/honduras-coup-was-

answer-to-prayer-for-many-evangelicals.html. For a discussion of Evangelical Protestantism as a social and political force in Latin America see, Garrard-Burnett and Stoll eds., *Rethinking Protestantism in Latin America*.

28. *National Catholic Reporter*, October 12, 2001.

29. This incident was widely reported in both Honduran and international news media (e.g., BBC), and by various international lawyers' and human rights organizations. Some do not mention that Trejo was a minister as well as a lawyer.

30. Some of Cardinal Rodriguez's statements related to the coup appeared for a time at, http://bonoc.files.wordpress.com/2009/07/edificar-desde-la-crisis.pdf, and, https://www.aciprensa.com/noticias/cardenal-hondureno-afirma-que-no-apoyo-golpe-ni-legitimo-a-nuevo-presidente. Many Hondurans interpreted the wording of these statements as coded support for the 2009 coup, especially in the context of other actions of Rodriguez in the days after the coup, despite the statement's apparent denial of support.

31. Excerpt from the full Spanish text published in *Vida Laboral*, September, 2009, 4.

32. Carmen Manuela Delcid, "Espiritualidad y derechos humanos en el contexto actual," *Envío Honduras* 8:24 (April, 2010): 46–48.

33. Delcid, "Espirtualidad y derechos humanos," 48 (translation mine).

34. Andres Perez-Baltodano, *Entre el Estado Conquistador y el Estado Nación: Providencialismo, pensamiento político, y estructuras de poder en el desarrollo histórico de Nicaragua* (Managua: Instituto de Historia de Nicaragua y Centroamérica de la Universidad Centramericana, 2008).

35. Equipo de Reflexión, Investigación, y Comunicación, *Religión, Ideología, y sociedad: Una aproximación a las iglesias en Honduras* (El Progreso: Editorial Casa San Ignacio, 2013), 90.

36. The quotation is from Golbery do Couto e Silva, *Geopolítica do Brasil* (Rio de Janeiro: José Olympio, 1967), 101. Quoted in José Comblin, *The Church and the National Security State* (Maryknoll, NY: Orbis Books, 1984, orig.1979), 78. Comblin's translation from Portuguese.

37. Comblin, *The Church and the National Security State*, 78.

38. Gustavo Gutierrez, *A Theology of Liberation* (Maryknoll, NY: Maryknoll Press, 1973). This was among the first, and one of the more influential, in a proliferation of theological and pastoral studies that elaborated different dimensions of the so-called theology of liberation and the so-called popular church. This theology received much impetus from the Second Vatican Council (1963–1965) and the attempts of Catholic and some Protestant scholars, priests and ministers to apply the general direction of Vatican II in the context of daily life and experience in Latin American communities.

39. Miguel d'Escoto, Catholic priest and Foreign Minister in the Nicaraguan revolutionary government, television interview, c. 1985.

40. Phillips, "Body and Soul," 15–16, 27–28.

41. Berta Oliva, personal interviews, September, 2013. Other Honduran religious and human rights leaders and longtime social activists also express this concern.

Chapter Ten

The United States in Honduras

Intervention, Solidarity, and Resistance

Since before its independence in 1824, Honduras has been a place much affected and shaped by external forces. The conditions that Hondurans face today and the popular resistance that we have traced through previous chapters are shaped by such external forces that intervene in various ways in Honduran life. The United States has exercised a particularly powerful hegemony over Honduras since at least the end of the nineteenth century. This relationship has been such that it prompted Honduran peasant leader Elvia Alvarado to exclaim in 1987 that "It is hard to think of change taking place in Central America without there first being changes in the United States."[1]

This intervention is apparent in Honduran history, and can be interpreted in the light of world systems theory and dependency theory—the connectedness of the modern world in systems of production and control so that countries like Honduras on the periphery of the world economy are shaped, exploited by, and kept dependent upon those at the center of the global economy. As Honduran governments have tried to move Honduras more firmly into neoliberal globalization, the influence of external forces is likely to increase. Popular resistance of the sort we have described in this book provides a counterweight to neoliberal globalization, and is therefore seen as threatening to the plans of Honduran globally connected elites, the governments they control, and sometimes the foreign governments and investors that participate in the development plans of Honduran elites.[2] In this chapter we explore some of the international forces that intervene in modern Honduran life. Some of these are forces of economic exploitation or domination, others of international solidarity. In the next chapter, we conclude by setting popular resistance in Honduras within a larger context of popular resistance elsewhere in the hemisphere.

Most people in the United States seldom hear about Honduras. If they think of the country at all, it may be as the archetypal banana republic. But Hondurans often say that it is hard to overestimate the influence the United States exercises over Honduras. In previous chapters we caught glimpses of that influence. A common portrayal of the Honduran relationship to the United States is that of a pawn or a colony. While this may reflect much of the historical reality, it does not fully describe the complexity of the relationship between these two countries or their people. There are many people and organizations in the United States whose relationship or attitude to Honduras and its people is much more one of solidarity, mutual benefit, or simply a desire to stay out of Honduran affairs, not to reduce Honduras to a U.S. colony. There are many Hondurans whose popular activism and resistance shows that if the country is a U.S. colony, it is also a place of protest and struggle for sovereignty.

Honduras today supplies not bananas but important minerals and metals such as silver and antimony that is used in manufacturing cell phones and other electronic devices. The country supplies wood for paper, cardboard, and furniture, and a variety of agricultural products such as palm oil that U.S. citizens consume in large quantities in a variety of processed and packaged foods and other products of daily use. Hondurans who can afford them consume these commodities as well. People in countries such as the United States may criticize or even protest the way in which foreign corporations and some Honduran entrepreneurs exploit Honduran natural resources and treat workers and peasants, but they may also be uncomfortably aware that in some ways their own lives are enriched by the products of this exploitation. A sense of moral compromise can complicate the relationship of well-intended U.S. citizens, especially, in relation to Honduras.

In this chapter we explore briefly some of the complexities of the U.S.-Honduran relationship in regard to popular resistance in Honduras. This relationship is manifest at both a government/corporate level and a people-to-people level, with some in-between such as non-governmental organizations that vary in the proportion of government and grassroots involvement and support they enjoy. Agendas and motives range from making wealth to making "good neighbors." Motives are often mixed, and the relationship may be conceived in a range from hierarchical (colonial) to some form of equal partnership, a mutual learning and sharing. The U.S. government routinely portrays its relationship to Honduras as a partnership with a sovereign, neighboring country. This portrayal strikes a chord with Hondurans who want to believe in a partnership and a sovereign Honduras, but they know that history seems to betray, or at least complicate this characterization.

AN UNRULY COLONY: INTERVENTION AS CONTROL

Any student of U.S. history is aware of the Monroe Doctrine (1823) that warned European powers to stay out of the Western Hemisphere, and effectively announced that the hemisphere, especially Central America and the Caribbean, were within the sphere of influence and interest of the United States—its so-called "back yard." The long litany of U.S. military and diplomatic interventions in these regions throughout the nineteenth and twentieth centuries amply illustrates the serious nature of this claim of dominance. The countries of Central America and the Caribbean seemed to be pawns in the internal struggles of the United States. For example, as the slavery question came increasingly into conflict in the United States in the 1850s, members of the U.S. Congress hatched a plan to seize Cuba from Spanish control and turn it into another U.S. state—a slave state.

With a weak government and little territorial or political integration or unity as a sovereign country, Honduras was vulnerable to such wild schemes. The so-called Walker Affair was one of the more outlandish of these schemes. In the mid-1850s, a Californian named William Walker gathered a band of U.S. fortune seekers, traveled to Nicaragua, and intervened in a political war between conservative and liberal factions there. Walker gained enough control to declare himself ruler of Nicaragua. When he decreed that English would replace Spanish as the country's official language, Protestantism would replace Catholicism as its religion, and slavery would be legal, Nicaraguans revolted and threw him out, with the support of troops from neighboring Central American countries and powerful economic interests in the United States who saw Walker as a hindrance to their plans for economic development in Central America. After a short time in the United States, Walker mounted an expedition to Honduras, landing near Trujillo on the Caribbean coast, an area then under British influence. British soldiers took Walker into custody and turned him over to Hondurans who promptly executed him in 1860.[3]

U.S. economic interest in Honduras began to develop with mining in the late 1800s, as U.S. companies gained generous silver and iron mining concessions. Honduran workers employed in some of these mining operations staged some of the first organized manifestations of worker agitation for better conditions (see chapter 4). U.S. influence expanded greatly with the expansion of the U.S.-owned banana empire in northern Honduras in the first half of the twentieth century. Again, Honduran workers staged increasingly large and organized strikes and work stoppages to demand better conditions, leading to the great banana strike of 1954 and the rise of organized labor and peasant activism. These popular protests became symbols of a struggle for national sovereignty in the face of foreign economic and political influence. They also became a concern for interests in the U.S. government and business that wanted to maintain their unrestricted access to Honduras. In 1962, leaders of the powerful U.S. AFL-CIO labor union conglomerate founded the American Institute of Free Labor Development (AIFLD) with financial and political support from the U.S. Central Intelligence Agency and a variety of corporation and labor executives in the United States. The official purpose of AIFLD was to provide training and support for labor leaders and unions in Latin American countries. Its major goals, however, were to prevent "communist" infiltration and control of labor unions in Latin America, to control or neutralize labor activism, and to foment labor unrest against "communist" governments. AIFLD supported alternative labor and peasant unions in countries like Honduras so as to divide and weaken the influence of less pliant and more militant unions. Thus, in Honduras ANACH provided a counterforce to the more militant FENACH and UNC. This aim of keeping labor movements docile and subservient to business elites and governments fit well with Honduran elite and government agendas.[4] AIFLD operatives were also implicated in fomenting labor unrest against "communist" governments in Brazil, Guyana, and several other Latin American countries in the 1960s and 1970s.[5] Since the 1980s, AIFLD has been subsumed within an expanded organization that continues involvement in Latin American countries. But as Dana Frank points out, the AFL-CIO abandoned its anticommunist campaign in 1997, abolished AIFLD, and created the American Center for Labor Solidarity that, "for the most part channels true solidarity to the labor movement in Latin America."[6]

One of the many lessons or contradictions of this kind of intervention is that it involved U.S. labor unions—the very sector of U.S. society that would be expected to ally with Honduran workers—and instead tried to divert them into supporting, albeit unwittingly, tactics of division that weakened the Honduran labor movement. In the process, the U.S. labor movement itself seemed compromised as an instrument of the agendas of big business. One explanation for why this divide-and-conquer strategy might succeed was the relative upward mobility and benefits enjoyed by U.S. workers in the "golden years" from 1950 to 1970 which was said the be a result not of their activism but of their compromise, their "social contract" with American enterprise, in comparison to the unruly and militant labor unionists of Latin America—an explanation that conveniently ignores the kind of oppressive tactics against popular activism in Latin America that we have described for Honduras in earlier chapters.[7] The crises that Central American countries experienced in the 1980s revealed further aspects of U.S. involvement in Honduras and the rest of Central America, and widespread criticism and resistance to aspects of that involvement. As we have seen, "Reaganomics for Honduras," the presence of Contra army training camps, and the development of the U.S. military presence in Honduras were all met with popular protest. Some of the policies of Reaganomics, such as the proposal to eliminate collective and community land ownership in favor of private individual title, were especially opposed.[8]

Honduras was the base from which a small group of Guatemalans directed and supplied by the United States staged a coup against the government of Guatemalan President Jacobo Arbenz in 1954, beginning more than thirty years of civil conflict and genocide in that country. By 1980, with the rise of armed "leftist" movements in El Salvador and Guatemala and the Sandinista revolution in Nicaragua, Honduras was the strategic location from which the United States could exert control in the region. The Honduran Constitution forbade the establishment of foreign military bases in the country, so the Honduran government "leased" the use of Honduran bases to U. S. military forces. The expanding U.S. military presence was said to be "temporary," but it continued and was even expanding in the years after the 2009 coup. From the members of rural farming communities near the Nicaraguan border to members of the Honduran Congress and the military, there was criticism of the Contra presence because it displaced Hondurans and further compromised Honduran sovereignty.[9] This critique was also directed against the United States for having forced Honduras into the role of host country to the Contras. Some Hondurans asked why their country was made to bear the burdens of becoming the frontline in a war that the United States wanted to wage against Honduras' neighbor Nicaragua. The great expansion of the U.S. military presence in Honduras brought protests from rural communities that this represented a loss of land for Honduran farmers. A priest in Comayagua reported that his parishioners were complaining about the conduct of U.S. soldiers on leave in the city.[10] Members of the Honduran Congress worried about national sovereignty, and some Honduran military officers were at least uncomfortable with the U.S. military presence that promised more military aid but also threatened to relegate the Honduran army to a subservient position in its own country. The ramped up economic, political, and military pressure and presence of the United States in Honduras during the early 1980s was considered a major impetus and support for the draconian national security measures initiated by General Gustavo Alvarez. Ironically, the repression also triggered increased protests and resistance from popular organizations, and the formation of several human rights groups in Honduras, including CODEH and COFADEH.[11] When other officers engineered Alvarez's ouster in 1984, they did so for several reasons. But it also seemed to be yet another protest against some of the consequences of U.S. intervention in Honduran institutions.

In the past two decades, the U.S. military presence in Honduras has been projected in four ways: the actual presence of U.S. soldiers on Honduran bases; security aid to the Honduran military and police through bilateral and regional agreements, especially the Central American Regional Security Initiative (CARSI); the presence of other enforcement agencies in Honduras, in particular the U.S. Drug Enforcement Agency (DEA); and the training of Honduran military officers, primarily at the School of the Americas (SOA) in Georgia. These trainees return to military posts in Honduras, and some of the school's alumni have been identified as the agents of various assassinations and other human rights violations.[12] The removal of U.S. military presence has been a focus of popular resistance in Honduras since the 1980s, and has become an objective also of groups of U.S. citizens concerned about their government's actions. In addition to military presence, U.S. influence is exercised by the Embassy that has a history of telling Honduran governments how to operate, a history that began at least with gunboats and diplomatic letters in the early1900s, continued through the Reaganomics for Honduras proposals from the embassy to the Suazo government in 1981, and is reflected even in accusations about the role of the embassy in trying to influence the Zelaya government before the 2009 coup. Foreign aid, including food aid and development funds through the Agency for International Development (AID) are additional channels of U.S. influence over Honduran government policy and practice.

Beginning in the 1990s, a major objective of U.S. policy in Honduras was the integration of the country into a global neoliberal economic system in a way that the United States could shape or control, especially through bilateral and regional "free trade." Earlier U.S. government initiatives had focused on providing the kind of economic and military aid that could prepare the region's countries for such integration. The Kennedy Administration's Alliance for Progress in the early 1960s was not a free trade scheme but provided assistance for the "modernization" of Latin American economies, including improvement of basic infrastructure needed for manufacturing, mining, and other enterprises and policies to "rationalize" agricultural production. In the 1980s, the Reagan Administration's Caribbean Basin Initiative (CBI) combined a modernizing and developmental approach with some aspects of a regional trade scheme. The Central American Free Trade Agreement (CAFTA) that was conceived and then promoted by both the Clinton and Bush Administrations finally became reality in the early 2000s. By then, President Hugo Chavez of Venezuela was promoting the Bolivarian Alliance (*Alianza Bolivariana*, ALBA) among Latin American countries as a truly Latin American alternative to a U.S.-dominated CAFTA. Honduras's neighbor, Sandinista-led Nicaragua became part of ALBA in 2006. President Zelaya's promotion of the entry of Honduras into ALBA was not well received among sectors of the Honduran elite and their economic partners in the United States, and became one more reason to remove Zelaya from office in the 2009 coup. Suspicion about the possible role of the U.S. government in the coup continued, fueled by reports that Zelaya was flown to the U.S. side of the Soto Cano military base on his way into exile, and by documents revealed by the so-called Wikileaks revelations. One year after the coup, a new de facto Honduran government and a new U.S. ambassador to Honduras who had a global trade background began to promote the "Honduras is open for business" initiative to attract international (including United States) investment to the country amid ongoing massive popular protests.

By the early 2000s, U.S. agencies were working with Honduran security forces to engage the growing narcotics trade in Honduras. As we saw in chapter 5, this drug war directly affected local Honduran communities, especially in the east of the country among the Miskito and other indigenous people. The increased presence of U.S. enforcement agencies, especially the DEA, working in collaboration with Honduran military and police, and the flow of U.S. security aid to Honduran military and police for anti-drug operations has probably contributed to the increasing militarization of Honduran society that some Hondurans applaud and others denounce, worry about, and try to resist (see chapter 3).

U.S. security aid in Honduras since at least the 2009 coup has taken two important forms. One is the militarization of Honduran society (see chapter 3) that is underwritten—economically and ideologically—by U.S. security aid through the Central American Regional Security Initiative (CARSI) and other programs. The second is the deployment of Foreign-Deployment Advisory Support Teams (FAST) composed of U.S. Drug Enforcement Agency units and U.S. military special forces whose roles include working with Honduran and other regional military and intelligence agencies to detect and stop narcotics trafficking. A FAST team was implicated in the killing and injury of Honduran civilians near Ahuas in the Mosquitia in 2012 (see chapter 5). U.S. security assistance, especially counter-narcotics funding and logistical assistance has been tied directly to an increased ability of repressive governments to further repress their unruly populations. A report issued in March, 2015, by the Global Drug Policy Observatory at Swansea University (UK) clearly describes this link:

> Latin American governments, often made up of groups that see their own people as threats to their social and economic position, have historically accepted "counter-narcotics" money from the United States, which has in turn improved their repressive capabilities and allowed Washington to dictate local policy related to drugs. The significant U.S. role in drug policy in Latin America historically has meant the emboldening of corrupt, repressive regimes and abusive militaries; the stifling of progressive political movements; and increased violence.[13]

In private conversation with U.S. citizens and in interviews, prominent human rights advocates and labor, peasant, and indigenous leaders point out that most of the narcotics flowing through Honduras are destined for the U.S. "market," and that the United States is by far the largest consumer of illegal narcotics in the hemisphere. They ask why the U.S. government insists on fighting "its" drug war on Honduran soil instead of dealing with the drug trade in the United States by working to reduce the market demand there. They suggest that if this shift in U.S. policy and practice were to occur, it would undercut the power of the drug trade, and the level of violence in Honduras might be significantly reduced. The possibility that such a shift might require major adjustments in U.S. society gives pause to U.S. officials and citizens who would engage the question.

These are some of the aspects of what might seem a neo-colonial relationship between Honduras and the United States, despite the continuing reference in the public relations statements of both countries to a mutually beneficial partnership between the two. But this relationship has been characterized as one in which the U.S. government speaks to and partners with only certain limited sectors of Honduran society—government officials, members of the economic and political elite and the military, but not with leaders and activists in popular organizations, environmentalists, middle-class professionals, human rights advocates, or indigenous leaders. Some Hondurans said the United States should broaden the scope of those it was talking to and involve new partners in Honduras drawn from other groups, including those involved in popular resistance.[14]

There are tensions in the "official" Honduran-U.S. relationship. The public image of Honduras as a violent country sometimes served the limited interests of Honduran politicians and military leaders who wanted more U.S. military aid. But an image of violence was bad for business and made more difficult the task of attracting foreign investment. Neither government wanted the violent Honduras image, but the policies of both seemed to contribute to it, or at least seemed powerless to end it. National sovereignty is an ongoing source of tension between Hondurans and the United States, given the weakness of the Honduran state and the overwhelming influence of the United States in Honduran life. The rising levels of daily violence in Honduras in the years after the 2009 coup finally became a source of tension for the United States as thousands of Honduran youth arrived at the U.S.-Mexico border in the summer of 2014 to seek asylum or a better life in the United States. U.S. citizens were divided over this "crisis at the border." Some demanded the speedy deportation of most of the "illegal aliens," while others argued that their plight was in part a product of U.S. policies and actions in Honduras.

Underpinning the ideological perspective that justifies this ongoing "colonial" relationship with Honduras for the United States is a sense that it is proper, or at least necessary and unavoidable that the sacrifices Hondurans make serve the greater good of the United States and the regional war on drugs and greater economic development. According to this, Honduras is a "sacrifice zone"—a part of the world whose environment, natural resources, and even its people must be sacrificed for the greater good of others, specifically the United States, and there is some tolerance for this within the sacrifice zone itself. The term originated during the U.S.-Soviet Cold War to justify U.S. atomic bomb testing in the Marshall Islands and later in Nevada as necessary for the defense of the free world against communism. It is now applied to those areas in the United States and those foreign countries that are used as sites of toxic chemical or extractive industries.[15] This time the justification has more to do with maintaining U.S. leadership in the global economy and the ability to resist terrorism. Honduras, with its sizeable mineral, forest, and other resources and its geopolitical position vis-a-vis Mexican and South American drug trafficking, contains such zones of exploitation, and even the entire country may be seen as a sacrifice zone whose government and some members of an elite tolerate the sacrifice of the country's resources and the sacrifices demanded of large numbers of its people. There, the added fact that much of the sacrifice is demanded of indigenous peoples—Lenca, Tolupan, Garifuna, and Miskito—adds a hint of environmental racism to the ideology. But this ideological justification has been increasingly challenged by both Hondurans, as we have amply seen, and by foreign groups, organizations, and communities, as we shall discuss next.

THE PEOPLE INTERVENE: SOLIDARITY

In April 2015, Lenca activist Berta Cáceres of COPINH received the Goldman Award, presented each year to a few outstanding environmental and human rights defenders from different countries. Her receipt of this award was an example of how Honduran popular resistance has gained international recognition and solidarity.

Solidarity is a term used to describe the ways in which people offer support and accompaniment to others, especially in situations of conflict or difficulty. Many U.S. citizens were engaged in acts that some characterized as solidarity with the people of Central America during the wars and crises of the 1980s, although others did not use this term to characterize their activities. At that time, the focus of solidarity actions was in the three countries of Nicaragua, Guatemala, and El Salvador. El Salvador was then one of the largest recipients of U.S. military aid in the world (behind Israel and Egypt). Many U.S. citizens thought that this official U.S. aid was supporting a government that killed its citizens and trampled on their human rights as it pursued a war against the Farabundo Marti Front for National Liberation (FMLN). A political cartoon in some alternative U.S. media depicted Uncle Sam feeding a cartridge belt to a Salvadoran Army gunner. Uncle Sam says, "I hope this is for human rights." The Salvadoran soldier replies, "Almost. It's for the humans who are left." In Nicaragua, the political situation was the reverse. The U.S. government's active support for the Contra forces trying to overthrow the revolutionary Sandinista government was abhorrent to many U.S. citizens. Especially terrible was the "low intensity conflict" waged with U.S. training and support against Nicaraguan rural communities. Some characterized this as terrorism. Here solidarity focused on support and accompaniment for Nicaraguan communities. In addition, many solidarity activists thought the Nicaraguan revolution was a hard-won example and a sign of hope for many oppressed people in the hemisphere, and they wished it to succeed. Solidarity was also seen as reparation for the destruction and terror the U.S. government was inflicting on the Nicaraguan people.[16]

In the United States, solidarity work for Honduras in the 1980s was complicated by an often unspoken perception of Honduras as the U.S. ally facilitating U.S. government policies and actions against neighboring countries—the very thing solidarity opposed. The legacy of this pattern of selective solidarity is reflected today in the many and strong U.S. and international groups and organizations that continue to work in and with Guatemala, El Salvador, and Nicaragua. Recent movements of solidarity with Honduras do not enjoy the same historical basis. The forms of solidarity U.S. citizens engaged in for Honduras during the 1980s were focused especially on trying to effect changes in U.S. policies primarily directed at neighboring countries, policies that also seemed to harm the Honduran people—using the country as a military staging ground, promoting economic policies that seemed to make life harder for many Hondurans, and supporting a militarized and repressive national security state.

During the Contra War, in March, 1988, U.S. government agencies and some news media reported that units of the Nicaraguan Sandinista Army were invading areas of Honduras along the countries' mutual border. Washington announced the deployment of three thousand troops to Honduras to assist the country in repelling this "invasion." Within a few hours of this announcement and continuing for more than one week afterward, popular street demonstrations and rallies organized in Durham, North Carolina; San Francisco; New York; Chicago; Minneapolis; Atlanta; and Boston, where organizers and police expected one thousand protesters and more than seven thousand actually participated. Groups of protesters occupied federal offices and blocked traffic in some cities. Other groups demonstrated and rallied in front of military bases in California and elsewhere. Protesters demonstrated in front of the White House in Washington, D.C.[17] Some of these protests included civil disobedience, and hundreds were arrested. This outpouring of popular resistance in the United States was directed against the further militarization of Honduras and the U.S. government's use of Honduras as the staging ground for operations against its neighbors, but also the use of Honduras itself as a pawn or colony in the Central American wars.

Other forms of solidarity tried to address the problems of Honduran communities that the Contra War, the U.S. military presence, and the Honduran national security state of the 1980s were causing. International organizations such as Caritas (a Christian relief and development agency based in Europe) addressed some of the immediate needs of Honduran rural communities displaced by Contra activity along the country's southern border. International relief and aid arms of religious denominations such as the Mennonites provided international accompaniment and aid to thousands of Salvadoran refugees in Honduras. Human rights discourse characterized some of the solidarity activity of the period, and this work had both a political and an immediately practical focus. Some U.S. and European citizens joined organizations such as Peace Brigades International that provided direct accompaniment to Honduran human rights activists in organizations such as COFADEH and CODEH, as well as in Guatemala and El Salvador. The U.S.-based organization Witness for Peace that deployed dozens of U.S. volunteers to accompany rural communities in Nicaragua devastated by the Contra War and hosted hundreds of North Americans on fact-finding delegations in Honduras and Nicaragua began to explore possibilities for more expanded solidarity work in Honduras.[18]

During the 1990s, some of the groups and organizations that engaged in the activism of the 1980s in Guatemala, El Salvador, and Nicaragua continued, often with a different emphasis. For example, Witness for Peace continued to work in Nicaragua in reduced capacity, and expanded into work in Colombia and Mexico where conflict and violence seemed to be escalating. The Quest for Peace that had channeled millions of dollars of aid from U.S. people and institutions for Nicaragua during the 1980s continued to gather aid from U.S. citizens but the purpose shifted from direct humanitarian aid for the victims of the Contra War to support for community development projects and local empowerment. There was little comparable continuity of solidarity for Honduras.

Non-governmental organizations (NGOs) constitute another form of intervention in Central American countries. There had been various NGOs in Honduras and other Central American countries for decades. Their presence continued and even increased with the end of the conflicts in Central America in 1990. They varied widely in the degree to which they encouraged or limited the participation of U.S. citizens in their work. Some encouraged participation only in the form of charitable contributions to the NGO's work. Others actively promoted and acted as a bridge for more direct encounter between peoples.[19] Some NGOs had a particular political agenda that might align with that of governments, while others tried to say clear of involvement with governments, but rather to channel the concerns of ordinary citizens.

With the coup of 2009 in Honduras and the rise of both a broad protest movement and state initiated repression, an older generation of people in the United States who had been activists in Central America during the 1980s began to think what Hondurans were already expressing. The post-coup situation of repression in Honduras seemed like a return to the crisis of the early 1980s. But there were at least two significant differences between then and now. There were new sources of violence in post-coup Honduras, especially narcotics trafficking and the desperate lack of opportunity for many of the country's youth that fueled gang (*mara*) violence that joined with the older patterns of state-sponsored repression and conflict over economic inequity. The other difference was that the popular resistance that quickly arose and organized after the 2009 coup was a product of many years of struggles by many different sectors of Honduran society whose concerns and discourse had evolved and converged in ways that may have facilitated the rapid organization of broad popular resistance in the wake of the coup. A sense of heightened and randomized violence in Honduras after the 2009 coup, and U.S. responsibility in this, coupled with a strong popular resistance among the Honduran people who said they could not succeed without change in the United States presented challenges to an older generation of U.S. solidarity activists to turn attention again to Honduras, and to educate a newer generation in the United States about the history of U.S. involvement, repression and resistance. As violence and insecurity increased in post-coup Honduras, the increasing influx of young Hondurans seeking asylum at the southern U.S. border, erupted into the news media and awareness of the U.S. population in 2014 with the so-called crisis at the border. This revealed some of the difficult reality of Honduras and how United States policies may have shaped some of that reality. But these lessons were often hard to highlight amid the emotional, deeply politicized, and factually deficient national argument over these "illegal aliens." Solidarity with the Honduran people has therefore operated in a difficult political and social climate.

Without entering into detailed listing or description of all the forms of solidarity and involvement that U.S. citizens began to engage in Honduras after the 2009 coup, we can observe some major themes around which much of this work seemed to be organized. Most prominent was human rights. State sponsored repression and generalized violence were often denounced with a discourse of violation of basic human rights to life, safety, free expression and movement, and basic legal and judicial guarantees. Accompaniment was a related form of solidarity. U.S. citizens accompanied Honduran activists who were the objects of threats in situations where the Hondurans requested some form of international accompaniment. The idea that the presence of U.S. citizens or other internationals might bring international attention and dissuade those intending to commit violence was a tenuous hope that drew its strength from the extent to which the international volunteer was connected to a larger U.S. or international network that would go into action if a violent act occurred or was attempted. Accompaniment was sometimes the work of individuals who described it as long hours of boredom interspersed with occasional moments of intense concern. As violence in

Honduras seemed to become increasingly widespread and seemingly random in the years after the 2009 coup, questions were raised about the efficacy of some forms of accompaniment, and about how to adapt it to the new situation. By 2012, the increasing level of violence in Honduras began to draw attention even in the U.S. Congress, and encouraged another form of solidarity worked to provide information to members of Congress, and to encourage them to work for a review of U.S. security aid in light of U.S. law that prohibits sending aid to foreign military units that are implicated in human rights violations.[20] Over the next three years, members of Congress sent several letters to the U.S. secretary of state. They also held hearings that explored the Honduran situation and heard testimony from prominent Hondurans and U.S. activists.

By mid-2014, the developing "crisis at the border," in which thousands of young people from Honduras, Guatemala, and El Salvador arrived at the Mexican-U.S. border seeking asylum in the United States further increased the opportunity to capture U.S. public attention about conditions in Honduras, despite a counter-narrative from the Honduran government that tried to assuage fears about what might happen to the children if they were returned to Honduras. U.S. officials began to deport planeloads of Honduran children, despite evidence of killings of children in Honduras. This situation provoked a series of actions in the United States including providing food, shelter, and direction to the newly arrived children; demonstrations in U.S. cities against the deportations; and city and state declarations supporting the young asylum-seekers. Some churches and religious congregations began to discuss reviving aspects of the Sanctuary Movement of the 1980s.

SECOND THOUGHTS: SOLIDARITY IN RESISTANCE

In September 2013, a small church group from the United States traveled to the Rio Blanco area in Honduras where Lenca activists were maintaining a roadblock and a protest presence in opposition to the building of a dam on the Gualcarque River. One of the Lenca leaders told the church group, "We are really grateful for all the international solidarity we have been shown. We don't feel alone, we feel supported by your presence and by others who have come. So thank you for that" (translation mine). Solidarity is especially about people and communities, and is really a people-to-people initiative, even when activism takes to the halls of the U.S. Congress to promote a change in foreign policy or patterns of aid.

Some forms of solidarity with the Honduran people bring U.S. citizens face-to-face with an uncomfortable sense of privilege. They become more aware that they enjoy certain benefits because of their citizenship in a hegemonic state, and especially the material benefits that are products of some forms of exploitation in countries like Honduras. People invent creative ways to avoid or mitigate the embarrassment they might otherwise feel at their privilege. Hondurans and other Central Americans do express the expectation that U.S. solidarity activists will use their privileges to help rather than to oppress. But the question of privilege remains for some a puzzling part of the relationships between the United States and Honduras. For many Hondurans, a true test of solidarity seems to be whether an action builds and promotes more equitable people-to-people relationships or merely increases overt and subtle divisions between "us" and "them."

At times, acts of solidarity with the people of Honduras may bring U.S. citizens into direct resistance to the policies and practices of their own government. A particularly clear example is that providing certain kinds of direct support to "illegal aliens" from Honduras and elsewhere has in the past landed U.S. citizens in jail or legal trouble. In this, solidarity takes on another meaning—solidarity in resistance. For Hondurans, the price of resistance is often much higher. But from this perspective, solidarity is not simply something U.S. citizens do for Hondurans. It is also something U.S. citizens seem to do for their own country, to make it more "humane" or to make it obey its own laws, even as they collaborate with and are inspired by the resistance and resilience of Hondurans. Solidarity and resistance in both countries cannot easily be separated, just as the histories of the two countries have been bound together.

NOTES

1. Elvia Alvarado quoted in Alison Acker, *Honduras: The Making of a Banana Republic* (Boston: South End Press, 1988), 88.

2. Andre Gunder Frank, "The Development of Underdevelopment," in James D. Cockcroft, Andre Gunder Frank, and Dale Johnson, eds., *Dependence and Underdevelopment* (Garden City, New York: Anchor Books, 1972). Immanuel Wallerstein, *The Modern World System*, in three volumes discusses the development of global systems from the sixteenth century to 1840, and lays a basis for general world systems theory (New York, Academic Press, 1974, 1980, and 1989).

3. Thomas W. Walker, *Nicaragua: Living in the Shadow of the Eagle*, fourth ed. (Boulder, CO: Westview Press, 2003).

4. Alison Acker, *Honduras: The Making of a Banana Republic* (Boston: South End Press, 1988), 84–85. Richard Swedberg, "From Legalization to Repression: The Labor Movement after 1954," in Nancy Peckenham and Annie Street, *Honduras: Portrait of a Captive Nation* (New York: Praeger Publishers, 1985), 89–91, reprinted from Richard Swedberg, *The Honduran Trade Union Movement, 1920–1982* (Cambridge, MA: Camino, 1983). Peckenham and Street, 89–91.

5. Cheddi Jagan, *The West on Trial: My Fight for Guyana's Freedom* (London: Michael Joseph, Ltd., 1966).

6. Dana Frank, *Bananeras: Women Transforming the Banana Unions of Latin America* (Cambridge, MA: South End Press, 2005), 98.

7. Richard Flacks, *Making History: The American Left and the American Mind* (New York: Columbia University Press, 1988).

8. For an overview from a Honduran perspective of the many ways in which the United States intervened and shaped affairs in Honduras during the 1980s see, Margarita Oseguera de Ochoa, *Honduras Hoy: Sociedad y Crisis Política* (Tegucigalpa: Centro de Documentación de Honduras, 1987), 78–97. For a larger discussion of Honduras and the United States in the 1980s see, Marvin Barahona, *Honduras en el siglo XX: Una síntesis histórica* (Tegucigalpa: Editorial Guaymuras, 2005), 233–75. Also, Ross Everton, "Justifying Militarisation: Counter Narcotics and Counter-narcoterrorism," Global Drug Policy Observatory, Swansea University, *Policy Report 3*, www.swansea.ac.uk/Militarisation%20FINAL%20.pdf, (March, 2015): 15–16.

9. For a detailed chronology of events relating to the Contra presence in Honduras see, Centro de Documentación de Honduras CEDOH, "La Contra en Honduras," Serie: Cronologias no. 7 (April, 1987).

10. Personal interview, August, 1984.

11. Barahona, *Honduras en el siglo* XX, 240–42. Swedberg, "From Legalization to Repression," 109.

12. For example, Honduran military graduates of the School of the Americas have been implicated: as members of Battalion 316 identified as a death squad in the 1980s; as members of the military that carried out the 2009 coup d'état against President Zelaya; the colonel who commanded the military's Catrucha Task Force implicated in killings of peasants in the Aguán Valley in the years after the 2009 coup; officers implicated in the killing of Ebed Yanez in 2013; and many other incidents. Honduran military graduates of the SOA have publicly denounced human rights activists, and an army general and SOA graduate publicly justified the killing of Lenca activist Tomas Garcia during a peaceful protest in Rio Blanco in 2014.

13. Ross Everton, "Justifying Militarisation," 14.

14. For example, Ishmael Moreno, SJ, director of Radio Progreso and ERIC, interview, April, 2013.

15. A study of the concept and practice of sacrifice zones in the United States itself is provided by, Steve Lerner, *Sacrifice Zones: The Front Lines of Toxic Chemical Exposure in the United States* (Cambridge, MA: MIT Press, 2010). The ideology is the same.

16. James Phillips, "When Governments Fail: Reparation, Solidarity, and Community in Nicaragua," in *Waging War, Making Peace: Reparations and Human Rights*, Barbara Rose Johnston and Susan Slyomovics eds. (Walnut Creek, CA: Left Coast Press, 2009), 69–70.

17. Centro de Documentación de Honduras CEDOH, *Boletín Informativo* 85 (May, 1988): 2. CEDOH's sources for some of the information were new reports in the *Guardian* during the period March 30 to April 6, 1988.

18. Information from the author's field notes from the period based on his research and participant observation in some of these activities in the region.

19. Phillips, "When Governments Fail," 70. Also see James McGinnis, *Solidarity with the People of Nicaragua* (Maryknoll, NY: Orbis Books, 1985).

20. The so-called Leahy Law or Leahy Amendment forbids the United States from sending security aid to foreign military units that are implicated in human rights violations against their own citizens.

Chapter Eleven

Conclusion

Honduran Resistance in a Global Context

In this study, we have seen some aspects of the society in which Hondurans live. In this society there are different and contrasting versions of reality. A powerful elite presents a version of reality in which its control of people and resources is right and natural. But people also experience in their fears and in their bodies a reality of horrendous and pervasive violence that seems very far from being right and natural. This experienced reality seems to contradict and yet reinforce the control of the powerful. The contradiction comes from a sense that even the traditional elite cannot control the violence or deliver the natural order that their ideologies promise. But the seemingly random violence also performs the task of raising a pervasive sense of fear and widespread "depression" in Honduran society, and this keeps the population docile and resigned—at least in theory. This is achieved by incorporating the experienced violence into the elite version of reality, so that the new violence is acknowledged and shown to be either the "new normal" or a reason why the elite must increase their already strong hold on Honduran society. This is an ingenious reality myth that would be a powerful instrument of control—at least in theory.

Not given to obeying meekly what should happen in theory, Hondurans keep trying to construct an alternative reality. This costly work has at least two interdependent aspects. People must conceive an idea, or many related ideas, of what an alternative reality would be like. They must begin to put it into practice, to construct it. The formation of the idea and the attempts to construct or live it daily form a sort of praxis, each dependent upon and informing the other. Sometimes people start doing things to resist the oppressive reality or to solve a practical problem in small ways without thinking of these small acts as part of a grand vision for a new society. But we have seen that when Hondurans find the conditions to form community or even communication with others, new ideas about what is and could be do begin to form. The organized actions of a few ignite the long endured grievances, concerns, and hopes of many. A sense of strength in numbers may not be enough to overcome the fears that pervade Honduran society, but for some people numbers plus trust may result in some form of community in which new ideas are born out of collective experience and need.

In Honduras, this process has been developing over many years despite attempts to instill distrust and cooptation, so that this interplay, this praxis of actions and ideas about a better life has become pervasive, not perhaps in the sense that everyone is actively involved in it, but rather in the sense that everyone sees and is in some way aware of the daily occurrence of large and small acts of resistance. It is as if resisting, protesting, and expressing demands for what should be have become so much a part of Honduran society and consciousness in broad aspects of daily life—food, land, subsistence, resources, legal and penal processes, political activity, popular cultural expression, religion, and spirituality—that we can speak of a culture of resistance. This culture of resistance has evolved in ways that bring together sectors of Honduran society across social class, urban-rural, ethnic, and generational divisions in a developing consciousness of the relatedness of each struggle, and with a sort of common discourse based in such universal and yet particularized concepts as human rights. Middle class academics and professionals engage in workshops and other forms of sharing with working class laborers and peasants. They form human rights and other organizations whose concerns overlap with those of peasants and workers. Indigenous organizations such as COPINH and OFRANEH work to establish mutual support relationships with many other popular and professional organizations in Honduran society, and to have indigenous concerns and struggles interpreted as struggles for all Hondurans. They position long marginalized indigenous people at the center of the evolving culture of resistance, and so squarely in the middle of current Honduran history. The culture of resistance includes the experience, judgment, and patience of older longtime activists like Margarita and Manuel, and the energy of young people in their expressions of popular culture for resistance, their dedication and willingness to risk in organizations like Radio Progreso and other investigative media that seek other accounts and perspectives of events and issues, and the exuberance of a youth run through the streets, accompanied by a few slower elders, to take back the public spaces.

It is important to remember that all of this—both the repression and violence and the resistance and building elements of a better society—is the work of human beings who carry their own weaknesses, vulnerabilities, anxiety, greed, prejudices, and forms of ignorance. Within the movement of popular resistance people change their minds, accept bribes, betray others, drop out, argue endlessly over ideology that divides them from others in resistance, or spread rumors and suspicions about others. What is remarkable is that despite all of the temptations and weaknesses of human beings, they manage to fashion movements and cultures of resistance that survive, evolve, and attain various small and sometimes large victories that are not vindication over others but rather attempts to free themselves and others from the worst aspects of human weakness and failure.

HONDURAN RESISTANCE: GLOBALIZATION FROM ABOVE AND BELOW

The inclusive dynamic of this evolution of resistance takes on a global dimension, as well. One may interpret the conflict and resistance happening in Honduras in the context of a society's confrontation with globalization. The culture of resistance in Honduras is deeply rooted in local and national situations and concerns that are shaped by larger, global economic decisions and forces. In this context, we can interpret popular resistance in Honduras as an effort not so much to reverse time and cling to a disappearing past, but rather as an effort to engage a different kind of globalization.

Some students of globalization speak of two kinds of globalization. Globalization from *above* penetrates local and national life from the outside. It can be characterized in different ways, among them the processes of converting environmental, social, and cultural capital into financial capital.[1] It is easy to see this process at work in Honduras. The attempt to convert environmental capital into financial capital is seen, for example, in the shift from community to private land titling, the often coercive and violent attempts to absorb peasant farmland into corporate export plantations, the great increase in mining concessions, and the general trend of government policy and practice toward freeing land and natural resources from the claims and demands of local communities and local needs so as to convert land and resources into global commodities. Social capital is disengaged from locality by the massive dispossession and eviction of rural communities from the land and their traditional place, and their conversion into a landless labor pool for maquiladoras and other industries. The mayanization policies that homogenize history and ethnic diversity into a "folkloric" myth and package ethnicity for easy foreign consumption convert cultural capital to attract dollars. The deliberate attempt to create a new dependency on imported foods and food tastes many also affect cultural identity. The emphases on privatization, individualization, and the conversion of local connection and "rootedness" into mobile resources—attempts directed especially against indigenous and peasant communities—underscore this movement to globalize. The invasion and pervasive presence of international narcotics adds to the violent braking open of Honduran society, subjecting it to an international criminal network whose only real concern is money. Inviting the establishment of Charter Cities in Honduras symbolizes the advancement of globalization and serves notice to Honduran society that the country has lost its identity and sovereignty in a globalized world.

In contrast, globalization from *below* is a process by which local and national communities and groups try to fashion ways of living that preserve their most valued aspects of local life, society, and culture while connecting or integrating this process with international networks and struggles.[2] What ties these struggles together is in part a sense that processes of globalization from above are doing bad things to ordinary people everywhere, in both wealthy and poor countries. Thus protests in the streets of Seattle against the World Trade Organization are related to the struggles of people in Central America because the same global economic system affects both negatively. The discourse of universal human rights also helps to connect these worldwide manifestations of resistance. In Honduras, globalization from below also has the dimension of international networking and solidarity. We have seen how the different popular organizations and their particular concerns began to converge in some significant ways beginning at least in the 1980s. Since then, many of the organizations and groups that form part of the larger culture of resistance have developed levels of networking or solidarity with like organizations and groups internationally. LGBT, indigenous, and environmental groups in particular, and to some extent progressive religious and human rights organizations in Honduras have strengthened their ties to international groups and movements.[3] The awarding of the international Goldman Environmental Defender Award to Lenca and COPINH activist Berta Cáceres in April, 2015 is emblematic of this, and it garnered attention in international news media. The culture of resistance in Honduras is globalizing its local resistance struggles by linking them to larger, global concerns and organizations, protecting the local with the global. This is a mutual outreach that is likely to influence in some as-yet-unknown ways both Honduran popular organizations and the culture of resistance as well as the international organizations and groups.

HONDURAN RESISTANCE AND POST-NEOLIBERAL SOCIETY

Students of popular social movements in Latin America have begun to describe the exhaustion, collapse, or loss of hegemony of the neoliberal development model that has held sway in much of Latin America since the early 1980s.[4] In Honduras, a neoliberal development model appeared in the early 1980s with the so-called Facussé Memorandum of APROH and the U.S.

Embassy's set of recommendations—the so-called Reaganomics for Honduras—to the new civilian government of Roberto Suazo Cordova. But the model could not be fully implemented until the end of the Central American conflicts of the 1980s, and finally emerged with the package of neoliberal measures (the *paquetazo*) and the Agricultural Modernization Law set forth by the government of Rafael Callejas in the early 1990s. Since then, several important developments have emerged to interfere with the smooth implementation of the neoliberal model in Honduras. Popular resistance grew and converged over the succeeding decades fueled by the displacements, disenfranchisement, and human rights abuses that were the price paid by sectors of the population for the implementation of the neoliberal model in Honduran society. The top-down enforcement of this model during the 1990s and 2000s promoted an increasing corruption of power and its handmaid, impunity. It also encouraged more state-sponsored or permitted violence as a vehicle that elites sometimes used to further their implementation of neoliberal policies and practices. And it fueled rising popular frustration with the traditional elite-controlled and restricted model of governance, coupled with an increasing demand for a widening of the avenues of popular political participation.

The Zelaya government (2005–2009) seemed to many Hondurans to represent the chance for such a widening of the legal constitutional mechanisms of political participation, but the 2009 coup that removed Zelaya from power ended that possibility. The coup and its aftermath reinforced the implementation of the top-down implementation of neoliberal policies and practices, and the burgeoning of violence that seemed increasingly random, uncontrollable, and threatening even to the neoliberal model itself. The combined widening and internationalization of Honduran popular resistance and the level of violence can be interpreted as symptoms of the internal contradictions emerging in the neoliberal model and its ideology, and as portends of its loss of hegemony as the way to national salvation. Neoliberalism will continue in strength, but it is increasingly delegitimized by these emerging forces of violence on the one side and resistance on the other. From this perspective, the argument that the level of violence in Honduras still serves the purposes of an elite-controlled neoliberal model must be weighed against further and future studies of how such extreme and seemingly random violence actually shapes the future of both governance and resistance in Honduras—for example, whether it is leading to increasing "areas of ungovernabilty." These studies may further the understanding of Honduras as it is transformed into a post-neoliberal society whose outlines and direction are still mostly unknown. In this book, we have seen some of the beginnings of this post-neoliberal society. At present, the term *late neoliberalism* might be a more apt characterization of the Honduran reality.

HONDURAS AND LATIN AMERICAN POPULAR RESISTANCE MOVEMENTS

Honduran popular resistance is increasingly globalized not only in its ties to the international networks of its various organizations and constituencies, but also by what it shares in common with other rising social movements and forms of popular resistance in Latin America and elsewhere. One of these shared characteristics is an internal tension between two different ideas or tendencies about the way such movements should organize and where their power resides. Horizontalism or horizontal organizing promotes a wide and relatively inclusive involvement in governance and decision-making. Vanguardism assumes the need for a forceful and relatively restricted leadership for social movements, such as a political party or a charismatic leader—for example, Hugo Chavez in Venezuela. In Honduras, Manuel Zelaya, and then Libre came to represent this tendency for some groups in popular resistance, while others favored a broader, shared vision of collective action and were skeptical of allowing Libre to monopolize or become synonymous with popular resistance in the country.

Horizontalism in Latin American social movements has identifiable characteristics. It rejects vanguardism and vertical structures of power in the movement and in national political structures. It contests the power of financial and corporate elites. It rejects the strategy or aim of taking state power as a primary goal of radical change, but searches instead for ways to create change without taking state power. John Holloway, *Changing the World without Taking Power* (London; Pluto Press, 2002).[5] We have seen that the culture of resistance in Honduras exhibits all of these tendencies. Creating change without taking state power, for example, includes the efforts to construct pieces of a new society in the midst of the old, a central characteristic of Honduran popular resistance manifest in many small and often little-noticed ways.

Thus, the culture of resistance that has evolved in Honduras in the past century now shares some fundamental characteristics with other social change and popular resistance movements in Latin America that are characterized by increasing ties to regional and international networks and elements of horizontalism tempered by the temptation to rely on a political party such as Libre or a charismatic leader such as Manuel Zelaya to secure the better future. As Clifton Ross and Marcy Rein point out, the problem of integrating the strengths of horizontalism and vanguardism or verticalism into a powerful new vision of society is an ongoing concern in Latin American social movements.[6]

THE NEXT GENERATIONS

All discussions about the future direction of Honduras must hinge in large part upon what happens to the country's future generations. Manuel's concern for the young people (chapter 4) is a major theme in the culture of resistance in Honduras, and it is a well-founded concern. Since at least the early 1980s, children and youth, especially street kids and poor youth have been depicted as expendable objects for "social cleansing," or as gang members and criminals, or they are simply ignored in government policy, as Wolseth suggests. Conditions in Honduran cities before the 2009 coup were already destroying opportunity for young people, pushing some into gangs or making them the target of gang violence and the violence of security forces. The heightened level of killings of children and the intensified criminalization of youth after the 2009 coup made the fate of the next generation of Hondurans an increasing concern. For some, the massive brutality that produces so many murdered and dismembered children can only be interpreted in the context of a spiritual struggle. At the same time, youth as a criminal and violent category becomes a subtext of Honduran cultural discourse in news media and political pronouncements. The pervasive presence and power of narcotics traffickers and their interactions with youth gangs provide another excuse for criminalizing Honduran youth. The arrival of tens of thousands of young Hondurans seeking asylum at the U.S. border and elsewhere in 2013 and 2014 seemed to prove the validity of the fears of Honduran activists that the country was losing its future generation through violence and flight. This was the loss of a generation that might have guaranteed the future of popular resistance and the building of a better society. The young people who remain and actively and consciously try to better their society, or simply to live a "normal" and dignified life risk much, live bravely, and become even more precious for the better future envisioned in the culture of resistance. Some of them marry and have children in the midst of a violent reality. Some of their elders in the resistance say it is surely a sign of great faith in the future of the country. Jon Wolseth describes the coping strategies of Honduran youth in a violent society in terms of resilience.[7]

RESILIENCE

Perhaps the question that most haunts this exploration of resistance and resilience is how Hondurans manage to maintain hope and to keep despair at bay even as they live in a society that has been characterized as *hundamente deprimida* (profoundly depressed). What does hope or resilience mean in this context? Finding an answer to this question is not so easy, even after we have reviewed the many and risky ways in which the struggle evolves and is expressed. The question of keeping hope alive and despair at bay seems to be closely related to the question of why and how Hondurans manage to organize resistance that is both critical and creative—critical of what is and creative about building something better. How can people engage in risky forms of resistance unless they have some hope that their actions will have some desired effect? But this question could be asked in reverse. How can people have some hope of a better future if they do not engage in some form of resistance that critiques and creates? From this perspective, engaging in resistance becomes a living out of hope even if one does not feel very hopeful. What would move people to do that? There are many possible answers—desperation, tiredness, a need to make something a bit easier, expectations of friends or community who are engaged in some form of resistance, guilt, or even a blind faith that is difficult to describe or explain.

When I ask Hondurans how they overcome their fears about engaging in resistance, they often give a simple answer that goes something like this: "If because of fear we did nothing, if we did not resist and try to build, it would be even more risky, difficult, or overwhelming." This response tempts one to turn the paradigm around. People resist not (or not only) because they are somehow resilient, rather they are resilient because they resist, and the living out of their resistance is precisely what resilience means. Although this observation does not "explain" why people resist, it does give *resilience* an empirical, living meaning. At least in Honduras, resistance is both very personal and very communitarian, and it is difficult to understand how it could be one without the other. The evolution of a culture of resistance that we have traced in Honduras is an evolution of individuals forming groups and movements fraught with weaknesses, limitations, and setbacks, but still evolving and growing.

This evolution inevitably encompasses the historic and problematic relationship of Honduras to the United States whose many interventions and influences in Honduran life have appeared repeatedly in these pages. People in the United States are already and have long been some part of the daily reality of life for Honduras. What is done in the United States—how policy is shaped and changed, how foreign aid is conceived and given, how young people seeking asylum are received at the U.S. border—all of this and more will affect Hondurans, their society and institutions. The idea of solidarity between people is built on this realization. It is as if the culture of resistance that is evolving in Honduras must also be evolving in the United States, where people reshape what their country is and does.

NOTES

1. James Phillips, "Democratic Socialism, the New International Economic Order, and Globalization: Jamaica's Sugar Cooperatives in the Postcolonial Transition," *The Global South* 4:2 (Fall, 2010): 180–82.

2. I was first introduced to the idea of seeing globalization from above and below by conversations with a sociologist colleague, S. M. Shamsul Alam, in the early 2000s.

3. This characteristic of other Latin American social movements is discussed in Richard Stahler-Sholk, Harry Vanden, and Marc Becker eds., *Rethinking Latin American Social Movements: Radical Action from Below* (Lanham, MD: Rowman and Littlefield, 2014), 9–10 and throughout the volume.

4. Mark Goodale and Nancy Postero, eds., *Neoliberalism Interrupted: Social Change and Contested Governance in Contemporary Latin America* (Stanford, CA: Stanford University Press, 2013). Rovina Kaltwasswer, "Toward Post-Neoliberalism in Latin America?" *Latin American Research Review* 46:2 (2011): 225–34. Eric Hershberg and Fred Rosen, *Latin America after Neoliberalism: Turning the Tide in the Twenty-first Century?* (New York: The New Press, 2007).

5. Stahler-Sholk, Vanden, and Becker, 8. One of the contributions to this volume specifically discusses the problematic relationship between the FNRP and Libre and the broader popular protest movement in Honduras in the context of this tension and of the resistance objective of re-founding the state (*refundacion*), Suyapa Portillo Villeda, "Honduras: Refounding the Nation, Building a New Kind of Social Movement," 121–46, esp. 132–33.

6. Clifton Ross and Marcy Rein eds., *Until the Rulers Obey: Voices from Latin American Social Movements* (Oakland, CA: PM Press, 2014), 22–23.

7. Jon Wolseth, *Jesus and the Gang: Youth Violence and Christianity in Urban Honduras* (Tucson: University of Arizona Press, 2011), 133.

Bibliography

Acker, Alison. *Honduras: The Making of a Banana Republic*. Boston: South End Press, 1988.
Aguilar Urbina, Francisco José. "Justicia transicional y comisiones de esclarescimiento de la verdad." *Envío Honduras* 9:31 (December 2011) 16–21.
Alvarado, Elvia. *Don't Be Afraid, Gringo! A Honduran Woman Speaks from the Heart.* New York: Harper Perennial, 1989 [San Francisco: Institute for Food and Development Policy, 1987].
Anaya, S. James. "The CIA with the Honduran Army in the Mosquitia: Taking the Freedom out of the Fight in the Name of Accountability." Report on a Visit to the Honduran Mosquitia during April, 1987. Unpublished report, 1987.
Anderson, Mark. *Garifuna Kids: Blackness, Tradition, and Modernity in Honduras*. Austin: University of Texas Ph.D. Thesis, 2000.
———. "When Afro Becomes (like) Indigenous: Garifuna and Afro-Indigenous Politics in Honduras." *The Journal of Latin American and Caribbean Anthropology* 12:2 (November 2007) 384–413.
———. "Garifuna Activism and the Corporatist Honduran State Since the 2009 Coup." In *Black Social Movements in Latin America: From Monocultural Mestizaje to Multiculturalism*. Edited by Jean Muteba Rahier. New York: Palgrave MacMillan, 2012, 53–73.
Appadurai, Arjun. "Disjuncture and Difference in the Global Cultural Economy." *Theory, Culture & Society* 7 (1990): 295–310.
Asociación de Jueces por la Democracia (AJD). "Administración de justicia y persistente fragilidad institucional." Statement of AJD for public hearing 147, Human Rights Situation in Honduras, Washington, DC (March 2013). Reprinted in *Revista Justicia* 6:12 (July, 2013): 39–67.
Assmann, Hugo. *Theology for a Nomad Church*. Maryknoll, NY: Orbis Books, 1976.
Avila, Jennifer. "La explotación minera, tan dura como la dictadura." *Envío Honduras* 11:38 (June, 2013): 28–34.
Banfield, Edward C. *The Moral Basis of a Backward Society*. New York: Free Press, 1958.
Barahona, Marvin. *Honduras en el siglo XX: Una síntesis histórica*. Tegucigalpa: Editorial Guaymuras, 2005.
———. *Pueblos indígenas, Estado, y memoria colectiva en Honduras*. Tegucigalpa: Editorial Guaymuras, 2009.
———. "El contexto histórico de las iglesias Cristianas en Honduras en el Valle de Sula," in *Religión, Ideología, y sociedad: Una aproximación a las iglesias en Honduras*. Equipo de Reflexión, Investigación, y Comunicación. El Progreso: Editorial Casa San Ignacio, 2013. 34–82.

Becerra, Longino. "The Early History of the Labor Movement." In *Honduras: Portrait of a Captive Nation*. Nancy Peckenham and Annie Street, eds. New York: Prager Publishers, 1985. (This chapter is a reprint and translation from sections of *Evolución Histórica de Honduras*, by Longino Becerra. Tegucigalpa: Editorial Baktun, 1983.)

Beezley, William, et al. "Introduction: Consructing Consent, Inciting Conflict." In, William H. Beezley et al eds., *Rituals of Rule, Rituals of Resistance: Public Celebrations and Popular Culture in Mexico*. Wilmington, DE: Scholarly Resource Inc., 1994. xiii–xxxii.

Bernard, Eben. "Critical Resistance: Can Such Practices Ever Have a Meaningful Impact?" *Critical Social Thinking: Policy and Practice* 13:2 (2011).

Bird, Annie, and Alexander Main with Karen Spring. "Collateral Damage of a Drug War: The May 11 Killings in Ahuas and the Impact of the U.S. War on Drugs in La Moskitia, Honduras." Washington DC: Rights Action and the Center for Economic and Policy Research, August, 2012.

Boff, Leonardo, and Virgil Elizondo, eds. *1492–1992: The Voices of the Victims*. London: Concilium-SCM Press, 1991.

Brondo, Keri Vacanti. *Land Grab: Green Neoliberalism, Gender, and Garifuna Resistance in Honduras*. Tucson: University of Arizona Press, 2013.

Bryceson, Deborah, Cristóbal Kay, and Jos Mooij, editors. *Disappearing Peasantries? Rural Labour in Africa, Asia, and Latin America*. London: Intermediate Technology Publications, 2000.

Canin, Eric. "Mingüito, Managua's Little Saint: Christian Base Communities and Popular Religion in Urban Nicaragua." In *Contemporary Cultures and Societies of Latin America: A Reader in the Social Anthropology of Middle and South America*. Dwight B. Heath, ed. Long Grove, IL: Waveland Press, 1974.

Cardenal, Fernando. *Sacerdote en la Revolución: Memorias, Tomo 1*. Managua: Anama Ediciones, 2008.

Caritas El Salvador. "Mitos y Realidades de la Minería de Oro en Centroamérica." http://www.stopesmining.org/j25/images/pdf/mitos%20y%20realidades (August, 2014).

Carney, James Francis. *To Be a Revolutionary*. New York: Harper-Collins, 1985.

Carter, Jon Horne, "Gothic Sovereignty: Gangs and Criminal Community in a Honduran Prison." *The South-Atlantic Quarterly* 113:3 (Summer, 2014): 475–502.

Cassel, Doug. "Honduras: Coup d'Etat in Constitutional Clothing?" *Insights*. (American Society of International Law) 13:9 (October 15, 2009).

Centro de Documentación de Honduras (CEDOH). "La Contra en Honduras." *Serie: Cronologias* 7 (April, 1987).

———. "La ayuda alimentaria estadouidiense en Honduras." *CEDOH Numero Especial 41* (May 1989).

———. *Boletín Informativo 85* (February, 1992).

Chapman, Anne. *Los hijos del copal y la candela*. Volumen I y II. Mexico: Universidad Nacional Autónoma de Mexico (UNAM), 1986.

Comaroff, Jean and John Comaroff. *Of Revelation and Revolution*. Chicago: University of Chicago Press, 1991.

Comblin, José. *The Church and the National Security State*. Maryknoll, NY: Orbis Books, 1984 (original printing 1979).

Comité para la Defensa de los Derechos Humanos en Honduras (CODEH). *Boletín* 62 (March, 1990).

———. *Boletín* 70 (November 1990).

———. *Boletín* 80 (September 1991).

———. *Boletín* 85 (February 1992).

Conferencia Episcopal de Honduras (Honduran Catholic Bishops' Conference). "A la opinión pública nacional." Unpublished official copy (August, 1992).

Cuffe, Sandra. "Militarization of the Mesoamerican Barrier Reef Harms Indigenous Communities." Truthout (Truth-out website) May 12, 2014. http://www.truth-out.org/news/item/23729-militarizatin-of-the-mesoamerican-barrier-reef-harms-indigenous-communities.

Delcid, Carmen Manuela. "Espiritualidad y derechos humanos en el contexto actual." *Envío Honduras* 8:24 (April, 2010): 46–48.

Del Cid, Rafael. "Las clases socials y su dinámica en el agro Hondureño." *Estudios Sociales Centroamericanos* 18, (1977): 154.
DeLuca, Danielle. "In Pursuit of Autonomy: Indigenous Peoples Oppose Dam Construction on the Patuca River in Honduras." *Cultural Survival Quarterly* 35:4 (December 2011): 12–15.
Dilling, Yvonne. *In Search of Refuge.* Scottsdale, PA: Herald Press, 1984.
Dore, Elizabeth. *Myths of Modernity: Peonage and Patriarchy in Nicaragua.* Durham, NC: University of North Carolina Press, 2006
Duncombe, Stephen. "Cultural Resistance." *Blackwell Encyclopedia of Sociology.* Edited by George Ritzer. London: Blackwell, 2007.
Durrenberger, E. Paul. "Anthropology and Globalization." *American Anthropologist* 103:2 (June 2001): 531–35.
Equipo de Reflexión, Investigación, y Comunicación (ERIC-SJ). *Nuestra Palabra: Radio Progreso y ERIC-SJ.* El Progreso: Editorial Casa San Ignacio, 2011.
———. *Religión, Ideología, y sociedad: Una aproximación a las iglesias en Honduras.* El Progreso: Editorial Casa San Ignacio, 2013.
———. "¿Qué mentalidad y conciencia predominan en la sociedad hondureña según los sondeos de opinión pública realizados por el ERIC?" *Envío Honduras* 12:41 (March 2014): 1–7.
Equipo de Reflexión, Investigación, y Comunicación (ERIC-SJ) y Universidad Centroamericana José Simeón Cañas. *Sondeo de opinión publica: Percepciones sobre la situación hondurena en el ano 2012.* El Progreso: ERIC-SJ, 2013.
Euraque, Dario. *Reinterpreting the Banana Republic: Region and State in Honduras, 1870–1972.* Chapel Hill, NC: University of North Carolina Press, 1996.
———. *El golpe de estado del 28 de junio del 2009, el patrimonio cultural y la Identidad Nacional de Honduras.* San Pedro Sula: Centro Editorial, 2010.
Everton, Ross. "Justifying Militarization: 'Counter-narcotics' and 'Counter-Narcoterrorism.'" *Policy Report* 3. Swansea, UK: Global Drug Policy Observatory, Swansea University (March, 2015).
Faber, D. "Imperialism, Revolution, and the Ecological Crisis in Central America." *Latin American Perspectives* 19:1 (1992): 17–44.
Fiallos, Maria. "Honduran Indigenous Community in Standing Forest Area." *Honduras This Week* (June 9, 2003).
Flacks, Richard. *Making History: The American Left and the American Mind.* New York: Columbia University Press, 1988.
Frank, Andre Gunder. "The Development of Underdevelopment." In *Dependence and Underdevelopment.* Edited by James Cockcroft, Andre Gunder Frank, and Dale Johnson. Garden City, NY: Anchor Books, 1972.
Frank, Dana. *Bananeras: Women Transforming the Banana Unions of Latin America.* English ed. Cambridge, MA: South End Press, 2005.
Frei Beto. *Fidel and Religion: Castro Talks on Revolution and Religion with Frei Beto.* New York: Simon and Schuster, 1988.
Freire, Paulo. *Pedagogy of the Oppressed.* New York: Herder and Herder, 1970.
———. *Education for Critical Consciousness.* New York: Seabury, 1973.
Freire, Paulo, Ana Maria Araújo Freire, Walter de Oliveira, and Donald Machado. *Pedagogy of Solidarity: Qualitative Inquiry and Social Justice.* Walnut Creek, CA: Left Coast Press, 2014.
Galtung, Johan. "Violence, Peace, and Peace Research." *Journal of Peace Research* 6:3 (1969): 167–91.
Garrard-Burnett, Virginia, and David Stoll, eds. *Rethinking Protestantism in Latin America.* Philadelphia: Temple University Press, 1993.
Geneva Academy of International Humanitarian Law and Human Rights. "Honduras: Non-state Actors." Rule of Law in Armed Conflicts Project (RULAC), University of Geneva, 2014.
Goodale, Mark, ed. *Human Rights at the Crossroads.* New York: Oxford University Press, 2013.

Goodale, Mark and Nancy Postero eds. *Neoliberalism Interrupted: Social Change and Contested Governance in Contemporary Latin America.* Stanford, CA: Stanford University Press, 2013.
Greaves, Tom, Ralph Bolton, and Florencia Zapata, eds. *Vicos and Beyond: A Half-Century of Applying Anthropology in Peru.* Lanham, MD: Altamira, 2011.
Grigg, Greg. "Honduran People Say No to Stone." *Focus on Honduras* (Summer 1993): 1–3.
Gutierrez, Gustvo. *A Theology of Liberation.* Maryknoll, NY: Maryknoll, 1973.
Hale, Charles R. "Does Multiculturalism Menace? Cultural Rights and the Politics of Identity in Guatemala." *Journal of Latin American Studies* 34 (2002): 485–524.
Handler, R. "Romancing the Low: Anthropology vis-à-vis Cultural Studies vis-à-vis Popular Culture." *Political and Legal Anthropology Review* 17: 2 (1994): 1–6.
Hansen, Thomas Blom, and Finn Stepputat eds. *States of Imagination: Ethnographic Explorations of the Postcolonial State.* Durham, NC: Duke University Press, 2001.
Hershberg, Eric and Fred Rosen. *Latin America after Neoliberalism: Turning the Tide in the Twenty-first Century?* New York: The New Press, 2007.
Holloway, John. *Changing the World without Taking Power.* London: Pluto Press, 2002.
Instituto Nacional de Estadística. *XVI Censo Nacional de Población.* Tegucigalpa: Instituto Nacional de Estadística, 2001.
Inter-American Commission on Human Rights. *Report No. 39/07, Petition 1118–03, Admissibility: Garifuna Community of Cayos Cochinos and Its Members, Honduras* (July 24, 2007).
———. *Honduras: Human Rights and the Coup d'Etat.* Organization of American States (Organización de Estados Americanos) OEA/Ser.L/V/II. Doc. 55, (December 2009). Spanish version published in same volume.
———. "Preliminary Observations of the IACHR on Its Visit to Honduras on May 15–18, 2010." Organization of American States, OEA/Ser L/V/II, Doc. 68 (June 3, 2010). English version.
———. "IACHR Expresses Concern over Violent Deaths of Children, Adolescents, and Youth in Context of Citizen Insecurity in Honduras." Press release, Organization of American States, May 14, 2014.
Intercontinental Cry. "Declaration of the International Meeting of the Landless in San Pedro Sula, July 24–28, 2000." Intercontinental Cry website, July 14, 2007. https://intercontinentalcry.org.
International Court of Justice. *Case Concerning Military and Paramilitary Activities in and against Nicaragua (Nicaragua v. United States of America) Jurisdiction and Admissibility 1984 ICJ REP 392 (June 1986).* New York: United Nations Press, 1986.
Jagan, Cheddi. *The West on Trial: My Fight for Guyana's Freedom.* London: Michael Joseph, Ltd., 1966.
Jansen, Kees. "Structural Adjustment, Peasant Differentiation, and the Environment in Central America." In. *Disappearing Peasantries? Rural Labour in Africa, Asia, and Latin America.* Deborah Bryceson, Cristóbal Kay, and Jos Mooij, editors. London: Intermediate Technology Publications, 2000.
Kaltwasser, Rovina. "Toward Post-Neoliberalism in Latin America?" *Latin American Research Review* 46: 2 (2011): 225–34.
Kavanagh, Tom. "Honduras is 'open for business.'" *New Statesman* (May 8, 2011).
Kearney, Michael. *The Winds of Ixtepeji: World View and Society in a Zapotec Town.* New York: Holt, Rinehart, Winston, 1972 [reissued by Waveland Press, 1986].
Kincaid, Douglas. "We Are the Agrarian Reform: Rural Politics and Agrarian Reform." In *Honduras: Portrait of a Captive Nation.* Nancy Peckenham and Annie Street, eds. New York: Praeger Publishers, 1985.
Kressen, Tanya. *Land Grabbing: The New Struggles for Land, Power, and Democracy in Northern Honduras.* Oakland, CA: Food First, Institute for Food and Development Policy, 2013.
Kroeber, A. L., Clyde Kluckhohn, and Wayne Untereiner. *Culture: A Critical Review of Concepts and Definitions.* New York: Vintage Press, 1952.

Lerner, Steve. *Sacrifice Zones: The Front Lines of Toxic Chemical Exposure in the United States.* Cambridge, MA: MIT Press, 2010.
Lernoux, Penny. *Cry of the People.* New York: Penguin, 1982.
Levy, Jordan. *The Politics of Honduran School Teachers: State Agents Challenge the State.* University of Western Ontario Electronic Thesis and Dissertation Repository. Paper 2142 (2014). http://ir.lib.uwo.ca/edt/2142.
Lovell, W. G. *Conquest and Survival in Colonial Guatemala: A Historical Geography of the Cuchumatan Highlands, 1500–1821.* Montreal: McGill-Queens University Press, 1992.
MacEoin, Gary. *Unlikely Allies: The Christian-Socialist Convergence.* New York: Crossroads Publishing, 1990.
Marsh, Michael. "Honduras Is Worth More than Gold." Asociación de Organismos No Gubernamentales (ASONOG), 2002, at asonog@hondudata.com.
McGinnis, James. Solidarity with the People of Nicaragua. Maryknoll, NY: Orbis Books, 1985.
McSwenney, Kendra, Zoe Pearson, Sara Santiago, and Ana Gabriela Domínguez. "A River Tale: Protecting a Tawahka Way of Life." *Cultural Survival Quarterly* 35:4 (December 2011): 16–20.
Mendez, Marilyn. "'Honduras Is Open for Business' cambiará la historia del país." *La Prensa* (April 10, 2011).
Merrill, Tim. *Honduras: A Country Study.* Washington, DC: Government Printing Office, for Library of Congress, 1995.
Merry, Sally Engel. "Transnational Human Rights and Local Activism: Mapping the Middle." *American Anthropologist* 108:1 (June, 2006): 38–51.
Mersky, Marcie. "Las Comisiones de Verdad como herramientas no judiciales de lucha contra la impunidad." *Envío Honduras* 9: 31 (December 2011): 22–25.
Meyer, Peter J., and Clare Ribando Seelke. *Central American Regional Security Initiative: Background and Policy Issues for Congress.* Washington, DC: Congressional Research Service (May 6, 2014).
Meza, Victor. *Historia del Movimiento Obrero Hondureño.* Tegucigalpa: Editorial Guaymuras, 1980.
Mintz, Sydney. *Caribbean Transformations.* New York: Aldine Publishing, 1974.
———. "The Rural Proletariat and the Problem of Rural Proletarian Consciousness." *Journal of Peasant Studies* 1 (1974): 291–325.
———. *Sweetness and Power: The Place of Sugar in Modern History.* New York: Viking, 1985.
———. *Tasting Food, Tasting Freedom: Excursions into Eating, Culture, and Past.* Boston: Beacon Press, 1996.
Mintz, Sidney, and Christine M. DuBois. "The Anthropology of Food and Eating." *Annual Review of Anthropology* 31 (2002): 99–117.
Moreno SJ, Ismael. "Déficit de ciudadanía: Una interpretación del sondeo de opinión pública UCA-ERIC." *Envío Honduras* 8:28 (March 2011): 1–8.
———. "Porque la violencia en Honduras?" *Envío Honduras* 10:34 (June 2012): 1–9.
———. "Dimensión social de la misión de la Iglesia Católica: Una mirada nacional desde la región noroccidental de Honduras." In *Religión, Ideología, y sociedad: Una aproximación a las iglesias en Honduras,* Equipo de Reflexión, Investigación, y Comunicación. El Progreso: Editorial Casa San Ignacio, 2013. 102–52.
———. "Tercer sondeo de opinión del ERIC: Retrato de un país que va de mal a peor." *Envío Honduras* 11:37 (March 2013): 1–8.
———. "Una caminata en repudio a la Ley de Minería." *Envío Nicaragua* 32:373 (April 2013): 24–30.
———. "Que mentalidad y conciencia predominan en la sociedad hondureña, según los sondeos de opinión publica realizados por el ERIC?" *Envío Honduras* 12:41 (March 2014): 1–7.
Nairn, Allan. "The United States Militarizes Honduras." In *Honduras: Portrait of a Captive Nation.* Edited by Nancy Peckenham and Annie Street. New York: Praeger, 1985, 292–97.
Nelson, Richard T. "Honduras Country Brief: Property Rights and Land Markets." Madison, WI: Land Tenure Center, University of Wisconsin, June 2003.

Nolan, Mary Lee. "The European Roots of Latin American Pilgrimage." In, *Pilgrimage in Latin America.* Edited by N. Ross Crumrine and Alan Morinis. New York and London: Greenwood Press, 1991.
Organización Fraternal Negra Hondureña OFRANEH. "The Supposed War on Drugs and the Demonization of the Indigenous Peoples of the Mosquitia." OFRANEH, March 13, 2014. Friendship Office of the Americas website March 14, 2014 (trans. by Adrienne Pine).
Oseguera de Ochoa, Margarita. *Honduras hoy: Sociedad y crisis política.* Tegucigalpa: Centro de Documentación de Honduras CEDOH, 1987.
Peckenham, Nancy, and Annie Street. *Honduras: Portrait of a Captive Nation.* New York: Praeger Publishers, 1985.
Pedraz Gonzalez, Antonio. "Sondeo de opinión pública y percepción religiosa." *Envío Honduras* 10:33 (March 2012): 29–34.
Pérez-Baltodano Andrés. *Entre el Estado Conquistador y el Estado Nación: Providencialismo, pensamiento político, y estructuras de poder en el desarrollo histórico de Nicaragua.* Managua: Instituto de Historia de Nicaragua y Centroamérica de la Universidad Centramericana, 2008.
Phillips, Arthur. "Charter Cities in Honduras?" *Open Security* (January 2014).
———. "Media Reports on Charter Cities Ignore the Larger Context." Center for Economic and Policy Research (February 27, 2014).
Phillips, James. "Nicaraguan Peasants and the Search for Peace." *Human Peace* 10:2 (Winter, 1994)
———. "Resource Access, Environmental Struggles, and Human Rights in Honduras." In *Life and Death Matters: Human Rights and the Environment at the End of the Millunnium.* Ed. Barbara Rose Johnston. Walnut Creek, CA: AltaMira Press, 1997, 173–84.
———. "Repatriation and Social Class in Nicaragua." In *Coming Home? Refugees, Migrants, and Those Who Stayed Behind.* Lynellyn D. Long and Ellen Oxfeld eds. Philadelphia: University of Pennsylvania Press, 2004.
———. "When Governments Fail: Reparation, Solidarity, and Community in Nicaragua." In *Waging War, Making Peace: Reparations and Human Rights.* Barbara Rose Johnston and Susan Slyomovics eds. Walnut Creek, CA: Left Coast Press, 2009.
———. "Body and Soul: Faith, Development, Community, and Social Science in Nicaragua." NAPA (National Association for the Practice of Anthropology) *Bulletin* 33 (2010): 12–30.
———. "Democratic Socialism, the New International Economic Order, and Globalization: Jamaica's Sugar Cooperatives in the Post-Colonial Transition." *The Global South* 4:2 (Fall, 2010): 180–82.
———. "Resource Access, Environmental Struggles, and Human Rights in Honduras." In *Life and Death Matters: Human Rights, Environment, and Social Justice.* Second edition. Ed. Barbara Rose Johnston. Walnut Creek, CA: Left Coast Press, 2011, 209–32. (This article is an entirely new update to the 1997 version listed above.)
———. "Challenging Impunity with Memory in Today's Honduras." Unpublished paper read at American Anthropological Association Annual Meeting, San Francisco, November 2012.
Phillips, Susan. *Wallbangin': Graffiti and Gangs in L.A.* Chicago: University of Chicago Press, 1999.
Pine, Adrienne. *Working Hard, Drinking Hard: On Violence and Survival in Honduras.* Berkeley, CA: University of California Press, 2008.
Portillo Villeda, Suyapa. "Honduras: Refounding the Nation, Building a New Kind of Social Movement." In, *Rethinking Latin American Social Movements: Radical Action from Below.* Edited by Richard Stahler-Skolk et al. Lanham, MD: Rowman and Littlefield, 2014, 121–46.
Posas, Mario. *Notas sobre las Sociedades Artesanales y los Orígenes del Movimiento Obrero Hondureño.* Tegucigalpa: Esp Editorial 1978.
Programa Latinoamericano de Etudios Religiosos (PROLADES) and Visión Mundial Internacional-Honduras. *Estudio Socio-Religioso de Honduras.* Tegucigalpa: Visión Mundial Internacional-Honduras, 1986.

Proyecto de Acompanimiento de Honduras (PROAH). "La Comisión de Verdad presenta su informe, 'La voz más autorizada es la de las victimas.'" PROAH website, proah.wordpress.com (Spanish). Posted October 22, 2012.

———. "Summary of Human Rights Issues and Events in Honduras for October–December 2013." PROAH website, proah.wordpress.com. (Spanish) and honduranaccomanimentproject.wordpress.com. (English).

Radio Progreso y Equipo de Reflexión, Investigación, y Comunicación (ERIC-SJ). *Impunidad: La ley de los fuertes que aplasta a las victimas.* El Progreso: Radio Progreso y ERIC, 2013.

Rainwater, Lee. "Crucible of Identity: The Negro Lower-class Family." *Daedalus* 95 (1966): 212.

Redfield, Robert. *Peasant Society and Culture: An Anthropological Approach to Civilization.* Chicago: University of Chicago Press, 1956.

Reilly, Kevin, ed. *Worlds of History. First Edition.* Boston: Bedford St. Martins, 1999.

Richard, Pablo. "The Violence of God and the Future of Christianity." In, *1492–1992: The Voices of the Victims.* Edited by Leonardo Boff and Virgil Elizondo. London: Concilium-SCM Press, 1991.

Riley, Hannah C. and James K. Sebenius. "Stakeholder Negotiations over Third World Resource Projects." *Cultural Survival Quarterly* 19:3 (Fall 1993): 39–43.

Rosenthal, Jack. "A Terrible Thing to Waste." *New York Times Magazine* (August 2, 2009).

Ross, Clifton and Marcy Rein eds. *Until the Rulers Obey: Voices from Latin American Social Movements.* Oakland, CA: PM Press, 2014.

Rosset, Peter. "Food Security and the Contemporary Food Crisis." *Development* 51:4 (December 2008): 460–63.

Ruiz, Elias. *El Astillero: masacre y justicia.* Tegucigalpa: Editorial Guaymuras, 1992.

Salomón, Leticia. "La doctrina de la seguridad national en Honduras." *Honduras Boletín Informativo,* Centro de Documentación de Honduras, (May 1984).

Sanabria, Harry. *The Anthropology of Latin America and the Caribbean.* Boston: Pearson, 2007.

Sanchez R, Magaly. "Insecurity and Violence as a New Power Relation in Latin America." *Annals of the American Academy of Political and Social Science* 606:1 (July 2006): 178–95.

Schlesinger, Stephen and Stephen Kinzer. *Bitter Fruit: The Story of the American Coup in Guatemala.* New York: Doubleday, 1982.

Scott, James C. *Weapons of the Weak: Everyday Forms of Peasant Resistance.* New Haven, CT: Yale University Press, 1985.

Skidmore, Thomas E. and Peter H. Smith. *Modern Latin America.* Fifth Edition. New York: Oxford University Press, 2001.

Smyth, Tim. "Garifuna People Are Risking Everything to Flee Their Ancestral Homeland." VICE News website,https://news.vice.com/contributor/tim-smyth, posted August 21, 2014.

Spring, Karen. "Evidence the DEA Attempted to Alter Testimony on Drug War Massacre in Honduras." Center for International Policy Americas Program, www.cipamericas.org (January 30, 2015).

Stahler-Sholk, Richard, Harry Vanden, and Marc Becker eds. *Rethinking Latin American Social Movements: Radical Action from Below.* Lanham, MD: Rowman and Littlefield, 2014.

Stern, S.J. Peru's Indian People and the Challenge to Spanish Conquest: Huamanga to 1640. Madison: University of Wisconsin Press, 1982.

Stewart, Charles, and Rosalind Shaw eds. *Syncretism/Anti-Syncretism: The Politics of Religious Synthesis.* London: Routledge, 1994.

Stock, Anthony. "Land War." *Cultural Survival Quarterly* 16:4 (1992): 16–18.

Stoll, David. *Is Latin America Turning Protestant? The Politics of Evangelical Growth.* Berkeley, CA: University of California Press, 1990.

Stoll, David and Virginia Garrard-Burnett, eds. *Rethinking Protestantism in Latin America.* Philadelphia: Temple University Press, 1992.

Stonich, Susan. "The Political Economy of Environmental Destruction: Food Security in Southern Honduras." In *Harvest of Want: Hunger and Food Security in Central America and Mexico.* Scott Whiteford and Anne E. Ferguson, eds. Boulder, CO: Westview Press, 1991.

Stonich, Susan, and Billie R. DeWalt. "The Political Ecology of Deforestation in Honduras." In *Tropical Deforestation: The Human Dimension*. Eds. Leslie E. Sponsel, Thomas N. Headland, and Robert C. Bailey. New York: Columbia University Press, 1996.

Suazo, Javier. "¿Una minería benigna para Honduras?" *Envío Honduras* 10:36 (December, 2012): 36–40.

Swedberg, Richard. *The Honduran Trade Union Movement, 1920–1982*. Cambridge, MA: Camino, 1983.

———. "From Legalization to Repression: The Labor Movement after 1954." In, *Honduras: Portrait of a Captive Nation*. Edited by Nancy Peckenham and Annie Street. New York: Praeger Publishers, 1985. 89–91.

Taylor, W.B. "Landed Society in New Spain: A View from the South." *Hispanic American Historical Review* 54:3 (1974).

Telesur. "Almost 4000 Youth Killed in Honduras in Last Six Years." www.telesurtv.net, (November 20, 2014).

Tojeira, José Maria. *Los hicaques de Yoro*. Tegucigalpa: Editorial Guaymuras, 1982.

Torres, Edelberto. "Francisco Morazan and the Struggle for a Central American Union." *Ariel* 21: 233 (June 1971).

Valladares, Edmundo. "La miseria financiando el modelo de desarrollo," *El Tiempo* (January 5, 1981).

Vigil, James Diego. "Group Processes and Street Identity: Adolescent Chicano Gang Members." *Ethos* 16:4 (1988): 421–445.

Volk, Steven. "Land Pressures Lead to War between Hondurans and El Salvador." *NACLA Report on the Americas* 15:6 (December, 1981): 20–22. Reprinted in *Honduras: Portrait of a Captive Nation*. Nancy Peckenham and Annie Street eds. New York: Praeger Publishers, 1985.

Walker, Thomas W. *Nicaragua: Living in the Shadow of the Eagle*. Fourth edition. Boulder, CO: Westview Press, 2003.

Wallerstein, Immanuel. *The Modern World System*. (Three volumes.) New York: Academic Press, 1974, 1980, 1989.

Weismantel, Mary. *Food, Gender, and Poverty in the Ecuadorian Andes*. Long Grove, IL: Waveland Press, 1988.

Winthrop, Robert. *Dictionary of Concepts in Cultural Anthropology*. New York: Greenwood Press, 1991.

Wolf, Eric R. "Closed Corporate Peasant Communities in Mesoamerica and Central Java." *Southwestern Journal of Anthropology* 13:1 (1957).

———. *Peasants*. Englewood Cliffs, NJ: Pentice-Hall, 1966.

———. *Peasant Wars of the Twentieth Century*. New York: Harper and Row, 1969.

———. "The Vicissitudes of the Closed Corporate Peasant Community." *American Ethnologist* 13:2 (1986).

———. *Envisioning Power: Ideologies of Dominance and Crisis*. Berkeley: University of California Press, 1999.

Eric Wolf and E. C. Hansen. *The Human Condition in Latin America*. New York: Oxford University Press, 1972.

Wolseth, Jon. *Jesus and the Gang: Youth Violence and Christianity in Urban Honduras*. Tucson: University of Arizona Press, 2011.

York, Suzanne. "Honduras and Resistance to Globalization." International Forum on Globalization website. http://.ifg.org/analysis/globalization/Hoonduras.htm (Winter 2003).

Index

Acción Católica (Catholic Action): founding and purposes of, 199. *See also* Catholic Church in Honduras, and rise of popular organizations

African palm (palm oil): and Garifuna communities, 110; expanded production of, 23, 41

Afrocaribbean, 24–25

Agrarian Reform Law 1974: attempts to weaken or revoke, 44, 46, 53; example of, 2; passage of, 41, 43, 76. *See also* land, and landlessness

Agricultural Modernization Law of 1992: and individual land ownership, 53, 129; criticisms of, 130, 132; impact of on food production and security, 129; passage of, 45. *See also* food, and structural adjustments of 1990s; peasants, and Agricultural Modernization Law

Aguán Valley, 21, 23; forcible evictions of peasant communities in, 52

Agua Zarca Dam. *See* Lenca

Ahuas: anti-narcotics raid on, as international incident, 104

Alianza Bolivariana (ALBA): and Manuel Zelaya, 86; and United States concern about, 225

Alvarez Martinez, Gustavo: and imposition of national security measures 1981, 3, 224; and warnings re. Nicaragua repeated after 2009 coup, 48; removal of, from office, 57. *See also* national security, Gustavo Alvarez and implementation of

American Institute of Free Labor Development (AIFLD): anti-communist labor union activity of, 77, 222

amoral familism: and weakness of Honduran institutions, 30

appropriate technology: as resistance, 136–138

artistic expression: and revolution, 170; and Dia del Arte y la Cultura en Resistencia, 173; and FNRP, 173; as act of resistance, 171; as image of better reality, 171; as source of emotional and imaginative context for resistance, 172; as subversive or public, 171

Association for Campesino Development of El Progreso (ADCP): and Magdalena Morales case, 149

Association for the Promotion of Honduras (APROH): national development plans of, 45, 96. *See also* Facussé Memorandum, as blueprint for neoliberal national development

Association of Judges for Democracy (*Asociación de Jueces por la Democracia* AJD): and defense of judges and lawyers against threats and corruption, 152; and hunger strike of judges, 164; critique of the judicial system by, 164. *See also* judicial system, collapse of at local level

Association of Non-Governmental Organizations (ASONOG): and anti-mining campaign, 134

AZUNOSA. *See* Morales, Magdalena

banana plantations: conditions on, 70; labor strikes on, 70–72; of United Fruit in northern Honduras, 2

banana strike of 1954: achievements and results of, 73–74; and manifestations of popular culture during, 72; as example of popular resistance, 74; description and analysis of, 72–74; displacement of local communities as factor in, 23; popular support for, 72

Battalion 316: seen as death squad in national security state of 1980s, 3

Black Fraternal Organization of Honduras OFRANEH (*Organización Fraternal Negra de Honduras*) : and opposition to Agricultural Modernization law, 53; seen as more militant than ODECO, 110; formation of, 107. *See also* Garifuna, emphasis on indigenous identity and land rights of; Lenca, relations of with popular organizations and interests

British: and early relations with Miskito communities, 101; and early relations with Garifuna communities, 106

Broad Movement for Democracy and Justice (*Movimiento Amplio por la Democracia y Justicia* (MADJ): support of for communities and lawyers under attack, 152

Cáceres, Berta: as example of women leaders in popular organization, 66, 150; legal charges against and hearing of, 118; opposition to REDES and Charter Cities, 33. *See also* Civic Council of Popular and Indigenous Organizations of Honduras (COPINH), and demonstrations for Berta Cáceres

Café Guancasco. *See* music and resistance

Callejas, Rafael: and formation of National Human Rights Commission (CONADEH), 160; implements neoliberal reforms (*el paquetazo*), 45, 129

caminata. *See* marches

campesinos. *See* peasants

Carias Andino, Tiburcio: and attempt to nationalize Catholic Church, 198; and repression of popular activism and organizations, 72; and repression of political and intellectual expression, 78; dictatorship of, 68

Caritas: and Hondurans displaced during Contra war, 4

Carney, James Francis (Guadalupe): and Guadalupe Carney Day, 184–186; importance of, 184

casa malla (mesh or screen house): and self-reliant agricultural technology, 137

Castro, Xiomara: and concern about REDES, 33; as candidate in election of 2013, 162

Catholic church in Honduras: and accord with Villeda government re. anticlericalism, 200; and anticlericalism of Honduran governments, 198; and rise of popular organizations, 199, 200; and support of cardinal for 2009 coup d'etat, 213; and bishops' critique of 1992 Agricultural Modernization Law, 130, 132; different tendencies and tensions within, 205; image of, as Honduran or foreign institution, 198; institutional weakness of, and difficulty changing, 200; post-Vatican 2 activism of, as challenge to powerful interests, 203–204; repression of, and retreat of from social and political activism, 204; role of, in evolution of popular resistance after 1990, 205–207; role of, in Spanish colonial period, 197–198; support for and opposition to 2009 coup d'etat, 207–208; threat against priests of, active with popular organizations, 206–207. *See also* Delegates of the Word; *doctrina socialcristiana*

Central American Free Trade Agreement (CAFTA): and *Alianza Bolivariana*

(ALBA), 86

Central American Regional Security Initiative (CARSI): and human rights violations in Honduras, 60; and United States security aid to Honduras, 226

Charter Cities (Model Cities): basic ideological assumptions of, 35–36; declared unconstitutional, 53; legal maneuvers for and opposition to, 33–36

Christian base communities (*comunidades eclesiales de base CEB*): description and importance of, 83. *See also* Vatican Council 2 and Christian base communities (CEBs)

Christian Commission for Development, Honduras (CCD): and community development, 139

Civic Council of Popular and Indigenous Organizations of Honduras *(Consejo Cívico de Organizaciones Populares e Indígenas de Honduras* (COPINH): accusations against leaders of, 53, 118; and demonstrations for Berta Cáceres, 54; and protest of hydroelectric dam, 53; founding and early activity of, 114; popular demonstrations at court hearing of leaders of, 118; role of, in major regional protest conferences in 2003, 115; role of, in national popular resistance, 119. *See also* Lenca, relations of with popular organizations and interests; coffee; and peasant farmers,

Comisión de la Verdad y Reconciliación (CVR) Truth and Reconciliation Commission (government): formation and mandate of, 165; critique of, 165; report of, 166

Comisión de Verdad (CDV) Truth Commission (independent): formation and mission of, 165; report of, 166; significance of name of, 165; work of and threats to, 166

Comité de Organizaciones Populares e Indígenas de Intibuca (COPIN): and Lenca activism leading to COPINH, 113, 114

Committee for Defense of Human Rights in Honduras (CODEH): and work for accountability, 154; formation and work of, in 1980s, 80, 81; formation of, as response to conditions in 1980s, 3

Committee of the Families of the Detained/Disappeared in Honduras (COFADEH): and work for accountability and defense, 154; formation and work of, in 1980s, 80, 81; formation as response to conditions in 1980s, 3

community development: as aspect of resistance and resilience, 138–139, 141; criteria for, as used by ERIC, 141; example of, described (La Unidad, *pseudonym*), 139–141

compliant society: and ideologies of domination and submission, 22–23

Constitution of 1982: Article 3 and people's right to popular resistance, 88; Article 107 prohibiting foreign land ownership, 44, 45; Article 347 and recognition of indigenous land rights, 44; attempts to weaken Article 347, 45; limitations of, 161

Constitutional Court (*Sala Constitucional*): critique of role in 2009 coup d'etat and other matters, 164; declares REDES unconstitutional, 7, 33; rejection of Garifuna request to block Charter Cities, 156

Contras: and displacement of Honduran communities, 4; and United States in Honduras, 224; in Nicaragua, 79; presence of, in Honduras, 3; relationship of, to Miskito communities, 102–103

cooperatives (peasant and rural production): form Federation of Honduran Agrarian Reform Cooperatives, 75; in revolutionary Nicaragua, 79; promoted by Catholic Church, 75; promoted by INA, 75; reduced government support for, 76, 131. *See also* land cooperative and collective ownership of

Copán, bishop of (Luis Santos): and statement of Diocese of Copán after

2009 coup d'etat, 192, 207–208; denounces powerful landowner, 52; opposition of, to government abuses of human rights, 208

corruption: accusations of, by popular organizations, 51; and popular protests after 2009 coup, 6; attempts by officials to combat, 155; image of, among elite and powerful, 28

coup d'etat of 1963: and popular resistance to, 87; and repression of agrarian reform and FENACH, 75

coup d'etat of 2009: arguments over legality of, 53; described, 5, 87; distorted characterization of, by U.S. observers, 49; popular resistance to, 87

culture: and cultural missions to Miskito people, 102; and cultural policy, 25; and power, 10–11; concept, 8–9; of poverty, as element in ideology of Charter Cities, 35; of resistance, 5, 9–10, 65, 237

Cuyamel Fruit Company: 1916 labor strike at plantations of, 70

death squads (*sicarios*): and reduction of safe public spaces, 180; ease of hiring, in context of poverty and arms, 19

Delegates of the Word: formation and description of, 84; involvement in social change and popular movements, 202–204

Desarrollos Energeticos (DESA). See Lenca

disappearances (of individuals): attempts to investigate, 50; changes in pattern of (who is disappeared), 50; described as a way of erasing popular memory, 49; memory work of popular organizations as challenge to, 155; of memorial symbols, 50; of youth from government policy, 50

doctrina socialcristiana (social doctrine of the Catholic Church): and Los Horcones massacre, 55; and Vatican Council 2, 56

domination: ideologies of, 17, 18, 20

drug/narcotics trafficking: and personal wealth accumulation, 28; and popular protests after 2009 coup, 6

Drug Enforcement Agency (DEA, U.S.): and anti-narcotics raids in Mosquitia, 104; and Operation Anvil, 104–105; and U.S. presence in Honduras, 226

El Astillero massacre: description and importance of, 17

elite class (ruling class, powerful): and ideologies of dominance, 26; and image of a violent reality, 236; and new entrepreneur class in banana areas, 41; and official history, 24; and perceived threat of Nicaraguan Revolution, 79; conflict among factions of, 69; historical evolution of, 20–21, 22–23; power of, in relation to Honduran state and institutions, 167

El Salvador: and FMLN insurrection, 3; refugees from, in Honduras, 4; and 1969 Soccer War with Honduras, 76

encomienda. *See* Spanish colonial rule

environment: degradation of, by extractive industries, 41, 47, 96; and community spiritual values, 47

Escuela Radiofonica: as vehicle for popular education and social activism, 66, 85

Evangelical churches. *See* Protestant churches

extractive industries: and indigenous and peasant communities, 95–97. *See also* logging; mining (all sub-entries)

extra-judicial killings: of "criminals" and street youth, 58

Facussé Memorandum: as blueprint for neoliberal national development, 33, 36, 45, 96

Farabundo Marti Front for National Liberation (FMLN): and guerrilla war in 1980s, 3

fear: as mechanism of social control, 59

Federation of Xicaque Tribes of Yoro (FETRIXY). *See* Tolupán

fiestas: as expression of a people's power, 171; example of, described and analyzed (Guadalupe Carney Day), 184–186 food: and natural food movement as form of resistance, 143–144; and obstacles to natural food movement, 144; and transforming ways of thinking, 144; as area of popular resistance, 127, 128; as aspect of identity, 127; as form of power, 128; as reflection of history, 127; declining production of, 1952-1985, 41, 128; opposition to policies regarding, 132–133, 134; policies regarding as threats to Honduran society, 127

food aid (from U.S.): and Honduran policy of agricultural export expansion, 132; as form of economic aid, 132; as wheat, 126; description and impact of, on households and government policy, 130–132

food insecurity: and declining food security, 129; and food dependency, 127; and policy of export expansion, 129; and structural adjustment of 1990s, 129

Fourth Mesoamerican Forum against Plan Puebla-Panama: demands of, 115

Foreign Deployment Advisory Support Teams (FAST): and U.S. anti-narcotics intervention in Honduras, 226

Franciscans: activism of, 205

Freire, Paulo: and culture as instrument of change, 9

gangs (*maras, pandillas*): and distrust of Honduran institutions, 30; and Garifuna communities, 112; and graffiti, 46; as form of popular resistance, 46; as identity and community, 46; image of teenagers as involved in, 51

Garifuna: and ILO Convention 169, 109; and indigenous identity, 25; appeals to Inter-American Human Rights Commission, 111, 156; attitude of early Honduran governments toward, 107; effects of drug and gang violence on, 112; effects of Hurricane Mitch on, 110; emphasis on indigenous identity and land rights of, 108–109; ethnic identity of and the problem of *mestizje*, 106; historical resistance of, 106–112; origins of, 106; racism toward, 107; relationship to English presence in Honduras, 106; threatened by and opposition to Charter Cities, 111; threats against since 2009 coup, 111; traditional culture of, 106. *See also* Black Fraternal Organization of Honduras (OFRANEH), formation of

globalization: and world economy's affects on Honduras, 44; as context for conflict and resistance in Honduras, 238; from above, 238; from below, 239

graffiti: as forms of resistance, 176–177; political and gang types of, 176; and gangs (*maras*) as form of resistance, 176–177; and future of youth in Honduras, 177

guancasco. *See* Lenca

Guardians of the Fatherland (*Guardianes de la Patria*): and militarization of Honduran society and youth, 59

Guatemala: and Honduran banana strike of 1954, 72, 73

hacienda. *See* Spanish colonial rule

hegemony: and ideology, 26

Hernandez, Juan Orlando: and Charter/Model Cities, 33; and emigrating youth, 32; and formation of military police (PMOP), 58; and militarization of Honduran society, 58, 212; anti-crime campaign pledges of, 58

history: official version of, 24–25; of the people, 68; reinterpretations of, 49

Honduran Documentation Center (*Centro de Documentación de Honduras*, CEDOH): as response to repression of 1980s, 3; formation and activities of, in 1980s, 80

Honduran National Human Rights Commission (CONADEH): creation and work of, 160–161. *See also* human rights; Reina, Carlos Roberto; Valladares, Leo

Honduran Women's Committee for Peace (*Comité Hondureño de Mujeres por la Paz "Visitación Padilla"*): mentioned, 66; activism of and involvement of different social classes in, 81

"Honduras is open for business": as example of attempt to erase trauma of 2009 coup d'etat, 48; contradicted by popular protests, 26

human rights: 1954 banana strikers invocation of, 74; as discourse of popular resistance, 82–83, 159; devastation caused to Garifuna communities by and tourism development, 45, 110; modern concept of, 158; national security and violations of, 52; organizations promoting in Honduras, 80–82, 160; processual and adaptive nature of, 82, 158–159; promoted in religious or theological discourse, 160; threats to organizations and activists of, 160; violations of, and formation of new organizations, 80. *See also* National Commission for Human Rights (CONADEH) creation and work of; Callejas, Rafael and formation of National Human Rights Commission (CONADEH); Reina, Carlos Roberto and defense of human rights; Valladares, Leo

Hurricane Mitch

hydroelectric dams: and Charter Cities plans, 34; as source of energy for mining and factories, 44; affect of, on indigenous communities, 44

identity economics: as component in ideology of Charter Cities, 35

ideology: and Charter Cities, 35–36; and discontent, 26; as support for power relationships, 18; hegemonic ideology, 26; of dominance, 27–28; of subordination, 29–32; success and failure of, 32–33

immigration: of Honduran youth to United States, 68, 230; of Garifuna youth to United States, 112

impunity: and demands for accountability, 154; and popular education about, 154; erasure of memory as defense of, 51; impunity and repression, 52; memory work as challenge to, 154–155; supported by doctrine of national security, 56, 153; ways of challenging, 153–155

indigenous communities: "inferiority" of, 20; in official history, 24–25; caciques and Spanish indirect rule of, 23; attempts to privatize land of, 45; major groups and numbers of in Honduras, 91–92; historic and current geographical distribution of groups of, 92; special characteristics of, 93–95; and problematic relationship to extractive industries, 95–97; reclaiming history and identity of, 97; and Honduran acceptance of ILO Convention 169, 109; and government policy of "neoliberal multiculturalism", 109; attempts to undermine resistance of, 120–122; resistance of to neoliberal globalization, 122. *See also* Garifuna; Miskito; Lenca; Tolupán

Inter-American Court of Human Rights: and Garifuna petition for legal protection, 156

Inter-American Human Rights Commission (IACHR): and Garifuna petition for legal protection, 156; report of, on violations of rights in post-coup Honduras, 157

international law: appeals to, when Honduran law fails, 156–157

International Labor Organization Convention 169 (ILO 169): Honduras becomes signatory to, 114

International Meeting of the Landless (2000): as response to hunger and landlessness, 133

Jesuits: and activities for social justice and human rights, 81, 205; mentioned, 2. *See also* Radio Progreso; Reflection, Investigation, and Communication Team (ERIC) formation and work of

judicial system: and delayed justice, 52; and redefining crimes, 53; as instrument to suppress popular resistance, 148; attacks against and defense of judges and lawyers in, 151–152; collapse of at local level, 148; loss of political independence of, 148; use of to defend accused activists, 149, 150; weakened legitimacy of, after 2009 coup, 164. *See also* Association of Judges for Democracy, critique of the judicial system by; technical coup, as factor in weakening legitimacy of judicial system

labor: activism transcending localism, 69; and early formation of unions, 69; appropriation of as linchpin of colonial economy, 41; organization of and early strikes, 70–72

land: and conflicts among peasant and indigenous groups, 136; and environmental deterioration, 47; and landlessness, 4, 133; and "neoliberal multiculturalism", 109; and peasant critique of resettlement schemes, 135; cooperative and collective ownership of, 44–46; evictions, 2, 18–20, 23, 44, 52, 133; loss of, and peasant activism, 128; privatization of (individual property title), 45, 129; promotion of individual title to, 45–46; shrinking base of and pressures on, 41, 128–129; threat to communal ownership of from Agricultural Modernization Law, 53, 129

land takeovers (*tomas de tierra*): as protest against hunger and food insecurity, 134; by United National Peasant Front (FUNACAMH), 76; by UNC (National Peasant Union), 76; criminalization of, 53, 80; example of, 2; example of judicial process in (CNTC-AZUNOSA case), 149. *See also* land, and landlessness; land, loss of and peasant activism; peasants, and criminalization of land takeovers

La Prensa: and popular criticism of, 182

Lara, Karla. *See* music and resistance

laughter: as weapon of popular resistance, 187

Lempira, indigenous leader: claimed by Lenca as ancestor and resistance leader against Spanish colonization, 113; image of, in official national history of Honduras, 24

Lenca: and *guancasco* as part of popular resistance, 116; and use of pilgrimages (*caminatas*) as expressions of protest, 115, 116; culture and way of life in colonial times, 92, 112; cultural origins of, 112; cultural syncretism and peasant identity of, 112; historical resistance of, 112–119; legal action against leaders of, 53, 118; relations of, with popular organizations and interests, 113–114; resistance to Agua Zarca hydroelectric dam project, 117; resistance to Spanish conquerors, 112; role in Honduran adoption of ILO Convention 169, 114; role within national popular resistance in Honduras, 119; spirituality and religious beliefs in popular resistance, 112, 119. *See also* Civic Council of Popular and Indigenous Organizations of Honduras (COPINH), founding and early activity of

Ley forestal (2001): as attempt to remove forests from indigenous stewardship, 45. *See also* logging, and forestry law (*Ley forestal*) of 2001

Liberal Party: and popular distrust of politicians, 30

liberal oligarchic state: and impunity, 153; as aspect of ideology of domination, 27; desire for change away from, after 1949, 78; formation of in late 1800s, 24

Liberal reforms of 1870: and construction of Honduran history, 24

liberation theology. *See* theology

Lobo, Porfirio (Pepe): and Charter Cities, 33

Locomapa: killing of Tolupán activists at, in 2013, 99

logging: and disruption of rural communities, 96; and forestry law (*Ley forestal*) of 2001, 45; by Stone Container Corporation, 44; illegal, 45; in early development of in Honduras, 96; of mahogany on Tolupán lands, 19. *See also* extractive industries, and indigenous and peasant communities

Lopez Arrellano, Osvaldo: and Agrarian Reform Law of 1974, 2, 41, 76

Los Horcones "massacre" (1975): and retreat of Catholic Church from social and political activism, 204; and UNC members, 76; as attack on progressive Christians, 55; described, 55

marches (pilgrimage, *caminata, peregrinación*): and "take back the streets" run, 183; as protests involving risk and safety in numbers, 181–182; creativity and popular culture displayed in, 182; forms of, and what they express, 181. *See also* public spaces, reclamation of, 181

Maya: and mayanization of Honduran ethnic diversity, 25

memory: as challenge to impunity, 154; attempts to erase collective memory, 48–49; use of by popular organizations and popular resistance, 155

Mendoza Peña, Mireya: killing of, 51, 151

mestizo and mestizaje: and construction of Honduran identity, 24–25

middle class: presence of in early independent Honduras, 21; and intellectual basis for popular resistance, 77–78

militarization, Honduras: and violence, 29; of Honduran society, 59

military, Honduran: and arms sales in Honduras, 6; and enforcement of land evictions, 52; and military rule, 56; independence of, from civilian government, 56; mentioned, 3; response of, to labor strikes, 70, 71–72; role of, in controlling Lenca resistance to Agua Zarca Dam project, 117; role of, in protecting mining projects, 117; social class differences within, 56–57. *See also* militarization, of Honduran society; Military Police for Public Order (PMOP) and creation of

military governments: and military coup of 1962, 87, 161; and repressive period after 1962, 75–76; end of most recent period of, 56

Military Police for the Public Order PMOP: and creation of, 58; and ideology of subordination, 29

mining: and anti-mining campaign "Honduras is worth more than gold", 134; and dislocation of rural communities by water pollution, 96; and hydroelectric dams, 34; and labor strike of San Juancito Mine 1909, 70; and land evictions, 19; early conditions of, 70; indigenous resistance to, 47, 97; moratorium during Zelaya government, 44, 46; revocation of moratorium on, 46. *See also* extractive industries, and indigenous and peasant communities; Mining Law of 2013, provisions of

Mining Law of 2013: and Honduran Army, 117; attempts to subvert informed consent provision of, 46–47; provisions of, 46, 117; selective opposition to, 54

Miskito: and Ahuas incident 2012, 104; and MISURISATA, MISURA, KISAN, 102; and Moravian and Catholic missionaries, 101–102; colonial attempts to "civilize", 100, 101; communities in Nicaragua during Contra War, 102, 103; effects of narcotics traffic and Operation Anvil on, 104–105; government "cultural missions" to in 1900s, 102; historical resistance of, 100–105; involvement in Contra War of 1980s, 102–103; MASTA as representative of, 104; opposition to hydroelectric dam projects, 103–104; origins of, 100; problematic relations of, to both sides in Contra War, 102–103; relations with English presence in colonial Honduras, 101; way of life in colonial times, 92; way of life threatened by development of oil exploration, 105

Model Cities. *See* Charter Cities

Montecinos, Antonio: and condemnation of Spanish colonial treatment of native people, 196–197

Morales, Magdalena: as regional leader of CNTC, 66; arrest of, and legal process against, 149–150

moral revolution. *See* Reina, Carlos Roberto

Moravian missionaries: and Miskito, 101

murals: and resistance, 175–176; as ancient and widespread political, social, religious expression, 175; two examples of, described, 176

music and resistance: as form of remembrance and memory work, 172; as portable or mobile resistance, 172; Karla Lara and, 174; of Café Guancasco, 173

National Agrarian Institute (INA): and Agrarian Reform law of 1974, 76; formation of, 75

National Association of Honduran Peasants (ANACH): as rival union to FENACH, 75

National Confederation of Farm Workers (CNTC). *See* Magdalena Morales

National Federation of Honduran Peasants (FENACH): formation and repression of, 75

National Party: and popular distrust of political parties, 30

National Peasant Union (*Unión Nacional de Campesinos* UNC): and land takeovers, 76; and relation to Catholic social teaching, 55; formation and early activism of, 75; members killed at Los Horcones, 55, 75

national police: formerly Public Security Forces FUSEP under military, 56

National Popular Resistance Front (FNRP): and LIBRE party, 162; and *refundación*, 162; incorporation of artistic expressions by, 173, 174; women in, 66. *See also* refundación, as objective of popular resistance

national security (doctrine, practices): as support for impunity, 56; Gustavo Alvarez and implementation of, 57, 80; mentioned, 3, 4. *See also* theology and national security doctrine, description and critique of

national sovereignty: and Charter Cities proposal, 111; and concerns about United States military presence, 224; and Honduran military, 57

neoliberalism: and "neoliberal multiculturalism", 109; indigenous resistance to, 122; in Honduras in 1980s, 44; weakening and loss of legitimacy of, and post-neolibaralism, 239

Nicaragua: and revolution of 1979, 3, 79; and Sandinista National Liberation Front, 3, 79; and Somoza family, 3, 79; Christian participation in 1979 revolution in, 204; warnings about by Honduran officials, 48

non-governmental organizations (NGOs): and levels of intervention in Honduras, 230

North American Free Trade Agreement (NAFTA): and abolition of communal land in Mexico, 46; and Zelaya government, 86

oil: exploration and discovery of, and effect on Miskito communities, 105

Oliva, Berta: threats and public denunciation against, 66, 150. *See also* Committee of Families of the Detained Disappeared in Honduras (COFADEH) formation and work of, in 1980s

Operation Anvil. *See* Drug Enforcement Agency, and Operation Anvil; Miskito, effects of narcotics traffic and Operation Anvil on

Organización Nacional Indígena Lenca de Honduras (ONILH): founding as Lenca organization, 113

Organization for Ethnic Community Development (ODECO, Garifuna): as alternative to OFRANEH, 110

paquetazo (the package).: as package of neoliberal reforms proposed in 1991 by Callejas government, 45, 129

Party of Liberation and Refounding (*Partido de Liberación y Refundación* LIBRE): and election of 2013, 162; and popular resistance, 68, 162; and teachers, 30. *See also* refundación, as major objective of popular resistance

patriarchy: and *refundación* as attack against patriarchy, 163

peasants (*campesinos*): activism 1955-1980, 74–76; and 1992 Agricultural

Modernization Law, 130; and balance between short and long term resources, 142; and criminalization of land takeovers, 80, 149–150; and effects on, of Contra presence in Honduras, 80; and environmental degradation, 47; and peasant dilemma, 42, 136; at El Astillero, 17; causes of land loss of, 21, 23, 41, 47; economic stratification and ideological diversity among, 42–43; Eric Wolf's description of, 42; impact on, of U.S. food aid, 131; landless, 4, 47, 132–133; organization and unions, 43; use of term *campesino* for, 42

physicality: importance of in popular resistance, 188

pilgrimage. *See* marches (*caminata*)

political parties: and election of 2013, 162; as help and hindrance to popular resistance, 67, 162; challenge of LIBRE to, 68, 162; complex popular attitudes toward, 30; increasing number of, 68

popular culture: and resistance, 170–172

preferential option for the poor: and Second Vatican Council, 83; mentioned, 56

Prisión Verde (*Green Prison* by Ramon Amaya Amador): and conditions on banana plantations, 70; and middle class intellectuals, 78

private security industry: and military involvement with, 56; as replacement for military and police, 58; criticism of as death squads, 58; size of, 57

protective measures (*medidas cautelares*): and journalist Luis Galdamez, 151; failure of Honduran government to implement, 157

Protestant churches in Honduras: and rise of evangelical Protestantism in Honduras, 199; attempts of, to address needs of rising popular organizations, 199; role of, in evolution of popular resistance after 1990, 205–207; support for and opposition to 2009 coup d'etat, 207; threats against ministers of, active with popular organizations, 206–207

providentialism. *See* theology, of providentialism

public spaces: as context for popular culture, 180; loss of, as loss of community and society, 180; loss of, in Honduras due to violence, 180; reclamation of, 181

Radio Progreso: as vehicle for popular education, 81, 85

Reagan Administration: and emphasis on anti-communism in Central America, 60; and expansion of military in Honduras, 79, 224; revolution reaction of, to Nicaraguan, 3

"Reaganomics for Honduras": and ongoing U.S. economic intervention in Honduras, 224; and role of extractive industries in Honduran development, 96; as blueprint of Honduran development for Suazo government, 45; popular protests against, 223

Reflection, Investigation and Communication Team (ERIC): and community development project described, 140–141; formation and work of, 81; formed in response to oppression of 1980s, 3

Refundación (refounding or re-structuring the constitutional and political order): and curbing power of elite, 163; and poll of 2009, 162; as attack against patriarchy, 163; as major objective of popular resistance, 148, 162

refugees: in Honduras, 4

Reina, Carlos Roberto (Beto): and defense of human rights, 161; "moral revolution" and civilian control of the military, 56

religion: and critique of treatment of native people, 196–197; and dynamic between belief and material conditions, 193; and "spiritual struggle", 214–216; potential efficacy of, for social change, 194; relation of, to popular resistance, 192; religious symbols and ideology, 33; treatment of, in social scientific analysis, 193; used to dampen popular resistance, 55

resilience: meaning of, 242–243

resistance movements: and individuals, 65; and tension between horizontalism and vanguardism, 241

Rosario Mining Company. *See* mining, and labor strike of San Juancito Mine 1909

sacrifice zones: and United States relationship to Honduras, 227

salvese quien pueda: and lack of security in Honduran society, 30

School of the Americas: and national security and militarization of Latin America, 60

"see, judge, act" (*ver, juzgar, y actuar*): meaning of, described, 84

Sinohydro: and hydropower dam projects, 53, 117, 119

social class: as factor in acceptance of ideologies, 32

social science: and liberation theology, 213; critical nature of, 6

Sociedad Cultural Abraham Lincoln (Garifuna): and Garifuna organizing against racism, 107

solidarity: and mutual connection of resistance in Honduras and United States, 243; and popular protests in U.S. against plan to invade Nicaragua in 1980s, 229; and sense of privilege, 232; and support of U.S. groups for Hondurans affected by Contra War, 229; as people-to-people initiative, 232; discussion of, and U.S. grassroots solidarity with Honduras, 228–233; expressed as U.S. citizens' opposition to militarization of Honduras, 229; lack of for Honduras in 1990s, 230; of U.S. citizens with Central America struggles in 1980s, 228

Somoza, Anastasio, 72

sovereignty: and role of Honduran elite, 28; threatened by Charter Cities, 33. *See also* vendepatria, meaning of, 48

Spanish colonial rule: characterization of by Spanish colonial authorities, 92; early local resistance to, 69; indirect rule of indigenous communities during, 23; land and labor systems of (encomienda and hacienda), 20, 40–41

Special Development Regions (REDES): declared unconstitutional by Constitutional Court, 7, 33

spirituality. *See* religion

Suazo Cordova, Roberto: and APROH, Facussé Memorandum, and Reaganomics, 45; and U.S. military expansion in Honduras, 79

sustainability: agricultural and environmental as aspect of resistance, 134; and critique of traditional peasant farming methods, 135; meanings of for families and communities, 134–135

syncretism (religious): and use of religious symbols in construction of group identity, 195; as a form of survival and empowerment, 195

teachers: and political parties, 30

Teatro La Fragua. *See* theater

technical coup: as factor in weakening legitimacy of judicial system, 164; described, 53

theater: and Teatro La Fragua, 178–179; as exploration of critical social themes, 178; as part of Honduran culture and history, 178; as training in social awareness for youth, 178

theology (and social activism): and national security doctrine, description and critique of, 211–212; as collection of cultural symbols, 212–213; of dispensationalism and Second Coming, 210–211; of dualism, 209; of gospel of prosperity, 211; of hierarchy of being, 210; of providentialism, 31, 210; of liberation, 213, 216; of spiritualism, 209; that undermines social activism, 55, 209–213

Third Forum on Biological and Cultural Diversity (2003): and COPINH network of relationships, 115

Tierra Nuestra (Our Land peasant movement): eviction of, 133

Tolupán (Xicaque): and formation and evolution of FETRIXY, 99; and killing of activists at Locomapa 2013, 100; and land evictions, 18–20; and peasant unionism, 98; and protests against corruption and impunity, 100; and resistance to mining and logging, 99, 142; historical resistance of, 97–100; in conflict over land, 99, 136; labor exploitation of, 98; under colonial rule, 97; way of life in colonial times, 92

toma de tierra. See land takeovers

tourism: and Garifuna communities, 110; as part of national development plans, 96; plans for development of, after Hurricane Mitch, 110. *See also* Garifuna, threats against since 2009 coup; Garifuna, effects of Hurricane Mitch on

Trejo Cabrera, Antonio: killing of, 51, 151

trova. See music and resistance

T-shirts: and Artists in Resistance, 174; and COFADEH, 175; and FNRP, 174; as expressions of resistance and memory, 174–175

United Fruit Company: 1932 strike on plantations of, 71; and 1954 banana strike, 72–73

United States: and coup d'etat of 2009, 225; and critique of counter-narcotics operations in Central America, 61; and Foreign Deployment Advisory Support Teams (FAST), 226; and labor strikes in banana plantations, 222; and militarization of Honduras, 60; anti-narcotics activities of, and DEA in Honduras, 226; as problem for Honduran national sovereignty, 222, 224; complexity of relations with Honduras, 221; economic interventions and development plans of, for Honduras, 224–225; Embassy in Honduras, 3, 45, 224; Honduras as a "sacrifice zone" for, 227; military presence in Honduras, 3, 224; Monroe Doctrine and hegemony of, in Caribbean region, 222; role of in 1932 United Fruit Company strike, 71; role of in overthrow of Arbenz government in Guatemala 1954, 72; support for anti-communist labor agitation in Honduras, 222–223; tensions in relationship of, to Honduras, 227. *See also* AIFLD anti-communist labor union activity of; CAFTA and *Alianza Bolivariana* (ALBA); CARSI and United States security aid to Honduras; Contras, and United States in Honduras; Reaganomics for Honduras, and ongoing U.S. economic intervention in Honduras

United Nations Declaration of Universal Human Rights: and modern concept of human rights, 158; and use of in 1954 banana strike, 81

Valladares, Leo: and human rights, 160; and *In Search of Hidden Truths* (1998), 160; and *The Facts Speak for Themselves* (1993), 160; threats against, 160. *See also* National Commission for Human Rights (CONADEH) creation and work of

Vatican Council, Second (1962-1964): and global context of need and inequity, 201; and preferential option for the poor, 201–202; and Christian base communities (CEBs), 202; and Delegates of the Word, 202–203; influence of, on Honduran Catholic Church, 56, 83. *See also* Catholic Church in Honduras, post-Vatican 2 activism of as challenge to powerful interests

vendepatria: as characterization of ZEDES, 111; meaning of, 48

Via Crucis (Way of the Cross). *See* marches

Villeda Morales, Ramón: against priests and ministers of religion, 206; and passage of agrarian reform law of 1962, 75; and lessened anticlericalsm re. Catholic Church, 200

violence: and ideology, 40, 236; becoming generalized in Honduran society, 67; causes of violence in 1990s, 6; image of Hondurans as violent people, 26, 59; inappropriate use of by police, example of, 151; individual and structural, 39–40

Walker Affair: and sovereignty in Honduras and Nicaragua, 222

women: leaders as targets of criminal accusations, 150; organizing across social classes in 1920, 77; women in popular organizations and resistance, 66–67. *See also* Honduran Women's Committee for Peace (*Comité Hondureño de Mujeres por la Paz "Visitación Padilla"*), activism of and involvement of different social classes in

workshops: as instruments of popular activism and resistance, 84–85

Xicaques. *See* Tolupán

Yanez, Ebed: killing of, 1, 51

youth (young people): and future of Honduran resistance, 68, 242; assumed guilt of, 51; contributions of, to popular resistance, 68; emigration of, 32, 68; killing of, 32

Zelaya, Manuel: 2009 coup d'etat against, 5, 49, 162; and national sovereignty, 86; popularity of, 68, 86

Zones of Employment and Economic and Social Development (*Zonas de Empleo y Desarrollo Económico y Social, ZEDES*): passage of law to create, and critique of, 33, 111

About the Author

James J. Phillips made his first visit to Honduras in 1974, and has been a student of Central America and the Caribbean region for forty years. His major concern has been to understand societal change, popular movements, and social and political revolution. He has conducted extensive fieldwork in Jamaica, Nicaragua, and Honduras, and has published many articles and chapters about change in peasant and plantation societies, refugee populations, and the role of human rights and religion in societal change. After receiving his PhD in anthropology from Brown University, he was a writer and speaker on international political economy with the American Friends Service Committee, and later a policy analyst on the staff of Oxfam America. He has taught at several universities. For the past seventeen years he has taught anthropology and international studies at Southern Oregon University.